TOM STOPPARD

CASEBOOKS ON
MODERN DRAMATISTS
(Vol. 1)

GARLAND REFERENCE LIBRARY
OF THE HUMANITIES
(Vol. 794)

TOM STOPPARD
A Casebook

Edited by
John Harty, III

GARLAND PUBLISHING, INC. • NEW YORK & LONDON
1988

Library of Congress Cataloging-in-Publication Data

Harty, John, 1945–
Tom Stoppard: A Casebook.

(Garland Reference Library of the Humanities;
vol. 794. Casebooks on Modern Dramatists; vol. 1)
1. Stoppard, Tom—Criticism and interpretation.
I. Title. II. Series: Garland Reference Library of
the Humanities; v. 794. III. Series: Garland
Reference Library of the Humanities. Casebooks on
Modern Dramatists; vol. 1.

PR6069.T6Z657   1987   822'.914   87-25812
ISBN 0–8240–9023–3 (alk. paper)

Printed on acid-free, 250-year-life paper
Manufactured in the United States of America

CONTENTS

Lord Malquist & Mr Moon (1966)

Rosencrantz & Guildenstern Are Dead (1967)

The Real Inspector Hound (1968); *After
Magritte* (1970)

Brazil (1984)

Acknowledgments

To Marie Nelson for typing this with
painstaking care and more. To the essayists for
their hard work and patience. To the staff at
Garland Publishing, especially Phyllis Korper for
editorial assistance and encouragement. To
Series Editor Professor Kimball King in Atlanta,
New York, Hawaii, Chapel Hill, the World. To
Matthew Simon for excellent assistance. To all
librarians at the University of Florida,
especially Dolores Jenkins and Pam Pasak. To the
English Department at the University of Florida,
especially Professor Melvyn New and Professor Sid
Homan. To countless others. To Tom Stoppard.
For this relief, much thanks.

GENERAL EDITOR'S NOTE
CASEBOOKS ON MODERN DRAMATISTS

Tom Stoppard: A Casebook, by John Harty, III, is the
first of a series of collected essays on contemporary
playwrights which will be published by Garland. Other
casebooks will include my own volume on Sam Shepard, one
on Samuel Beckett edited by Douglas McMillan, one on
Lanford Wilson by Jackson Bryer, one on Caryl Churchill
by Phyllis Randall, and one on Christopher Hampton by
Robert Gross. Professor Harty's book contains his own
survey of Stoppard criticism, a chronology and an annotated bibliography. Some of the articles in his text
have previously appeared in distinguished scholarly
journals and provide valuable insights into the complexities of Stoppard's canon. Garland's emphasis in subsequent casebooks will focus on articles specifically com-
missioned for publication in this series. Our task,
admittedly an ambitious one, is to give thorough coverage to dramatists whose reputations have been mainly
established in the years following World War II and who,
after several decades, continue to merit the scrutiny of
leading drama critics.
      Every attempt will be made to include discussions of
the artists' major works and to represent a variety of
critical approaches to the playwrights' major artistic
statements. The series should be valuable to scholars
seeking new materials on major literary figures, professors who welcome a wide range of critical viewpoints when
preparing lectures and seminars, students who wish to
grasp the significant attributes of exciting new writers,
and general readers who, like myself, simply enjoy the
theatre and appreciate "sharing" ideas with others who
have studied the craft.

   As general editor I hope to introduce as many as
three or four new volumes a year during the next decade.
I particularly want to thank Phyllis Korper and Gary
Kuris of Garland Publishing, Inc. for their careful
planning, encouragement, and assistance on this long-
range project.

                                          Kimball King
          General Editor, Casebooks on Modern Dramatists

Editor's Note

Tom Stoppard: A Casebook contains
eighteen articles -- eleven original essays and
seven reprints. The book has been arranged as
much as possible so that the essays correspond to
the chronological order in which Stoppard's
published works appeared. An advantage to this
format is that insights of an early essay often
contribute to a better understanding of a later
one. For example, "Stoppard's **Lord Malquist &
Mr Moon**: The Beginning" examines how characters and themes in Stoppard's only novel recur in
his later works. The annotated selected
bibliography has been arranged in the same
manner.

INTRODUCTION

Tom Stoppard (pronounced STOP-PARD, with the accent on both syllables) appears to be the product of a natural progression of humor in Great Britain, a country that has produced **The Goon Show**, the Beatles, **Monty Python's Flying Circus**, and **Benny Hill**. In studying Stoppard's works it is important to remember that he never attended college, that he worked as a journalist for several years, and that he decided in his early twenties to become a playwright. A glance at his works reveals a structure that is uninhibited by the restraints of formal training. In fact, Stoppard's lack of a formal education may have served as an advantage in the long run.

In 1960 Stoppard resigned as a journalist for the **Bristol Evening World** and began writing plays. In a bold and defiant move he became a playwright, supporting himself as a free lance writer who in 1963 gained valuable experience by seeing 132 plays in a seven-month period as the drama critic for the short-lived **Scene** magazine.[1]

Stoppard's concern about the theater has overridden all other concerns in constructing his plays, which are intended primarily to do the obvious, that is, succeed as theater. His main goal has been to create comedies, and he has attempted to make almost everything he has ever written, including his novel, his short stories, and even a large part of his journalism, funny. If audiences do not find the work, for whatever reason, to be funny, then Stoppard considers that work to have failed.

In order to accomplish this, each play is designed with the theatrics of show business in mind; one finds in Stoppard's plays murders, real and feigned madness, women disrobing, a symphony orchestra, acrobatics, gun shots, a reliance on the thriller genre for suspense, vaudeville routines, and magic. Closely related to this is the device of mimicking which includes burlesque, farce, parody, and travesty.

Stoppard's ethos is derived from the British tradition despite the fact that he was born in

Zlín, Czechoslovakia (since renamed Gottwaldov),
on July 3, 1937. After spending a portion of his
childhood in India, his family relocated in
England where he became as time passed more
British than the British.

Exactly how did the British environment
affect the young Stoppard? One can only
speculate on such matters but there are obvious
points one might make. British culture has
always stressed both the spoken and the written
word, with the highest attainment of this
possibly having been reached in the drama of
Shakespeare. If one studies the various historical myths, he discovers a culture that has been
very successful worldwide based on its sense of
order and discipline, a sense that fills each day
with such occurrences as tea at assigned times
(even during wartime), orderly queues, the ride
on the underground, the care of gardens and pets,
the discipline of children, and in almost every
imaginable activity.

The "stiff upper lip" for which the British
are proud was never more vividly demonstrated for
the world than during the German bombings in
World War II. With their characteristic dark
humor, the British refused to let this annoyance
disrupt their daily lives (the same might be said
of the current bombings), and the current soccer
or cricket match usually remained a topic of more
importance than the activities of the war.
Anticipating the mad humor of **Beyond the
Fringe** and **Monty Python**, one man asked on
the second day of the war: "Pardon me, but have
I time to get to Victoria before the devastation
starts? I have to get a train for Haywards
Heath."[2]

England is well known for its eccentrici-
ties. The British people as a whole are a very
tightly knit group compacted onto one island
where space is always at a premium. Yet the
class system has always separated the various
groups of people; even those of the same class
rarely speak to someone they do not already know.
Reserve, aloofness, and irony seem to be elements
of the mythical John Bull. The national character of aggression, another paradox, counterpoints

the self-discipline and order. The worldwide
colonization and exploitation of foreign
countries is probably the best example of these
qualities.

These national characteristics can be seen
warring within Stoppard. His sense of order and
self-discipline triumphs over aggression and
other evils through the construction of plays,
plays which always debate such propositions and
paradoxes, with no clear-cut winner or solution
provided for the debate.

Metaphorically, the world Stoppard finds
himself in resembles a bombed-out London. The
next bomb may well have your number on it. (Two
bombs, one false and one real, explode in **Lord
Malquist & Mr Moon.**) Why not make a joke about
it and laugh while still alive? Stoppard's
method of fighting against the world's absurdity
is that of the comedian.

This same world finds itself at times on the
verge of self-destruction, both with the bomb
perched precariously high overhead since 1945 and
with the destruction of the nuclear family.
Stoppard's own life has experienced these
destructions. His father was killed in 1942 by
the Japanese in Singapore after he, his mother,
and brother had resettled in India.[3] And his
first marriage to Jose Ingle ended in divorce
with Stoppard getting custody of their two
children.[4]

These events plus those of the world at
large must be considered an influence. It is the
Age of Anxiety, an age of heart transplants, of
computers and Xerox. It is the Age of jet travel
on this globe and space travel to the moon and
beyond. It is an Age in which the copy receives
almost as much respect as the real thing, as
evidenced in recent art exhibitions in which a
giant photograph of Da Vinci's **Last Supper**
was displayed to great acclaim or such art
exhibitions as those containing thousands of
television sets arranged in some geometrical
order and tuned to the same station. Perhaps
Stoppard and his characters are "Protean men"
which Robert Lifton has defined as a result of
"historical dislocation," the breakdown of the

cultural tradition embedded in religion and the
family, and caused in part by the flooding of
imagery one experiences in the modern mass
communication networks.[5]

      This collection of essays roughly follows
the chronological order in which the novel **Lord
Malquist & Mr Moon** and the plays have appeared.
John Harty's "Stoppard's **Lord Malquist & Mr
Moon**: The Beginning" discusses Stoppard's only
novel as a watershed for many of the works that
followed, works which often contain plays-
within-plays.
      William E. Grubar's "'Wheels within wheels,
 etcetera': Artistic Design in **Rosencrantz and
Guildenstern Are Dead**," one of the most thought
provoking pieces available on **Rosencrantz**,
concludes that **Rosencrantz** "has no clear
theatrical precedent," and that the "workshop
vocabulary proves unable to explain what occurs
when the script of **Hamlet** mingles with the
script of **Rosencrantz**." Although
Rosencrantz is conceived in terms of emptiness,
Gruber finds it neither absurdist nor existential. **Rosencrantz**, like all of Stoppard's
works, develops a debate, and its staged events
are found to have little in common with the
events of **Hamlet**.
      J. Dennis Huston's "'Misreading' **Hamlet**:
 Problems of Perspective in **Rosencrantz &
Guildenstern Are Dead**" contends that Stoppard
has attempted a modern misreading of **Hamlet**
within **Rosencrantz** and Huston addresses the
following three issues: (1) the ambiguity of
Stoppard's title, (2) the large amount of magic
found in **Rosencrantz**, and (3) the simultaneous presence in **Rosencrantz** of two
Hamlets --Shakespeare's and Stoppard's.
Stoppard's **Rosencrantz** challenges Shakespeare's **Hamlet** by offering audiences an
updated, though skewed, version of **Hamlet**
through the perspective of Rosencrantz and
Guildenstern, originally insignificant courtiers
within the earlier prototype.
      Gabrielle Robinson's "Plays Without Plot:
The Theatre of Tom Stoppard" overviews Stoppard's

works and points out that "Stoppard's principal
means of generating both the uncertainty and the
laughter is [through] the intermingling of the
logical with the absurd: fantastic incidents are
made to appear logical, while ordinary and
apparently rational occurrences are presented as
if they were absurd and inexplicable." Rosencrantz and Guildenstern's "attempts to impose
logic on their lives merely lead them into
absurdity." Stoppard is at his best when he
parodies, when he plays with other people's ideas
as in **Jumpers** and **Travesties**, or with
plots as in **Rosencrantz** and **Travesties**.
All attempts in **Jumpers** at a rational understanding of existence are overwhelmed by
absurdity.

Robinson then extends and enlarges her
arguments in her essay "Nothing Left But Parody:
Friedrich Dürrenmatt and Tom Stoppard." She
emphasizes that Dürrenmatt and Stoppard plays
often contain parody in one form or another.
Both playwrights detest sentimentality and
incorporate parody to avoid it. "Parody becomes
inevitable since it discloses the breakdown of
meaningful, coherent concepts. Man now feels out
of control, alienated and at the mercy of absurd
accidents that his reason proves pathetically
incapable of explaining." Characters become
pathetic as "the parodist turns tragedy into a
farce and heroes into clowns." **The Real
Inspector Hound** is found to be a "bewildering
mixture of the absurd and the commonplace. . . ."
Like **Hound**, **Jumpers** parodies the thriller
and provides a lively and farcical plot.

Weldon B. Durham's "Ritual of Riddance in
Tom Stoppard's **The Real Inspector Hound**" uses
Kenneth Burke's critical apparatus in Burke's "On
Human Behavior Considered 'Dramatistically'" and
Burke's **Rhetoric of Religion** to examine
Hound as "a purgative ritual." Puckeridge
within **Hound** utilizes the combined efforts of
the play-within-the-play and the audience, except
for the two critics, to set a trap for both Moon
and Birdboot. The violence and deceit witnessed
in the play-within-the-play interrelates with the
motives of Moon and Birdboot.

Jeffrey D. Mason's "Foot-prints to the Moon: Detectives as Suspects in **Hound** and **Magritte**" highlights the interplay between the detective and the suspect in both **Hound** and **Magritte** and examines each play as a ritual of observation. Mason analyzes scenes in **Hound** (different scenes than those in Durham's essay on **Hound**) to reveal, as did Durham, the interrelationship between the play-within-the-play and the two critics. Mason emphasizes that in both **Hound** and **Magritte** there is a relationship established in which the various characters observe each other. For example, in **Hound** Drudge always manages to overhear apparently important fragments of conversation which she later reports to Inspector Hound (Moon). **Magritte** opens with the policeman Holmes looking in the Harris window. Hence Stoppard points out that observation and testimony are often unreliable and that the rational order often sought by such people as detectives cannot always be assumed to exist. Or, in other words, what appears rational may, in reality, be irrational and vice versa.

Like Gabrielle Robinson, Lucina Gabbard in her "Stoppard's **Jumpers**: A Mystery Play" concludes that **Jumpers** contains the elements of Absurdism: ". . . The farce, the satire, the contemporary milieu--even the Brechtian screen-- are all elements of Absurdism. Stoppard's slapstick takes place in the midst of cosmic tragedy and metaphysical inquiry." Archie's amorality and the Coda are typical of the Absurdist's world.

G. B. Crump's "The Universe as Murder Mystery: Tom Stoppard's **Jumpers**" takes one giant step toward an explication of Stoppard's philosophy play. The protagonist George Moore argues for a belief in God and moral absolutes and against the beliefs of the logical positivists, the "jumpers." The murder of McFee (which has been disparaged as gratuituous by other critics) is found to be central to a play in which George approaches the answer to the large question of who created the universe and why. McFee's murder metaphorically represents the essential mysteries of creation.

The next section of essays discusses
Travesties, Stoppard's most important work to
date. Rodney Simard in his "Seriousness
Compromised by Frivolity: Structure and Meaning
in Tom Stoppard's **Travesties**" reminds the
reader that the construction of **Travesties** is
centered upon an explanation of ideas about art
and its relationship to politics. Carr and
Stoppard pose the following question: Which
[Joyce or Lenin] was the more important as a
creative genius? Tzara, without really realizing
it, has agreed with "Carr's notion of the artist
as a representative of civilized ideals."
Stoppard's subtle shift in his treatment of
political matters in **Travesties** "suggests a
new, increased awareness of the realities of
human existence."

Weldon Durham in his "The Structure and
Function of Tom Stoppard's **Travesties**"
analyzes **Travesties'** source play **The
Importance of Being Earnest** and closely
scrutinizes the structure of **Travesties**.
Earnest serves as a nearly perfect mirror for
Stoppard to gaze into "as he sought to perfect
his portrait of himself as an artist." As is
well known, Act I is the "art" act while Act II
is the "politics" act. Act II is structured
inversely to Act I, and Durham compares the two
Acts, scene by scene, to demonstrate this
structure. The two ideas which serve as poles in
Travesties are the two ideas of the function
of art--"to gratify through caprice man's urge
for immortality and to serve socialism through
sympathy with the working millions."

Shirley Shultz and Russell Astley in their
"**Travesties**: Plot and the Moral Tilt"
emphasize that **Travesties** consists of a spy
thriller. Their questions are (1) "Why does
Stoppard use **The Importance of Being Earnest**
plot in the first place? and (2) Why isn't it
sustained once imported?" The short answer to
both questions is that the **Earnest** plot is
rooted in the psychology of an internal author--
Henry Carr--whose design cannot be realized
within the confines of that plot. Carr
"therefore blends his **Earnest**, with a

conventionally melodramatic spy thriller, casting
himself as hero, a transformation which has the
effect of elevating his private conflicts to the
level of international urgencies."

After **Travesties**, Stoppard's work began
to emphasize political concerns. Much like his
protagonist George Anderson who made a decision
in **Professional Foul** to smuggle a thesis out
of Czechoslovakia, Stoppard reached a turning
point and decided to relinquish to an extent what
he had always written for a new direction--
political comedies. Katherine Kelly's "Breaking
the Stalemate: The Stoppard Comedies Since
Travesties" argues that the political comedies
--**Every Good Boy Deserves Favor, Professional Foul**, and **Dogg's Hamlet, Cahoot's
Macbeth**--"accomplish the poetic shift [to
politics] and lay the groundwork for the more
ambitious stage plays, **Night and Day** (1978)
and **The Real Thing** (1982). . . ." "**Night
and Day** also reflects Stoppard's shift away
from a symmetrically split stage towards a
shifting of stage locations, accomplished by a
cyclorama, that corresponds to the characters'
shift from absolutist to relativist beliefs." In
The Real Thing, a play about playwrighting
among other things, Stoppard consolidates his
shift and moves "towards a new flexibility in
thought and staging."

Joan Dean's "Unlikely Bedfellows: Politics
and Aesthetics in Tom Stoppard's Recent Work"
also discusses Stoppard's shift to political
concerns. She points out that "in each case
[**Travesties, Night and Day, Professional Foul,
Every Good Boy Deserves Favor, Cahoot's Macbeth,
Squaring the Circle**, and **The Real Thing**]
the social and political backdrop is essential to
the thematic concerns--specifically, those
regarding the nature of playwriting--in a way
that is not at all characteristic of the plays
before **Jumpers**." **Squaring the Circle**,
Stoppard's most "Brechtian" play, "does not
distance the work in an imaginary setting, but
directly addresses a political reality [Poland]
as well as the problems involved in presenting
that situation." Politics and playwrighting

become curiously interrelated in Stoppard's most
recent stage play **The Real Thing**.

Richard Corballis's "Tom Stoppard's
Children" emphasizes that in six of Stoppard's
recent plays--**Professional Foul, Every Good Boy
Deserves Favor, Night and Day, Dogg's Hamlet/
Cahoot's Macbeth, The Real Thing,** and **Squaring the Circle**--children play a major role "in
defining the moral issues which are at stake."
Children are simply not "clever enough" to be
skeptical about their natural impulses. Stoppard
himself has spoken about the importance of
children's perceptions, and he has placed this
idea in his plays with children. As Miss Prism
or the Player in **Rosencrantz** might have put
it: "When children are attended to things end
happily; when children are coerced, exploited or
ignored things end unhappily." Corballis points
out that Stoppard's stage children served a very
useful purpose during the 1977-1982 period "by
providing the prop which helped him out of his
early phase of intellectual 'leap-frog' into
social and political involvement."

Katherine Kelly's "Tom Stoppard's Dramatic
Debates: The Case of **Night and Day**" finds
Night and Day the least successful of the five
major stage comedies to date, probably "because
it marks a change in Stoppard's style of dramatizing uncertainty." Stoppard's shifts include
parody that is sporadic rather than pervasive,
speech that is flat rather than clever, and plots
that have a primary line of action rather than
many converging ones. **Night and Day** preoccu-
pies itself with "the absolute good of the free
flow of information," which is refined through
the "characters' repeated attempts to describe
the proper relation between free expression and
news reporting." Both can go afoul as demonstrated by the death of the idealist Milne in
search of a story and by Mageeba's idea of a
relatively free press as being one that is edited
by his relatives.

Hersh Zeifman's "Comedy of Ambush: Tom
Stoppard's **The Real Thing**" untangles the hall
of mirrors and the ambushes contained in **The
Real Thing** and concludes that "[a]ll of

Stoppard's plays are about defining 'the real
thing'; the only element that varies from play to
play is the nature of the particular 'reality'
under debate: philosophy, art, political
freedom, the press. What remains constànt is the
debate formula itself, and the method of dramatizing it."
        G. B. Crump's "Art and Experience in
Stoppard's **The Real Thing**" approaches
Stoppard in semiotic terms: "To put it in a way
defenders of Stoppard's early non-mimetic plays
have found congenial, both a drama and the
objective world present a set of signs which man
must decode, and all man can know is that
decoding, not some ultimate message or truth, if
any, behind the signs he perceives." **The Real
Thing** shifts away from symbolic modes and the
play of ideas toward mimetic drama and a concern
for the emotional lives of the characters.
        Crump's essay in part examines Tom
Stoppard's linguistics and states that "while the
play's [**The Real Thing**] insights into literary language exemplify the intricacy of
linguistic codes, its romantic story hinges on
correct or incorrect readings of non-linguistic
codes." Crump concludes that "[w]hat saves **The
Real Thing** is the witty surprises of the
dialogue evoking Wilde and Shaw, the clever
manipulation of structure and plot to form a
metaphorical investigation into aesthetics and
epistemology, the structural and linguistic
'ambushes' created by punning and by juxtaposing
real and imaginary scenes--in other words, the
very symbolic and verbal ingenuity which marked
Stoppard's non-mimetic, early works."
        Felicia Hardison Londré's "From Zurich to
Brazil" contains an overview of Stoppard's
works and describes the screenplay **Brazil**
(1985), of which he was one of three collaborat-
ors, as a metaphoric voyage for Stoppard from the
real setting of Zurich in **Travesties** to
"'somewhere in the twentieth century' **Brazil,**
a state of the mind." **Brazil** splices together several Stoppardian motifs from past works:
the film echoes other literary works, especially
George Orwell's **1984;** the ineffectual Sam is

related to Albert in **Albert's Bridge**, George
Moore in **Jumpers**, the title characters in
Lord Malquist & Mr Moon and others; the
disembodied ducts in Sam's apartment link up
visually with a severed wrist; and other connections exist such as questions of identity
("Buttle" or "Tuttle"), a crisis (the identity
error) is brought on through the swatting of a
fly (Donner fell to his death swatting a fly in
Artist); and a collection of Stoppardian
symbols such as boots, bandaged hands, and
twisted quotations such as the inscription "The
truth shall make you free" at the Ministry of
Information where truth is made inaccessible.

   Stoppard's critics have expressed a wide
divergence of views, some at total odds with each
other. The essays in this collection have been
assembled to include some of the best work done
on Stoppard and to provide both an overview of
the works and material on works which have not
received much critical attention, such as **Night
and Day**. The authors of reprinted essays have
with scrupulous meanness gone over their work and
corrected items, such as typographical errors,
within the original publication and have amended
their work if such was desired.

   Stoppard studies continue to come forth. To
date there are twelve dissertations devoted
solely to Stoppard and fourteen full length books
of criticism. Articles, reviews, and notes
continue to appear in journals. The plays
themselves are on the road and keep popping up in
cities like Reston, Virginia (**Hound** and
After Magritte, March 1985); Gainesville,
Florida (**Every Good Boy Deserves Favor**, March
1987); and Memphis (**The Real Thing**, summer
1987) and so on.

   The essays in this casebook will hopefully
lead the reader to further essays, to Stoppard's
texts, and to the theater itself for which no
substitute is available and where the real thing
comes to life as it jumps for joy and travesties
with a comic cosmos.

Notes

1. Ronald Hayman, **Tom Stoppard**, Third
Edition (Totowa, New Jersey: Rowman and
Littlefield, 1979), p. vii.

2. Daniel Snowman, **Britain and America**
(New York: New York University Press, 1977),
p. 85.

3. Hayman, p. vii.

4. Kenneth Tynan, "Withdrawing with style
from the chaos--Tom Stoppard," in **Show People**
(New York: Simon and Schuster, 1979), pp. 65,
90.

5. Robert Jay Lifton, "Protean Man,"
Partisan Review, 35 (Winter 1968), 16. AT&T
in an advertisement in **Atlantic Monthly**
(December 1986), p. 19 looks to the future and
suggests their intended goal and what could
happen: "We [AT&T] envision a vast global
network of networks, the merging of communications and computers, linking devices so
incredibly capable, they will bend to the will of
human beings, rather than forcing humans to bend
to theirs."

TOM STOPPARD

Stoppard's **Lord Malquist & Mr Moon:**
The Beginning

John Harty

Richard Corballis has written that
Rosencrantz & Guildenstern Are Dead is "indeed
the novel's [**Lord Malquist & Mr Moon**] sister
work."[1] Most recently Tim Brassell has also
alluded to the importance of **Lord Malquist:**

> . . . his novel [Stoppard's **Lord
> Malquist**] is in several respects a highly
> theatrical achievement. . . . Moon's lament
> in the novel that 'hardly anyone behaves
> naturally any more' (**Lord Malquist,**
> p. 53) is an aphorism for Stoppard's
> characters in two distinct senses. First,
> it is true of a particular strain of
> polished, precomposed, stylish characters
> who seem almost to speak as performers, in
> inverted commas. The first embodiment of
> this type is Moon's own opposite, Malquist;
> later examples include the Player in
> **Rosencrantz**, Archie in **Jumpers** and
> Tzara in **Travesties.** . . . On the other
> hand, there is Stoppard's own organization
> of **all** his characters into ostentatious-
> ly 'composed' edifices, schematized
> according to highly theatrical principles
> and governed by his desire to provide as
> much entertainment as possible for his
> audiences.[2]

I wish to expand on these two statements and
to show how **Lord Malquist** mirrors **Rosencrantz** which preceded it and looks ahead to
many of the plays that were to follow.

Before proceeding further a discussion of
Lord Malquist's plot is necessary since the
novel is certainly an unknown work. To get both
a sense of the novel and where the author's heart
really lies one need only glance over the table
of contents:

ONE   Dramatis Personae and Other
        Coincidences

TWO   A Couple of Deaths and Exits

THREE   Chronicler of the Time

FOUR   Spectator as Hero

FIVE   The Funeral of the Year

SIX   An Honourable Death[3]

Stoppard created a theatrical scaffold for his
novel and he has never repeated the novel form.
    The characters in **Lord Malquist** are all
British eccentrics who live as fashionable
(stylish) a life as possible. Malquist sees
himself as a modern Dr. Johnson and Mr Moon is
hired to be his Boswell. It is through Moon's
eyes that the reader obtains most of the novel.
Moon is our spectator as hero whose marriage to
Jane has never been consummated. Jane ends up
flirting with Malquist while Moon is seduced by
Lady Malquist.[4]
    The novel is filled with other eccentrics
such as O'Hara, Malquist's coachman, who sounds
Jewish but is actually an Irish Catholic anti-
Semitic Negro, one of Stoppard's characters in
this work who embodies the role of scapegoat.
Two cowboys, Long John Slaughter and Jasper
Johns, fugitives from a Pork'n'Beans commercial,
seek out Jane's affections and kill each other in
a gunfight at Trafalgar Square, the memorial to
another gunfighter of sorts. In an earlier
gunfight at Moon's house the French maid Marie is
killed by stray bullets as she hides beneath the
chesterfield. The General, a photographer,
arrives at Moon's house and takes pictures of the

dead Marie in strange positions, and Moon smashes
him over the head with a bottle and kills him.
To get rid of the two bodies Moon convinces
another eccentric visitor who calls himself the
Risen Christ to wrap the bodies in a carpet and
to take them away on his donkey--which he does.
    The relationship between Moon and Lord
Malquist results from Moon's attempts to become
Malquist's official writer and in an effort to
collect important quotations Moon rides with
Malquist in an eighteenth-century coach, a coach
which eventually hits and kills a Mrs. Cuttle.
    All the principal characters in the novel
are brought together at the funeral of the great
statesman (presumably Churchill). Moon decides
to explode the bomb he has been carrying with him
and has referred to throughout the novel. It
turns out to be nothing more than a large balloon
with obscenities written on it (presumably "fuck
you"). The novel ends with Moon borrowing
Malquist's coach to return home, only to be
killed by Mr. Cuttle's real bomb in a case of
mistaken identity. Lord Malquist has become
bankrupt and he loses his family home in the
process.
    The novel can be labelled "literature of
exhaustion," that is, a work that echoes and
parodies literary works that have preceded it.
John Barth developed the term in an article
entitled "Literature of Exhaustion," and in a
follow-up article "Literature of Replenishment."
Barth has stated that what he did **not** mean
was that literature was **kaput** but rather that
the matrixes of art are subject to being used up.
What is now a possibility Barth states is ". . .
that artistic conventions are liable to be
retired, subverted, transcended, transformed, or
even deployed against themselves to generate new
and lively work."[5] The literature of exhaustion in Stoppard's works includes various motifs
of open systems which are used to give the
illusion of infinity and include the following:
(1) Chinese boxes, (2) mirrors, (3) labyrinths,
and (4) infinite series and the infinite regress.

Many of Stoppard's plays can be labelled
literature of exhaustion and **Lord Malquist**
mirrors **Rosencrantz**, Stoppard's first literature of exhaustion, and looks ahead to the others
which include **The Real Inspector Hound,**
After Magritte, Jumpers, Travesties,
Dogg's Hamlet / Cahoot's Macbeth, The Dog It
Was That Died, and **The Real Thing.**

Lord Malquist has several examples of
images of exhaustion. One occurs when Moon
examines a can of Pork'n'Beans:

> On the table was a jumbled pyramid of tins
> identically labelled with a picture of a
> cowboy holding a tin with a picture of a
> cowboy holding a tin with a picture of a
> cowboy, and the words, "Western Trail
> Pork'n'Beans."
>
> **(Lord Malquist,** p. 38)[6]

Another occurs when Moon looks at his reflection
in a mirror:

> When he [Moon] leaned forward between the
> hinged mirror-leaves he caught the reflec-
> tion of his reflection and the reflection of
> that, and of that, and he saw himself multi-
> pled and diminished between the mirrors,
> himself aghast in the exact centre of a line
> that stretched to the edges of a flat
> earth.
>
> **(Lord Malquist,** p. 81)[7]

Stylistically Stoppard uses parody to mirror
the works of others. **Lord Malquist** in a way
is a watered-down parody of Joyce's **Ulysses,**
in which each chapter was done in a different
style. Besides the overall parody of **Ulysses**
two sections of **Lord Malquist** appear to echo
"Ithaca." In one of the "Ithaca" parodies Moon
questions himself about his bomb:

> **So you carry this bomb about with you**
> **expressly for the purpose of throwing it at**
> **someone?**
> Well, yes. I suppose there's no
> getting away from that. . . . I mainly
> think of throwing it.

> **At whom?**
> I don't know. I've got a list.
> **Now why exactly--**
> I don't know. Exactly.
> >   (Lord Malquist, p. 12)

Later in the novel Moon again has a conversation
with himself:

> Moon smirked.
> **Schizo.**
> What?
> **Would you describe yourself as a**
> **schizophrenic?**
> Oh really. . . .
> **Wha'?**
> I mean I'm not bigoted--I can see both sides
> of a question.
> **And subscribe to both.**
> That doesn't make me a schizophrenic.
> **What about interviewing yourself?**
> No harm in that, nothing sinister in that at
> all, merely an attempt at rationalization.
> >   (Lord Malquist, p. 74)

Stoppard's question-and-answer format is similar
to that of Joyce's "Ithaca" as can be seen in the
following excerpt:

> Why did Bloom experience a sentiment of
> remorse? Because in immature impatience he
> had treated with disrespect certain beliefs
> and practices.
> As?
> The prohibition of the use of fleshmeat and
> milk at one meal, ...
> How did these beliefs and practices now
> appear to him? Not more rational than they
> had then appeared, not less rational than
> other beliefs and practices now appeared.[8]

Stoppard himself seemed to hint at a desired
connection between **Lord Malquist** and **Ulysses** when he stated in an interview:

> Stoppard: The action of the novel [**Lord**
>   **Malquist**] takes place within twenty-
>   four hours in contemporary London. The

> characters have a sort of eccentricity
> that moves them into a Surrealistic
> context, but the book isn't in the least
> Surrealistic. Nothing in it is unreal or
> distorted, although some of it is
> heightened to a degree of absurdity. I
> think that realism has room for absurdi-
> ty. It's a sort of funny book. I wrote
> it to be funny.[9]

The novel is a funny one and the butt of
most of the jokes is Moon who can't help but
remind the reader of Bloom. Moon as well as his
employer Lord Malquist is the spectator as hero.
Like Bloom, he passively watches a lot as he
rambles about the city that is home. We are
reminded of Joyce writing about Bloom in Dublin
when we read:

> He [Moon] crossed the road, because that was
> southerly, and looked through the railings
> into Green Park which shined wet and wind-
> swept, desolate as Arctic tundra. Then he
> turned to his left, easterly, and began to
> walk towards the Circus, but without hope,
> and stopped again when he reached the
> right-angle of Queen's Walk which cut south
> down the side of the Ritz and straight
> across Green Park joining the parallels of
> Picadilly and the Mall; . . . It occurred
> to him that the labyrinthine riddle of
> London's streets might be subjected to a
> single mathematical formula, one of such
> sophistication that it would relate the
> whole hopeless mess into a coherent logic.
>   (**Lord Malquist**, p. 113)

Like Bloom, Moon is overwhelmed by the mass
of things which surround him. Like Bloom, he has
a sexual problem with his wife who gives off the
appearance that she is unfaithful to him. Like
Bloom, he makes his living by writing and has the
touch of the poet about him (he thinks). Like
Bloom, he constantly gets things mixed up as when
Malquist's utterance "cosmic accuracy" becomes
"comic inaccuracy" (**Lord Malquist**, p. 3) in

Moon's notebook. Like Bloom, Moon is careless.
He allows his notebook to get wet and then burns
it up when he tries to dry it by a fire.

So Moon bears a direct resemblance with
Bloom. He is mistreated by everyone, especially
his wife. Moon plays verbal games, thinks often,
and makes literary allusions to T. S. Eliot,
Waugh, and others. Unlike Bloom he does get some
sexual comfort (from Lady Malquist). But Moon's
real situation is like Bloom in that events seem
to be in control of his life.

Stoppard pays homage to Joyce's **Ulysses**
when he parodies so many different authors and
styles. Critics have pointed out the use of
old-fashioned melodrama, drawing-room comedy,
Heyer Regency romance, westerns, vaudeville,
film, absurdity, Oscar Wilde, Kingsley Amis,
Salvador Dali, Hemingway, T. S. Eliot, Joseph
Conrad, Evelyn Waugh, P. G. Wodehouse, Pepys,
Boswell, Nabokov, and others.[10]

Stoppard creates another nod to Joyce when
Moon discusses his project, a history of the
world:

> Meanwhile I retired to my desk to work on my
> book **The History of the World**. Today I
> toyed with one or two openings but at once
> felt uneasy about committing myself to the
> narrative before I was in full possession of
> all the elements that will go into it. When
> the time comes perhaps Jane will help with
> typing. It will be quite pleasant I feel.
> (**Lord Malquist**, p. 86)

This history can't help but remind the reader of
Joyce's **Finnegans Wake**. Moon will never
write it, will never even write the first
sentence.

Moon's situation seems best exemplified in
the many cuts and the bleeding he undergoes. He
appears to be a comic-Christ figure who cuts his
hand while opening a can of Pork'n'Beans. He
soaks the bread with blood, bread intended for
another Christ figure of sorts, the character
known as the Risen Christ. Londré goes so far
as to say that this scene evokes the body and
blood (bread and wine) of Christ.[11]

Moon later cuts his feet on a broken mirror, one that Jane hit him with, and he is even scratched by Lord Malquist's lion. Throughout the novel he bounces about with his various wounds until he is finally killed by a bomb thrown by Mr. Cuttle who thinks he is Lord Malquist. His life ends as it was lived, pathetically.

As with Joyce, Stoppard can be said to relish parody. As does **Ulysses** on a much grander scale, **Lord Malquist** has noticeable design. For example, Chapter 5 is a stylistic repeat of Chapter 1 as the main characters all reassemble, this time at Trafalgar Square at the funeral of the great statesman. Like Joyce, Stoppard presents apparent chaos and then allows the reader to put the puzzle together. For both Joyce and Stoppard the battlefield is turned into a farce.

Like Joyce, Stoppard relishes the pun and the clever twist of well-known quotations. For example, Lady Malquist who has just gotten out of jail for drunkenness devises the following puns when she tells Moon, "No booze in jail, you know, Bosie. They put me in a temperance prison. Without bars. Witty?" (**Lord Malquist**, p. 126). And an example of the corrupted quotation occurs when Malquist prophetically tells Moon: "I am an island, Mr Moon, and when the bell tolls it tolls for thee" (**Lord Malquist**, p. 4).

Stoppard's characters often appear in pairs as do Lord Malquist and Mr Moon. Examples include Rosencrantz and Guildenstern, Birdboot and Moon, Foot and Holmes, George Moore and Archibald Jumper, Henry Carr and Tristan Tzara. Dean has pointed out that rarely is one the dominant and one submissive. Instead one appears more systematic while the other comes to depend on his partner.[12]

Like Rosencrantz and Guildenstern, Malquist and Moon withdraw from the chaos around them and attempt to make sense of it. There appears to be a connection between Malquist and Guildenstern and between Moon and Rosencrantz. Guildenstern does not have a Boswell but he does have a

faithful listener in Rosencrantz. Like Guildenstern it is Malquist who tosses out the deeper
thoughts for Moon's ears. When Malquist says,
"Since we cannot hope for order let us withdraw
with style from the chaos" (**Lord Malquist**, p.
21), he sounds like the clever Guildenstern.

Looking at Stoppard's works overall, Lord
Malquist becomes the paradigm for the "Boot"
character, that is, one who kicks, albeit lightly. The Boot character has more control over his
destiny, yet his fate is almost always disastrous.

And, of course, Moon serves as the paradigm
for the "Moon" character throughout Stoppard's
works. By sheer accident, Moon bends over, it
seems, and gets kicked every time for his
efforts.

There is no play-within-the-play in **Lord
Malquist** but ordinary life, the life of modern
London, might be said to be that play. Where
Hamlet served as the hostile world for
Rosencrantz and Guildenstern, modern London
serves as such for Malquist and Moon. Like
Rosencrantz and Guildenstern, Malquist and Moon
withdraw from the normal flow of life and instead
live within their imaginary worlds, which allows
for strange events such as swapping wives and
Malquist's eighteenth-century coach (his
malquist), his falcon, and his pet lion.

What the main characters in both these works
discover is never revealed. Rosencrantz,
Guildenstern, and Moon all die while Malquist,
though dispossessed of his home, lives on. What
one reads in **Lord Malquist** is the same pondering one experienced in **Rosencrantz**. Lord
Malquist voices his thoughts while Moon thinks
his over and over; neither gets anywhere.
Between their extremities of "style" and
"substance," Malquist and Moon vacillate throughout the novel and this vacillation often is
witnessed in future plays. Stoppard's plays,
especially **Rosencrantz**, end up in the air as
does **Lord Malquist**.

Brassell has pointed out that the difference
in attitude between the Players and Rosencrantz
and Guildenstern resembles the contrast between

Malquist and Moon. The Players like Malquist
survive on the philosophy that "things don't
stand much looking into." The Players revel in
the illusion of their world of acting while
Rosencrantz and Guildenstern are unaware of their
confinement in this world and pass their play in
a search for clues and connections in a quest for
identity and meaning.[13]
     Lord Malquist echoes many of the senti-
ments in **Rosencrantz.** For example, Lady
Malquist and Moon sum up so much of the pondering
in **Rosencrantz** when they discuss Moon's
projected history study:

> "But isn't it all mixed up, Bosie?"
> "Yes, that's it--when I've got everything I
> can put it all down in the form of a big
> chart, all over a wall, with different races
> and so on, . . . like a diagram of every-
> thing that counts, so it might be possible
> to discover the grand design, find out if
> there is one, or if it's all random--if
> there's anything to it." . . .
> "Why?"
> "I just want to know."
> "I mean, does it matter?"
> "Yes." **Doesn't it?**   "I mean, whether
> it's all random or inevitable."
> "But what difference does it make?"
> "What?"
> "Whether it's all random or inevitable."
> . . . He floundered--"Well, you want to know
> that there is something going on besides a
> lot of accidents." . . .
> "But if it's all random then what's the
> point?"
> "What's the point if it's all inevitable?"
>   (**Lord Malquist,** p. 129)

     The early plays are diverse but in each the
protagonist takes refuge from the real world.
Riley in **Enter a Free Man** becomes an "inven-
tor"; Albert in **Albert's Bridge** resorts to a
life as viewed from atop a bridge; John Brown in
A Separate Peace retires to a hospital for
escape; George Moore escapes to his room where he

prepares a lecture which as far as **Jumpers** is
concerned he never gives. Each of these early
protagonists has attempted to withdraw from the
chaos, preferring to live in his own private
dream world.

The seeds for **Jumpers** can also be found
in **Lord Malquist**. Like both marriages in
Lord Malquist, the marriage between George
and Dotty Moore is a troubled one. Dotty has had
an emotional breakdown caused in part by the
explorations on the moon. Like both Moon and
Lord Malquist, George is incapable of helping his
wife and like those two, the appearance is given
in **Jumpers** that someone else, Archie Jumper,
enjoys Moore's wife's sexual favors. George is
like Moon in that he wishes to capture everything
in a written document, his lecture about the
existence of God. Marie's dead body under the
chesterfield in **Lord Malquist** becomes McFee's
dead body on the back of a door in **Jumpers**.
Archie is a latter-day Malquist in that style
rather than substance is what matters. Both men
care nothing at all about others. In **Jumpers**
the circumstances are changed a bit but the
action of Malquist's and Moon's domiciles are
simply moved to the house the Moores occupy in
Mayfair.

Hound and **After Magritte** must be
thought of in conjunction with **Lord Malquist**.
The important thing there is that all three deal
intently with perception. At the beginning of
Lord Malquist one reads about the variety of
eccentrics and only later does it become a clear
how such a group blends together to make a novel.
In both **Hound** and **After Magritte** one discovers puzzles, puzzles with more clues given as
the play proceeds.

In **Hound** the names Birdboot and Moon
reappear (Birdboot is the butler in charge of
Malquist's estate) and the play opens with a dead
body on the floor, a body reminiscent of Marie's
dead body in **Lord Malquist**. **Hound** is one
of the most confusing of Stoppard's plays but by
play's end the dead body is revealed to be Higgs,
both Birdboot and Moon are shot dead, and
Puckeridge alias Magnus alias Hound alias Albert
Muldoon stands up to reveal his subterfuge.

After Magritte like **Lord Malquist**
begins with a puzzle: why are things as they are
in the Harris house? There is an explanation for
each of the strange occurrences. For example,
all the furniture is stacked against the door not
to keep anyone out but to allow the Harrises to
practice dancing.

The other puzzle in **After Magritte** is
the identity of the strange man reported seen
committing a crime. Harris, Thelma, Mother, and
Inspector Foot each have a different description.
The purported criminal is variously described as
a black-and-white minstrel with a broken crutch,
a blind one-legged man in pajamas carrying a
tortoise (George Moore carries his tortoise Pat
to the door in **Jumpers**), a West Bromwich
Albion footballer with his face covered with
shaving cream, and an escaped prisoner with a
handbag and a cricket bat. It turns out that the
person was Inspector Foot of the Yard who was
putting money in a parking meter and, in fact, no
crime occurred.

One point to be stressed is that Stoppard
has a vision of life that is both comic and
serious. His novel and plays are characterized
by the constant sense that life is comically
absurd, but behind all the bizarreness runs the
question: how do we cope with existence in such
a mad world?[14]

I have mentioned that **Lord Malquist**
opens with a puzzle, the six sections which
describe each of the eccentrics in the novel.
The Prologue to **Travesties** acts as a Stoppard
play in miniature. The audience is teased by the
mischief of an opening of silence in a library (a
possible reference, as in the opening silence of
Hound, to both Pinter and Beckett) followed by
an incomprehensible flow of language from the
characters, except for Cecily's "Ssssssh." Tzara
opens the play with the following incoherent
poem:

> Tzara: Eel ate enormous appletzara
>   key dairy chef's hat he'll learn
>   oomparah!

> Ill raced alas whispers kill later nut
> east,
> moon avuncular ill day Clara!
> (**Travesties**, p. 18)

Inevitably one must turn to commentary to discover that what is spoken is a limerick in near-French which translates as follows:

> He is a man called Tzara
> who has unparalleled
> talent
> He stays in Switzerland
> Because he is an artist
> "We have only art," he
> declared.[15]

Joyce the character mystifies the audience by dictating to Gwendolen "Deshill holles eamus" and other phrases which appear in the opening to Joyce's "Oxen of the Sun." And the final puzzle occurs when Lenin and his wife begin speaking in Russian about the revolution ("revolutsia") in St. Petersburg.

Like **Lord Malquist**, **Travesties** is a series of parodies. The word travesty itself means to burlesque or parody something, and **Travesties** is Stoppard's finest example of parody to date.

The central parody, of course, is Wilde's **The Importance of Being Earnest** (hereafter referred to as **Earnest**). The syntax of the play is sometimes Wildean, sometimes Joycean, sometimes Dadaistic. In **Travesties** Stoppard draws on Shakespeare, Wilde, Joyce, Tzara, Lenin, and others.

As in **Lord Malquist**, Stoppard again parodies Joyce's technique of switching from one style to another (sometimes in mid-narrative). The most obvious of these is the catechism section (**Travesties**, pp. 56-61) which parodies both Lady Bracknell in **Earnest** and the question-and-answer section in **Ulysses** ("Ithaca").

Travesties is the logical outcome of the plays which preceded it, combining the two kinds

of fiction found in **After Magritte** and
Jumpers. Carr's reminiscences, which form the
structural focus of the play, are fictionaliza-
tions of his personal life; like the fictions of
After Magritte they put the individual's
imaginative stamp upon his experience. And the
philosophy-fictions of **Jumpers** are found in
Travesties's four-sided debate about what
constitutes art as seen through the memory of
Henry Carr.[16]

   Travesties is the story of Carr, the
"spectator as hero" (a chapter title in **Lord
Malquist**). This spectator daydreams about his
past frustrations and his neglected fame, and he
recreates his past as he would have liked it.
As Pearce has stated, "**Travesties** is like a
hall of mirrors, character mirroring character,
art mirroring world, stage mirroring art reflecting world, artist reflecting world reflecting
artist, present reflecting past."[17] **Travesties** is like a Cubist painting that attempts
to portray events from as many different directions as possible, something begun in Stoppard's
Lord Malquist.

   The cover of the Faber and Faber edition of
Stoppard's latest play **The Real Thing** (1982)
alerts the reader to the play's themes by depict-
ing a mirror image of a man standing on a stage
in front of a mirror with a mirror image of a man
standing on a stage in front of a mirror which is
endlessly repeated to give the illusion of
infinity as in an endless series of Chinese boxes
or in an infinite regress, of which so many
appeared in **Jumpers**. This pictorial representation of **The Real Thing** welcomes the
reader to a play filled with examples of the
literature of exhaustion and one need only to
return to **Lord Malquist** to find early
illustrations of this.

   Lord Malquist may be the most important
early work with which to compare **The Real
Thing**. In that novel Lord Malquist and Moon
swap wives for sexual purposes. The swapping
goes much further in **The Real Thing** for Henry
marries (or so we are led to believe) Annie,
Max's first wife. Stoppard teases us by not

revealing exactly who it is that Max marries at
the end of the play, but we are told she is an
actress and we are led to believe that it is
Charlotte, Henry's first wife. Although **Lord
Malquist** is much more bizarre than **The Real
Thing**, both concern themselves, **Lord
Malquist** less so, with the topic of love versus
adultery.

   Stoppard had to write two political plays,
Dirty Linen (1976) and **Night and Day** (1978)
as lead-ins before he could write **The Real
Thing** (1982). **Dirty Linen**, Stoppard's
"knickers farce," handled the theme of love
versus adultery from only one angle of the
debate. The action of that play stems from the
fact that Maddie Gotobed has had affairs with
almost everyone on the Select Committee on
Promiscuity in High Places, and she is the
committee's secretary. Rather than explore the
topic of love deeply in **Dirty Linen**, Stoppard
instead allows the action of illicit sex to
function as a concise metaphor for the
imperfections of governmental processes.

   With **Night and Day** Stoppard began a
deeper treatment of the subject of love. Ruth
Carson, married to Geoffrey Carson who runs a
successful mining industry in a fictitious former
British colony in Africa, has an affair with Dick
Wagner, a journalist she meets in London while
picking up her son in prep school. But the
tensions in Ruth's marriage are not fully
developed and are overshadowed by the topics of
British Imperialism in Africa and the value and
duty of journalism to tell the true story.

   Therefore a close reading of **Lord
Malquist** now serves as a watershed filled with
the characters and themes that Stoppard developed
in many of his later works, especially those that
might be labelled "literature of exhaustion." On
both ends of the present spectrum, one can see
that Stoppard kicked off things, more or less, as
a playwright when he examined and exhausted for
himself the theme of Death in **Rosencrantz &
Guildenstern Are Dead** (1967). Within **The
Real Thing** (1982) he exhausted for himself, the

topic of Love, thereby encompassing the second
of literature's two great themes.

    Stoppard's plays that contain plays within
them, his literature of exhaustion, are metaphoric marriages and include his three best works--
Rosencrantz, Jumpers, and **Travesties.**
Stoppard has stated that the "perfect marriage"
on stage is one between a "play of ideas and
farce or perhaps even even high comedy."[18]
Stoppard's choice of the phrase "perfect
marriage" enlightens auditors who can look back
to **Lord Malquist's** farcical plot about the
marriage state and who can scrutinize **The Real
Thing** and find the farce all but gone for the
sake of high comedy.

Notes

1. Richard Corballis, **Stoppard: The
Mystery and the Clockwork** (New York: Methuen,
1984), p. 17. Hereafter **Rosencrantz &
Guildenstern Are Dead** will be referred to as
Rosencrantz and **Lord Malquist & Mr Moon**
will be referred to as **Lord Malquist.**

2. Tim Brassell, **Tom Stoppard: An
Assessment** (New York: St. Martin's Press,
1985), p. 263.

3. Tom Stoppard, **Lord Malquist & Mr
Moon** (New York: Alfred A. Knopf, 1968), n.p.
All further references to this novel will be from
this edition. Arriving at workable dates for
Rosencrantz and **Lord Malquist** resembles
Stoppard's doubling of characters in his works.
Rosencrantz came first since Stoppard
composed the rough drafts and the burlesque
version that evolved into the final version while
participating in a Ford Foundation grant in
Berlin from May until October in 1964. **Tom
Stoppard: An Assessment** p. 7 points out that
the Anthony Blond edition of **Lord Malquist**
was published during the same week in August 1966
that **Rosencrantz** (in a slightly shortened
form) was first produced at the Edinburgh
Festival. The first professional production of
Rosencrantz was given at the Old Vic Theatre
on April 11, 1967. Both Faber and Grove
published **Rosencrantz** in 1967. **Stoppard:
The Mystery and the Clockwork** pp. 189-94 lists
the various editions of Stoppard's works up to
1982.

4. This switching of partners will occur again
in Stoppard's **The Real Thing**, that is, if one
concludes that Max marries Charlotte.

5. John Barth, "Literature of Exhaustion,"
Atlantic Monthly (August 1967), pp. 29-34;
"Literature of Replenishment," **Atlantic
Monthly** (January 1980), p. 71.

6. In Stoppard, **Night and Day** (New York: Grove Press, 1979), p. 93 the audience gets a glimpse of "Ruth"'s thoughts which includes another example of exhaustion related in type to the one about the tins of Pork'n'Beans:

> "Ruth": On a packet of salt used in my grandmother's kitchen there was a label showing a girl holding a packet of salt with the label showing, and so on. It is said, with what authority I do not know, that this was the inspiration of Whistler's famous painting of my grandmother painting her self-portrait, the one he was painting. A different school holds that it was in fact the inspiration of Turner's painting of a packet of salt. During a storm at sea. Sorry. I was miles away. Come and sit down. I talk to myself in the middle of a conversation. In fact I talk to myself in the middle of an **imaginary** conversation, which is itself a refuge from some other conversation altogether, frequently imaginary. I hope you don't mind me telling you all this.

7. The image of the mirror is a popular one with Stoppard. His stage directions call for one between the stage and the audience in **Hound.** George Moore looks at an imaginary mirror in **Jumpers.** The film **The Romantic English-woman** for which Stoppard was scenarist includes many reflections in mirrors, windows, and vases. The cover of the Faber and Faber edition of **The Real Thing** depicts a man on stage in front of a mirror which reflects a man on a stage in front of a mirror and so on.

8. James Joyce, **Ulysses** (New York: Random House, 1961), p. 724. All further references to **Ulysses** will be to this edition.

9. Anon., "The Talk of the Town," **The New Yorker,** 44 (May 4, 1968) rpt. in Felicia Londré, **Tom Stoppard** (New York: Frederick Ungar, 1981), pp. 101-102.

10.   Londré, p. 106; David Gordon, "Some Recent Novels," **Yale Review**, 58 (October 1968), 123; Phoebe Adams, "Potpourri" **Atlantic**, 221 (May 1968), 114.

11.   Londré, p. 103.

12.   Joan Dean, **Tom Stoppard** (Columbia, Missouri: University of Missouri Press, 1981), p. 18.

13.   Brassell, p. 52.

14.   Brassell, p. 265.

15.   Jim Hunter, **Tom Stoppard's Plays** (New York: Grove Press, 1982), p. 240.

16.   Susan Harland, "Play, Game, and Playfulness in Tom Stoppard's Plays," Diss. University of Pittsburgh,1979, p. 210.

17.   Howard D. Pearce, "Stage as Mirror: Tom Stoppard's **Travesties**," **MLN**, 94 (December 1979), 1148.

18.   Tom Stoppard, "Ambushes for the Audience: Towards a High Comedy of Ideas," **Theatre Quarterly**, 4 (May – July 1974), 7.

"Wheels within wheels, etcetera":
Artistic Design in
Rosencrantz and Guildenstern Are Dead

William E. Gruber

Tom Stoppard's **Rosencrantz and
Guildenstern Are Dead** ought to cause us to
acknowledge some inadequacies in the vocabulary
we currently use to discuss plays, and the nature
of our shortcoming can be demonstrated, I think,
with some representative summaries of Stoppard's
art. Ruby Cohn, for example, suggests that
Stoppard proved "extremely skillful in dovetail-
ing the **Hamlet** scenes into the **Godot**
situation"; Ronald Hayman writes that "Stoppard
appeared at the right moment with his beautifully
engineered device for propelling two attendant
lords into the foreground"; Charles Marowitz
comments that "Stoppard displays a remarkable
skill in juggling the donnees of existential
philosophy"; and Thomas Whitaker argues that "the
raisonneur of this clever pastiche is of
course The Player . . . [who] knowingly plays
himself."[1]
    Such language--"skillful in dovetailing,"
"beautifully engineered," "clever pastiche"--
condemns while it praises, subtly labeling
Stoppard's play as a derivative piece of
workmanship. We tend to mistrust anything which
is not obviously new, not wholly original; yet
surely our modern bias here obscures crucial
differences between Stoppard's play and, say, the
Hamlet-collages of Marowitz and Joseph Papp.
These latter works may be summarized accurately
as examples of skillful joinery. But Stoppard's
drama does not simply "fit" together different
pieces of theater. His play has no clear
theatrical precedent, and a workshop vocabulary

proves unable to explain what occurs when the
script of **Hamlet** mingles with the script of
Rosencrantz and Guildenstern Are Dead.

Part of the reason this subject has not been
clarified is that it is impossible to assess
accurately the extent to which the audience will
recognize allusions to **Hamlet.** Even one of
Stoppard's stage directions poses insoluble
problems: "**Hamlet enters upstage, and pauses,
weighing up the pros and cons of making his
quietus.**"[2] Is this a reference which only
readers who are familiar with Hamlet's soliloquy
can pick up? Or can the actor who mimes Hamlet's
actions somehow call the audience's attention to
a specific portion of an unspoken soliloquy? Or,
to cite a related problem, what is the audience
to make of references to **Hamlet** which occur
out of immediate literary context? For example,
Guildenstern, on board the ship for England,
suddenly speaks portions of Hamlet's
"pipe-playing" speech, a speech he had heard (yet
can we really assume this?) during an earlier
scene from Shakespeare's play which Stoppard does
not reproduce. Is it possible that Stoppard here
intends to show that Guildenstern ironically is
locked into the text of **Hamlet?** But if this
is Stoppard's intent, how many viewers, in
passing, could make the necessary connections
between the two plays? Because of these and
other similar instances, it is clear that
different kinds of audiences are going to
experience significantly different responses to
the various allusions to **Hamlet.** Those who
read **Rosencrantz and Guildenstern Are Dead**
are more acutely aware of the numerous subtle
references to **Hamlet;** and, of course, those
readers and viewers who are thoroughly familiar
with Shakespeare's drama will recognize many more
interactions between the two plays than those
members of the audience who know **Hamlet** only
as a famous old tragedy.

The key to Stoppard's design, however,
cannot be found by wrestling with ambiguities
such as these, and there is no point in laboring
to answer what percentage of what audience
catches which **Hamlet** allusion. Instead, it

will be more profitable to speculate regarding
the general expectations of one who comes to see
or to read the play. It would be a mistake to
underestimate the pervasive influence of
Shakespeare's most famous tragedy, even among
those whose interest in the theater is minimal.
Our belief that **Hamlet** is **the** central
drama of our culture has been growing since late
in the eighteenth century, so that the language
of the play shapes our idiom, governs the way we
think on certain critical matters. Indeed, the
play's status is mythic.[3] Stoppard can assume
of every member of his audience an almost
religious attitude toward **Hamlet**, a belief
that this play comes closer than any other to
capturing the mystery of human destiny. The
audience does not expect **Hamlet** itself, and
this is an important distinction. Stoppard's
audience is not prepared for any specific
response to the **Hamlet** material; and the
great secret of his method is that he offers us a
wonderfully suggestive way of seeing human action
performed simultaneously in several modes.

If one assumes that Stoppard is using
Hamlet as ancient playwrights used myth--and
not for irony or for plot line or for laughs--one
sees his play in ways which are wholly invisible
to those who mistakenly treat it as a "worm's
eye" view of tragedy, or as a witty experiment in
Absurdist drama, or as a clever Shakespearean
pastiche.[4] From this perspective, I plan to
review three noteworthy features of **Rosencrantz
and Guildenstern Are Dead.** My aim is to
correct a number of misconceptions regarding the
play, misconceptions which have persisted for so
long that they are in danger of becoming accepted
as facts.

The first thing that impresses one about the
play is its peculiar "literariness." So marked,
in fact, is this quality that no one seems able
to avoid mentioning it. Though there has been no
agreement as to its effect, it is generally taken
to be more-or-less undesirable. Robert Brustein,
for example, once called the play a "theatrical
parasite"; Normand Berlin has dissected the play
into specific borrowings from Shakespeare,

Beckett, and Pirandello, concluding that the play
exists exclusively on an intellectual level
rather than an emotional one; Andrew Kennedy
believes that "the real pressure in the play
comes from thought about the theater rather than
from personal experience"; and almost every other
commentary or review of **Rosencrantz and
Guildenstern Are Dead** stresses Stoppard's
indebtedness to Absurdist dramatists, Beckett in
particular.[5]   Clearly, **Rosencrantz and
Guildenstern Are Dead** is so consciously a
distillation of literature and literary method
that, to paraphrase Maynard Mack's point about
Hamlet's mysteriousness, the play's
literariness seems to be part of its point. We
feel this literariness in numberless ways. We
feel it in the particular use of the
Shakespearean materials: in the characters,
certainly, and in the numerous scenes or
part-scenes from **Hamlet**, in the broad sweep
of the action, and in the incessant probing of
familiar questions as to Hamlet's madness, his
motives, his ambitions, fears, loves. And we
feel it in a less specific sense, too: partly
because of The Player, of course, who points the
thought of the play with his frequent discussions
of tragedy, of melodrama, and of the significance
of playing and acting; but partly, too, because
of the general bookish consciousness which seems
to be diffused evenly throughout the play,
manifest in a score or more of literary or
linguistic biases: syllogisms, puns, rhetori-
cians' games, pointed repetitions, along with a
host of allusions to literature and literary
topics that at times threaten to make the play
into an exclusively literary epistemology,
shifting our attention from pictorial to verbal
theater.

     In this respect, in fact, the play is
remarkably exploratory. "Like a Metaphysical
poet," Hayman writes, "or a dog with a bone,
Stoppard plays untiringly with his central
conceit, never putting it down except to pick it
up again, his teeth gripping it even more
firmly."[6]   One feels here enormous pressures of
language operating through the characters,

pressures which, say, in the work of Ionesco or
Beckett, are distinguished only in a negative
sense, as they are in the broken discourse of
Lucky in **Godot** or in the ludicrous
absurdities of **The Bald Soprano.** Here,
however, language is not an imperfect instrument,
a thing to be scorned. There is so much
conscious experimentation with language, it is as
if Stoppard were permitting his characters the
freedom to strive for the linguistic combination,
so to speak, that will unlock their mystery. Ros
and Guil often exchange banalities, to be sure;
but sometimes, too, their words frame truths, as
when they analyze the history of Hamlet's
condition (end of Act I), or when they discover
(on board ship in Act III) the purpose of their
voyage to England.

     For these reasons, the dramatic power of
Rosencrantz and Guildenstern Are Dead
involves more than skillful juggling or witty
commentary, and Stoppard has done more than to
dovetail his story with an older one in the
manner, for example, that Eugene O'Neill created
Mourning Becomes Electra. The staged events
of **Rosencrantz and Guildenstern Are Dead** in
fact have little in common with the events of
Hamlet; they are not the same play, but
different plays jostling for the same space. And
the outcome of the duel, so to speak, between the
respective plots of **Rosencrantz and**
Guildenstern Are Dead and **Hamlet** is hardly
a foregone conclusion. Stoppard's play is not an
"interpretation" of **Hamlet** if by
"interpretation" one refers merely to a modern
rendering of a fixed text. The real technical
innovation of **Rosencrantz and Guildenstern Are**
Dead can be understood only when we see that,
for Stoppard, the text of **Hamlet** is
potentially invalid, or at least incomplete--
something to be tested, explored, rather than
accepted without proof, just as a myth may
generate endless versions of itself, some
contradictory. Hence Stoppard is not using
Hamlet as a script; rather, the script of
Hamlet forms part of the material for a
discursive experiment, a literary exercise, as it

were. In this most superficial sense, Stoppard's
play may be considered simply an honest effort to
clarify some matters of Hamlet's story that
Shakespeare for unknown reasons ignored. Thus
Brian Murray commented on the play: "This
strikes a blow for everyone who was ever puzzled
by a minor Shakespeare part."[7]

In a more profound sense, however, the play
does not clarify mysteries, only multiplies them.
Yet this does not mean that Stoppard equivocates,
teases his audience with a methodical changing of
signs. Like its famous Elizabethan predecessor,
Rosencrantz and Guildenstern Are Dead
attempts to close with the fact of meaninglessness, to enfold it with words. Here we touch the
core, I think, of the play's literariness,
perceive the motive behind its experimentation
with a variety of scripts. What, this play asks
again and again, is valid dramatic language, and
what is its relationship to the modes of human
action? Is that relationship heroic? or is it
comic, a poignant statement of our own
insignificance? Two possible and variant texts,
one willed and one predicted, here compete for
the same stage in a contest which is mediated by
the figure of The Player, who moves easily
between the heroics of Hamlet's court and the
anterior world of Ros and Guil. It is important
when experiencing Stoppard's play to be alive to
its rich variety of contrasts.[8] We must wince
at the jolt, so to speak, whenever the play
shifts from one mode to another, from one cast
and its story to its alternate, and back again.
Iambics and prose, vigor and lassitude,
seriousness and silliness, skill and ineptitude,
all coexist, alternately and repeatedly testing
the efficacy and theatrical appeal of each. We
must not hold up one mode at the expense of the
other, but must be sensitive to each of the two
as an element in an ongoing dialectic. Moreover,
we ought not to see these incompatible elements
as an experiment in Absurdist drama, either in
philosophy or in form. For the play does not
advance a simplistic philosophy by means of its
constantly shifting perspectives, but develops a
debate: Do we wish our drama in meter, or in

prose? Do we prefer silly gaming, or coherent
action? Do we, like Ros, want a "good story,
with a beginning, middle and end" (80)? Or do
we, like Guil, prefer "art to mirror life" (81)?
And finally, are these ancient classical
directives of any relevance nowadays, times being
what they are?[9]
        Thus the literariness of Stoppard's play is
pervasive, total. Its significance cannot be
grasped simply by documenting the numerous
specific echoes of earlier plays and playwrights,
"intellectualizing" the play and its author,
assigning them the appropriate thematic and
technical camp, or postcamp. Not a failure of
words, which proves the playwright's lack of
originality or demonstrates his place in the
Absurdist ranks, but a bold assertion of
language's worth: for all the theatrical and
literary elements, it turns out, are not ends in
themselves, but help clearly to frame deeply
personal considerations of human action, its
motives and limitations and values. From its
earliest moments, Stoppard's play reopens a
number of very old questions related to the
meaning of the simple **event**, questions which
Waiting for Godot had effectively closed.
The play begins by posing such questions: a coin
falls "heads" almost ninety times in succession.
It must, as Guil says, be "indicative of
something besides the redistribution of wealth.
List of possible explanations. One: I'm willing
it. . . . Two: time has stopped dead. . . .
Three: divine intervention. . . . Four: a
spectacular vindication of the principle that
each individual coin spun individually is as
likely to come down heads as tails and therefore
should cause no surprise each individual time it
does" (16).
        Since the operations of their world lie
generally beyond their comprehension, it is not
surprising that critics, used to modern theater,
have found in Ros and Guil's plight yet one more
image of humans' bafflement as to their proper
roles. Ros and Guil have usually been seen (in
Thomas Whitaker's words) as "two characters in
search of an **explication de texte,** two

muddled players in reluctant pursuit of the roles
they already play."[10] It is in this respect,
of course, that the play seems most closely to
resemble Beckett's **Godot.** For we hear echoes
of Vladimir and Estragon in the repetitious
emptiness of Ros and Guil's conversations as
they, like Beckett's clowns, wait to play their
parts: "Where's it going to end?" "That's the
question." "It's **all** questions." "Do you
think it matters?" "Doesn't it matter to you?"
"Why should it matter?" "What does it matter
why? Doesn't it **matter** why it matters?"
What's the **matter** with you?" "It doesn't
matter." "What's the game?" "What are the
rules" (44)? Whether or not Ros and Guil's
bewilderment suggests the play's essential
kinship with the work of Beckett is a matter I
would like to take up later. One final point
concerning the two courtiers: it is clear that
their essence--hence their character--is
conceived in terms of emptiness: **Two
Elizabethans** [establishes the opening stage
direction] **passing the time in a place without
any visible character**" (11).
        Concomitant with this emptiness of act and
motive, of course, is a second important feature
of **Rosencrantz and Guildenstern Are Dead,** an
emphasis on play and playing. Like **Hamlet,
Rosencrantz and Guildenstern Are Dead** examines
human acts and acting within a variety of
contexts ranging from practical to the
metaphysical to the theological. Central to
Stoppard's play are the figures of Rosencrantz
and Guildenstern, two of literature's most
unimportant people, mere concessions to the
expediencies of plot. Shakespeare jokes about
the courtiers' lack of individuality by playing
on their metric interchangeability. And
Stoppard, as did Shakespeare, first conceives his
creations as broadly comic. That there should
exist two persons with a corporate identity, as
it were, mocks some of the fundamentals of human
order both on stage and off. The world may well
be a stage; if so, however, the metaphor requires
identities to be unique: each must play his
part. Hence the concept of identical twins--two
actors playing one role--is inherently chaotic,
traditionally comic. In fact, we may trace the

dramatic lineage of Ros and Guil back much
further than Beckett and the music hall, back at
least to Roman comedy, and even further to the
primitive notion that there is something
downright foolish in two people who compete for a
single identity.

But if the actions of Ros and Guil seem
foolish and aimless, it is equally true that
divine secrets seem to govern their madness.
There is no doubt that the various collisions of
identity and motive that occur in **Rosencrantz
and Guildenstern Are Dead**--taken singly--are
humorous. Yet here, as is true of the comic
elements that are characteristic of mature
Shakespearean tragedy, what is funny and what is
serious seem interchangeable--or, rather, seem
independent analogues of a grim reality. We
realize very soon, for example, that the Fool's
witticisms in **Lear** are "no play." Something
similar conditions our appreciation of Stoppard's
drama: grappling with the concept of death as a
state of negative existence, for example,
Guildenstern concludes that, "You can't not-be on
a boat," a statement which is mocked immediately
by Ros's foolish misinterpretation, "I've
frequently not been on boats" (108). Yet the
courtiers' inept mishandling of language does not
long remain a comic malapropism, but bends, to
use Robert Frost's image, with a crookedness that
is straight. Both twisted syntax and twisted
logic are appallingly true: wherever they
are--on boats, on the road, within a court--it is
the fate of Ros and Guil never to be.

The play returns us, then, to thoroughly
familiar territory, to a consideration of some of
the fundamental perplexities that gave shape and
lasting meaning to **Hamlet**. We of this
century do not know with any greater clarity what
it might require for a man "to be." Nor are we
any closer to the secret which resolves the
separate meanings of "play," that art which
defines for us human time endowed with maximum
meaning, maximum consequence. Here it has seemed
to many that Stoppard's answer lies with The
Player: always in character, always in costume,
The Player's essence is his abiding

changeability. The simple fact of his endurance
argues for his wisdom. At the play's end,
corpses litter the stage. Yet The Player, like
Brecht's Mother Courage, seems infinitely
adaptable, infinitely resourceful. Although his
numerous "deaths" are impressive and even
credible, he inevitably returns to life for his
next performance. In a world in which everyone
is marked for death, The Player's survival
capabilities seem especially significant.

Because of the apparent emphasis Stoppard
places on "play," it has been frequently
suggested that Stoppard wants us to believe that
mimesis fosters understanding.[11] In Act I,
for example, Ros and Guil deepen their awareness
of Hamlet's transformation through an act of
role-playing, whereby Ros questions Guil, who
pretends to be Hamlet:

> Ros (lugubriously): His body was still
> warm.
> Guil: So was hers.
> Ros: Extraordinary.
> Ros: Hasty.
> Guil: Suspicious.
> Ros: It makes you think.
> Guil: Don't think I haven't thought of
> it. (50)

Even more important is their playing in Act
III, in which they act out a possible script for
their arrival in England. Here Ros, who is
taking the part of the King of England, becomes
so convinced of the reality of his situation that
he tears open their letter of instructions and
discovers the order for Hamlet's execution.
Suddenly, unexpectedly, Ros and Guil are
illuminated by moral crisis; "Their playing,"
Robert Egan writes, "has made available to them
the opportunity to define significant versions of
self through a concrete moral decision and a
subsequent action, even if a useless
action."[12]

It is inevitable, perhaps, in this shadow
world made of parts of old plays that one of the
largest roles should be that of the Player. And

it is also inevitable that in such a shifting and
ofttimes morally weightless world the advice of
The Player should carry the negative equivalent
of weight. Regarding the question of how to act
in their situation, for example, he advises
Guildenstern to "Relax. Respond. That's what
people do. You can't go through life questioning
your situation at every turn" (66). Or, later,
his professional comments seem universally
applicable: "We follow directions-- there is no
choice involved. The bad end unhappily, the
good unluckily. That is what tragedy means"
(80). And, finally, it is The Player who
convinces Guil (and us) of the impressive
efficacy of mimetic understanding. Indeed, for a
time it seems as if **mimesis** represents the
only valid mode of knowing: the play's closing
scenes forcefully demonstrate that what we
considered a "real" stabbing and a "real" death
was merely competent acting, merely the
fulfillment of the bargain between actor and
audience. "You see," The Player explains to the
dumbfounded Guildenstern, "it is the kind they do
believe in--it's what is expected" (123). And
the truth of this seems to be reinforced a few
lines later, when we truly witness "real" deaths
as merely an actor's casual exit. Ros simply
disappears, disappears so quietly that his friend
does not notice his passing. And Guil makes
death into a game of hide-and-seek: "Now you see
me, now you--" (126).

There is a series evident here, of course:
Hamlet is to Ros and Guil as Ros and Guil are to
Alfred. And naturally this projects an engulfing
form, an engulfing dramatist for **Hamlet,** and
so for Stoppard's audience. Yet we ought not to
presume to have uncovered the message of the play
within this problematical series of regressions.
The mind wearies of such esoteric speculations;
and Stoppard's aim here may well be to cause us
eventually to reject any fancies regarding our
own wispy theatricality. Indeed, the line of
argumentation which makes play the only reality
can be pursued too far, resulting at best in
empty theatricality, at worst in excessively
sophisticated dogma. It is, in Horatio's words,

"to consider too curiously." This is not to deny
the concept of playing an important place in
Stoppard's work. Nevertheless, to make The
Player exclusively into a source of affirmation
betrays the meaning of the remainder of the
characters, ultimately of the entire drama.   "Do
you know what happens to old actors?" inquires
The Player, setting the context for still one
more joke about occupations. Ros, here playing
the comic-hall straight man, obediently asks
"What?" "Nothing," replies The Player, "They're
still acting" (115). Here, in a single word, is
focussed the whole of the play's chilling
analysis of human freedom and providential
design. Actors are **nothing.** As The Player
admits elsewhere, actors are the opposite of
people. It is not a matter of how we take the
sense of "nothing"; for in a play whose deepest
levels of meaning concern the minimum essentials
for human action and human identity, "nothing"
can refer only to a waste of being, the
squandering of human potential through
cowardice.[13]   Perhaps the play's literariness
may help clarify this crucial point: to be
"nothing," in literary terms, has been considered
the most terrible fate of all. Recall, for
example, the horde of lost souls whirling
endlessly outside Dante's Hell, desperately
pursuing all banners, any banner that might
ultimately give them human shape, human meaning.
        As is true of so much of the superficial
horseplay in **Rosencrantz and Guildenstern Are
Dead,** then, words here turn on their user,
twisting themselves into enigmatic truth. The
Player, because his role is eternally to be
someone else, is thus no one in particular. Free
of every human limitation, he exists wholly
within the sphere of play. Thus nothing happens
to the actor because nothing can: he is wholly
amorphous, wholly uncertain, without identity,
feeling or meaning apart from that conferred on
him by his audience, without--and this is most
important--responsibility for who he is. What
The Player espouses is that a person should "act
natural." That is, he argues that one should
merely respond to circumstances, secure in the

belief that in the end all one can do is to
follow one's script. This is of course an
acceptable concept to propose to explain human
activity, but let us acknowledge it for what it
is: fatalism. And there is little evidence in
this play--less in later plays--that Stoppard
holds such a view. The point is this: in this
play, as in most of the important tragic
statements of Western theater, there is no single
perspective that hits the mark.

        We are left, then, with a third problem,
possibly the most intriguing: what sort of play
is **Rosencrantz and Guildenstern Are Dead**? To
call the play a burlesque or a parody betrays
one's insensitivity to its rich and manifold
significances; and "tragicomedy" is a term grown
so vague as to be almost without meaning.
Clearly, Stoppard has surrealist longings in him
(**After Magritte; Travesties; Artist Descending
a Staircase**), but **Rosencrantz and
Guildenstern Are Dead**, despite its veneer of
gimmickry, proves instead the lasting power of
straightforward theater. There is a small
measure of truth in Brustein's term for the
play--"theatrical parasite"--for it is obvious
that Stoppard needs **Hamlet** if his play is to
exist at all. Stoppard's play seems to vibrate
because of the older classic, as a second tuning
fork resonates by means of one already in
motion.

        Nevertheless, the tone of the modern play is
distinct.[14] Properly speaking, Stoppard has
not composed a "play within a play," nor has he
written a lesser action which mirrors a larger.
The old text and the new text are not simply
"joined"; they exist as a colloidal suspension,
as it were, rather than as a permanent chemical
solution. Or, to change metaphors to illustrate
an important point more clearly, the texts of
Hamlet's play and Ros and Guil's play form two
separate spheres of human activity which, like
two heavenly bodies, impinge upon each other
because of their respective gravitational fields.
The history of Rosencrantz and Guildenstern
swings into line the scattered chunks of
Hamlet; and the courtiers' story in turn is

warped by the immense pull of Hamlet's world.
Even though we cannot see much of that world, we
may deduce its fulness. Though it exists largely
offstage, or on another stage, we nevertheless
sense that world's glitter, its nobility, and its
grandeur, and we feel its awesome power.

This is not to imply that the sum of the two
texts results in determinism, or that we leave
the theater pitying Ros and Guil for being
victimized. To the contrary: Helene Keyssar-
Franke speculates that the juxtaposition of
Hamlet scenes and invented scenes "creates a
sense of the possibility of freedom and the
tension of the improbability of escape."[15]
Such is Stoppard's economy of technique that he
chills us with Fate's whisper without a single
line of exposition, without an elaborate setting
of mood or of theme. As the play begins, our
attention is mesmerized by the two courtiers
spinning their recordbreaking succession of
coins. The atmosphere is charged with dramatic
potential, tense with impending crisis. The coin
which falls "heads" scores of times in succession
defines what has been called a "boundary
situation"; the technique is notably
Shakespearean, reminding one of the tense,
foreboding beginnings invoked by the witches of
Macbeth, or, of course, by the ghost of
Hamlet. Ros and Guil's playing is not the
aimless play of Beckett's tramps, with which it
has been compared, but a play obviously freighted
with imminent peril. We are impressed not by the
absurdity of their situation, but by its terrible
sense; one senses the chilling presence of
Hamlet, waiting menacingly in the wings.

But **Hamlet**, as is true of all myths, is
what is predicted, not what is ordained. The two
courtiers are not sniveling, powerless victims of
time and circumstance, and their story does not
illustrate the baffling absurdity or the blind
fatality that has sometimes been said to arrange
their lives. This is the conclusion which many
who comment upon the play have reached, guided,
in part, by the anguish of Guil: "No--it is not
enough. To be told so little--to such an end--
and still, finally, to be denied an

explanation--" (122). We are wrong here to view
events wholly through the eyes of the characters,
and our pity for them must be conditioned with a
little judgment. It is necessary to recognize
that the Ros and Guil whom we see in the final
scene are in no important way different from the
Ros and Guil of the opening scene, and that such
implied insensitivity to their world--puny though
that world may be--bespeaks a deeper, mortal
insensitivity to humanity and to themselves.
Facing death, speaking his final lines of the
play, the burden incumbent upon him to touch the
shape of his life and so give it meaning, Ros one
last time chooses to evade responsibility: "I
don't care. I've had enough. To tell you the
truth, I'm relieved" (125). Nor is the more
speculative Guil alive to his context: "Our
names shouted in a certain dawn," he ponders;
". . . a message . . . a summons. . . . There
must have been a moment, at the beginning, where
we could have said--no. But somehow we missed
it" (125).

The context of men's action remains forever
a mystery. It was a mystery for Hamlet, it is a
mystery for Ros and Guil, it is a mystery for us.
Yet between the two plays there exists an important difference in the quality of the characters'
responses to what must remain forever hidden from
their sight. We do not here--as we did in the
closing scenes of **Hamlet**--discover new men.
Hamlet, it is true, submits to his world with
weary resignation. But Hamlet acknowledges human
limitations without lapsing wholly into despair.
The difference is between Hamlet, who accepts an
ambiguous world while yet believing in the need
for human exertion at critical junctures in time,
and Ros and Guil, who quail before their world's
haunting mysteries, wishing never to have played
the game at all. Guil despairs, groping for his
freedom "at the beginning," when he might--so he
reasons--have refused to participate. He
wishes--there is no other way to put it--to avoid
human responsibility. Thus his undeniably moving
cry must be understood in the light of our clearer knowledge that his real opportunity came not
at the beginning, but near the end of the play,

when he accidentally discovered that his mission
was to betray Hamlet. He misunderstands the
nature of his freedom, misunderstands as well the
meaning of his choice. Too, we must not overlook
the fact that Guil's misreading of his life
provokes one final confusion of names: unaware
that Ros has silently departed--died--Guil asks,
"Rosen--? Guil?" In a play in which the
floating identities of the two central characters
has steadily deepened in seriousness, this final
misunderstanding is especially important. Guil's
fate is never to know who he is. Ultimately, as
Robert Egan has pointed out, "Guildenstern does
die the death he has opted for."[16]

     To insist on Ros and Guil's freedom, and
therefore on their responsibility, may seem
wrongheaded, particularly because one is reluctant to condemn them for being confused by a
script which they have not read. The courtiers
are baffled by offstage events; hence it is not
surprising that critics and playgoers have been
tempted to draw parallels between this play and
Waiting for Godot. Yet in truth the
dramaturgy of Stoppard does not simply grow out
of the theater of Beckett. True, Stoppard
employs elements of that theater; but the effect
of this is to call the validity of Absurdist
theater into question. Stoppard uses Absurdist
techniques, as he uses the **Hamlet** material,
to frame questions concerning the efficacy and
significance of these diverse ways of understanding human action.

     Evidence for this may be found by examining
Stoppard's handling of the **Hamlet** material,
and by noting how this handling varies over the
course of the three-act structure of
Rosencrantz and Guildenstern Are Dead. Act I
first poses the dilemma, defining, as it were,
the conflict of the play as a struggle between
two plots, between the story an individual (here,
two individuals) wills for himself and the story
the myth tells about him. Here the two texts
seem most at odds, for **Hamlet** intervenes in
two large chunks, each time unexpectedly, almost
forcing its way on stage. In the second Act,
however, the compositional pattern shifts: here

Shakespeare's text intrudes more frequently, and
in shorter bits, as if the completed play were
being broken down and assimilated by--or accommodated to--the play in the making. In this second
Act we feel the maximum presence of **Hamlet**,
the increased pull of the myth. Structure here
may be clarified by reference to classical
terminology: in this Act we witness the
epitasis, the complication, or the tying of
the knot. Between the growing design of
Hamlet, and the intertextual freedom of Ros
and Guil's discussions there develops maximum
tension, maximum interplay between what
Keyssar-Franke calls "the possibility of freedom
and the improbability of escape." Then, in the
final Act, the process whereby **Hamlet** is
accommodated to **Rosencrantz and Guildenstern
Are Dead** seems completed. Here is staged the
famous sea voyage of Hamlet, for which no
dramatic precedent exists. No lines from
Shakespeare's play can here intrude, for none is
available. In **Hamlet**, we learn of the events
of the voyage only in retrospect, during a
subsequent conversation between Horatio and
Hamlet. So, even though those of us who know the
the play remember what happened at sea, we know
nothing of the causes of that action. Even
knowledgeable playgoers, then, assume that the
events at sea had resulted from chance, or, as
Hamlet later suggests, from heaven's ordinance.
This is an important point: most of Act III of
Rosencrantz and Guildenstern Are Dead exists
between the lines, as it were, of **Hamlet**, in
what has always represented an undefined,
unwritten zone. Stoppard here invites his
characters to invent their history according to
their will. He offers them alternatives, if not
absolute choice. This is confirmed by the
courtiers' imaginings concerning their arrival in
England. Ros mourns:

> I have no image. I try to picture us
> arriving, a little harbour
> perhaps . . . roads . . . inhabitants
> to point the way . . . horses on the
> road . . . riding for a day or a

> fortnight and then a palace and the
> English king. . . . That would be the
> logical kind of thing. . . . But my
> mind remains a blank. No. We're
> slipping off the map. (107-108)

The passage chills us, and invites us to recall
that for Rosencrantz and Guildenstern there will
be no future. Yet does it not invite us equally
to reflect upon the courtiers' imaginative short-
comings, their own sinful--not too strong a
word--despair? Indeed, soon afterwards they are
graced with the opportunity to devise their own
script, but they fail to do so because they
cannot transcend their own banality, cannot for
one moment rise out of their slough. Upon
reading the letter which discloses the King's
intent to have Hamlet executed, Guil lapses into
an empiricism so bland, so callous as to lack
utterly moral context:

> Assume, if you like, that they're going
> to kill him. Well, he is a man, he is
> mortal, death comes to us all, etcet-
> era, and consequently he would have
> died anyway, sooner or later. Or to
> look at it from the social point of
> view--he's just one man among many, the
> loss would be well within reason and
> convenience. And then again, what is
> so terrible about death? As Socrates
> so philosophically put it, since we
> don't know what death is, it is illogi-
> cal to fear it. It might be . . . very
> nice. Certainly it is a release from
> the burden of life, and, for the godly,
> a haven and a reward. Or to look at it
> another way--we are little men, we
> don't know the ins and outs of the
> matter, there are wheels within wheels,
> etcetera--it would be presumptuous of
> us to interfere with the designs of
> fate or even of kings. All in all, I
> think we'd be well advised to leave
> well alone. Tie up the
> letter--there--neatly--like that.--
> They won't notice the broken seal,
> assuming you were in character. (110)

Only by considering Guil's comments in full
can we appreciate their slowly deepening
repulsiveness. They are spoken, recall, while
our hearts are yet moved by Ros' intuitive
reaction to the letter ordering Hamlet's death:
"We're his **friends**." As Guil speaks, the
stage grows quiet, empty: we feel the crisis,
feel the awful pressure of a thing about to be
done, feel that (in Brutus' words) "between the
acting of a dreadful thing and the first motion,
all the interim is like a hideous dream." Given
the opportunity for meaningful action, Guil (and
thus, by way of tacit compliance, Ros) refuses to
act. Given suddenly--one is tempted to say
beneficently--ample room and time to define their
selves, the courtiers cannot swell to fit their
new roles. For a moment, **Hamlet** is swept
away, suspended powerless; for a brief interim we
sense that the fate of the prince and his play
rests in Ros and Guil's hands. That interim is
theirs alone; it does not belong to **Hamlet**.
And they refuse to act. To choose not to choose,
of course, is a manner of choosing. Ros and Guil
fill their moment of time, their **season**, with
emptiness--until the text of Shakespeare's
Hamlet rushes back to fill the vacuum.
Scarcely has Ros concluded, "We're on top of it
now" (111), than Shakespeare's text looms to meet
them.

In this light, then, Guil's desperate
attempt to slay The Player who brings the
courtiers the news of their deaths seems triply
ironic. Guil is wrong about death, in that it
can be counterfeited by a successful actor.
And he is wrong about the shape of his life, too,
and about the meaning of human action. No
one--not Fate, not Shakespeare, and not Tom
Stoppard--"had it in for them." Where Guil and
Ros erred was not in getting on a boat; they
failed when they chose freely to be cowards,
chose freely, that is, to be themselves.
Stoppard stresses their cowardice, not their
ignorance, and his irony here flatly contradicts
those who see Ros and Guil as powerless victims.
And Guil is wrong, finally, in his desperate
attempt to murder The Player. Guil seems here to

hope to win dramatic stature by an act of
violence, to gain identity from a conventionally
heroic act of will. In fact, Stoppard seems to
be saying, such conventional heroism is not
necessary; all that was required of Guil was the
destruction of a single letter.

Thus it is inevitable that the stage lights
dim on Ros and Guil's play and shine in the end
on **Hamlet**: "immediately," Stoppard directs,
"the whole stage is lit up, revealing, upstage,
arranged in the approximate positions last held
by the dead tragedians, the tableau of court and
corpses which is the last scene of **Hamlet**"
(126). The text of Shakespeare's play suddenly
appears to overwhelm its modern analogue, as the
old play and the new play here converge in a
genuine **coup de théâtre**. Yet the point
here is more than mere theatrics, more, too, than
weary fatalism or anguish at the absurdity of
human life. The sudden sweeping reduction of Ros
and Guil completes Stoppard's play at the same
time it affirms unconditionally the morality of
Shakespeare's. On this crucial point, Stoppard
is unequivocal: in rehearsals, and in all
published editions of the play after the first,
Stoppard excised a bit of action which brought
his drama full circle, so that it ended with
someone banging on a shutter, shouting two
names.[17] Stoppard's alteration moves his
play away from the cultivated theatricality and
ambiguity one finds often in Absurdist drama; and
we are left with the clear knowledge that Ros and
Guil, despite their being given an entire play of
their own, have not advanced beyond the
interchangeable, nondescript pair who took the
boards more than three hundred years ago. Just
as he disappears from view, Guil quips, "Well,
we'll know better next time" (126). But the
evidence from **two** plays, now, suggests that
they won't. Oddly, Stoppard is here not
following Shakespeare's script so much as he is
redefining and reasserting its tragic validity:
Rosencrantz and Guildenstern Are Dead proves
that Shakespeare had it right after all. For
this reason, Ros and Guil are not permitted to

"die" on stage; they merely disappear from view.
Is this not one final demonstration of Stoppard's
consistent dramatic technique?--for he merely
whisks the courtiers off the stage, lest their
corpses--visible proof that they had lived--
convince an audience of their dramatic
substance.

Wheels within wheels: **Rosencrantz and
Guildenstern Are Dead** is deeply ironic, yet the
irony is not at all the mocking, ambivalent irony
we have come to expect of the modern theater. To
be sure, to rank the orders of reality in this
haunting play is to invert **mimesis**, for here
the admitted fiction--the world of **Hamlet**--
possesses most substance. It turns out, in fact,
that even The Player is more real, that is, of
more worth, than Ros and Guil. But this does not
mean that The Player--whose essence is his
artifice--forms the play's thematic center. Like
Hamlet, Rosencrantz and Guildenstern Are Dead
brings into conjunction a number of states of
being, examines from a variety of perspectives
some modes of human action. What the play
means, it means largely by virtue of these
numerous contrasts and resulting tensions. No
one perspective is so broad as to embrace the
whole; each, by itself, is faulty, both intellectually and morally. Nevertheless, together they
assert a view of human activity that stresses
men's ultimate responsibility-- whether prince or
actor or lackey--for what they do, and so for who
they are.

It is simply incorrect, for this reason, to
call **Rosencrantz and Guildenstern Are Dead** an
example of Absurdist drama, even to call it
"post-Absurdist" drama (in all but the literal
sense). In the first place, we do not find here
a "sense of metaphysical anguish at the absurdity
of the human condition," a theme which Martin
Esslin long ago defined as central to Absurdist
playwrights.[18] Certainly, Ros and Guil die
without knowing what their lives were all about.
But the whole point of the **Hamlet** material is
to define for the audience--if not for Ros and
Guil--a knowable logic that shapes men's
fortunes, even as it permits them a part in the

process. We must distinguish here the difference
between two varieties of offstage material, such
as one finds, say, in **Waiting for Godot** or in
The Birthday Party, on the one hand, and in
Oedipus Rex and in **Rosencrantz and
Guildenstern Are Dead**, on the other. In the
former plays, the offstage material functions
exclusively to deepen the audience's awareness of
human ignorance; it is mockingly obscure,
purposely baffling to characters and to
spectators. But in the latter plays, the
offstage material functions both as mystery
and as myth, the myth with its powerful
implications of logic, design, even--in the right
circumstances--knowability.

In other ways, too, **Rosencrantz and
Guildenstern Are Dead** rejects much of the
Absurdist canon. It is not "antiliterary"; it
does not "abandon rational devices and discursive
thought," but instead depends upon them; and
finally, it does not lament the loss of
opportunities for meaning, even for heroism,
because Ros and Guil enjoy, albeit briefly, such
potential.[19] This play, as has been said of
Stoppard's **The Real Inspector Hound**, is
"comfortingly classical."[20] It testifies to
the informing aesthetic power even today of a
tragic dramatic form far older than the
Elizabethan play which inspired it.
Rosencrantz and Guildenstern Are Dead offers
its audience the vision of two characters caught
in the agony of moral choice. At a moment when
they least expect it, and in a place they had
never forseen, they must decide the shape of
their lives. To be sure, the information upon
which they must base their decision comes to them
in the form of riddles, half-truths, things only
partly-known; but when has it ever been
otherwise? Like other tragic protagonists before
them, Ros and Guil must choose, and they choose
in error. Leading up to and away from this moral
crisis which forms the dramatic center of his
play, Stoppard constructs a linear plot, set in
time, and moved by a group (or, if you will, two
groups) of characters who are consistent in both

motive and response. Behind the play stands an
ancient way of ordering experience, a way which
is both mythic and ritualistic. And for his
theme, Stoppard (with the aid of **Hamlet**)
offers a version of justice: all the characters
get what they deserve. So simple, so moving, so
regrettable, but, finally, so consoling: what,
in the end, could be more like classical tragedy
than that?

Notes

1. Ruby Cohn, **Modern Shakespeare
Offshoots** (Princeton: Princeton University
Press, 1976), p. 217; Ronald Hayman,
Contemporary Playwrights: Tom Stoppard
(London: Heinemann, 1977), p. 34; Charles
Marowitz, "Confessions of a Counterfeit Critic,"
cited by Christian W. Thomsen, "Tom Stoppard,
Rosencrantz and Guildenstern Are Dead: Spiel
vom Sterben, Spiel vom Tod, Spiel vom Tod in
Leben," in **Maske und Kothurn**, 24 (1978), 124;
and Thomas Whitaker, **Fields of Play in Modern
Drama** (Princeton: Princeton University Press,
1977), p. 14.

2. **Rosencrantz and Guildenstern Are
Dead** (New York: Grove Press, 1968), p. 74.
All quotations from Stoppard's play are from the
Grove Press edition; page references appear in
the text.

3. See Maynard Mack, "The World of
Hamlet," **Yale Review**, 41 (June 1952),
502-23; Helene Keyssar-Franke, "The Strategy of
Rosencrantz and Guildenstern Are Dead,"
Educational Theatre Journal, 27 (1975),
85-97; Francis Fergusson, **The Idea of a
Theater** (Princeton: Princeton University
Press, 1949), pp. 98-142; Martin Scofield, **The
Ghosts of Hamlet** (Cambridge: Cambridge
University Press, 1980); and Cohn, **Modern
Shakespeare Offshoots**, pp. 106-231.

4. In fact, Stoppard called an early
version of the play "just a sort of Shakespearean
pastiche": "Ambushes for the Audience: Towards
a High Comedy of Ideas," **Theatre Quarterly**,
14 (1974), 6. But the finished play is very much
different from the early skit. See Thomsen,
p. 231, and Hayward, pp. 32-33.

5. Robert Brustein, "Waiting for Hamlet,"
New Republic (November 1967), p. 25; Normand
Berlin, "**Rosencrantz and Guildenstern Are
Dead:** Theater of Criticism," **Modern Drama**,

16 (1973), 269-77; Andrew K. Kennedy, "Old and
New in London Now," **Modern Drama**, 11 (1969),
437-46; see also Jill Levenson, "Views from a
Revolving Door: Tom Stoppard's Canon to Date,"
Queen's Quarterly, 78 (1971), 431-32, and
Julian Gitzen, "Tom Stoppard: Chaos in
Perspective," **Southern Humanities Review**, 10
(1976), 143-52.

   6. Hayman, p. 42.

   7. Cohn, p. 215.

   8. Hayman notes (p. 43) that "the
transitions into the modern vernacular make the
twentieth century look lame," but adds: "Not
that the vocabulary of the Elizabethan theatre--
verbal or silent--is always represented as
superior."

   9. Stoppard acknowledges his preference for
constructing a dialectic: see "Ambushes for the
Audience," pp. 6-7; Hayman, p. 40; and Thomsen,
p. 241.

   10. Whitaker, p. 13.

   11. See Whitaker, p. 17, and Richard Egan,
"A Thin Beam of Light: The Purpose of Playing in
Rosencrantz and Guildenstern Are Dead,"
Theatre Journal, 31 (March 1979), 59-69.

   12. Egan, p. 66.

   13. Keyssar-Franke puts it in slightly
different form (p. 96): "Within a life, within a
play, there is space for play, but the end is
set before we begin. . . . Without death, man is
amorphous and uncertain; within death, man must
take on character, feeling and meaning. This is
the dramatic outburst of Act III; it is the
underlying assumption of the entire play."

   14. Hayman, p. 34: "Stoppard was not the
first playwright to incorporate generous slabs of
Shakespearean dialogue into a modern text, but he

was the boldest and cleverest."

    15.   Keyssar-Franke, p. 87.

    16.   Egan, p. 69.

    17.   Hayman, p. 46.

    18.   Searching for appropriate modern terms,
one might possibly call Stoppard's position
"existentialist," insofar as he insists that Ros
and Guil are to be held responsible for their
lives. But the label seems to me inappropriate.
Stoppard comments ("Ambushes for the Audience,"
p. 6): ". . . I didn't know what the word
'existential' meant until it was applied to
Rosencrantz. And even now existentialism is
not a philosophy I find either attractive or
plausible. But it's certainly true that the play
can be interpreted in existential terms, as well
as in other terms." In any case, calling the
play "existential" does not move it much closer
to Absurdist drama. As Esslin points out, there
are numerous important differences between
Existentialist and Absurdist drama; indeed,
Esslin goes so far as to suggest that these
differences may be fundamental: "the beautiful
phrasing and argumentative brilliance of both
Sartre and Camus . . . by implication, proclaim a
tacit conviction that logical discourse can offer
valid solutions": Esslin, **The Theatre of the
Absurd** (Garden City, New York: Doubleday,
1961), pp. xix-xx.

    19.   Esslin cites these characteristic
features of Absurdist drama. See **The Theatre
of the Absurd,** p. xv-xxiv.

    20.   Kennedy, p. 437.

"Misreading" **Hamlet**: Problems of Perspective
   in **Rosencrantz & Guildenstern Are Dead**

J. Dennis Huston

   Tom Stoppard's **Rosencrantz & Guildenstern
Are Dead** does to critical categories what it
does to **Hamlet**: it skews perspectives and
disrupts expectations. Like Falstaff's Mistress
Quickly, it seems neither fish nor flesh, and the
critic knows not where to have it; for it mixes
genres, times, places, and characters into what
may seem only a confusing dramatic amalgam,
composed of odd bits and pieces from **Hamlet,
Waiting for Godot, Six Characters in Search of an
Author,** and **The Castle,** to name only the
most notable sources and influences cited by the
critics.[1] With alarming swiftness--and often
with no explanation--Stoppard moves his action,
as if in dramatic hyperspace, through the world
of Elizabethan tragedy, burlesque humor, mono-
mythic narrative, comic pornography,
contemporary metadrama, modern philosophy,
critical theory, and black comedy.
   The apparently arbitrary, pastiche-like
structure of the play, however, belies both its
ambitiousness and its originality, for in it
Stoppard attempts a literal revision, a modern
"misreading,"[2] of **Hamlet.** In so doing he
not only borrows ingeniously from pieces of
Shakespeare's play, fundamentally changing its
context while still preserving the letter of its
text, but he also partly challenges Shakespeare's
achievement by offering his audience a revised,
contemporary view of the **Hamlet**-world, skewed
from the perspective of the originally insignificant Rosencrantz and Guildenstern. When Stoppard
arbitrarily manipulates and "misreads"
Hamlet, then, he consciously dramatizes both

the modern playwright's bondage to and rebellion
against Shakespeare's imposing presence. That
bondage Stoppard emphasizes by appropriating
parts of **Hamlet**; that rebellion he enacts by
resituating Shakespeare's text and reconstituting
his characters and dramatic world. Metamorphosed
into representatively modern anti-heroes,
Stoppard's Rosencrantz and Guildenstern bemusedly
observe small pieces of **Hamlet** from its
periphery and confusedly live even smaller pieces
of it from its vortex. Powerlessly, they
confront a universe apparently arbitrary and
incomprehensible. But from their powerlessness
the playwright derives his power; in their
confusion, he finds vision. Out of apparent
chaos he shapes an imaginative world logically
disordered by its blurred dramatic perspective
but thematically coherent and theatrically
compelling.
         As a way of exploring both Stoppard's
"misreading" of **Hamlet** and his ingenious
manipulation of dramatic perspective, I mean to
address in this essay three aspects of
Rosencrantz & Guildenstern Are Dead which
critics of the play have ignored: the ambiguity
of the title, the preponderance of magic in the
work, and the simultaneous presence in it of two
Hamlets--Shakespeare's and Stoppard's. These
three aspects of the play variously reflect
problems of shifting, ambiguous perspective which
characterize this work and contribute to its
richly complex nature.

                              I
         Because it is a quotation from **Hamlet**,
the title announces the direct ties between this
play and Shakespeare's, but it also introduces
and embodies the self-contradictoriness and
slippery relativism of Stoppard's dramatic world.
For although this title may seem initially simple
and clear, its meaning expands into complexity
and collapses into self-contradiction as soon as
we try to situate it precisely. In this play
categories as distinct as night and day suddenly
come to confusion before the characters', and
Stoppard's, skewed dramatic perspective: "Yes,

it's lighter than it was. It'll be night soon.
This far north."[3] In such a world no statement
proves absolute, not even the apparently simple-
seeming assertion that Rosencrantz and
Guildenstern are dead.

To begin with the most obvious problem posed
by the title: What time does it define? The
tense of the statement is present, but in the
present depicted by the play Rosencrantz and
Guildenstern are certainly not dead. Therefore,
the Rosencrantz and Guildenstern referred to in
the title cannot be the Rosencrantz and
Guildenstern of this play; they are rather the
Shakespearean characters killed long ago in an
Elizabethan revenge-tragedy. The event thus
denoted by the phrase "are dead," though it
reaches out to touch the present, has as its
principal effect the differentiation of
Stoppard's Rosencrantz and Guildenstern from
Shakespeare's: the characters belong to
different dramatic worlds and times.

Or do they? What happens, for instance, if
we read "are dead" as truly present tense? Then
at least two more possible meanings emerge.
First, the word "dead" may refer to Rosencrantz
and Guildenstern metaphorically, as roles rather
than as characters: for actors these parts in
Shakespeare's play are "dead"; they offer little
in the way of range, challenge, or audience-
appeal. But although Shakespeare may have
created in Rosencrantz and Guildenstern two
"dead" theatrical parts, Stoppard may outdo
Shakespeare--within this limited context--by
resituating those characters in a play which
brings them to life. In this case his title
becomes ironic, for it asserts as fact a
situation he intends to alter dramatically; it
challenges Shakespeare's presentation of
Rosencrantz and Guildenstern as characters
without much dramatic life. Stoppard's title and
his play, then, announce simultaneously the
playwright's aspirations and his anxieties. He
means to revise the work of the world's greatest
dramatist, but he chooses as his center of
attention the confused comings and goings of two
minor characters, who seem to have gotten little
more consideration from Shakespeare than they got
from his principal character.

The second possible meaning which emerges
from a reading of "are dead" as truly present
tense suggests close correspondence, rather than
differentiation, between Shakespeare's and
Stoppard's Rosencrantz and Guildenstern. For if
the force of the verb is essentially upon the
present, the title implies that Stoppard's
characters are as good as dead; i.e., they are
doomed by some judgment already passed upon them.
Because in **Hamlet** Rosencrantz and
Guildenstern are sent to their deaths near the
end of the drama, the fate of Stoppard's characters, who now find themselves unaccountably
called forth to play their parts in **Hamlet**,
is sealed: Rosencrantz and Guildenstern are
dead; their end is inescapable.

        Such an interpretation of the title has, of
course, radically different implications than the
reading which distinguishes Stoppard's
Rosencrantz and Guildenstern from Shakespeare's
in world and time. Instead of differentiation,
we find identification. What happened to
Shakespeare's characters is happening to
Stoppard's, who mirror them--bearing their names,
speaking their lines, encountering the mad Prince
Hamlet on behalf of King Claudius, and ultimately
suffering their ignominious demise. And because
in this interpretation of the title Rosencrantz
and Guildenstern are perceived as dramatic
characters contained timelessly in an imaginative
world, time remains eternally present tense.
What happened in the past is happening again in
the present and will continue to happen, again
and again, in the future.

        This interpretation of the title depends
partly on an audience recognizing it as a
quotation from the closing moments of **Hamlet**.
For then Stoppard encourages us to feel both
correspondence and tension between the design of
Hamlet and of this play: he makes us
anticipate the moment when the words from
Hamlet, as a judgment upon Stoppard's
Rosencrantz and Guildenstern, shape their tragic
end. The words of the title thus become
something we as an audience wait for near the
conclusion of the play, when Rosencrantz and

Guildenstern's fate in Stoppard's dramatic world
will be fitted somehow to their fate in
Shakespeare's. By the example of a dramatic event
known to us in **Hamlet**, the words promise a
future remorselessly pressing upon the present:
we know that inevitably, near the end of the
play, we will hear that "Rosencrantz and
Guildenstern are dead."

But what we do not know is whether, when we
hear these words, they will be nullified by their
context. For so cleverly and imaginatively does
Stoppard play with the Shakespearean text he
appropriates that we may wonder throughout the
work if Rosencrantz and Guildenstern can escape
their **Hamlet**-shaped fate.[4] Because
Stoppard can find ways of fundamentally altering
Shakespeare's dramatic context, even while still
retaining his language, he may also be able to
deliver Rosencrantz and Guildenstern from death
by creating a new context in which to announce
it. The extent to which he and his principal
characters are bound by the language, action, and
overall outlines of **Hamlet** is never clear,
because Stoppard plays fast and loose with his
source.[5]

Stoppard's title, then, in spite of its
apparent clarity and simplicity, is neither clear
nor simple. The Rosencrantz and Guildenstern it
describes may be any one--or all--of four
different Rosencrantzes and Guildensterns: the
characters who appear in Shakespeare's play and
are to be differentiated from Stoppard's
Rosencrantz and Guildenstern; two contemporary
anti-heroes recognizably different from
Shakespeare's figures; two characters,
identifiable with Shakespeare's, who are caught
in a dramatic time warp where past, present, and
future exist simultaneously; or the actors'
roles, Rosencrantz and Guildenstern, which
Shakespeare created, apparently with cursory
attention, but which Stoppard reconstitutes,
newly infused with theatrical life. Even the
seemingly unambiguous word "dead" in the title
proves slippery in meaning. For its implications
may be literal or metaphorical, and its point of
reference, Shakespeare's play or Stoppard's.
"Dead" describes a fate either identifying or
differentiating Stoppard's and Shakespeare's

characters, but which of these alternatives it
will be, the play does not reveal until its
conclusion.[6]   Even after Hamlet has disappeared
from the boat late in act three, Stoppard offers
ambiguous evidence about the "dead"-ness of
Rosencrantz and Guildenstern:

> ROS. He's dead then, He's dead as far as
>   we're concerned.
> PLAYER. Or we are as far as he is. (p. 119)

This exchange may suggest that death is sometimes
only a matter of perspective: as far as
Rosencrantz and Guildenstern are concerned,
Hamlet, because he is absent from them, is
"dead," and vice-versa. Death may be sometimes a
relative, as well as an absolute, condition. But
this exchange may also suggest a chillingly
different and absolute meaning. By writing the
letter which orders Rosencrantz and
Guildenstern's execution, Hamlet has assured
their eventual murder: his concern for them has
been for their death.

In **Rosencrantz & Guildenstern Are Dead**
nothing escapes the swirling rush of Stoppard's
shifting dramatic perspective, in spite of the
heroes'--or the critics'--attempts to situate
meaning precisely. Early in act three
Guildenstern tries desperately to locate some
"fact" which gives understandable purpose to his
present circumstances: ". . . we are brought
round full circle to face again the single
immutable fact--that we, Rosencrantz and
Guildenstern, bearing a letter from one king to
another, are taking Hamlet to England" (p. 101).
But even this "fact" dissolves as Guildenstern
tries to give it expression, for his assertion
contains not a "single immutable fact" but two:
Rosencrantz and Guildenstern are taking Hamlet to
England; **and** they are bearing a letter from
one king to another. Nor does the statement, as
Guildenstern claims, prove immutable, since they
are actually taking Hamlet not to England but
into the company of pirates--or into a
disappearing barrel, whichever applies. In
addition, the letter they bear will eventually

become a letter not from one king to another, but
from a prince to a king--again whichever applies.
In a world where one fact proves to be two, and
one letter, another, a statement like
"Rosencrantz and Guildenstern are dead" confounds
absolutist interpretation by engendering four
Rosencrantzes and Guildensterns, a stereoscopic
array of verbal references, and no sure
definition of "dead," which may prove literal,
metaphorical, or merely mistaken.

II

Such shifting meanings may partly account,
too, for the preponderance of magic, another
source of ambiguous perspective, in this play.
For magic, like language in Stoppard's dramatic
world and like the theatrical medium itself,
works transformations. It changes one thing into
another--even when that change is from something
into nothing, as is often the case in
Rosencrantz & Guildenstern Are Dead. That is
because all the magic tricks in the play deal
with surprising appearances and disappearances:
Rosencrantz makes a coin vanish, so completely
that not even he can find it; at another time one
coin in his hands becomes two. In act three the
players make their entrance out of barrels, like
clowns unfolding themselves from a circus car.
Later, in the darkness following the pirate
attack, one of the barrels disappears; and then
the Players, Rosencrantz, and Guildenstern
surprisingly emerge from different barrels from
the ones they have just fled to. Near the end of
the play the knife blade Guildenstern means to
drive into the Player instead harmlessly
disappears into its handle. And finally,
Rosencrantz and Guildenstern make their final
exits simply by disappearing from the stage.

All of these magic tricks are, of course,
only stage devices, sleights of hand worked by
actors (and/or the characters), the stage crew,
or the set designer. And perhaps they ought to
be transparently obvious in their trickery. In
that way, they would contribute to other
"alienation effects"[7] in the play, other
moments which intensify an audience's awareness

of themselves as an audience to a theatrical
performance. Like the principal characters'
periodic sense that they face an audience, like
the puns--"What is your line?" (p. 23), and "It's
all the same to me, sir" (p. 81)--which call
attention to the play **as** a play, like the
self-consciously theatrical scene-setting of the
stage as a boat, the stage magic would ask an
audience to experience the work intellectually as
well as emotionally. For only then can the
audience remain alert to the fact, implicit both
in Stoppard's title and in his use of magic, that
meaning in theater, language, and world is
embedded in structures so complex and anamorphic
that they not only confound certain interpretation; they also encourage, indeed almost demand,
fundamental self-contradiction. "I write plays,"
Stoppard has claimed, "because dialogue is the
most respectable way of contradicting
myself."[8]

Furthermore, if the tricks which underlie
the magic in **Rosencrantz & Guildenstern Are
Dead** are obvious to the audience, such effects
may serve as a self-reflexive commentary on the
limitations of the dramatic medium itself. For
what the playwright who would create an
imaginative world has to work with is essentially
no more than an array of overworked tricks:
artificially constructed and enacted verbal
exchanges and actions built around just as
artificially motivated entrances and exits, all
accompanied by manipulations of costume, changes
of lighting, and sound effects. Add to this
observation the fact that Stoppard appropriates
whole sections of his play from **Hamlet**, and
the transparency of his stage medium seems
obvious and self-conscious. His art and, by
extension, the art of the contemporary dramatist
are constrained both by the binding artificiality
of the theater itself and by the achievements of
preceding dramatists, whose successes oppress the
imagination of the playwright and limit his range
of possibilities, leaving him with little
artistic choice but to produce imitations of
earlier plays and earlier forms of playmaking.

The magic tricks in this play do not,
however, have to be transparent, nor is
Stoppard's artistic power necessarily compromised

by Shakespeare's achievement. As earlier we saw
Stoppard's title embodying the self-contradic-
tions of his dramatic world, so here we see his
focus on magic in the theatrical medium
reflecting this same thematic concern. For what
from one perspective is a world constrained by
convention, whose magic is all overworked stage
business, is from another perspective a world
vitalized by imagination, whose magic is
genuinely transformative.[9] The claim of the
magician, after all, is that he has access to
forces operating beyond the pale of the natural
world, and that these forces give him unusual
control over ordinary, everyday occurrences. In
a way, the playwright can make similar claims,
since he, too, may exercise magical powers.
Within the charmed circle of the theater world he
may, if his play is successful, temporarily set
aside the laws governing the movement of things
in time and space. A play may be artificial in
form, constrained by convention, enacted by
players, dependent on obvious stage devices, and
transparently derivative. But that same play may
also magically transcend its artificiality,
limiting conventions, and derivativeness by
making its audience see old things in new ways.
Two minor characters from **Hamlet**, for
instance, take on vital dramatic energies when
they are viewed, sometimes simultaneously,
sometimes consecutively, from at least three
different perspectives: as participants in a
radically skewed version of **Hamlet**; as
contemporary anti-heroes trapped in a universe
they cannot understand or affect;[10] and as
characters inextricably caught up in some
discontinuous, deenergized play that they can
neither enliven nor abort, no matter what they
do, or do not do.
      Such perspectives, as Stoppard presents
them, work a kind of magic on Rosencrantz and
Guildenstern, transforming them from theatrically
insignificant Elizabethan nonentities to,
paradoxically, powerful dramatic representations
of modern impotence. Between these two views of
the characters there are, of course, correspondences, which Stoppard emphasizes by
appropriating Shakespearean characters to his
particular purposes. But there are also crucial

differences between these two views, a fact which
criticism of the play has generally ignored. For
Stoppard's Rosencrantz and Guildenstern are not,
as critics claim, trapped in the **Hamlet**-
world;[11] they are rather trapped in
Stoppard's dramatic world, which is quite a
different thing--even if Stoppard's theatrical
magic periodically conjures up pieces of the
Hamlet-world. Magic in **Rosencrantz &
Guildenstern Are Dead**, then, serves partly as
an image for the playwright's and the principal
characters' limits, since both dramatist and
characters are bound, though in different ways,
by the stage tricks indigenous to the dramatic
medium. But partly, too, Stoppard's stage magic
calls attention to his powers as a playwright by
paradigmatically embodying those powers, all
successful drama being a kind of stage magic.

III

One notable example of such dramatic power
is his complex and deliberately self-contradictory revision of the **Hamlet**-world. On the
one hand, the literal presence of **Hamlet** in
Rosencrantz & Guildenstern Are Dead
emphasizes the shrunken trivialities of the
modern condition. Its principal dramatic figures
are no longer recognizably tragic heroes,
summoned to terrible tasks by supernatural
forces, but merely minor characters living on the
edges of some ineluctable, death-dealing action,
which alternately swirls around and by them. And
from this perspective, the language of **Hamlet**
dwarfs the petti-fogging idiom with which
Rosencrantz and Guildenstern confront the
conundrums of their world. But on the other
hand, **Hamlet** is trivialized by **Rosencrantz
& Guildenstern Are Dead**, as the young playwright enacts his dramatic revenge on the
oppressive figure of the father-playwright. In
the context of Stoppard's dramatic world,
Shakespeare's verse may sound as archaic and
artificial as the language of "The Murder of
Gonzago" sounds in **Hamlet**; instead of
grandness, it may attain only to bombast. In
addition, the broken, discontinuous events of
Shakespeare's play as it appears in Stoppard's
reduce it to a comic pastiche, an effect further

emphasized by radical changes in stage
directions. And finally, when Stoppard at last
moves his Hamlet outside the literal boundaries
of Shakespeare's text, the character appears
grotesquely modern: lounging under a beach
umbrella like some contemporary vacationer, with
nothing surviving of his capacity for brilliant,
self-excoriating soliloquies but the mindless,
inarticulate act of spitting into the wind.

In effect, then, there are really two
Hamlets contained within the world of
Rosencrantz & Guildenstern Are Dead. The
first is Shakespeare's play, from which Stoppard
borrows his title, principal characters, and
whole sections of text, at least partly for the
purpose of reactivating his audience's knowledge
of that play. He chooses **Hamlet** as the basis
of his plot and action for much the same reason
that the Greek playwrights chose to build their
plays upon myths:[12] so his audience will
bring into the theater already-formed impressions
about his dramatic characters and action. But
unlike the Greek playwrights (Euripides sometimes
excepted), Stoppard wants to use his audience's
impressions disruptively, in at least two ways.
By implicitly contrasting Shakespeare's
Hamlet with his own play, he emphasizes that
tragic action, character, and language have been
reduced in the contemporary theater and world to
trivial, confused inaction. And by
"ambushing"[13] the audience's expectations--
creating a second **Hamlet** by distorting the
meaning even of the sections he borrows
verbatim from Shakespeare--he loosens the
audience's hold on the foundations of their
perceptions,[14] skewing their perspective. In
this dramatic world coins, barrels, and
characters disappear magically. And even such
certainties as the written text of **Hamlet** and
our knowledge of its plot--dissolve before our
eyes.

As an audience we may persist in thinking
that Rosencrantz and Guildenstern are trapped in
the **Hamlet**-world. From our detached position
as spectators who know what happens in
Hamlet, we think we know also what will happen

in **Rosencrantz & Guildenstern Are Dead.** But
Stoppard keeps surprising us by the way he uses
and abuses Shakespeare's play until we, too, may
begin to feel almost as confused as his principal
characters. Rosencrantz, trying to decipher King
Claudius' instructions about gleaning what
afflicts Hamlet, remarks: "He's not himself, you
know" (p. 46). And we share his opinion, though
our perspective makes us conscious of
implications not available to Rosencrantz; for
Hamlet is "not himself" in at least four ways:
because he is apparently mad, because
Guildenstern has assumed his part in a practice
exchange with Rosencrantz, because Hamlet is
always just a role played by an actor, and
because this play in which he appears is not
Hamlet. And since it is not, our assumed
"knowledge" of the fate which awaits Stoppard's
characters, as if they were Shakespeare's, may be
fallacious.

     Such uncertainty of perspective is further
compounded by the fact that Stoppard himself
seems differently bound to Shakespeare's text at
different times: sometimes he reproduces it
literally; sometimes he cuts it radically; and
sometimes he departs from it altogether. Thus
when Rosencrantz says at the end of act II, "And
besides, anything could happen yet" (p. 95), the
meaning of his words remains indeterminate. Is
the speech ironic: Rosencrantz desperately
trying to cheer himself up in the face of deeply
felt danger? Or is it ironic in a different way:
stressing the difference between Rosencrantz's
optimistic way of viewing his situation, as
almost infinite in possibility, and the
audience's way of viewing it, as circumscribed by
his inalterably fated death in England? Or,
again, is the speech essentially Stoppard's
metadramatic commentary on his characters'
situation, which the playwright may bring to a
conclusion in any way he likes? The reason why
Stoppard concludes act II in this way, I think,
is to emphasize dramatically his audience's, as
well as his characters', confusion: perhaps
anything **could** happen yet, the play being
Stoppard's to shape as he wishes, but perhaps the
conclusion is already predetermined by the
outlines of **Hamlet,** to which Stoppard feels
necessarily bound. In the third act of his play,

however, he makes clear that the dramatic world
which confines his principal characters is not
Shakespeare's but his: Rosencrantz and
Guildenstern are trapped not by **Hamlet** but by
Stoppard's **Rosencrantz & Guildenstern Are
Dead**, which means that anything **could**
happen yet.

IV

     In that third act the basic elements of
Shakespeare's plot still remain. Rosencrantz and
Guildenstern, accompanying Hamlet by boat to
England, carry from Claudius to the English king
a letter ordering Hamlet's death; Hamlet reads
the letter and substitutes for it one ordering
their execution; and then Hamlet disappears from
the boat during a pirate attack. But Stoppard,
who has earlier been constrained by the written
words of Shakespeare's play, now works entirely
beyond its textual boundaries, inventing
ridiculous correspondences between the particulars of his text and the implications of
Shakespeare's. Hamlet travels in a deck chair
under a gaudy beach umbrella; and later during
the pirate attack he disappears not by boarding
the pirate ship but by diving into a barrel.
Rosencrantz and Guildenstern open the letter to
the English king--twice--thereby learning of the
order not only for Hamlet's death but also for
their own as well; and yet they do nothing to try
to nullify the actions commanded by the letters.
They apparently cannot even choose to avoid
delivering the letter which orders their own
deaths.
     With the opening of this second letter,
Stoppard's play breaks completely free from the
constraining logic of Shakespeare's plot. For no
reader of **Hamlet** before Stoppard, I suspect,
ever imagined that Rosencrantz and Guildenstern
open and read the letter they deliver to the
English king. Within the context of the
Hamlet-world the thought is unimaginable.
But within **Rosencrantz & Guildenstern Are
Dead**--at least in the third act--"anything
[can] happen," even, in a sense, the
unimaginable. To be sure, such an event is no

longer unimaginable once it happens, because it
serves as a defining part of the dramatic world
which contains it: their inability to act even
when threatened by an imminent sentence of
death--written into a letter they possess and
could destroy--becomes the ultimate expression of
Rosencrantz and Guildenstern's powerlessness,
confusion, and imprisonment in the world Stoppard
has shaped for them. Their paralysis, though, is
a measure of Stoppard's power. Throughout this
play he has found ways of moving freely within
the apparently constraining form of his medium
and his model. Now he has discovered how to
explode dramatically the logic of Shakespeare's
plot while yet choosing to abide by its ending;
he replaces the logic of tragic inevitability
with the irrationality of incomprehensible
arbitrariness.   And in the process he brings to
dramatic fruition a theme originally sounded at
the beginning of the play.

There instead of the **Hamlet**-world the
title has encouraged us to expect, we encounter
a world modeled on **Waiting for Godot**. Nobody
comes; nobody goes, and two characters, waiting
for some undefined event of importance in the
future, pass the time in trivial activity--in
this case, flipping coins. But their trivial
activity takes on portentous importance because
the coins defy the law of averages and come down
heads ninety-two times in a row. In this
dramatic world, ordering rules of nature and
logic do not apply: the title encourages an
audience to expect Shakespeare's world, but the
audience initially finds Beckett's instead;
coins, when flipped, come down heads ninety-two
straight times; the trivial proves portentous;
and, as the pastiche-like scenes from **Hamlet**
shortly prove, the portentous is trivialized.
Nor do the usual laws of dramatic exposition or
characterization apply here: for almost twenty
pages of text the characters remain nameless and,
when they are at last identified, they prove to
have no past which they can remember before that
morning.

What Stoppard dramatically sets up by this
disorienting beginning, he brings to thematic

consummation in the scene when Rosencrantz and
Guildenstern open the letter ordering their own
executions. The force which arbitrarily shapes
Rosencrantz and Guildenstern's destiny, then, is
a play whose particulars they do not understand,
but that play is not **Hamlet**; it is
Rosencrantz & Guildenstern Are Dead. To them
this difference may be insignificant, for both
Shakespeare's Rosencrantz and Guildenstern and
Stoppard's are prevented by their perspectives
from understanding what eventually happens to
them. But from the audience's perspective the
distinction is crucial, because in Shakespeare's
dramatic world there is a logical explanation to
be discovered:

>   Their defeat
> Does by their own insinuation grow.
> 'Tis dangerous when the baser nature comes
> Between the pass and fell incensed points
> Of mighty opposites. (**Hamlet** V. ii.
> 58-62)

In the world of **Rosencrantz & Guildenstern
Are Dead,** however, no such explanation is
forthcoming because no such logical order
obtains. There shifting surfaces cover not
villainy or a disoriented sense of self, as in
Hamlet, but only indeterminate meanings,
dramatic embodiments of a world without any
secure foundations: where language derives its
logic from ephemeral and often irresolvably
confusing speech acts: "Yes, it's lighter than
it was. It'll be night soon" (p. 99); where the
identity of the King of England is unknowable;
where coins, barrels, and even characters
inexplicably disappear; and where not even the
text of **Hamlet** escapes trivialization. For
such events we can, of course, posit meanings,
though Stoppard's point, I think, is that these
meanings never prove fully verifiable and are
often self-contradictory; their shapes change
with Stoppard's shifting dramatic perspective.
And none of these changes in perspective proves
more elusive and self-contradictory than the ones
attending the trivialization of **Hamlet,** which
serves Stoppard's purposes in richly varied ways.
It radically reduces the power of Shakespeare's

play by a "misreading" so that Stoppard, as a
modern playwright, will not be intimidated into
silence by the magnitude of Shakespeare's
achievement. It demonstrates the fundamental
difference between earlier, heroic conceptions of
tragic action and the shrunken, contemporary view
of it. It calls attention to his own dramatic
brilliance, in radically altering Shakespeare's
meaning without altering any words of his text.
It "ambushes" his audience by using their
expectations against them. And finally, it
emphasizes the absence of any secure foundations
for meaning in his dramatic world by dislocating
the apparent bedrock source of plot and action in
his play. That Stoppard thus succeeds in
trivializing **Hamlet** without depriving it of
crucial thematic importance in his work, that he
also effects a kind of dramatic magic which
metamorphoses the trivial into the portentous,
and that he ultimately creates a dramatic world
at once both logically impenetrable and
thematically coherent, are important measures of
his achievement in **Rosencrantz & Guildenstern
Are Dead.**[15]

Notes

1.   Stoppard himself talks about Beckett's influence in Ronald Hayman, **Tom Stoppard** (London: Heinemann, 1979), pp. 6-7. And the similarities between the two plays, which Hayman particularizes, pp. 36-37, have been frequently noted by other critics. Norman Berlin, in **"Rosencrantz and Guildenstern Are Dead:** Theater of Criticism," **Modern Drama**, 16 (December 1973), 269-277, remarks that Stoppard borrows from Pirandello "the idea of giving extra-dramatic life to established characters" p. 269; and Kenneth Tynan suggests that **The Castle** may also be an important influence on the work, in "Profiles (Tom Stoppard)," **The New Yorker** (December 19, 1977), pp. 72-74.

2.   My use of this word here is shaped by Harold Bloom's discussion of the way a writer--for Bloom a "poet"--confronts the challenges posed by the success of earlier writers. See particularly **The Anxiety of Influence** (New York: Oxford University Press, 1973), p. 30: "Poetic Influence--when it involves two strong, authentic poets,--always proceeds by a misreading of the prior poet, an act of creative correction that is actually and necessarily a misinterpretation. The history of fruitful poetic influence, which is to say the main tradition of Western poetry since the Renaissance, is a history of anxiety and self-saving caricature, of distortion, of perverse, wilful revisionism without which modern poetry as such could not exist."

3.   Tom Stoppard, **Rosencrantz & Guildenstern Are Dead** (New York: Grove Press, 1967), p. 99. All subsequent references are to this edition.

4.   The critic who most directly suggests this possibility is Helene Keyssar-Franke, "The Strategy of **Rosencrantz and Guildenstern Are Dead**," **Educational Theatre Journal**, 27 (March 1975), 85-97: "For both Rosencrantz and

Guildenstern and the audience it appears through
Acts I and II that they may be existing or can
exist outside of their roles in **Hamlet**; if
this is true they may be free to escape the
deaths implied by their Shakespearean roles"
(p. 87).

     5. To name only a few, his notable
revisions include: 1) transposing the Player's
line, "Full thirty times hath Phoebus' cart . .
." from III.ii. in **Hamlet** to III.i., where
Stoppard presents a rehearsal of the play-
within-the-play, radically restructured to focus
on the events in **Hamlet** leading to the
execution of Rosencrantz and Guildenstern (pp.
76-84); 2) allowing Rosenscrantz and Guildenstern
to observe moments from **Hamlet** at which they
were not originally present; 3) having Hamlet
confuse Rosencrantz with Guildenstern when he
first encounters them; 4) making Rosencrantz, in
an uneasy attempt to alter the action of the
Hamlet-world around him, play "Guess who?!"
(p. 75) with the Queen, who turns out to be not
the Queen at all, but Alfred; 5) profoundly
altering the context of IV.iii. so that
Rosencrantz's "Ho! Bring in the lord" (p. 92) is
no longer a simple command, but instead a
cowardly betrayal of Guildenstern, who, like
Rosencrantz, is terrified of the murderous and,
he thinks, unguarded Hamlet; 6) and moving the
whole of his third act--which situates Hamlet,
the Players, and Rosencrantz and Guildenstern on
a boat to England--entirely outside the literal
boundaries of Shakespeare's text.

     6. And even here the issue **may** still be
in doubt. Rosencrantz and Guildenstern do both
disappear, suggesting death as Guildenstern has
earlier defined it: "a man failing to reappear"
(p. 84). But, like everything else in this play,
this definition is subject to conjecture, since
Polonius reappears after his death (p. 89).
Perhaps the disappearance of Rosencrantz and
Guildenstern is Stoppard's way of magically
delivering them from their deaths in the
Hamlet-world; they disappear (magically
escape?) before their demise is reported, not
presented, in that world.

7.   A number of critics have noticed
Stoppard's use of this kind of Brechtian
technique in the play. See particularly
Gabrielle Scott Robinson, "Plays Without Plot:
The Theatre of Tom Stoppard," **Educational
Theatre Journal**, 29 (March 1977), 45;
Keyssar-Franke, p. 89; and Felicia Hardison
Londré, **Tom Stoppard** (New York: Frederick
Ungar, 1981), p. 36.

8.   Tynan, p. 44.

9.   For a related discussion of
Shakespeare's manipulation of these two opposing
dramatic perspectives, see Alvin Kernan, **The
Playwright As Magician** (New Haven: Yale
University Press, 1979), particularly
pp. 155-159.

10.   Julian Gitzen, "Tom Stoppard: Chaos in
Perspective," **Southern Humanities Review**, 10
(Spring 1976), 143-152, notes that Stoppard's use
of sight gags in the play emphasizes his
characters' lack of control, even of objects, in
their world, and points "to an unpredictable
environment in which little can be taken for
granted" (p. 150).

11.   In one of the most perceptive essays on
the play, Robert Egan, "A Thin Beam of Light:
The Purpose of Playing in **Rosencrantz and
Guildenstern Are Dead**," **Theatre Journal**, 31
(March 1979), 59-69, claims that Rosencrantz and
Guildenstern find themselves "Adrift" in the
"same world" that Hamlet inhabits (p. 60).

12.   Keyssar-Franke, p. 88, makes a similar
argument.

13.   Stoppard himself uses this word to
describe the surprises he builds into his plays:
"I tend to write through a series of small,
large and microscopic ambushes--which might
consist of a body falling out of a cupboard, or
simply an unexpected word in a sentence."   Tom
Stoppard, "Ambushes for the Audience: Towards a
High Comedy of Ideas."   (Interview,) **Theatre
Quarterly**, 4 (May-July 1974), 6.

14.   Clive James, "Count Zero Splits the
Infinite," **Encounter**, 45 (November 1975),
68-76, argues of Stoppard's world that there the
space-time continuum "exists to be ungraspable,
its creator having discovered that no readily
appreciable conceptual scheme can possibly be
adequate to the complexity of experience. . . .
Here and now in Stoppard is a time and place
defined by an infinite number of converging
vectors each heading towards it at the speed of
light and steadily slowing down to nothing before
passing through it and speeding up again"
(pp. 72-73).

15.   As I struggled to find a way of ordering
Stoppard's richly confusing dramatic world, Frank
Lentricchia and Sidney Homan provided valuable
assistance.   I am much in their debt.

Plays Without Plot:
The Theatre of Tom Stoppard

Gabrielle Scott Robinson

The subjects of Tom Stoppard's theatre are
familiar to much of contemporary literature. He
writes of the anxiety and confusion of life, of
the helplessness of the individual caught up in
forces impervious to reason, of the loss of
identity and faith. He discusses in
philosophical terms the lack of absolute values,
the problem of freedom, the uncertainty of all
knowledge and perception. Stoppard's world is
implausible and irrational and also full of
cruelty and pain. His characters are the victims
of accidental calamities which threaten and
occasionally destroy them.

But to dwell upon his themes alone is to
falsify the effect of his plays, for Stoppard
adds such farce to his philosophy that the result
is more funny than painful. He develops his
ideas through a series of comical confusions,
leaving the hero in a bewilderment which is both
sad and funny. The characters may suffer from
the insufficiency of reason, but the farce makes
this very lack a cause for enjoyment.

Among Stoppard's principal means of
generating both the uncertainty and the laughter
is the intermingling of the logical with the
absurd: fantastic incidents are made to appear
logical, while ordinary and apparently rational
occurrences are presented as if they were absurd
and inexplicable. In the novel **Lord Malquist &
Mr Moon** (1966) Stoppard makes his hero spell
out this characteristic of his work. Moon,
looking at his wife's made-up face, is puzzled
and estranged by a vision of pink lips and green
eyes; in an instant, however, this strangeness

resolves itself into something as unexceptional
as lipstick and eyeshadow.   "Once more the
commonplace had duped him into seeing absurdity,
just as absurdity kept tricking him into
accepting it as commonplace."[1] Most Stoppard
heroes possess just such a capacity for
wonder--"finding mystery in the clockwork"[2]--
which distinguishes them from their fellows, even
if it is hazardous to their sanity.

Stoppard expresses his basic sense of
disorder in two ways: directly, by making it the
subject of his plays and having his characters
talk about and be thwarted by it; and indirectly,
in the form of his plays, by a lack of development and coherence in his plots, which are
constructed episodically of a chain of arguments
and counter-arguments. Stoppard himself sees it
as the greatest virtue of his plays that they
present "a series of conflicting statements made
by conflicting characters, and they tend to play
a sort of infinite leap-frog. You know, an
argument, a refutation, then a rebuttal of the
refutation, then a counter-rebuttal, so that
there is never any point in this intellectual
leap-frog at which I feel **that** is the speech
to stop it on, **that** is the last word."[3]
This working method produces both the farce and
the intellectual fireworks, but it also leads to
dramatic thinness, to characters who are
personifications of ideas, always subordinate to
a conceit.

By surveying first the subjects of the major
plays and then their form, I hope to reach some
understanding of Stoppard's achievement, of both
the success and the failure of his plays without
plot.

Stoppard's characters are unnerved by
uncertainty. They are plagued by the thought of
having to "take everything on trust"--the very
words recur in three of his plays--everything,
from the existence of a country ("a conspiracy of
cartographers"[4]) to the truth of their own
experiences and even their identity. This
troubles them particularly since they all live by
their heads, trying to order their world with the
power of reason.

Guildenstern: We only know what we're told,
and that's little enough. And for all we know it
isn't even true.

Player: For all anyone knows, nothing is.
Everything has to be taken on trust; truth is
only that which is taken to be true.

·Taking things on trust is all Rosencrantz
and Guildenstern can do since they are forced to
play their parts in **Hamlet**, ignorant of
either purpose or plot. They make desperate and
blundering attempts to establish a meaningful
connection between themselves and the action that
surrounds and at last engulfs them; but they fail
dismally, believing that "at last we're getting
somewhere" (88) when they have merely returned to
their original positions. Yet they will not
relinquish the hope of finding knowledge and
certainty; so they speculate about chance and
fate, wondering whether the chaos they perceive
is part of a larger pattern or just a "shambles."
But their attempts to impose logic on their lives
merely lead them into absurdity. The coins they
are spinning come down heads ninety-odd consecu-
tive times, and Guildenstern keeps betting--and
losing--on tails in a more and more frenzied hope
for a return to a meaningful order. Frustrated
in this, as in all else, he will not give up
trying to reason about the irrational. "The
scientific approach to the examination of
phenomena is a defense against the pure emotion
of fear" (17). But the bewildering flux of life,
or rather of the play in which the two have to
perform, will not be controlled and at the end
they have to accept the futility of it all.

Rosencrantz: I could jump over the side [of
the boat]. That would put a spoke in their
wheel.

Guildenstern: Unless they're counting on
it.

Rosencrantz: I shall remain on board.
That'll put a spoke in their wheel. (**The
futility of it, fury.**) All right! We don't
question, we don't doubt. We perform. (108)

Only the Player can relish this situation of
playing a part and no more. He blithely accepts
that life is a play, boasting that "there's a
design at work in all art. . . . Events must
play themselves out to aesthetic, moral and
logical conclusion" (79). The absurdity of life
does not pain him; he refuses to be baffled or to
suffer, maintaining a posture of cynical
detachment, content that circumstances are beyond
his control "ever so slightly." He behaves as if
he had an insight into the absurd forces which
control their destinies, and Guildenstern looks
to him for advice. But his superiority and air
of menace are only assumed and, in contrast to
the appealing vulnerability of Rosencrantz and
Guildenstern, the Player, forever unmoved, is a
somewhat sinister figure.

Stoppard's only novel, **Lord Malquist & Mr
Moon** (1966), is a storehouse of both his ideas
and methods, and it presents important perspectives for his plays. It is an account of two
days during which Malquist, accompanied by his
chosen biographer Moon, journeys across London
and becomes involved in absurd and fantastical
adventures. Moon and Malquist are the typical
Stoppard antagonists, a variation of Guildenstern
and the Player, or George and Archie in
Jumpers. In Moon we recognise the small man
with romantic yearnings who suffers in a bleak
and confusing world. He desperately seeks order
but finds himself in a world out of control.
"It's all got huge, disproportionate to the human
scale . . . and no one is controlling it" (12).
Moon's remedy is a bomb: "We require an
explosion. It is not simply a matter of
retribution, it is a matter of shocking people
into a moment of recognition--**bang**!" (108).
Through most of the novel Moon does console
himself by fingering a bomb concealed in his coat
pocket; but in the end even this fails him: the
bomb produces not a bang but a mere bubble
printed with an obscene message.

Finally, no nearer a solution, Moon dies a
martyr's death: he is blown up by the genuine
bomb of an anarchist who mistakes him for
Malquist. His martyrdom really extends all

through the book, beginning with a casual cut on his finger and ending with him barely able to move, one leg lifeless, his shoe filled with blood, his hands torn, being helped into Lord Malquist's coach, where he is blown to bits. But his is a martyrdom of accidents, of arbitrary and farcical mishaps: Moon stepping on a broken bottle, falling into a tub, or being hit on the head.

And yet who is to distinguish between accident and fate? It is a problem which troubles Moon as it had troubled Guildenstern before him. Moon's question, "But if it's all random then what's the point?" is countered by Lady Malquist: "What's the point if it's all inevitable?" "She's got me there," Moon admits (129). Moon is the victim of uncertainty; it is fitting that he dies being mistaken for someone else. He finds it impossible to take a stand about anything; and yet, like most Stoppard heroes, he craves moral absolutes. Ultimately, of course, he has to resign himself to the idea that "all the absolutes discredit each other" (48).

Malquist, by contrast, does not allow himself to suffer; he stands aloof, careless of everything save his appearance, "Since we cannot hope for order let us withdraw with style from the chaos" (16). The crucial word here is style, for Malquist's attitude is that of the artist. His aphorism, addressed to the unhappy Moon, that nothing has any reality "except when it aspires to art" (34), is reminiscent of those other artists, the Player and Joyce in **Travesties**.

In **Jumpers** Stoppard rephrases the questions of **Rosencrantz** in a more directly philosophical manner while at the same time integrating them better into the farcical plot. Here he achieves his best synthesis so far of ideas, characters, and comedy. Thematically the play revolves around witty exchanges between rival philosophical positions, generally representative of the clash between idealism and materialsm. But these discussions are carried on amidst farcical, although frequently fatal, accidents: one of the philosophers is shot--by

whom no one knows; the inspector who arrives to
solve the case leaves with an autographed record
of his favorite singer, but without notebook or
solution. Thus all attempts at a rational
understanding of existence are overwhelmed by
absurdity.

The central character is George Moore,
Professor of Moral Philosophy, who punctuates the
play with his long monologues--draft versions of
a rebuttal of the logician McFee--in which he
struggles to reestablish the existence of
ultimate values. Yet George is himself infected
with the nihilism of his age, and his convictions
are expressed as highly qualified and uncertain
propositions: "All I know is that I think that I
know that I know that nothing can be created out
of nothing, that my moral conscience is different
from the rules of my tribe, and that there is
more in me than meets the microscope. . ." (67).
Thus uncertainty is again the key issue: "for if
one can no longer believe that a twelve-inch
ruler is always a foot long, how can one be sure
of relatively less certain propositions, such as
that God made the Heaven and the Earth. . ."
(74).

To help him find his way through his
philosophical arguments George has equipped
himself with a hare, a tortoise, and an archery
set. With their aid he hopes to unravel the
famous paradoxes of Zeno. However--and this is
typical of his inadequacy as well as of the
nature of Stoppard's comedy--in the heat of his
reasoning he accidentally transfixes the hare
with an arrow and, trying to retrieve him,
crushes the tortoise.

George is plagued by uncertainty rather
closer to home as well. He never knows for sure
whether his wife Dotty is having an affair with
Archie, the suave Vice-Chancellor and leading
acrobat of his university. In fact George is
farcically and pathetically oblivious to what
goes on around him. McFee is shot in the very
first scene and during much of the play Dotty and
Archie try to dispose of the body. But although
his rival is murdered in George's own house,
under his very eyes, he only learns about it at
the end of the play.

In both **Rosencrantz** and **Jumpers**
Stoppard uses a background which, by way of an
ironic commentary, throws both the meanness and
the meaninglessness of modern life into relief.
In the earlier play it is, of course, the tragedy
of **Hamlet**, while in **Jumpers** it is the
first British landing on the moon. The set shows
a huge television screen picturing the moon and
we hear a report on the British expedition. The
spaceship, having developed a defect, can carry
only one of the two astronauts back to earth.
Captain Scott, victorious in the struggle at the
entrance, leaves behind his colleague Oates, "a
tiny receding figure waving forlornly from the
featureless wastes of the lunar landscape" (22).
Times have changed since that historic expedition
when another Oates sacrificed himself heroically
for his comrades.[5]

The moral implications of this moon
adventure play a decisive part in the dislocation
of the characters: "all our absolutes, the
thou-shalts and the thou-shalt-nots that seemed
to be the very condition of our existence, how
did **they** look to two moonmen with a single
neck to save between them?" (74-75). Dotty's
reaction is a nervous breakdown which means the
end of her career as a singer. Her romantic
world, which centered on the moon of the poets,
"the fair paradise of nature's light" (41), has
all at once dissolved; she can no longer fit
words to tunes, rhyme "moon" with "June." Her
yearning for romantic and mystical experience
must forever remain unfulfilled. Stoppard felt
"that the destruction of moon mythology and moon
association in poetry and romance, superstition
and everything, would be a sort of minute
lobotomy performed on the human race, like a tiny
laser making dead some small part of the
psyche."[6]

The political background of **Jumpers**
further reflects the general moral anarchy. The
party at which McFee dies is a victory
celebration for the Radical-Liberals who have
already shown their true colors, ruling the
country despotically with contempt for moral
values: newspaper proprietors are arrested, the

police force is dismissed, and the church is
dispossessed and "rationalised." The spokesman
for agriculture is appointed Archbishop of
Canterbury. Thus the background to **Jumpers**
is drawn with a bitterness which hides nostalgia
for a lost romantic idealism. The moon, once
seen as man's inspiration and ideal, is violated;
political freedom and decency are destroyed; it
is the fashion to denounce morality and to use
the chapel as a gymnasium.

Stoppard's recent work **Travesties,**
unlike **Jumpers,** is historically recognizable;
however, as will be seen in an analysis of the
form of the play, it is Stoppard's least
successful attempt at combining farce and ideas.
He incorporates historical characters and events
and, as in **Rosencrantz,** uses the plot of
another play--this time it is Wilde's **The
Importance of Being Earnest**--as frame for his
own. But it seems that neither literary and
historical parody nor Stoppard's own themes and
humour are worked together to produce a statement
which can stand on its own.

The place is Zurich during the First World
War. Stoppard portrays three men of genius who
lived in Zurich then, although not all at the
same time. They are Tristan Tzara, involved in
his Dadaist revolution, James Joyce at work on
Ulysses, and Lenin laying the foundation for
his political and ideological triumphs of 1917.
Setting the play in Switzerland serves two
functions: Stoppard finds there a cross section
of ideas on art and society, which forms the
thematic center of the play; and he exploits the
ludicrous qualities of "Whitest Switzerland,"[7]
"the still centre of the wheel of war" (26). He
is presented with a ready-made farce in Joyce's
lawsuit against Henry Carr over, among other
things, the cost of the trousers worn by Carr as
Algernon in **The Importance of Being Earnest.**

Stoppard uses these giants to discuss ideas;
he pits philosophies of life against each other
and analyzes moral positions. But he is really
trying to come to terms with a personal problem:
the play "asks whether an artist has to justify
himself in political terms at all."[8]

Stoppard had been troubled by this problem of the
amorality of the artist long before
Travesties, and he dealt with it in his
treatment of the Player and Lord Malquist. In
each case he describes the artist as the ultimate
in detachment. As Carr remarks in
Travesties, "To be an artist **at all** is
like living in Switzerland during a world war"
(38).

The radio play **Artist Descending a
Staircase** (1972) also discusses the artist,
formulating many of the same ideas and sometimes
even using the same phrases that we find in
Travesties. The painter Donner is plagued by
the question, "How can one justify a work of art
to a man with an empty belly?"[9] For the moment
Stoppard resolves this conflict farcically:
Donner's answer is edible art! Despite his
ironic and critical attitude, Stoppard sees the
artist as the only one who can practice escapism
with impunity and even glory. This whole
question seems particularly relevant in England
because ever since Osborne's **Look Back in
Anger** (1956) the influence of plays written
from and about social commitment has been strong.
Indeed, the interviewers of **Theatre Quarterly**
(1974) pressed Stoppard a good deal about the
lack of a political position in his plays.

In **Travesities** Stoppard uses Tzara,
Joyce, and Lenin to dramatize his own conflict of
conscience, of how to overcome "that small sense
of shame which every artist lives with."[10]
Joyce celebrates the artist as "the magician put
among men to gratify--capriciously--their urge
for immortality. . . . If there is any meaning
in any of it, it is in what survives as art. . ."
(62). Tzara scorns Joyce's self-absorption and
rejects both the artist and the civilization he
represents: "It's too late for geniuses! Now we
need vandals and desecrators . . . to reconcile
the shame and the necessity of being an artist!"
(62). Insofar as Lenin is occupied with the fate
of the artist, he believes that "literature must
become a part of the common cause" (85). The
artist must serve the purpose of history. This
contradicts Tzara's idea of chance as the sole

determinant of historical events as well as
Joyce's indifference as expressed by his Mr.
Dooley who "doesn't care a damn" (50).

This account of the ideas of the play does
not mention its hero, another--though
unrenowned--historical figure by the name of
Henry Carr. Carr was a minor official at the
British Consulate in Zurich who accidentally, and
without realising it, came into contact with
great men. Carr is, of course, another version
of Riley in **Enter a Free Man** (1968),
Guildenstern, and Moore--the man, thrown into an
incomprehensible world, who is constantly trying
to catch up with events and constantly out of his
depth. He is that most typical Stoppard
character, "the spectator as hero."[11]

The problem of uncertainty is compounded by
the fact that the play is set in old Carr's
memory: we watch the events in Zurich in 1917,
while at the same time the now senile Carr tries
to remember them. Stoppard indicates his
character's floundering and self-contradictory
memory by presenting different versions of the
same scene. This may sound like the probing of
memory in Beckett or Pinter, but Stoppard's
effect is different. He presents the
contradictions of Carr's memory as a series of
scenes, each of which opens with the same lines
and then works up to its own climax. (In Peter
Wood's production at the Aldwych the beginning of
each repetition was indicated by the striking of
a cuckoo clock.) In this way each scene appears
almost like a music hall routine. Memory as such
does not really become problematical; it is
rather a means of bringing comic variety and
intellectual antithesis into the play while yet
retaining some sort of unity in the shape of
Carr's consciousness.

Nevertheless, this technique brings out the
theme of uncertainty and confusion and it does so
in a farcical manner. In fact the events we have
witnessed have been delusions, travesties all of
them. Stoppard seems to have taken his cue from
The Importance of Being Earnest where Cecily
asserts that memory "chronicles the things that
have never happened, and couldn't possibly have

happened."[12] Thus old Carr sees himself as
consul, naming his butler after the real consul.
He believes that he could have prevented Lenin
from reaching Russia, if only he had not been
uncertain (81). Like Guildenstern he cherishes
the dream that he could have said "no" at the
right moment; even if he missed it, he did have
the opportunity to act meaningfully. But, of
course, this is an illusion. He never even met
Lenin. All along Carr is trying to define his
existence in terms of the significant events that
take place around him. But his predicament is
that of Rosencrantz and Guildenstern with the
action of **Hamlet**: their lives look all the
more futile in contrast to that action. The end
of the play makes this point in a somewhat
Beckettian vein. Carr is defending his faulty
memory. What does any of it matter? "I was
here. They were here. They went on. I went on.
We all went on" (98).

The travesties of Carr's life are played out
against a background which is potentially more
significant than in any of the other works; it is
also, for the first time, based on historical
facts: the great war, trench warfare, the
Russian revolution, a literary revolution. Set
against such monumental events, the life of the
confused Carr appears all the more pointless.
Yet Carr is not a sufficiently developed
character and, for that reason, his farcical
misadventures fail to make much of an impact.
Moreover, in this play the farce tends to render
innocuous the terror of war--which merely "ruined
several pairs of trousers" (37)--and the futility
of life, which is here represented by sketchy
even if witty figures.

Stoppard's characters are trapped in their
roles and are constantly foiled by inexplicable
events. It is no wonder that they indulge in
dreams of escape. The form of these dreams
indicates the condition as well as the secret
romanticism of his characters. Driven to the
breaking point by having to act in an unknown
play, Guildenstern sees his ideal in a boat. "I
like the way they're--contained. You don't have
to worry about which way to go, or whether to go
at all" (100). Riley, in Stoppard's **Enter a**

Free Man, also feels the strain of performance
and dreams of a life away from life. Again a
boat symbolises this ideal. "I sometimes think
of myself as a sailor . . . with home as a little
boat, anchored in the middle of a big calm sea,
never going anywhere, just sitting, far from
land, life, everything. . . ."[13]
     Just such an escape from reality and
humanity is the subject of the radio play
Albert's Bridge (1967). Albert, a student of
philosophy destined for his father's thriving
business, gives up everything to spend his life
painting a railway bridge. To him this is the
only occupation which is both satisfying and
meaningful. Up on the bridge Albert meets
Fraser, who is also trying to climb out of the
chaos of reality since he fears--as does
Moon--that sooner or later everything will
collapse. He becomes calmer the higher he
climbs, away from "the enormity of that
disorder."[14] In the end Albert's bridge is
shown to be an illusion, a false refuge from
life, and it collapses, ironically, under the
impact of human feet--hundreds of workers who
have been ordered to help with the painting. As
we have seen, the artist is the most extreme and
the most successful example of the deliberate
withdrawal from life.
     "Incidents! All we get is incidents! Dear
God, is it too much to expect a little sustained
action?!" (118). On considering the structure of
Stoppard's plays one finds this remark by
Rosencrantz to be universally applicable; herein
lies both their strength and their weakness. His
plays consist of a sequence of farcical situations and abstract ideas put together in a
parodistic and seemingly aimless fashion. There
is little development, no evolution of characters
and relationships. Stoppard admits that "I have
enormous difficulty in working out
plots. . . ."[15] He tells interviewers that
he tends to write his plays "through a series of
small, large, and microscopic ambushes--which
might consist of a body falling out of a
cupboard, or simply an unexpected word in a
sentence. But my preoccupation as a writer,

which possibly betokens a degree of insecurity,
takes the form of contriving to inject some sort
of interest and colour into every line, rather
than counting on the general situation having a
general interest which will hold an
audience."[16]   As a result, Stoppard's plots
are episodic rather than linear.

   As for the characters, they are vehicles for
the ideas, personifying argument and counter-
argument; they are intellectually rather than
psychologically complex. At the same time they
are the bewildered victims of hostile circumstances and therefore figures of farce. Take,
for example, the figure of the Risen Christ in
the novel **Lord Malquist & Mr Moon**: he is
introduced to create new situations to keep the
farce going and to motivate a discussion of
God--again, farce and philosophy--and he is
dropped as soon as Stoppard has exhausted his
possibilities. The same can even be said of
heroes like Rosencrantz, Guildenstern, and
Joyce.

   But on the positive side this structural
characteristic of Stoppard's plays is both
dramatic and theatrical in its tension between
conflicting ideas and its juxtaposition of farce
and philosophy. Moreover it is itself part of
the theme, or even a necessary consequence of
Stoppard's world view. Sustained action would
bring some degree of coherence to the chaos of
the world and meaning to the absurd lives of his
characters. Stoppard allows the plot to unfold
in a seemingly uncontrolled manner because the
characters have no control over their destinies.
They are at the mercy of every situation and, as
noted in **Rosencrantz**, "without possibility of
reprieve or hope of explanation" (140).

   Moreover the lack of plot turns the play
away from sentiment and melodrama. It works as
an alienation effect, preventing the spectator
from becoming too involved in any one character's
dilemma and keeping the often cruel and depressing circumstances from weighing him down with
suffering and despair. It also keeps the
spectator alert to the intellectual fireworks of
the play, serving to create that crisp, detached,
and extremely funny effect that is Stoppard's
trademark.

All of this may help to explain why Stoppard
is so successful with parody. Parody is a way of
reducing the stature of characters and events, of
destroying a known model and revealing its
absurdity, of looking at ideas from an angle
which fractures their meaning. But when the
great truths can no longer be taken on trust,
parody seems the only way of at least
appproaching them. It makes an indirect
statement on life. Stoppard is at his best in
parody when he plays with other people's ideas,
as in **Jumpers** and **Travesties**, or with
plots, as in **Rosencrantz** and **Travesties**.
The pleasure derived from parody is largely
intellectual.

In **Rosencrantz** the lack of sustained
action lies at the heart of the comic situation
since the play is silhouetted against **Hamlet**,
with the heroes never becoming part of that
drama. Instead they are entangled in a series of
farcical incidents which bear no relation to each
other and in which they can discern neither
progress nor direction.

There is, however, one moment in the play
when Rosencrantz and Guildenstern seem to exert
control and establish a plot of their own. In a
fit of fury at the Player's superior airs,
Guildenstern stabs him with a dagger. This, he
believes, will show the actor that death is more
than stage action, more than mere illusion. As
the Player writhes in his final agony, the two
watch in awe. The actors, however, applaud
warmly when the Player moves no more.
Rosencrantz and Guildenstern have been shamefully
taken in, believing themselves in the presence of
death when in fact they have merely been watching
a performance. And the spectator, too, has been
tricked, since he has been led to mistake for
plot what is really another inconsequential
incident leading nowhere.

After this tense moment the actual deaths of
Rosencrantz and Guildenstern are as anticlimactic
as were their lives. Their ineffectualness in
the dramatic structure underlines the pointless-
ness of their lives. And Stoppard conveys this
not merely by words, but by the form of the
dramatic situation.

From the conceit of two actors with a
narrowly prescribed part in a--to them--unknown
play springs both the comedy and the philosophy
of **Rosencrantz**. And as long as Stoppard
stays within this conceit both come off successfully. But when he tries to deepen the
spectator's response with a profound statement he
fails, for he sounds either banal, as with his
thoughts on death, or sentimental, as in such
attempts at poetry as Guildenstern's metaphor of
autumn (94).

Since there is no necessary progression of
events, Stoppard has some difficulty with the
endings of his plays. In **Rosencrantz** he is
helped by Shakespeare and indeed quotes some of
the last lines of **Hamlet**; nevertheless his
own conclusion is a rather arbitrary fading out
of the two heroes. The fading out is
appropriate, as we have seen, but the moment when
it occurs seems arbitrarily chosen.

None of Stoppard's plays is quite so laden
with incidents as his novel, where he could more
easily defy the rules of realism. **Lord
Malquist & Mr Moon** is blatantly episodic in
structure. The title of the first chapter is
indicative of this: "Dramatis Personae and Other
Coincidences."   Among these we see a lion
rampaging through Hyde Park, a cowboy named Long
John Slaughter wooing Moon's wife, and a rival
cowboy accidentally shooting the French maid
while the Risen Christ, perched high on a carpet
roll stuffed with bodies, rides off on his
donkey. The series of vignettes at first appears
utterly incoherent, but there exists a wild and
strange sort of logic in these happenings, even
though they remain fundamentally "without
possibility of reprieve or hope of
explanation"--words, again, from **Rosencrantz**
(140).

Jumpers opens dramatically with a
murder. Yet, again, this is not so much the
beginning of a plot as the first in a series of
farcical incidents, coincidences, mistaken
identities, and misunderstandings. The very
presentation of the murder shows that its
function is to provide a comic and dramatic

moment for its own sake. Professor McFee is shot
during the formation of a human pyramid by his
colleagues. Here is Stoppard's stage direction:
"One Jumper . . . is blown out of the pyramid.
He falls downstage, leaving the rest of the
pyramid intact. . . . Dotty, chanteuse, walks
through the gap in the pyramid" (21).

McFee's body will be on view for much of the
play, hung from a door or slumped in a chair, for
no other reason than to give rise to hilarious
complications. Its eventual removal is an excuse
for more theatrical tricks. Like the incident
with the pyramid, this is a stylized comic scene,
contributing to the alienation effect which we
have mentioned before. The Jumpers arrive in
yellow tracksuits to pick up the body.

> Dotty continues to sway and snap her fingers
> as she moves about welcoming the troops, and
> the Jumpers lightly respond, so that the
> effect is a little simple improvised
> choreography between the Jumpers and Dotty.
> Archie moves downstage, facing front,
> and like a magician about to demonstrate a
> trick, takes from his pocket a small square
> of material like a handkerchief, which he
> unfolds and unfolds and unfolds until it is
> a large plastic bag, six-feet tall, which he
> gives to two Jumpers. . . .As the climax of
> the 'dance' the four Jumpers throw the body
> into the bag. (56)

Throughout **Jumpers** the spectator knows
more than the characters--that is part of the
farce--but he, too, learns essentially nothing
and thereby becomes implicated in the
unpredictable situation. "Life," observes
Archie, possibly the arch-villain of the play,
"does not guarantee a denouement; and if it came,
how would one know whether to believe it?" (81).
We cannot be certain why McFee is killed and who
killed him, or whether Dotty is Archie's
mistress; much less can we answer George's
philosophical questions.

In this play Stoppard largely avoids the
attempts at poetry and at the direct philosophizing that we find in **Rosencrantz**. Again he is

at his best in parody--here of the complexities
of philosophy--and at his weakest when he wants
his characters to express a meaning or feeling of
their own--as, for example, when Dotty steps out
of her part to show that she suffers.

Jumpers has a somewhat chaotic ending:
a "coda" consisting of the symposium for which
George has been preparing himself, but in
"bizarre dream form" (83). It compounds the
terror and confusion we have witnessed throughout
the play--there is yet another murder--and ends
with an answer to George's agonized search, put
into the mouth of the cynical nonbeliever Archie:
"Do not despair--many are happy much of the time;
more eat than starve, more are healthy than sick,
more curable than dying . . . and one of the
thieves was saved" (88).[17] Stoppard uses the
coda to repeat the main themes, this time
distorted into nightmare, but he handles this in
a confusing manner and there appears to be no
dramatic reason for the mock trial of Scott and
the shooting of the Archbishop. It seems rather
as if Stoppard is carried along by his inspiration, piling incident upon incident. Then,
abruptly, he ends his play.

The plot of **Travesties** is made up of a
string of all too loosely connected travesties of
Joyce, Shakespeare, Beckett, Wilde, the limerick,
the law. "I did intend, throughout, a minor
anthology of styles-of-play, styles-of-
language."[18] Like the Player and Malquist,
Stoppard is obsessed with style; as he says, "I'm
hooked on style."[19] Again he excels in wit,
farce, theatrical dialogues, funny confusions,
and equally funny resolutions. But this time he
does not seem to arrive at a coherent subject.
The backbone of the plot, such as it is, is a
burlesque of historical fact and **The Importance
of Being Earnest.** As in Wilde there is a havoc
over the identity of the non-existent brother
Jack and the formal pairing off of Cecily and
Gwendolyn. The mix-up with the travelling bag
turns, here, into the confusion of folders
containing the manuscripts of Joyce and Lenin.
There are innumerable quotations from Wilde's
play wittily worked into Stoppard's situation

(such as Joyce speaking Lady Bracknell's lines),
and the play is studded with borrowed refer-
ences--down to the vintage of the champagne which
the butler cannot resist. Yet much of this will
be missed in performance, giving the plot an even
less coherent appearance. In his use of Wilde,
Stoppard has again taken up his favorite concept
of life as a play. While Carr plays Algernon in
The Importance of Being Earnest,
Travesties itself is a parody of that play.

The one figure who does not fit into the
Wildean plot is Lenin. His character, in fact,
remains a problem. Especially in the second act,
which he dominates, his presence upsets the
balance of the play. Stoppard uses excerpts from
Lenin's letters and his wife's diaries most
effectively to create the drama of Lenin's situation. Although this is a powerful scene, it does
not seem to belong in this play and, indeed, it
is the only part of the play which is not
simultaneously used for comedy. Lenin's scene is
followed by another farcical exchange between
Cecily and Gwendolyn speaking in rhymes, an
exchange which now sounds frivolous. The contrast of highminded seriousness with farce is, of
course, Stoppard's speciality, but in this case
the two styles jar.

Stoppard's ideas may be largely
derivative--as can be seen from his preference
for parody--but he performs theatrical feats in
playing with contemporary concepts; he is
sensitively attuned to the ideas of his time. He
initiates us into a world in which the commonplace is seen as absurd and absurdity accepted as
commonplace. Disorder is the order of the day,
which is reflected in the incoherence, the lack
of "sustained action" of his plays. Stoppard
portrays this state from the standpoint of the
average thinking man who cannot relinquish all
hope of a reasonable as well as a moral world.
This man struggles to direct his life according
to rational principles and higher laws but is
frustrated in the attempt. Circumstances
invariably defeat him. But--and this no doubt
adds to the broad popularity of the plays--
Stoppard treats his hero's bewilderment as farce.

Metaphysical questions are aired but, like the
characters themselves, they are submerged in
farcical mishaps. This makes the plays both
painful and funny. Furthermore, with his
"intellectual leap-frogging," Stoppard opposes
his confused, struggling hero with a man who
neither believes in nor cares about anything
except "style." Whether or not these figures are
actually artists like Joyce in **Travesties**,
they are all artists and performers in their
attitude to life.

It is Stoppard's self-declared aim to find
"the perfect marriage between the play of ideas
and farce or perhaps even high comedy."[20]   At
his most intense Stoppard is like Moon, overwhelmed by the confusion around him, contriving
to force his audience into a moment of recognition with the farcical bomb of his plays.

Notes

1.   Tom Stoppard, **Lord Malquist & Mr Moon** (New York: Alfred A. Knopf, 1968), p. 30. Subsequent references to this work appear in parentheses in the text.

2.   Stoppard, **Jumpers** (London: Faber and Faber, 1972), p. 72. Subsequent references to this work appear in parentheses in the text.

3.   Stoppard, "Ambushes for the Audience: Towards a High Comedy of Ideas," **Theatre Quarterly**, 4 (May-July 1974), 6-7.

4.   Stoppard, **Rosencrantz & Guildenstern Are Dead** (New York: Grove Press, 1968), p. 107.   Subsequent references to this work appear in parentheses in the text.

5.   The reference is to Captain Oates, a member of Scott's ill-fated antarctic expedition of 1912.

6.   Stoppard, "Ambushes for the Audience," p. 17.

7.   Stoppard, **Travesties** (London: Faber and Faber, 1975), p. 23. Subsequent references to this work appear in parentheses in the text.

8.   Stoppard, "Ambushes for the Audience," p. 16.

9.   Stoppard, **Artist Descending a Staircase** (London: Faber and Faber, 1973), p. 25.

10.   Stoppard, **Artist**, p. 26.

11.   This is the title of the fourth chapter of **Lord Malquist & Mr Moon**.

12.   "The Importance of Being Earnest," **The Complete Works of Oscar Wilde**, intro. by John Drinkwater (New York, 1927), 8:66.

13. Stoppard, **Enter a Free Man** (London: Faber and Faber, 1968), p. 75.

14. Stoppard, **Albert's Bridge** (London: Faber and Faber, 1969), p. 31.

15. Stoppard, "Ambushes for the Audience," p. 8.

16. Stoppard, "Ambushes for the Audience," p. 6.

17. Parts of this passage are taken from **Waiting for Godot.**

18. In Charles Marowitz, "Tom Stoppard--The Theater's Intellectual P. T. Barnum," **The New York Times,** 19 October 1975, sec. 2, p. 5.

19. Interview with Giles Gordon, **Transatlantic Review,** 29 (Summer 1968), 25.

20. Stoppard, "Ambushes for the Audience," p. 7.

RITUAL OF RIDDANCE
IN TOM STOPPARD'S
THE REAL INSPECTOR HOUND

Weldon B. Durham

The critical response to **The Real Inspector Hound**[1] identifies the play as satire and its author as an inveterate critic of "a concept of drama which defines itself in terms of the enactment of a riddle and its answer."[2] The specific target of Stoppard's mockery is, of course, Agatha Christie's **The Mousetrap**. While the thriller's famous devices are everywhere ludicrously apparent, C. W. E. Bigsby reads the play as a deeper commentary on the relationship of theater to life, arguing that the play's intricate action works up the statement that "performance at all levels implies the existence of an audience."[3] Indeed, the interfacing of reality and appearance is vitally present, but this is not, I believe, the soul of Stoppard's neatly formed drama. A satiric tone pervades **Hound**; the parodic thrusts at the mechanical conventions of the whodunit and the challenge to the validity of rational structuring are inescapable features of the play. However, one can, though at some risk, echo Moon, Stoppard's compleat criticaster, with "there is more to it than that."

Stoppard's satiric attitudinizing is sustained by two structures. In the first place, an intrigue of the very sort he vilifies provides a narrative framework for the satire. We witness in **The Real Inspector Hound** a story of revenge and ambition centering on Puckeridge's cunning efforts to become the first string critic on Moon's paper. More importantly, as it is implicated in Puckeridge's scheme, an audience in the theater participates in a purgative ritual.[4]

    As the play begins, "We are in a theatre,
waiting for the play to begin." Moon, (young,
tall, tense--a critic), waits too. Soon Birdboot
(plump, middle-aged--also a critic) joins him.
Moon and Birdboot are to critique a play the
action of which takes place at Muldoon Manor,
home of the widowed Lady Cynthia Muldoon. Lady
Cynthia's houseguests include her invalided
brother-in-law, Major Magnus Muldoon, and her
vivacious girlfriend, Felicity Cunningham.
Puckeridge, third string critic behind Higgs
(whose dead body is hidden under the sofa on the
Muldoon Manor set) and Moon, is the author of
this skeleton of a mystery drama. Moon and
Birdboot are unaware of the identity of their
host for this evening's entertainment, just as
they are unaware of the end toward which they are
being steered. As the play begins, a radio
onstage warns of an escaped madman "on the loose
in Essex." The first of a series of telephone
calls from an anonymous source disrupts Mrs.
Drudge, the housekeeper, as she dusts. Simon
Gascoyne, a feckless roué who courts both
Cynthia and Felicity, confronts Mrs. Drudge
(which occasions the awkward spilling of detail
about the manor, its inhabitants past and
present, and its misty milieu). Simon takes a
second mysterious call, then listens nervously to
yet another radio warning about the madman at
large. Felicity enters pursuing an errant tennis
ball, and Simon musters the courage to tell this
girl that he loves another. Mrs. Drudge
overhears Felicity threaten to kill Simon
Gascoyne, but she says nothing as she and Simon
set up a table for a game of cards. Simon then
begins his unwelcome seduction of Cynthia, only
to be interrupted by Magnus's jealous attack.
Simon is invited to play cards with Felicity,
Magnus, and Cynthia, but the table talk is larded
with murderous innuendo, concluding with
Cynthia's threat, a precise echo of Felicity's
"I'll kill you for this, Simon Gascoyne!"
    The second act of the play within begins
smartly with a third mysterious call, then
founders in a protracted and apparently pointless
coffee-serving scene. To this Inspector Hound

enters seeking the escaped madman. He explains
his mission to the befuddled residents of Muldoon
Manor, then discovers a body under the sofa. The
house must be searched; all exit and Simon
wanders on, likewise discovers the body, and is
then killed by a shot from the dark. Act III
begins with a fourth call, but no one is on stage
to answer it. Moon, attempting desperately to
compose his convoluted response to the play, is
addled by the jangling phone. Since it is within
reach from his box, he grabs it up, listens, then
hands it to Birdboot with "It's for you."
Birdboot finds the call is from his wife, Myrtle.
From this point the play within repeats itself
with Birdboot in the role of the recently
murdered Simon Gascoyne and Moon as "Inspector
Hound." The actors once seen onstage as Simon
and Hound take the critics' box seats.

Both the narrative and the ritual
structures come into focus for the audience in
action vividly burlesquing the thrilling
reversals at the conclusion of **The Mousetrap**.
Magnus Muldoon reveals himself to be "the real
Inspector Hound." Seconds later Moon recognizes
Puckeridge whom he has seen in the dual role of
Magnus and the "real" Inspector Hound. Moon then
realizes that Puckeridge, frustrated (as is
Moon!) in his efforts to get ahead at the office,
has murdered Higgs and Birdboot and will kill
him, too. More importantly, the audience in the
theater comes to realize the part it has played
in springing Puckeridge's "mousetrap." This
scheming killer has written a playlet, rented a
theater, ordered scenery, hired a cast, rehearsed
it, and, to complete the illusion of a play in
progress, he has assembled an audience. Clearly,
the young actress playing Felicity, a recent
Birdboot conquest (Birdboot trades favorable
notices for sex), was bait to draw out this
womanizer. Birdboot's intrusion into the play
within has softened Moon's reluctance to get
involved in the play, and Birdboot's death
compelled Moon to set foot on the stage. The
body of Higgs functioned as magnet holding Moon
onstage until he could be properly prepared for
his death.[5] In this view, a production of
The Real Inspector Hound is theater like

theater, a similitude of itself, containing a
complicated conspiracy to delude and destroy
Birdboot and Moon. The auditor is treated to the
illusion of a theater, the appearance of a play
in progress, and the experience of involvement as
an accomplice in Puckeridge's murder plot.

     While the auditor must reconstruct the
narrative from hindsight, it should be clear that
when Birdboot answers the stage phone, we are
not, as Edith Oliver maintained in a review of
the New York production, "suddenly . . . in a
different kind of play."[6] The "critical" phase
of the narrative of Puckeridge's revenge has
begun--the "mousetrap" is baited and about to be
sprung. Puckeridge has selected the early scenes
with an eye for their appeal to the preoccupations of his prey. The warning of "a madman on
the loose," a murderously spiteful psychotic, as
we learn in Hound's analysis, is calculated to
appeal to Moon's appetite for bloody revenge.
Early on, Birdboot recognizes the plot
machinations in the play within, picks Magnus as
the killer, and declares his motive to be
"Revenge, of course . . . the paranoid grudge."
Birdboot's analysis of the madman's motives
meshes neatly with symptoms Moon displays.
Simon's churlish behavior, on the other hand,
amplifies the auditor's emerging understanding of
Birdboot. Both are types of the guileful rapist.
Simon's seductions are based on promises he has
no intentions and no means of keeping; Birdboot
elicits sexual favors from actresses in return
for favorable press notices. If one examines the
play within not as burlesque but as a part of an
elaborate intrigue, the patchwork scenes merge to
reveal unity. The scenes of violence and deceit
in the play within are keyed to motives that
compel the two critics. From the perspective of
satire, the play within is a hodgepodge of
familiar scenes from melodrama; from the perspective of narrative, the superficially disparate
scenes wholly develop the relationship between
the critics and the actors up to the point of
Birdboot's entry into the action. When Felicity
enters to Birdboot, the critics and the players,
once similarly motivated, now become identical.
Birdboot echoes Simon's lines with Felicity, with

Drudge, and with Cynthia. Moon's imprecations
have no effect on him; the obsession with sexual
conquest--implied in Moon's chiding and Birdboot's all too vehement denials--now dominates
Birdboot's consciousness. His behavior "on
stage" is fully consistent with all we've learned
about him earlier. Furthermore, no bait could be
more effective than Higgs' body in drawing Moon
into the scene. His soliloquies have firmly
established the intensity of his hatred for his
superiors. And no better challenge could be
calculated to keep Moon on stage than the
challenge of assuming the role of analyst. As he
compulsively (and ineptly) worried about the
meager facts of the play within for their
metaphysical significance, so he must explain why
Higgs and Birdboot have been killed. Puckeridge's "mousetrap" works perfectly. However,
the narrative of Puckeridge's revenge amounts to
little more than an amusing solution to the
problem of hastily and economically rationalizing
an absurd set of circumstances, a problem
Stoppard solved brilliantly in **After
Magritte**. The formal appeal of such an
exercise is negligible. Adroit manipulation of
the dramatic materials creates a complex experience for the auditor, but the emotional power of
the drama derives from an underlying pattern
which the narrative at once masks and ramifies.

The ritual process submerged in the intrigue
is the main source of the play's emotional
appeal. The root of the comic effect of **The
Real Inspector Hound** is a covert process
whereby certain types of anti-social behavior
invested in Moon and Birdboot are ceremonially
drawn out, perfected in action, and then expelled
from the world of play. The complicity of the
audience in Puckeridge's intrigue enhances the
potential for their further participation in and
appreciation of the method whereby exploitive and
nihilistic impulses are purged.

The ritual process suffusing the action of
The Real Inspector Hound is made up of seven
qualitative moments. The moments are "qualitative" in the sense that they are found in the

drama without strict regard to the temporal
progression of incidents. They are parts of an
idea, or form, which give intellectual and
emotional life to the incidents. The first of
the moments, and the one from which the others
may be extrapolated, is the quality of **order**.
Stoppard organizes the world of the play in terms
of several hierarchies which provide a structure
of values, standards by which the elements of
that world--objects, utterances, characters,
activities, and themes--are ranked. The most
obvious of these is the hierarchy upon which the
narrative feeds: the professional "depth chart"
that locates Higgs and Birdboot on "the first
string" and relegates Moon and Puckeridge to
lower status. Stoppard establishes his hierarchy
in the first few minutes of the play, and it
energizes the entire narrative of Puckeridge's
rise. Other miniature orderings are imbedded in
it and amplify our sense of the relatedness of
elements of the fictive world. Birdboot
understands the play being reviewed to be an
elementary thriller; Moon sees the murder mystery
as merely coincidental to a more vital drama
about man's search for identity. In Moon's mind,
such a drama of high consciousness is superior to
a drama of simple intrigue. As Moon repudiates
Birdboot's taste in theater, so he also denies
his taste for candy. Birdboot's offer of a
caramel from his box of "Black Magic" chocolates
elicits a disdainful "No thanks." Later Moon
asks for a chocolate and Birdboot obligingly
offers "Cherry? Strawberry? Coffee Cream?
Turkish Delight?" But the snobbish Moon will
have "montelimar" or "gooseberry fondue," or
"pistachio fudge," and so on, listing exotic
confections of another order entirely. Moon's
rejection of Birdboot's chocolates is part of a
rich pattern of hierarchical placement, for Moon
also assumes a superior moral position from which
to judge Birdboot's sexual adventures. Birdboot
has abandoned his "homely but good-natured wife,"
Myrtle, to pursue the conquest of more exciting
women. He has apparently seduced the young
actress playing Felicity Cunningham, but her
sweet, youthful ways lose their attraction when

he sees the svelt, sophisticated woman playing
Lady Cynthia Muldoon. Not only is Birdboot
obsessed with "mounting," but he is also driven
to seek new heights of excitement with a succession of ever more alluring sexual partners. Not
at all coincidentally, Simon Gascoyne follows an
identical pattern in moving up from a conquest of
Felicity Cunningham to a seduction of the
socially and sensually superior Lady Cynthia.

Hierarchical patterning is evident in
details of character and object, but it is no
less characteristic of the satiric attitudinizing
of **The Real Inspector Hound**. Brian Crossley
notes that "Stoppard repeatedly sets up the
standard classical thriller situations with the
deliberate intention of knocking them down. . . .
Thus, the well-made thriller is nominally and
theatrically 'hounded' to death, while the kind
of fatuous critiques of **The Real Inspector
Hound**, especially those of the critic Birdboot,
are shown to be a dead letter."[7] Like
Crossley, C. W. E. Bigsby treats **Hound** as
literary burlesque aimed at circumventing the
auditor's easy dissociation from the fantastic
and irrational qualities of the theatrical event.
According to Bigsby, Stoppard aims to undermine
"the conviction that reality is susceptible of
rational analysis, since it turns so clearly on
causality."[8] Crossley and Bigsby correctly
maintain that the play asks the auditor to mount
up the scale from rationally structured,
Apollonian drama to Dionysian ceremony and to
accept the disconcerting conclusion that
theatricality has surpassed realism not only in
the order of art but also in the order of life.

The second moment of the ritual process is
revealed in the way a character responds to
order. The "grading system" in the world of the
play breeds psychological uneasiness in Moon most
pointedly, but in Birdboot and Puckeridge as
well. In Moon the hierarchic psychosis is
manifest as a nihilistic obsession that
infiltrates his every behavior. The death of
Higgs is foremost in his mind: "Sometimes I
dream of revolution, a bloody **coup d'etat** by
the second rank. . . . Sometimes I dream of

Higgs" (pp. 6-7). His analysis of the play is
cast in images much more violent than the simple
events can suggest: "Already in the opening
stages we note the classic impact of the
catalystic figure--the outsider--plunging through
to the centre of an ordered world and setting up
the disruptions--the shock waves--which unless I
am mistaken will strip them of their shells and
leave them exposed as the trembling raw meat
which, at heart, is all of us" (pp. 20-21).
Moreover, his critical pronouncements have about
them a resentful, sometimes sneering quality:
"there are moments, and I would not begrudge it
this, when the play, if we can call it that, and
I think on balance we can, aligns itself
uncompromisingly on the side of life," (p. 33)
and "If we examine this more closely, and I think
close examination is the least tribute that this
play deserves, . . ." (p. 45). When they usurp
his position "on the aisle," Hound and Simon
redouble Moon's malice: "Simon: To say that it
is without pace, point, focus, interest, drama,
wit, or originality is to say simply that it does
not happen to be my cup of tea . . . Hound: I'm
sorry to be blunt, but there's no getting away
from it. It lacks pace. A complete ragbag"
(p. 59).

The third moment of the ritual process is
found in the assertion of the negative, a ringing
contravention of order. Both Moon and Birdboot
are infested with negativity. The world's order
rankles Moon. He is bound by the deadly spell he
seeks to cast over Higgs and over every other
element of his world. His dreamy meanderings,
his relations with Birdboot, and his response to
the play are all expressions of his efforts to
contradict accepted classifications. Moon fairly
reeks of death and denial. His identity as a
critic, as one who discriminates, fits him
admirably for the role of criminal. His way
of mounting up the hierarchy, of becoming
somebody, is to reduce the world about him to a
nihil, a mere nothing.

Birdboot is no less psychotic in his efforts
to scale the hierarchy, but his way of mounting
up is different. An approving soul of simple

tastes, he has acquired a powerful position as a
kind of St. Peter guarding the gates to the
theatrical heaven of critical approval and
popularity. Birdboot succeeds from critic to
criminal by exploiting his power over young
actresses. As a critic, he is inclined to accept
order, but he uses the threat of the negative,
the threat of disapproval, to gain sexual
advantages denied him by the social conventions
of monogamy. His marital faithlessness and his
professional dereliction are but manifestations
of his characteristic irresponsibility. Thus we
have in Moon and Birdboot two demons who prowl
the paths of theatrical success, each using his
power and position for purposes of self-
aggrandizement--one a nihilist, one a chauvinist.
Lord Chesterfield defined dirt as "matter out of
place," a definition which implies two conditions: a set of ordered relations, in this play,
"the theatre," and a denial of that order:
nihilistic and exploitive uses of criticism.
Moon and Birdboot are thus "dirt," "pollution,"
and their expulsion from the play world is
accomplished in a comic ritual of riddance.

The fourth and fifth moments of the ritual
process are involved with cleansing. The fourth
is mortification, a type of self-cleansing, and
the fifth is victimage, cleansing of the polluted
agent at the hands of another agent or agents.
Moon and Birdboot are both mortified and
victimized. In the first half of the play, they
are inept and preoccupied auditors, continually
misunderstanding each other and the play. Their
unwitting intrusiveness and their witless
critical pronouncements are ridiculous. The
appropriate response to this revelatory spectacle
is laughter, which the critics bring on themselves. Once, however, they are swept into the
action of the play they have come to review,
they are victimized by the the cast of the play
within. Stoppard's stage direction at Felicity's
entrance says "Everything is as it was. It is,
let us say, the same moment in time" (p. 47). In
fact, the pattern of the action indicates
precisely that this is not "the same moment in
time," but suggests rather that temporal

progression is inherent in the motive of the
play. Birdboot's exploitive manner of "mounting
up" becomes radiant when he assumes the role of
Simon and when Felicity emerges as a suitable
scourge. The safely confined intrigue in which
Simon abandons Felicity (thereby establishing her
motive for killing him) has broken out into the
"real world." "Felicity" plays the scene as
"actress playing Felicity"--Birdboot "plays"
Birdboot only to find himself doubled as "Simon
Gascoyne" in the last line of the scene. An
auditor witnesses a scene in which a critic
advises an actress he has no more use for her as
a concubine. Felicity's dialogue with Birdboot
repeats what she has said to Simon, but the words
are infused with a different animus. The
enlarged circumference of the action implies
deepened emotions. The venom in "I'll kill you
for this . . ." is doubled by the crossing of
roles.

Similarly, Lady Muldoon repeats to Birdboot
words she had said to Simon, but the tone is
altered by the circumstances. The "Cynthia" of
the text is not the same "Cynthia" who earlier
responded so passionately to Simon Gascoyne.
Here, "Cynthia" is a sly actress using her
physical charms and her dramatic dialogue to
ensnare a victim. "Birdboot as Simon" thinks
he's the hunter/seducer when he is actually the
object of the hunt/seduction.

The victimization of Birdboot accelerates
and intensifies. Magnus's wheelchair knocks him
to the floor, despite effort to avoid it. The
physical abuse here is a precursor of what's to
come. The madcap card game is clearly a device
for making Birdboot sense most strongly his alien
status. Each player threatens "Birdboot as
Simon" with table gibberish made up of equal
parts of bridge lingo and chess talk. Birdboot
hardly notices his predicament; he thinks he,
like Simon before him, has "won" Cynthia, the
prize in the game. When he capers into the body
and recognizes it as Higgs, his function has been
fulfilled. He has completed Simon's pattern; he
has wholly, albeit unwittingly "confessed" his
characteristic sinfulness, and he has passed the

lure to Moon. The shot that kills Birdboot is
the ultimate act of victimzation and the wages of
his sin. The conferring of the new identity--an
identity we have already seen to be that of "the
perfect victim"--is an act of victimage, a ritual
assault upon the character of Birdboot. In part,
he is victimized by being forced to assume a
false and degrading identity, but he is also
duped and seduced into playing **himself.** His
ironic and ambiguous identity is crucial to his
suitability as a ritual scapegoat: He is
punished not for what he has done, but for what
he would be--not for his deeds, but for the
symbolic quality they radiate.

Moon undergoes treatment similar to that
accorded Birdboot. He is reidentified as
"Inspector," subjected to degrading criticism
from "Simon" and "Hound," encircled by Cynthia,
Magnus, Felicity, and Mrs. Drudge, and challenged
to display his characteristic analytical
abilities. He tries to explain why Higgs is dead
and why Birdboot was killed, but the explanation,
typically, makes no sense. Like Birdboot, his
fate is sealed when he assumes the "reality" of
the on-stage conditions--when he refers to
Birdboot's corpse as "Simon." Again, like
Birdboot, he is fit to kill when he acknowledges
the power of his destructive fantasies, when he
pleads "I only dreamed . . . Sometimes I
dreamed." Finally, he recognizes Puckeridge,
sees the trap he has fallen into, and tries to
run, only to be gunned down "in the name of the
law." His victimization, too, is complete in
death. The silliness that ensues as Magnus
reveals himself to Cynthia as her beloved Albert
is an obvious parody of the classical
anagnorisis. More importantly, however, Moon
recognizes Puckeridge as one who has by cunning
realized what he could only fantasize. Though a
"bastard," and not the properly blessed heir to
Higgs' place of prominence, Puckeridge will
"mount up" to it over the ritually slain bodies
of his professional betters.

The sixth moment of the ritual process is
the catharsis, a resolution actualized in the
drama and seeded as potential in the auditor.

The resolution actualized in the drama is the
result of the efforts of the playwright and the
producing agency to identify Moon and Birdboot as
nihilist and exploiter, then to reconfirm and
amplify these identities through the critics'
involvement in the play within, and finally, to
victimize these characters unto perfection, that
is, unto death. The world of the play is thereby
"innoculated" with their filth and then purged of
it.

As with any purgation by victimization, the
cleanser becomes unclean in the process. If
Birdboot has exploited his professional powers,
so have the actors. Their natural powers of play
and improvisation are not simply exercised, they
are also used for effect. Nihilistic fantasy is
actualized most clearly in Moon, but the very act
of victimizing him is a critical act, and a
criminal act. Puckeridge and the unnamed
performers playing Felicity, Simon, Cynthia,
Drudge, and Hound become unclean in their act of
cleansing and they must be disposed of. The
audience, final arbiter and ultimate benefactor
of this process, obliges by dismissing them from
the stage with applause.

The resolution is seeded as potential in the
auditor by means of identification, as well. The
auditor's playful involvement in Puckeridge's
assassination conspiracy does much to promote
identification. As narrative plot meshes with
ritual process, the auditor's involvement in
Puckeridge's assassination conspiracy does much
to promote identification. As narrative plot
meshes with ritual process, the auditor's
involvement is transformed into something more
"serious," that is, into a relationship more
threatening to his sense of well-being. But, the
increased risk brings with it increased benefits,
as we shall see. Birdboot and Moon are
themselves represented as auditors. In the
proscenium staging Stoppard presumes in his stage
directions, "The first thing is that the audience
appear to be confronted by their own reflection
in a huge mirror . . . . It can be progressively
faded out as the play goes on, until the front
row remains to remind. us of the rest, finally

merely two seats in that row--. . ." (p.3). In
an arena staging of the play, the identification
of the critics with the audience is explicit, for
the critics are clearly seated in audience space
and the audience mirrors itself, as it encircles
the playing area. The critics behave like
auditors; they noisily thumb programs, they
gossip and comment on the play. They also
vocalize the usually unspoken thoughts of the
auditor. Electronic amplification of their
whispers is a technical requirement, but it also
creates an expressively auditory image of the
presence of the audience in the theater. The
critics are obviously present as critics when
they broadcast their pronouncements on the play.
More importantly, their response to the action of
the play within symbolizes the general relationship between auditor and stage action. The scene
in which Mrs. Drudge serves coffee is a case in
point. It parodies the ubiquitous moments of
mood intensification in the murder mystery
melodrama. Nervous, anxious characters wait for
a storm to break. A menacing atmosphere of
suspicion and dread permeates and distorts some
quiet, innocuous social ritual. As Mrs. Drudge
tediously serves coffee, cream, sugar, and
biscuits, the play's forward movement halts
entirely. The audience squirms restlessly and
their creaking chairs and stiffled coughs, their
nervous giggles and quiet exchanges become the
"menacing atmosphere," as far as the actor-
cum-character is concerned. The audience
thus takes intimate part in the action--it is one
with the play and wholly in accord with
Birdboot's note: "The second act, however, fails
to fulfill the promise . . . ," as well as with
Felicity's remark, "If you ask me, there's
something funny going on" (p. 35).
     The auditor's consubstantiality with both
the cleanser and the unclean is the fertile
ground in which the psychic and emotional effect
of the drama is seeded. The devices of the play
identify the auditor with both the ritual victim
and the scourge. Laughter at Birdboot's transparent lies about his faithfulness to Myrtle and
at his breathless pursuit of Cynthia, at Moon's

bloody obsession with Higgs and at his disruptive
criticisms, implicates the auditor in their
faithlessness and destructiveness. The laughter
acknowledges these behaviors as entirely human,
but it does not signal forgiveness. That comes
only when the victimage is complete, when
Birdboot and Moon are dead. By then the auditor
has dissipated some of the tension caused by his
own exploitive and nihilistic responses to his
own hierarchic situation, and he has transferred
part of them to the **dramatis personae.** The
final moment of the ritual process is the
redemption, the auditor's sense of "ransom from
capitivity," which succeeds the symbol-induced
catharsis. The symbolic death of Moon and
Birdboot and the conventional reward of applause
given the "Puckeridge Players" for services
rendered releases the auditor from the burden of
guilt once shared with the players. The sense of
well-being that ensues is partly the result of
the re-establishment of the hierarchical
relationship between the theater and the audience
and partly the result of the ritual unburdening.

Far from stopping "annoyingly short of
examining the implications of its central
premise," as C. W. E. Bigsby maintains, **The
Real Inspector Hound** is wholly and completely
responsive to its purgative-redemptive motive.
Without denying Stoppard's parodic aims, this
essay demonstrates that, in addition to being a
barbed satire and a somewhat less successful
exposition of a view of the relationship between
theater and life, the play is fully comprehens-
ible as a ritual of riddance. Its capacity to
exorcise an auditor's guilts about incipient and
real forms of exploitation and nihilism will
commend it for production when **The Mousetrap**
is as dead as **Uncle Tom's Cabin.** This
apparently light-weight comedy may be seen to be
a complex and powerful drama with multiple
structures simultaneously at work on the
auditor's consciousness. The complex narrative
of Puckeridge's revenge offers unique but trivial
satisfactions. The satirical thrust Brian
Crossley points out adds engaging ironies and
counterpoints that appeal to the sophisticated

and literate viewer. The statement about
theatricality Bigsby extracts is a theme of
contemporary interest. The narrative, the
parody, and the play's thematic statement
broadens the play's attraction, but the ritual of
riddance is the developmental principle of **The
Real Inspector Hound** and the primary source of
its formal appeal.

Notes

1. Page numbers in parentheses refer to the
Grove Press edition of 1968.

2. Brian M. Crossley, "An Investigation of
Stoppard's 'Hound and Foot,'" **Modern Drama**,
20 (March 1977), 88.

3. C. W. E. Bigsby, **Tom Stoppard**
(London: Published for the British Council by
the Longman Group, Ltd., 1976), p. 18.

4. The perspective on the ritual
functioning of drama is drawn from the theory and
critical practice of Kenneth Burke. On the
moments of the ritual process, see "On Human
Behavior Considered 'Dramatistically,'" in K.
Burke, **Permanence and Change**, Second Revised
Edition (Indianapolis: The Bobbs-Merrill Co.,
Inc., 1954, 1964), pp. 274-294; and the discussion of "the cycle of terms implicit in the idea
of 'order,'" in K. Burke, **Rhetoric of
Religion** (Boston: Beacon Press, 1961), pp. 183
ff. See also William F. Rueckert, **Kenneth
Burke and the Drama of Human Relations**
(Minneapolis: University of Minnesota Press,
1963), pp. 128-163.

5. My arena production of **The Real
Inspector Hound** in March, 1979, began with
Higgs' entrance. Before the play within could
begin, Higgs was called to the actor's lounge to
receive an urgent call (the ringing telephone
could be easily heard all over the theater and
foreshadowed the calls that eventually drew Moon
and Birdboot into the action). Shouts and then a
shot ensue, and Higgs' body was shortly returned
to the stage by the actors playing Hound and
Simon. "Puckeridge" helped them position the
body, sent them to their places, gave the
audience an impromptu welcome and vote of thanks,
then signaled the beginning of the play.

6. Edith Oliver, "At Lady Muldoon's," **New
Yorker**, 48 (May 6, 1972), 62.

7. Crossley, pp. 78-79.

8. Bigsby, p. 16.

Foot-prints to the Moon: Detectives as Suspects in **Hound** and **Magritte**

Jeffrey D. Mason

I'll give you a tip, then. Watch the girl.

--Birdboot in **The Real Inspector Hound**

Well, Constable, I think you owe us all an explanation.

--Foot in **After Magritte**

Late in **The Real Inspector Hound** (1968), the allegedly false Hound refers to the "unsuspected public" in a context that leaves the performer or reader wondering if he meant to say "unsuspecting." Yet the apparent typographical error is, as Birdboot would say, a "red herring," for Hound has said exactly what Stoppard intended. In both **Hound** and **After Magritte** (1970), everyone is suspect, so only those who are "unsuspected" are remarkable.[1]
    In each play, Stoppard designs networks of interlocking investigations that involve each character intimately, inextricably and excruciatingly with the others. The obvious link between the two plays is the figure of the detective, yet an investigation requires **two** participants: the detective and his quarry. In Stoppard's plays, an individual can fill both roles at once, so everyone is simultaneously the agent and the object of scrutiny. In **Hound**, the critics study the actors as they perform the play, the actors furtively check the critics' reactions, the characters in the play watch each other suspiciously within the structure of the murder mystery, and, if the entire evening is indeed an

elaborate scheme of Puckeridge's devising, the
actors **as conspirators** surreptitiously
observe the critics.   In **After Magritte,**
Holmes and Foot spy on the Harris family, who
earlier witnessed Foot's ambiguous, one-legged
appearance in the London rain. An investigator
is a bloodhound who follows tracks to find their
source, but Stoppard's detectives and
pseudo-detectives tend to discover that the
Foot-prints are their own.
        In Stoppard's world, no action goes
unnoticed. No matter how apparently trivial an
episode might seem, there is someone lurking
nearby to observe, interpret, and then comment.
When Moon asks, "Who was that lady I saw you with
last night?" (p. 13), Stoppard creates the
impression that Moon (or perhaps his stand-in!)
is always on hand to take note of Birdboot's
amorous affairs. Within the play they come to
review, Drudge manages to appear on stage just in
time to overhear each of several murderous
threats that create obvious suspense within the
murder mystery and less obvious mockery within
Stoppard's larger purpose. Cynthia keeps an eye
on Simon, saying, "did I hear you say you saw
Felicity last night?" (p. 28), and barely a
moment after he bursts on stage, Magnus bellows,
"I have witnesses!" (p. 26). So he does; so do
they all.
        While **Hound** opens with the image of
Moon--critic as witness--watching the empty
stage, **After Magritte** begins with the image
of Holmes--policeman as witness--watching the
Harris family. The former image is subtler,
wearing the veil of theatrical custom, but the
latter is overt, making Holmes look like a clumsy
voyeur.   In **After Magritte,** everyone seems to
be peering through windows as Foot looks out of
his bathroom to watch the Harris family drive
away from the curb, and they, in turn, see him
through their windshield as he hops madly towards
the street.
        Each play involves rituals of observation.
In **Hound,** the critics arrive at the play for
the specific purpose of bearing witness to their
readers, and the actors face the opening curtain

with full knowledge that their work is subject to
formal scrutiny. The ritual gives the critics
permission to examine the behavior of the actors,
just as it allows the actors to pretend that
there is no one watching them.   In **After
Magritte**, the ritual derives from the social
contract to sacrifice privacy in the name of
public safety, the agreement that makes the
police possible.   Here the threat is more severe,
for while Birdboot and Moon can only ruin an
actor's reputation, Foot can take away the Harris
family's freedom.
     Observation creates interdependence between
the agent and the object.   There can be no
critics without actors, no well-publicized actors
without critics, and no policemen without
suspects.   When a character lacks the customary
object of his observation, he is bereft; one of
the first actions in **Hound** involves both Moon
and Birdboot contemplating the possible where-
abouts of Higgs.   Birdboot is accustomed to
observing Higgs's style (even as he observes that
of his replacement, Moon), and Moon spends his
days watching Higgs and waiting for him to step
aside.   Moon realizes that Higgs must reciprocate
his scrutiny, and he has grown to believe that
his very existence depends on Higgs's attention.
He says, "I think I must be waiting for Higgs to
die. . . .   Half-afraid that I will vanish when
he does" (p. 18).
     Observation requires separation.   Holmes
watches unmolested while standing outside the
Harris family's window, but when he enters to
pursue the investigation, he is caught up in the
chaos and eventually gets down on his hands and
knees to locate a search warrant that he could
not recognize even if he found it.   Moon observes
Higgs passionately, but at a distance.

> It is as if we only existed one at a time,
> combining to achieve continuity.   I keep
> space warm for Higgs.   My presence defines
> his absence, his absence confirms my
> presence, his presence precludes mine. . . .
> When Higgs and I walk down this aisle
> together to claim our common seat, the
> oceans will fall into the sky and the trees
> will hang with fishes. (p. 9)

As long as Higgs is absent, Moon will look
nervously up the aisle behind him; were Higgs to
appear, there would be no reason for Moon to
investigate him.

If one's every move is noted, then actors
are not the only ones who perform: we **all**
perform, even though we may perform unwillingly.
Moon and Birdboot become reluctant, terrified
actors in the play they came to review, dragged
down from the complacent safety of their box
seats to deal with a world they have always kept
at a safe distance. Moon is especially aghast to
find himself subject to the scrutiny and
reportage of Hound and Simon, and he must wonder,
as we must, whether they appear as characters or
as actors.

The actor on stage performs with awareness
of his audience, but the individual on the street
may not always realize that others are watching
him. The Harrises do not execute their apparently bizarre opening scene for the entertainment of
an audience; each individual is trying to solve a
problem. Foot's profession requires him to
monitor the behavior of others, but it does not
occur to him until the end of the play that
someone else might study him with equal attention
and energy. Birdboot knows that others are bound
to see him **tête-à-tête** with the
actresses he claims to have seduced, so he tries
to make the best of the situation and enjoy his
reputation as a ladies' man. When it seems that
gossip might reach Myrtle's ears and inspire her
to restrict his freedom, he scoffs at his
accusers, describing himself with intuitive
accuracy as "the object of uninformed malice, the
petty slanders of little men" (p. 23). Both Moon
and Birdboot are aware that their readership will
study their reviews, just as Hound and Foot act
with constant awareness that their every move is
subject to study and evaluation by the public and
their fellow officers. Yet when the critics are
forced to move into an overt, rather than tacit,
mode of performance, the harsh light amazes
them.

Like the object of a scientific experiment,
the individual's behavior alters when he realizes

that someone observes him in a manner out of
keeping with his expectations or experience.   It
seems inevitable that during his first few
moments on stage, Birdboot constantly checks
around him to see who overhears his conversation
with Felicity. He expects the quick, knowing
leer scarcely seen over a crony's shoulder in a
pub, but he finds himself inhibited by the gaze
of the audience and especially by the clinical
eye of Moon as his colleague continues to take
his painfully detailed notes. Birdboot loses his
limited capacity for spontaneity, and his
carefully rehearsed suavity disintegrates.   He
assumes the uncomfortable position of the man who
is expected to "perform" sexually while someone
is watching him, and like that unfortunate
individual, he finds himself incapable. He makes
reference to Felicity's "technique" in an
interchange that creates an amusing ambiguity
between theater and sex.   The actor is remarkable
because he **can** perform under the public eye,
but Birdboot, developing the sexual parallel,
says that he "couldn't take it night after night"
(p. 48).

Stoppard's joke on the victims--and on the
audience--is that there is no point or purpose to
all of this observation.   The whole theory of
detection is founded upon the naive belief that
one can objectively observe evidence, intelli-
gently comprehend testimony, accurately interpret
both, and formulate dependable deductions.
C. W. E. Bigsby identifies the object of mockery
in **Hound**:

> . . . the play which Birdboot and Moon are
> reviewing is a whodunnit, the supreme
> example of rational art . . . a form which
> rests on the conviction that reality is
> susceptible of rational analysis, since it
> turns so clearly on causality.[2]

The detective is the champion of rationalism, the
man who claims to solve the puzzle by building a
structure of logically related deductions, and he
is therefore the victim of Stoppard's pen.   Both
Brian M. Crossley and Thomas R. Whitaker have

identified the detective as the philosophical
heir of Oedipus, the man who believes confidently
that he can resolve a disordered situation but
whose investigations lead to chaos.[3] Oedipus
fell from grace because his questions succeeded
too well in revealing a situation that demanded
his destruction, but Hound and Foot discover that
their very methods are unreliable. They are the
objects of Stoppard's derision because they
believe that effect follows cause, that phenomena
permit comprehension, that deduction reveals
truth, and that the future responds to planning.
They place their trust in the chain of observation, interpretation, testimony and deduction,
but it breaks down at every point. They assume a
rational order that does not exist, and when they
act according to that assumption, they stand
revealed as fools.

Observation, when not debilitatingly
subjective, is unreliable. In a production of
Hound, it is inevitable that the body of
Higgs lie fully visible to the characters in the
play for quite a while before Hound "discovers"
it. The corpse dominates the scene and its
presence suggests either that the characters fail
to notice it or that they choose to ignore it.
Moon sees the body from the first, and even
though Higgs is the object of his obsessive
fantasies, he fails to recognize the corpse until
Birdboot turns it over. The inability to observe
with any degree of reliability leads to comically
absurd statements, as when Foot finally enters
the Harris home, now virtually "normal" in
appearance, to say in response to its earlier
condition, "What is the meaning of this bizarre
spectacle?!!" (p. 82).

Testimony is equally suspect. Magnus
deflates Moon (and detectives in general) when he
says, "We have only your word for that,
Inspector. We only have your word for a lot of
things" (p. 57). In **After Magritte**, Harris,
Thelma and Mother present different versions of
what occurred in Ponsonby Place that afternoon,
while Foot places his professional credit in
jeopardy by basing his investigation on a
second-hand account; each insists that he or she

merely reports what was there to be observed, but
the act of observation is so subjective that
subsequent interpretation renders the reportage
useless. Each layer (observation, interpretation, testimony) creates another barrier between
the original phenomenon and the detective's
deduction.

If, as Felicia Hardison Londré has argued,
Hound is partly about wish-fulfillment, then
the detective represents mankind's wish for the
ultimate impossibility: reliable deduction from
available evidence.[4] Harris derides Holmes's
investigations, saying, "If he's found a shred of
evidence to back it up then get him in here and
let's see it" (p. 102), but his statement implies
that certain evidence, correctly presented, would
convince him to accept Foot's interpretaton. In
other words, he scorns Foot's viewpoint while
accepting the basic soundness of his methods.

Yet the rational approach is absurd when
applied to an irrational world. Moon begins his
work as the surrogate detective by proclaiming,
"I'm going to find out who did this!" (p. 55),
but he unconsciously ridicules his efforts
moments later when he says that "it is from these
chance remarks that we in the Force build up our
complete picture" (p. 56), which is to say that
the supposedly inviolate structure of rationality
is a jumble of random statements, and that which
purports to be investigation is actually a series
of lucky accidents. When he finally finishes his
tortuous reconstruction of past events, Felicity
dismisses it all as nonsense.

Moon's attempt to play detective is even
more foolish from another perspective. His
alleged purpose is to discover who killed
Birdboot, the critic, not Simon, the character.
Yet as he begins his investigation, he speaks to
the others not as actors but as characters,
allowing himself, as Birdboot did, to sink into
the fiction of the play. When he slips into
regarding Birdboot as Simon, his demise is
assured.

Stoppard further mocks the figure of the
detective by juxtaposing him with the figure of
the actor. A detective conventionally pursues

his quarry by putting himself in the suspect's
place and reconstructing past events; Sherlock
Holmes's most triumphant moments came when he
demonstrated to Watson exactly those actions the
criminal executed at the scene of the crime.
Both actor and detective ask the question, "What
would I do if I were such-and-such a person?" and
proceed accordingly. Yet the actor knows that it
is all artistic sham, that there is at least as
much of himself in his portrayal as of the
character he interprets. The detective insists
that he can impersonate the miscreant to such an
accurate degree that he can re-create the unknowable past. The detective is an actor whose own
pretense has seduced his belief, and both
Birdboot and Moon are actors forced to don the
detective's blinders and play the consequences.

If detection is impossible, then investigation is absurd and the detective is but a fool.
Stoppard's detectives seem unable to draw correct
conclusions. Hound visits the Manor due to the
erroneous understanding that someone has summoned
him. He goes on to assume that someone in the
house party is protecting the killer when in fact
none of them knows who the miscreant is (if,
indeed, there is a criminal **within the fiction
of the mystery**), and he compounds his folly by
concluding that the corpse is Lady Muldoon's
missing husband. His only defense is, "I seem to
have made a dreadful mistake" (p. 40). No one in
Hound ever unravels the various complications
of the several levels of action; the character of
Hound never even returns to pursue his investigation of Simon's murder.

Foot pursues the scent until the facts turn
around to assault him. He sets himself up with
his confident and unwittingly ironic remarks
about the conclusions he hopes to draw, until he
finally must confess his incompetence:

> My reconstruction has proved false in every
> particular, and it is undoubtedly being
> voiced back at the station that my past
> success at deductions of a penetrating
> character has caused me finally to overreach
> myself in circumstances that could hardly be
> more humiliating. (p. 101)

He tries to excuse himself, saying, "but bear in mind that my error was merely one of interpretation" (p. 102). But even this statement betrays his basic failure to understand that erroneous interpretation is unremarkable in a world without objective information. The more solemnly he behaves and the more firmly he clings to his rationalistic foundation, the more foolish he appears.

Life according to Stoppard does not submit to rational analysis. Either phenomena are too ambiguous to permit reliable conclusions, or, as in the case of Higg's corpse, evidence is so obvious that man can barely bring himself to acknowledge its presence. Mother Harris scorns Magritte's paintings because they don't represent her view of the tuba, complaining that the images weren't "life-like." She expects Magritte to express an experience that resembles her own, not realizing that even a tuba is too ambiguous to permit two people to perceive it identically.

In addition to its subjectivity, reportage may fail because of form or intent. When the critics frame their reviews and the Harris family make their statements, they all mimic the form of the detective's official report, using a style that attempts to create the impression of reliability even if the content is insubstantial. Moon and Birdboot sometimes plan their reviews for reasons extraneous to the quality of script and performance, as when they collaborate to promote the career of the actress playing Felicity. While the detective might argue that investigation and deduction form an objective science, the vagaries of reportage make the detective's work more a subjective art.

Twice in **After Magritte,** Thelma says that "There's no need to use language." She refers to coarse or abusive vocabulary, but she might as well warn against relying on language of any sort at all, for it cannot convey meaning effectively, it seldom helps the characters get what they want, and it raises a barrier to mutual understanding instead of illuminating ideas. As Joan Fitzpatrick Dean says,

> the comedy of **After Magritte** grows out
> of lexical misunderstandings, puns, and a
> keen sense of the limitations of language to
> communicate. . . . Language compounds
> rather than resolves the confusion and
> misunderstandings about the events that
> transpired on Ponsonby Place.[5]

Harris accidentally anticipates Foot's questions,
but the detective, true to form, mistakenly
concludes that the gentleman is answering the
questions in the wrong sequence. Foot refers to
the Harris home as a "disorderly house," meaning
a brothel, and Harris agrees, implying that the
place is chaotic. Moon and Birdboot seldom
understand each other, their conversations
intertwining like a double helix as they part
company, return for a moment of startled
recognition, and part again.
     As the characters fail to communicate, their
language becomes increasingly elaborate. Moon's
perorations limp and halt from the weight of
qualifiers, parenthetical remarks, and repeated
formulas, all symptomatic of the lack of true
content in his purportedly brilliant analyses as
well as his inability to find a position worthy
of his genuine commitment.

> There are moments, and I would not begrudge
> it this, when the play, if we can call it
> that, and I think on balance we can, aligns
> itself uncompromisingly on the side of life.
> **Je suis**, it seems to be saying, **ergo
> sum.** But is that enough? I think we are
> entitled to ask. For what in fact is this
> play concerned with? It is my belief that
> here we are concerned with what I have
> referred to elsewhere as the nature of
> identity. I think we are entitled to
> ask—and here one is irresistibly reminded
> of Voltaire's cry, "**Voilà**"—I think we
> are entitled to ask—**Where is God?**
> (p. 32)

Moon creates his script as he goes, contriving
his language to reflect the image of himself that

he hopes to display to his reading public and to
his colleagues on Fleet Street. Foot, too, is
the product of his own will as he struggles to
maintain his status in the eyes of the citizenry,
the non-detectives he alternately suspects and
protects, employing a mixture of casebook
cliché and stuffy formality.

> Everything I have heard about events here
> today convinces me that you are up to your
> neck in the Crippled Minstrel Caper. . . .
> Will you kindly stop interrupting while I am
> about to embark on my exegesis!! . . . The
> facts appear to be that shortly after two
> o'clock this afternoon, the talented though
> handicapped doyen of the Victoria Palace
> Happy Minstrel Troupe emerged from his
> dressing-room in blackface, and entered the
> sanctum of the box-office staff; whereupon,
> having broken his crutch over the heads of
> those good ladies, the intrepid uniped made
> off with the advance takings stuffed into
> the crocodile boot which, it goes without
> saying, he had surplus to his conventional
> requirements. (pp. 91-92)

Hound also retreats into stiffly polite
conventionality when it develops that no one
called him to Muldoon Manor and that there is no
emergency, saying that "this puts me in a very
difficult position" (p. 37).
    Keir Elam has analyzed the characters'
linguistic alienation in terms of the semiotic
perspective on the slippery relationship between
the object, the image and the word.[6] Harris
asserts that the apparition carried a white
stick, and when Thelma suggests that it was an
ivory cane, he cries, "An ivory cane IS a white
stick!!" (p. 77). His difficulty is that he does
not realize that "ivory cane" does not
necessarily equal "white stick." He grows
exasperated at the endless debate, saying "I am
only telling you what I saw" (p. 77), as if such
an assertion would resolve the difficulties. In
Hound, object is divorced from both name and
icon as the characters assume pseudonyms, roles,
and even disguises.

The players can exploit semiotic relativity when they answer the telephone, which rings four times during **Hound**. Stoppard does not reveal the name of the hapless caller on the first three occasions, but the director may choose to decide that it is Myrtle, asking each time for Birdboot. When Simon and Drudge answer, they refuse to concede Birdboot the name that Myrtle uses, but they can quite justifiably look furtively in Birdboot's direction before telling Myrtle, "I'm afraid there is no one of that name here." They are sensitive to the implications of the naming; only when Birdboot assumes the name of Simon will they admit him into their world.

Another production choice relates to the connection of icon with object, or of image with person. The role listed as Magnus is "actually" Puckeridge playing the triple role of Magnus, Albert Muldoon and the real Inspector Hound. If his disguise is subtle and convincing, then the audience is drawn into the deception. If, on the other hand, he wears a blatantly false beard--one which he can pull aside for selected "revealing" remarks--then the audience shares Stoppard's vantage, able to see that name or appearance do not denote essence.

Performance is, by definition, a process of re-naming, a semantic and semiotic manipulation of experience. Birdboot confuses the actor with the role when he chafes at the way Simon treats Cynthia, and again when he snaps at the bait Drudge offers by telling him that Lady Muldoon will miss his presence at the card game. He seems unable to make the distinction between the woman and the role she plays. Part of Birdboot's clumsy charm is that he writes unintentionally ingenuous criticisms like "the part as written is a mere cypher but she manages to make Cynthia a real person" (p. 31). There is no such thing as a "real person" in a play, and Birdboot's failure to understand the point is his weakness, for while he remains on stage in hopes of making progress with Cynthia (or with "Cynthia"), he cannot control the situation and the events sweep him under.

In **Hound**, the characters' inability to understand the truth protects them against disaster, for to comprehend all is to forfeit all. Both Birdboot and Moon face death only a moment after they discover the truth they seek. **After Magritte** concludes in a less sinister fashion as Foot goes to great lengths to complete his investigation but Stoppard offers him humiliation in place of destruction. Indeed, all who seek rational, explicable truth must admit defeat at Stoppard's hands, for each circumstance in **After Magritte**, no matter how bizarre it may seem, admits an elaborately--and therefore absurdly--logical explanation. The card games in **Hound** are bewildering mixtures of chess, bridge, poker and roulette, revealing that any such game involves a set of arbitrary rules and values which the players agree to accept. The so-called "rational" world is itself a pastiche of mutual agreements made by the participants, and when rationality is too neatly constructed, it looks as though someone has stacked the deck. Stoppard mocks us while he resolves the mysteries that piqued our attention.

The ubiquitous presence of the detective means that no one is safe from a sudden knock on the door in the middle of the night. The title of **After Magritte** carries several possible implications: that the play occurs after the Harris family visits the Magritte exhibit, that Stoppard wrote the play in the manner of Magritte, that Stoppard wrote the play in response to Magritte's ideas, or that Stoppard wrote the play after Magritte's work was established in the collective imagination. Yet it also indicates that Stoppard pursues the painter as the detective pursues his quarry, implying that Stoppard, like a bloodhound, will locate Magritte and flush him out, or even supplant him in the minds of the public.

The pursuer as potential supplanter is the image that pervades Moon's fantasies. He dreams of replacing Higgs, but he cannot abide the idea of someone else taking his own spot. Moon says that "no member of the human race keeps warm my bit of space" (p. 20), yet Higgs usually occupies the "bit of space" that Moon would like to claim. When the play approaches its climax, Moon looks

up in horror to find that Hound, or the false
Hound, or the actor playing either role, has
commandeered his seat. In this world of
detectives, there is always someone eager to step
in. Puckeridge would replace Moon, who would
replace Higgs. Birdboot envies Simon's intimacy
with Cynthia; he wins that place but trades away
his own in the process and finally forfeits his
life. Hound is merely taking the place of the
"real" Hound, who is not actually Hound at all,
but Puckeridge. Even Cynthia and Felicity
compete to see who will dominate Simon's
affections, and both ladies supplant poor Myrtle.
Moon finally gets his wish, following in Higgs's
footsteps as he dies on the same stage that
claimed his predecessor's life, and it is
relatively simple to stage the denouement so that
Moon collapses to complete the heap of corpses
that Higgs and Birdboot began. His demise is
especially poignant in view of his passionate
exhortation that finishes with his asking the
stand-ins of the world to unite and take what he
regards as their rightful places in society.

    Stoppard's investigations go beyond the
limits of these two plays to reach out into the
audience. The playwright investigates the
audience's beliefs, assuming the role of mock-
detective in order to accuse us of investing our
own detective status with naive trust. We
believe in a rational world that permits us to
control our destiny and maintain our privacy;
Stoppard reveals life as uncontrollably absurd,
characterized by ubiquitous but futile detection.
Hound is a classic exercise in realistic
farce, where the farceur sets up a familiar order
and dismantles it before the audience's amazed
eyes, while **After Magritte** is the precise
reverse, an apparent chaos which finally submits
to the tidy explanations that we all cherish but
which Stoppard knows are impossible.

Notes

1.   Tom Stoppard, "**The Real Inspector Hound
and After Magritte** " (New York: Grove Press,
1980), p. 54.   Subsequent references to these
plays will be to this edition and will appear in
the text.

2.   C. W. E. Bigsby, **Tom Stoppard**
(Harlow, Essex: Longman Group, 1976), p. 18.

3.   Brian M. Crossley, "An Investigation of
Stoppard's 'Hound' and 'Foot,'" **Modern Drama**,
20 (March 1977), 77; and Thomas R. Whitaker,
Tom Stoppard (New York: Grove Press, 1983),
p. 75

4.   Felicia Hardison Londré, **Tom Stoppard**
(New York: Frederick Ungar, 1981), p. 119.

5.   Joan Fitzpatrick Dean, **Tom Stoppard:
Comedy as a Moral Matrix** (Columbia: University
of Missouri Press, 1981), p. 55.

6. Keir Elam, "After Magritte, After
Carroll, After Wittgenstein: What Tom Stoppard's
Tortoise Taught Us," **Modern Drama**, 27
(December 1984), 469-85.

Nothing Left but Parody:
Friedrich Dürrenmatt and Tom Stoppard

Gabrielle Scott Robinson

Why do almost all things have to appear to me
as their own parody? Why must it seem to me as
if almost all, no, all means and conventions of
art today are fit only for parody?

Leverkühn's exclamation from Mann's
Doctor Faustus could be appropriated by an
increasing number of modern artists for whom
parody has become the only possible mode of
expression. Conspicuous among them are two
contemporary playwrights, Friedrich Dürrenmatt
and Tom Stoppard, who use parody similarly and
extensively. Their use of parody, we discover,
both expresses and satisfies similar artistic,
philosophical, and emotional concerns that,
despite their subjective nature, are symptomatic
of the larger, contemporary experience.

All Dürrenmatt's and Stoppard's plays
employ parody in one form or another. Stoppard
parodies **Hamlet** in **Rosencrantz & Guilden-
stern Are Dead**, and **The Importance of Being
Earnest** in **Travesties**. He parodies Shaw's
philosophical jargon in **Jumpers** and treats
the mystery story in **The Real Inspector
Hound**. Dürrenmatt in his **King John** and
Titus Andronicus also parodies Shakespearean
plays. His **Play Strindberg** is a take off on
The Dance of Death. In fact, many of
Dürrenmatt's plays are historical parodies.
The Blind Man (The Thirty Years' War),
**Romulus the Great, An Angel Comes to
Babylon** (the origin of the Tower of Babel),
It Is Written, and **The Anabaptists** (the
anabaptist movement of the sixteenth century).

121

From the perspective of artistic freedom,
parody helps the author choose a subject. Within
this form, Dürrenmatt finds the freedom which,
he feels, a "museum-ridden,"[1] fact-obsessed age
otherwise denies him. Seemingly suffocated by
worn-out modes and sterile facts, he imagines
that only parody offers him original material.
Stoppard puts it less theoretically when he says
that he has difficulty in finding plots--"I can't
invent plots." Therefore, he parodies existing
plots. Nor will he "invent" characters: "What I
like to do is take a stereotype and betray it,
rather than create an original character. I
never try to invent characters."[2] Parody frees
Stoppard from the need to invent and delivers
Dürrenmatt from the museum of inventions.

From a philosophical perspective, parody
represents a self-conscious, critical attitude.
As Dürrenmatt says: "We make theatre
consciously today; we know that we make theatre,
and therefore we are writing comedies."[3] Like
Mann's Leverkühn, the parodist cannot take
anything seriously. The form provides a sense of
distance and alienation that is or becomes a
basic mode of experiencing, controlling, and
expressing reality. The parodist is essentially
a player: he plays with life and art. He
regards all manifestations of both reality and
art as subjects for his play. Dürrenmatt's
statement "I think the world through by playing
it through"[4] typifies this attitude. And since
both Stoppard and Dürrenmatt are theatrically
oriented, they use their material to play with
theatrical possibilities and constellations.
They play with scenes and characters; they play
with paradoxical contrasts and symmetrical
reversals that are simplified and distorted but
always intensely theatrical. (It remains,
however, an open question whether the playwrights
enjoy parody because they love to be theatrical,
or whether they see reality as theatrical and
therefore as essentially simplistic and parodic.)
In the act of playing, the parodist exaggerates
and consequently reduces the stature of events
and characters. The parodist turns tragedy into
a farce and heroes into clowns. Dürrenmatt's

Play Strindberg changes Strindberg's bourgeois
marriage tragedy into a parody of bourgeois
marriage tragedies[5] by staging the lethal
battle between Edgar and Alice as a boxing match
in twelve rounds, each introduced by a gong and
exposed to the glare of ringlights.   In **The
Conformist** Dürrenmatt reduces the characters
to a comic-strip level.   In a world of stereotypes, Stoppard's statement about their
"betrayal" becomes a profound idea, and parody
becomes the only successful mode of expression.
     However, by tearing down worn-out traditions
and laughing at them in the very act of playing,
parody not only destroys but it also liberates.
It not only expresses but also subdues the
"nonsense of the world" (K, III, 392).
Parody creates distance, freedom, energy, a
clarity of vision as well as a form that enables
one to cope with its desperate message.   Parody
grants "a possibility (or even a necessity) for
approaching emotionally dangerous areas of
experience . . . and for making **erzählbar**
[expressible] and **erträglich** [bearable]
what otherwise would remain in the dark."[6]
Both authors use parody not only for theatrical
effect, but also for making reality
transparent--being precise about their perception
and controlling the image.   Through parody, they
focus on the condition of our world: the lack of
order, meaning, value, and, consequently, the
lack of heroism and justice that leaves man with
no alternative to victimization.   Moreover,
parody prevents the sentimentality inherent in a
perception of reality that views man as victim.
     Thus, despair in both Stoppard's and
Dürrenmatt's work coexists with an unquenchable
vitality.   Their parodies tend to express this
despair and vitality simultaneously.   To
Dürrenmatt the theatre expresses the creative
joy of life, an immediate life-force (T, 189)
that is embodied in most of his heroes.   This
same vitality is evident in Stoppard's
characters.   Kenneth Tynan observes that "While
it is clear that none of his characters control
their own destiny . . . it is equally obvious
that their unsinkable quality, their irrepressible vitality and eccentric persistence,

constitute what Stoppard feels to be an authentic
response to existence."[7]
    The dialectic of destruction and regenera-
tion, of despair and hope becomes apparent when
one considers parody from a moral perspective.
As ultimate values are lost, parody becomes
inevitable since it discloses the breakdown of
meaningful, coherent concepts. Man now feels out
of control, alienated and at the mercy of absurd
accidents that his reason proves pathetically
incapable of explaining. In Stoppard's
Jumpers, Dotty precisely formulates this
condition when she breaks out in tears: "Because
the truths that have been taken on trust, they've
never had edges before, there was no vantage
point to stand on and see where they stopped."[8]
Parody provides this vantage point, revealing a
world without certainty, order, or moral
absolutes. Dürrenmatt, when he portrays
similar situations, tends to emphasize the
problem of justice, while Stoppard concentrates
on the problem of identity and perception. But
both playwrights see man frustrated and often
destroyed in such a world, "without possibility
of reprieve or hope of explanation" as Stoppard
says in **Lord Malquist & Mr Moon** and in
Rosencrantz & Guildenstern Are Dead.
    The two playwrights use parody to force a
realization of this lack of absolutes. They
distort a situation to farcical extremes in order
to bring out the truth, to make us feel that
which has been lost. Perhaps **the** important
basis for their use of the form is that they
themselves continue to believe in the existence
of absolute moral standards, a "moral order
derived from Christian absolutes." Accordingly,
Tynan can see **Jumpers** as "a farce whose main
purpose is to affirm the existence of God."[9]
The parody, then, would insist that without moral
values life would be as nothing. Stoppard's
Malquist tells us that "Nothing . . . is the
history of the world viewed from a suitable
distance. Revolution is a trivial shift in the
emphasis of suffering."[10] Years later
Stoppard confirmed the logic of Malquist's
argument, but made his own position clear in
opposition: "I believe all political acts must
be judged in moral terms, in terms of their

consequences. Otherwise they are simply attempts
to put the boot on some other foot."[11]
Dürrenmatt often shows that the injustice,
defeat, and victimization exposed by parody stem
from human limitations. Thus the Angel in **An
Angel Comes to Babylon** counsels Nebuchadnezzar, proud of his justice and reason, "to learn
once and for all that ruling worlds befits heaven
and begging befits man" (K, I, 199). In **The
Marriage of Mr. Mississippi**, Ubelohe (disguised
as Don Quixote) ends the play saying "And eternal
comedy/That His glory be illuminated/Nourished by
our impotence" (K, I, 159). At other times
Dürrenmatt juxtaposes nihilism and faith,
making one parody the other, as at the end of
The Meteor. Shouting his anguish, the hero
sees nothing but the "monstrous disorder of
things" (K, III, 72), the deadness of life,
the "obscene aberration of carbon" and the
"incurable scab" (K, III, 74), but his words
are drowned out by the Salvation Army's rendering
of a hymn in praise of God's splendor. However,
nihilism and submission are not the only answers.
Another is to endure fully aware of the
"monstrous disorder." Many of Dürrenmatt's and
Stoppard's heroes are courageous enough to so
endure.

     With these general remarks about parody in
mind, I want to examine Dürrenmatt's "model
Scott" (K, III, 175) as it appears in his
"Dramaturgical Considerations to **The
Anabaptists**," which he appended to the play.
The death of the ill-fated antarctic explorer
Scott shows how for Dürrenmatt, as for Mann's
Leverkühn, everything appears as its own
parody, "betraying" characters and destroying
meaning through a farce both funny and terrible.
Dürrenmatt imagines Scott to be dying not
tragically amid the endless glaciers of
Antarctica, but accidentally, locked in a freezer
room while purchasing supplies for his expedition. The imprisoned Scott first knocks politely
on the freezer room door, later screams, bangs,
hops about to get warm, then desperately dashes
frozen foods against the door. Finally, he
circles in the smallest space, shaking, raging,

and powerless. Although a farce, the end of this
"**model** Scott" in the very heart of a populous
city terrifies. It is as Dürrenmatt himself
says, "the worst possible turn a story can take"
(K, III, 175-76).

Curiously, Stoppard also parodies Scott's
fate, but shifts the emphasis from the existential to the moral. In **Jumpers**, Scott is a
lunar explorer who knocks down a colleague
(Oates) in order to secure his place in the
spaceship, which can carry only one of them back
to earth. We recall that in Scott's historic
expedition of 1912 Oates had sacrificed himself
heroically for his comrades in the slim hope that
without him they would survive. In Stoppard's
version Oates is forced into his self-sacrifice
by a Scott without moral scruples. Oates becomes
a pathetic victim, "a tiny receding figure waving
forlornly from the featureless wastes of the
lunar landscape" (p. 22). His fate of farcical
victimization is made possible, or rather
inevitable, because "all our absolutes, the
thou-shalts and the thou shalt-nots that seemed
to be the very condition of our existence"
(p. 75) have been obliterated.

The main characters of both Stoppard and
Dürrenmatt are often parodied in much the same
way as the Scott of Dürrenmatt's "**model.**"
They are characters who, although engaged in a
great and meaningful purpose, are typically shown
as clowns, farcical victims of the accidents of
life as well as of their own grandiose and often
maniacal visions. And yet their fates can be
seen not only as farcical and terrible but also
as affirmative, since their spirit remains
undefeated. Dürrenmatt's **Romulus the Great**
is built on such ironic double vision. Dürrenmatt chooses the historical figure of Romulus
Augustulus as his hero and transforms the little
Augustus into Romulus the Great. But then his
great/little Romulus, the last Roman Emperor in
the West, plays the fool, rearing hens instead of
defending the empire. However, Dürrenmatt goes
on to show that Romulus is in fact not a fool but
rather a man of superior vision and the moral
judge of his world, having determined to impose

justice on an unjust Rome by destroying it.
Singleminded in his devotion to a moral law,
Romulus deliberately turns himself and his
decadent civilization into a victim. Yet
Dürrenmatt will not leave it at that either; in
the final parodistic reversal of the play,
Romulus ends up not dying tragically for his
ideal but surviving farcically, forced to accept
a pension and live on as the clown he had
pretended to be. Having conceived himself as a
tragic victim, he has to face being merely a
grotesque and foolish one. Nevertheless, he
attains a final greatness by bearing this
injustice heroically, as he suggests to Odoacer
at the end: "Let's play once more, for the last
time, our comedy. Let's act as if things turned
out all right on this earth, as if the spirit
would win over the material, man" (K, I, 75).
In Dürrenmatt's **An Angel Comes to Babylon**,
Nebuchadnezzar also makes justice his ideal, but
for him it is a social justice based on order and
reason.   Disguised as a beggar--a ruse to help
eradicate begging from his perfect state--he wins
the girl Kurrubi, sent down from heaven as a gift
for the lowest of men. Although he very much
desires Kurrubi, Nebuchadnezzar would have to
remain a beggar to keep her, for the girl can
love only the beggar. The king, proud and
confident in his own powers, refuses the gift of
the heavens, and his work subsequently fails: "I
sought perfection. I created a new order of
things . . . I wished to introduce reason. The
heavens despised my work. I remained without
grace . . ." (K, I, 260). He is condemned to
remain in the vicious circle where we found him
at the beginning of the play, being alternately
oppressor and victim. He rules for a time, using
Nimrod as his footstool, then a meaningless
reversal makes him into Nimrod's footstool, and
so on in senseless succession, while his idiot
son hops through the place. This is as futile
and grotesque a notion of history and human
endeavor as is that of Scott's being in the
freezer. And yet Nebuchadnezzar remains defiant,
aspiring to oppose "creation out of nothingness"
with the creation out of the spirit of man and
see which is better: "My justice or the
injustice of God" (K, I, 250).

The parody of Shakespeare's **King John**
offers another example of Dürrenmatt's parodic
reversals. In the play the Bastard tries to
order the affairs of state with justice and
humanity, steering clear of war, violence, and
unreason. But through this attempt at order,
Dürrenmatt's shows that the more man plans and
reasons, the more vulnerable to accident man
becomes, with increasing chaos and injustice
following upon all his endeavors. Here
Dürrenmatt spells out what he had already shown
in **Romulus**: a historical chronicle becomes a
"comedy of politics" (K, III, 281), a parody
portraying the inevitable defeat of the reasonable man. The Bastard has all but succeeded in
persuading England and France to accept a
peaceful compromise in their dispute over the
English crown when stupidity intervenes in the
shape of the mindless and bloodthirsty Duke of
Austria, who secretly brings up his troops and
forces a battle. After a bloody but inconclusive
encounter, Philip insists "out of caprice" on
combining forces with John in order to level the
town of Angiers, merely because its citizens
wanted peace, not war. Afterwards Philip makes a
pious speech in front of the ruined cathedral:

> You daughters, sons, this day shall yearly
> Be celebrated as a day of peace.
> It's a day of the spirit, too, which
> Over sinful nature has won out; a day
> In which Christian meditation has brought
> blessing.
>
> [K, III, 225]

And so it continues, as the Bastard concludes:
"Stupidity pulled the carriage of fate/And
accident" (K, III, 276). Foiled at every
turn and unable to come to terms with the
absurdity of life, the Bastard finally withdraws
from the world to end his days as his brother's
groom.

Titus Andronicus is the most farcically
reduced of Dürrenmatt's Shakespearean parodies.
After a series of futile attempts to obtain
justice for his family, attempts that result in

even greater atrocities against them, Titus takes
refuge in madness. Most of Dürrenmatt's heroes
would agree with his verdict that "The non-
sense/Of the world only insanity can still
subdue" (K, III, 392). Through parody
Dürrenmatt reduces his characters to madmen,
victims, and clowns, but implicit in this
reduction is a condemnation of the disorderly
world and its lack of moral values that by
contrast gives a manner of greatness to the
parodied heroes.

Stoppard's characters undergo much the same
experience. Moon, of the early novel **Lord
Malquist & Mr Moon**, is Stoppard's archetypal
victim, seeking order, purpose, and moral absolutes, but invariably finding himself the victim
of arbitrary, usually hostile and always farcical
mishaps. The world never makes sense to him, and
its absurdity finally destroys him. Clearly
Moon's despair has a metaphysical origin: "It is
something to do with no one being **good**
anymore . . . of things all getting out of
control, too big. I mean I'm not a crank fixed
on an individual--it's not vengeance, it's
salvation" (p. 12). All he can think of is
shocking people into a "moment of recognition."
To accomplish that end, Moon carries a bomb in
his coat pocket. When the bomb finally explodes,
he is dismayed to find in it merely a balloon
with an obscene message. This discovery is
particularly--and ironically--discouraging, since
he had kept the bomb in the vague hope that it
would somehow cure his physical impotence. Moon
dies, accidentally of course, when he is blown up
by the genuine bomb of an anarchist who mistakes
him for Malquist, the imperious lord.

When earlier Moon had said of himself "I've
got no direction, no momentum, and everything
reaches me at slightly the wrong angle" (p. 49),
it could have been either Rosencrantz or
Guildenstern speaking. For these two likewise
try to impose reason and order on their lives,
but are reduced to playing obscure and indefin-
able parts in another man's tragedy. They are
thrust into a play that may have meaning for the
other characters but whose only significance for
them is that it brings about their destruction.

When seven years later, he involved Henry
Carr of **Travesties** in the lives of Joyce,
Tzara, and Lenin, Stoppard was in a sense
repeating the Hamlet-Rosencrantz and Guildenstern
situation: another small man drifts in a world
without guidance or understanding.   Again
Stoppard uses parody to show the ironic
discrepancy between the character's limited,
misguided perception and a reality both farcical
and cruel.   Old Carr with his uncertain memory
tries to recapture his youth, or rather to imbue
its insignificance with meaning.   All that
results is a series of parodies as each scene is
replayed several times in different versions,
parodying Wilde, Shaw, Beckett, and Shakespeare.
     Against all odds and in the teeth of his own
uncertainty, George Moore in **Jumpers** tries to
cling to his belief that absolute values do
exist, claiming that "**Cogito ergo deus est**"
(p. 72).   But the parody of Scott on the moon as
well as the burlesque of his logical postivist
colleagues, one of whom is inexplicably shot
while taking part in a human pyramid, denies
this.   Scott dispassionately deserts Oates to
save himself, and the chief philosopher, Archie,
disposes of his murdered colleague in a large
plastic bag, arguing that the victim, in a fit of
depression, "wandered into the park, where he
crawled into a large plastic bag and shot
himself" (p. 64).   The point is that once order
has collapsed and moral values are seen as
relative, all things appear as their own parody,
and only parody can express this condition.
     To avoid being thus victimized by an
existence that reduces everything to a parody,
one must single-mindedly restrict oneself to
playing a game without any ulterior purpose, to
become, like Lord Malquist, the spectator as
hero, withdrawing "with style from the chaos."
Malquist cares about nothing except style, proud
of being "the man of inaction who would not dare
roll up his sleeves for fear of creasing the
cuffs" (p. 73).   His aloofness allows him to
escape unscathed every time, while his counter-
part, Moon, the man who always struggles, yearns,
and strives, invariably gets blamed, hurt,

beaten, and finally blown up. In **Rosencrantz &
Guildenstern Are Dead** the Player is the
Malquist figure who enjoys nothing more than
playing a part; in **Jumpers** it is Archie who
merely plays. Joyce, in **Travesties**, is a
slightly different version of this character,
living only for his art. It must be stressed,
however, that all these characters are artists:
the art, the style, the part to be played are
their exclusive concerns. By playing a game with
life, they want to turn it into an art for its
own sake.

Dürrenmatt too employs characters with
artistic interests to offset their roles as
farcical victim-heroes. Bockelson in **The
Anabaptists** is an actor not merely by profession but by philosophical conviction. One moment
his role is that of a beggar, the next that of a
king, but he regards both as parts to be picked
up or discarded at will, or as chance will have
it. Nothing matters except the game he plays
with life. As king he sees his part as acting
"comedian-like a farce interspersed with biblical
passages and dreams of a better world" (K,
III, 166). In common with the Player and other
Stoppard characters of this type, Bockelson, if
nothing else, does take his art seriously: "A
comedy which is only half ventured is bad; we,
too, have to venture our comedy completely"
(K, III, 115), recalling Malquist's "nothing
has any reality except when it aspires to art"
(p. 34). One could say that while the heroes
become victimized by the parody of life, these
characters survive by parodying the parody. And,
of course, one can see a parallel between the
characters and their authors, also players in the
broadest sense.

Although Stoppard's and Dürrenmatt's
characters come to grief over the same
obstacles--the irreducible disorder and accidents
of life--and although both playwrights formulate
this dilemma in farcically pointed situations,
there is one important difference between them:
Dürrenmatt tends to use extreme and extraordinary characters who become destructive in their
drive for order and justice, men like Romulus and

Möbius who are prepared to commit murder for
the sake of their plan. It is said of the
Bastard (another dangerous idealist): "You
brought nothing but calamity/Improving the world
you only made it the/More damned" (K, III,
275). As soon as a Dürrenmatt character tries
to realize his dream of justice and order, he
augments the chaos and violence around him.
Action "only heightens the confusion" (K, II,
72). But this is a reflection not only of the
hero's destructiveness, but also of the
desperation of the times, times in which "justice
only breeds murder" (K, III, 370).
Dürrenmatt's idea, although more limited than
Goya's famous "the dream of reason breeds
monsters," nevertheless introduces the same world
view, even, or particularly, in its reliance on
monstrosity. Dürrenmatt sees monstrosity
everywhere; it is one of his favorite terms. He
finds the world both "monstrous in its emptiness"
and "monstrous in its abundance," and, like his
characters, he tries to control the "monstrous
disorder of things" (K, III, 72).

   Instead of using extraordinary characters,
monstrous and grotesque distortions, Stoppard
formulates the dilemma from the viewpoint of the
average man, who is less concerned with justice
than with finding a place for himself in the
world. Stoppard's characters, as a result, are
not so much destructive as they are pathetic.
But both Dürrenmatt and Stoppard need parody to
avoid pathos and sentimentality. A world of
hostile and absurd forces in which nothing is
left but to become a victim offers only one
alternative: farce or sentimentality. And both
playwrights abhor sentimentality, using parody to
safeguard against it.

   So far we may have seen the effects of
parody in an overly abstract manner; and yet
despite its intellectual motivation parody must
also work on a level of farcical simplicity that
appears even anti-intellectual. In Dürrenmatt's plays, discussions of justice are
interrupted by questions about chicken feed, and
historical treaties are "sealed" by the arrival
of hot water bottles. In Stoppard's works, the

existence of God is discussed by the farcical
figure of the Risen Christ, who, uneasily perched
on his donkey, sways through the crowded London
streets high on a carpet roll stuffed with
bodies. In **Jumpers**, too, metaphysical
questions are aired amid farcical mixups, such as
the one involving a hare and a tortoise that
Moore keeps to help him sort out Zeno's paradox,
but that lead him into ever new confusions until
he finally but accidentally transfixes one and
crushes the other.

In many of their works Dürrenmatt and
Stoppard have made use of the "thriller" form,
both having written parodies of that dramatic
mode: Dürrenmatt in **The Pledge** and
Stoppard in **The Real Inspector Hound.** On one
level, **The Pledge** is a straightforward
mystery story in which Inspector Matthaei,
Holmes-like, using the power of reason, hunts
down a psychopath who assaults and murders
children. Dürrenmatt plays with the
conventional devices of the suspense story to
create a tense drama of discovery, but it is the
parody of the thriller that wins out in the end.
In long discussions throughout the novel an old
police inspector warns Matthaei that human reason
is ultimately insufficient in an absurd world.
But Matthaei, eager and confident, solves the
case and sets a trap for the murderer. At this
point, however, an absurd accident foils his
plan: the killer dies in a car accident while on
his way to the trap. Matthaei, refusing to give
up, waiting endlessly for his man to arrive,
subsequently goes mad. Here again we see
Dürrenmatt's idea that action, planning, and
reason are powerless in a world where chance
rules. The paradox is made more poignant by
being formulated within a detective story, a form
in which one expects the victory of order and
reason.

Says one character to another in **The Real
Inspector Hound**, "You're turning it into a
complete farce,"[12] summing up Stoppard's
parody of the detective story's conventions. His
seemingly intrepid and quick-witted inspector is
constantly beyond his depth. To this work
Stoppard has added a parody of theatre criticism,
as two critics, Birdboot and the second-string

Moon, watch and comment on the play. Like his
namesake in Stoppard's novel **Lord Malquist & Mr
Moon**, Moon is searching for metaphysical
explanations but can come up with only a muddle:
"**Je suis . . . ergo sum . . .** nature of
identity . . . Voltaire's cry **Voilà! . . .
Where is God?**" (pp. 16-17). The main parodic
reversal occurs when Birdboot and Moon end up on
stage taking parts; they repeat earlier scenes
from the play as a parody of a parody. Moreover,
Moon's murderous thoughts about his rival Higgs
become reality when Higgs's concealed corpse is
discovered. Once again the spectator appears as
hero--or rather, in this parodic world, as
victim, since both critics end up dead. The
mastermind turns out to have been the third-
string critic Puckeridge, who, by doing away with
his rivals, has secured his professional
position. Thus a rational explanation,
inpenetrable as it may seem, indeed exists behind
all the absurdity. As is so often the case with
Stoppard, the play adds up to a bewildering
mixture of the absurd and the commonplace that
imbues the everyday with the fantastic and makes
the fantastic seem ordinary. By contrast,
Dürrenmatt's parodies create a world of violent
and grotesque distortion from which there can be
no escape.

In addition to their overtly formal mystery
stories, both playwrights make more subtle use
within other plays of the detective-story
formula. For example, Dürrenmatt's **The
Physicists**, set in a prestigious sanatorium
housing "the whole spiritually confused elite of
half the Occident" (K, II, 288), opens with
the discovery of a murdered nurse and an
exasperated inspector attempting to establish the
facts in a place where everyone speaks only of
mishaps and patients instead of murder and
murderers. With the third murder, however, the
inspector gives up the fight for justice and,
with a sense of relief, gives in to the madness
around him. The patients turn out to be
physicists who murdered their nurses when the
young women discovered one of the scientists,
Möbius, playing the lunatic to keep his

discoveries from an irresponsible world. The
only true lunatic in the play is the hunchbacked
spinster doctor who runs the institution. She
ends in complete control, exploiting Möbius's
discoveries in order to build an empire of her
own. Because of the murders, the guilty physicists become her permanent captives.
Dürrenmatt here has used the thriller structure
to reveal the victory not of justice and reason,
but of madness and paradox, since even the hero's
plan, like that of Romulus, is mad to begin with
despite high ideals. The same theme occurs in
Dürrenmatt's parodic use of Solomon. Once a
"prince of peace and justice" (K, II, 351),
Solomon becomes the inspiration for madness and
murder when Möbius invokes his name both for
the scientist's turning to insanity and for his
killing the nurse he loves.
    Stoppard's **Jumpers** also begins with a
murder, and a good part of the plot is taken up
with the problem of disposing the body and the
vain attempt at identifying the murderer. Like
everyone else, the inspector is unable to
extricate himself from a net of farcical
misunderstandings. The murderer, however, is
ultimately associated with the general problem of
uncertainty, farcical impotence, and a valueless
world. These same conditions are part of Scott's
betrayal, Moore's anguished questions, and
Dotty's disillusionment and despair. Rather than
its being merely a heinous crime that goes
unsolved, the murder is in fact a symptom of a
climate wherein anything is permissible and
nothing matters. Once again the thriller is
parodied to highlight the opacity of reality, at
the same time furnishing a lively and farcical
plot.
    From whatever perspective one approaches the
work of Dürrenmatt and Stoppard, one discovers
that for these two nothing remains but parody--
whether one considers their self-conscious
attitude toward art, as they work from concepts,
dialectics, paradoxical reversals, as well as
from theatricality; or whether one considers
their view of a world distorted by stereotypes,
lacking moral absolutes. Both playwrights create

a world in which the individual, at the mercy of
accident, becomes a victim, taking on a fate both
farcical and terrible. Born out of a radical
alienation, their parodies nevertheless imply a
need for radical faith. Parody distorts,
degrades, and destroys; at the same time it opens
up life, not only to the vitality of farce, but
also to the hope of regeneration.

Notes

1. Juergen von Stackelberg, **Literarische Rezeptionsformen** (Frankfurt a.M.:   Athenäum, 1972), p. 11.

2. Kenneth Tynan, "Profiles," **The New Yorker**, 19 December 1977, pp. 51, 79.

3. Friedrich Dürrenmatt, **Theater - Schriften und Reden** (Zürich: Arche, 1969), p. 73; cited as T.

4. Dürrenmatt, **Monstervortrag über Gerechtigkeit und Recht** (Zürich: Arche, 1969), p. 95.

5. Dürrenmatt, **Komödien** III (Zürich: Arche, 1957, 1970), p. 349. All further references are to this edition, cited in the text as K, together with page notations. The translations are by the author.

6. Bertel Sigfred Pedersen, "The Theory and Practice of Parody in the Modern Novel: Mann, Joyce, and Nabokov," Diss. University of Illinois, Urbana 1972, p. 74.

7. Tynan, p. 51.

8. Tom Stoppard, **Jumpers** (London: Faber and Faber, 1972), p. 75. All further references are to this edition; page numbers are noted in the text.

9. Tynan, pp. 85, 86.

10. Stoppard, **Lord Malquist & Mr Moon** (New York: Alfred A. Knopf, 1968), p. 3. All further references are to this edition; page numbers are noted in the text.

11. Stoppard, "Ambushes for the Audience: Towards a High Comedy of Ideas," **Theatre Quarterly**, 4 (May-July 1974), 12.

12.   Stoppard, **The Real Inspector Hound**
(London: Faber and Faber, 1968), p. 29.   All
further references are to this edition; page
numbers are noted in the text.

Stoppard's **Jumpers**: A Mystery Play

Lucina P. Gabbard

Tom Stoppard's **Jumpers** is a
many-splendored mystery play--so many-splendored
that it is, metaphorically, a kaleidoscope.
Bright fragments of many forms and many themes
make new configurations with each twist of the
dial. The most obvious ingredients are rollick-
ing comedy and metaphysics. This combination
recalls the mystery plays of medieval times which
mixed morality and Bible stories with humorous
and grotesque details. Stopping there, however,
would misrepresent and oversimplify the generic
classification of **Jumpers**, for the kaleidoscope contains bits of many genres assembled in
the overall design of a "whodunit."
     Applied to form, the mystery is not
"whodunit?" but "whatisit?" Some critics call
the play a farce, and it does employ many
farcical techniques. It makes beautiful mischief
with mistaken identity. George assumes that
Dotty's casserole is made from his missing
rabbit, Thumper. So he tells Crouch, the porter:
"Do you realize she's in there now, **eating**
him?"[1] Crouch, thinking George refers to the
murdered Professor McFee, replies: "You
mean--raw?" Compounding Crouch's horror, George
answers crossly: "No, of course not!--
cooked--with gravy and mashed potatoes"
(p. 76). The play is alive with broad comic
action. McFee's corpse swings in and out of
sight on the back of the bedroom door. Nobody
drops his pants, but Dotty drops her robe,
revealing a lovely body naked from the thighs up.
Traditionally, however, farce is devoid of pro-
fundity, whereas **Jumpers** is not. Stoppard's
slapstick takes place in the midst of cosmic

tragedy and metaphysical inquiry. Astronaut
Oates has been abandoned on the moon, and George
addresses himself to the question, "Is God?"
(p. 24). Moreover, the play ridicules man's
institutions--education, justice, morality--
thereby taking on the weight of a satire.

Intermingled with these ancient forms are
all the cultural features of twentieth century
drama. The two astronauts on the moon represent
Space Age technology; their fight for the single
berth on the crippled space capsule depicts the
Darwinian commonplace of survival of the fittest.
The image of Astronaut Oates "waving forlornly
from the featureless wastes of the lunar landscape" (p. 22) objectifies man facing the
existential void. Dotty's analyst is a Freudian.
The Jumpers, flipflopping between political and
philosophical roles while Archie calls the tune,
suggest the Marxian masses controlled by society.
The amorality of Archie and his acrobats is
typical of the Absurdist's world which Richard
Corrigan describes well: "There are no value
judgments or distinctions in values in the world
of the Absurd. In Adamov's **Ping Pong**, the
aesthetic, economic, and philosophic implications
of pinball machines are discussed with religious
fervor. In Ionesco's **Jack, or the Submission**
the whole action is to convince Jack to accept
the family's chief value: 'I love potatoes with
bacon.'"[2] Another example in Corrigan's elaboration might well have been George's analogy
between McFee's beliefs about **good** and
bad and "the rules of tennis without which
Wimbledon Fortnight would be a complete shambles"
(p. 48).

Brechtian technique also contributes to this
kaleidoscope. In his description of the set,
Stoppard calls for a screen forming a backdrop
for film and slide projections. But the farce,
the satire, the contemporary milieu--even the
Brechtian screen--are all elements of Absurdism;
and to this accumulation, Stoppard adds his and
the Absurdists' principal method--the use of
concrete images to convey meaning. In **End-
game**, Beckett places Nagg and Nell in giant
garbage cans to represent the discarding of old

and useless parents. Stoppard makes a pyramid of
acrobats out of the university's Philosophy
Department, bodying forth the intellectual's
mental gymnastics. The Coda, a full-fledged
dream, adds still another Absurd ingredient.

Other nondramatic literary forms also claim
mention in **Jumpers**. Titles of novels and
songs constitute the charades which are the basis
of Dotty's relationship with George. Overt
allusions to classic poets--Milton, Keats--mingle
with covert references to modern masters like
Eliot and Beckett. The tortoise and the hare
recall an oft-told fable--as do Dotty's cries of
"Wolf!" A large portion of the play, however, is
devoted to George's preparations for the symposium. Thus, Stoppard daringly weaves a serious
philosophical dialectic in and out of this
Absurdist drama; the whole is thinly wrapped in
the Londoner's favorite genre--the detective
story. Inspector Bones and the characters of
Jumpers are confronted with three obvious
mysteries: who killed McFee? where is Thumper?
does God exist? Analysis of the play soon
reveals, however, that these three questions are
only starters. The kaleidoscope is as full of
posers as of forms.

Thus, the emphasis of this "whodunit" shifts
from "whatisit?" to "whatsitsay?" To investigate
this mystery requires examination of the play's
inseparable mixture of images and characters.
Like the fragments in the kaleidoscope, the
images, when juxtaposed, create meaningful
designs; they all deal with man's problems--with
himself, his beliefs, and his institutions. The
people within these images have dual roles. On
the one hand, they reveal the personal problems
and relationships of the characters in the murder
mystery; and on the other hand, they represent
differing facets of the troubled Space Age.

At the center of the design are George and
Dorothy Moore and Sir Archibald Jumpers. George
Moore is a professor of Moral Philosophy, but his
identity is diminished by his namesake, the famed
author of **Principia Ethica**. George is totally absorbed in preparing a paper to be presented
at the university's symposium on "Man--good, bad,

or indifferent?" (p. 46); his paper poses the
question--"Is God?" (p. 24). George's
eccentricity is captured in the image he presents
opening the door to Inspector Bones. Brandishing
a bow and arrow in one hand, holding a tortoise
in the other, George appears with his face
covered in shaving foam. The effect is
appropriate to his later self-description:
". . . I cut a ludicrous figure in the academic
world . . . largely due to my aptitude for
traducing a complex and logical thesis to a
mysticism of staggering banality" (p. 72).
George is also central to the "whodunit," even
though for a long time he seems unaware of the
tragedy. Nevertheless, the murder occurred at a
party at George's house; George summoned the
police by an anonymous complaint about the noise;
the victim, Professor McFee, was George's
philosophical adversary; and finally, the
discovery of George's absent-minded murder of
Thumper presents the possibility that he may also
have unwittingly killed McFee.

George is married to Dotty, "a prematurely-
retired musical-comedy actress of some renown"
(p. 13). Dotty is dotty: "unreliable and
neurotic" (p. 17), she calls herself. She can no
longer distinguish one moon song from another.
Nevertheless, her fans enthusiastically await her
comeback. At the party, scene of the murder,
they applaud despite her inability to remember
her song. She has withdrawn into the darkness
before the shot is fired; afterwards she steps
into the light only to have the dying man pull
himself up against her legs. The others quickly
depart, and Dotty is left, whimpering under the
weight of the corpse. Her frock stained with his
blood, she is the image of the prime suspect.
She calls out to George for help, and he, unaware
of the murder, responds indifferently. To gain
his attention she makes an offer which reveals
the emptiness of their marriage: "Georgie!--I'll
let you." He replies: "I don't want to be
'let.' Can't you see that it's an insult?"
(p. 31). Their only communication seems to be
through charades. Finding Dotty nude and
despondent on the bed, George responds quickly--

"The Naked and the Dead!" On the contrary,
Archie comforts Dotty by removing the corpse and
visiting her every day--in her bedroom. He
claims to be her doctor-psychiatrist, but
evidence indicates a love affair. The nature of
Archie's relationship with Dotty is another of
the mysteries with which George wrestles.
      Sir Archibald Jumpers is a man of many
talents? roles?--all of them authoritative. Near
the opening of the play, he stands in a white
spot as his voice barks out: "And now!--ladies
and gentlemen!--the INCREDIBLE--RADICAL!--
LIBERAL!!--JUMPERS!!" (p. 18). As the music
swells and eight Jumpers come somersaulting in,
Archie is the image of the ringmaster of this
whole circus. And indeed he is! He is
Vice-Chancellor of the university, thereby
George's boss. He is organizer of the
Jumpers--"a mixture of the more philosophical
members of the university gymnastics team and the
more gymnastic members of the Philosophy School"
(p. 51). As chief Jumper, he is also head of the
Radical Liberal Party which is celebrating its
victory at the polls. When he signs the report
on the cause of McFee's death, he insists he is
coroner. He is not only Dotty's psychiatrist but
also her legal adviser. He explains: "I'm a
doctor of medicine, philosophy, literature and
law, with diplomas in psychological medicine and
P.T. including gym" (p. 61). Archie is totally
amoral and pragmatical. He solves his problems
by lies, bribery, blackmail, or whatever is
necessary. In short, he is George's opposite--in
temperament and belief. Archie is very much
involved with the murder. The victim, Professor
McFee, was one of the Jumpers--holder of the
Chair of Logic. Archie disposes of the body and
attempts to defend Dotty. He also makes himself
a suspect by admitting that McFee, his faithful
protégé, was threatening to become "St. Paul
to Moore's Messiah" (p. 63).
      Also involved in the murder mystery are
three other characters: Inspector Bones, Crouch,
and a nameless secretary. Inspector Bones, like
all the others, displays Cognomen Syndrome; he is
a detective, a rattler of skeletons in closets.

(He also has a brother who was an osteopath!)
Bones has been summoned to the scene by two
anonymous telephone calls, but he comes, flowers
in hand, as one of Dotty's ardent fans. He hopes
for her autograph, perhaps even "the lingering
touch of a kiss brushed against an admirer's
cheek . . . ." Nevertheless, if he discovers the
allegations to be true, he will let her feel "the
full majesty of the law" (p. 45). Upon seeing
Dotty, however, he is struck dumb by infatuation
and desires only to protect her. He suggests an
eminent psychiatric witness might get her off.
Although incorruptible by Archie's attempted
bribery, he is easy prey to a blackmail scheme.
While he is alone in the bedroom with Dotty, she
cries "Rape!" Archie enters to find Bones--a
frozen image pleading with a smile: "It's not
what you think." Archie moves in quickly to "tsk
tsk" at the "tragic end" of "an incorruptible
career." To George, it is all another mystery:
"How the hell does one know what to believe?"
(p. 71). In any event, the investigation is
ended, and the "whodunit" is unsolved.

Crouch is the porter. As his name suggests,
he maintains a servile posture. He carries out
the rubbish and serves drinks at the party. In
this latter capacity, he was at the scene of the
crime. In fact, he made the second anonymous
report to the police. His involvement is deepened by his friendship with the deceased. He
used to converse with McFee when the learned
professor called for his girl--George's
secretary. As a result of these conversations
and "a bit of reading," Crouch has become
something of a philosopher himself. He demonstrates his knowledge by pointing to a flaw in
George's treatise. But when George rebuts his
point, Crouch, true to his name, withdraws
humbly: "I expect you're right, sir. I mean,
it's only a hobby with me" (p. 79).

The secretary is nameless and wordless. At
the party she strips while swinging from a
trapeze. Through the rest of the play she sits
silent and grim, taking George's dictation. Only
at the close of Act II is her involvement
revealed: she was secretly betrothed to McFee,

who was already married. Just before his death,
McFee had "to make a clean breast and tell her it
was all off" because he was going into the
monastery (p. 81). Thus, the failures of modern
marriage are reaffirmed, and the secretary joins
the list of suspects with a motive for murdering
McFee. This last message is transmitted vividly
by the image of the secretary turning to reveal
blood on her back.

Two other characters, appearing only on
Dotty's giant television screen, are too crucial
to be omitted--the astronauts Scott and Oates.
Their images are seen stalking the surface of the
moon, and the announcer reports their private
drama. Only one man could return in the crippled
space capsule. While the world of viewers
watched, the astronauts--the twentieth century's
heroes--struggled until Oates was knocked to the
ground by Scott, the commanding officer. Dotty's
word image speaks the rest: "Poor moon man,
falling home like Lucifer" (p. 38). Later she
adds: "it certainly spoiled that Juney old moon"
(p. 39). It also caused Dotty's breakdown and,
according to Crouch, McFee's reversal. So the
moon men are indirectly responsible for the
course of events.

A twist of the kaleidoscope and all these
private characters assume an almost allegorical
significance. Each becomes a symbol of some
segment of society; each becomes a fragment in a
new configuration showing the topsy-turvy world
of the Space Age and the mind-defying mystery of
life. Through all time man has sought to right
the world and solve the mystery of his presence
on this planet. All of his systems and institutions have been devised to approach one or the
other of these problems.

For centuries man's solution was belief in
God and the morality of man. George is the
defender of these beliefs, but his progressive
deterioration represents their precarious
position. From the outset George explains:
"There is presumably a calendar date--a
moment--when the onus of proof passed from
the aetheist to the believer, when, quite
suddenly, secretly, the noes had it" (p. 25).

This tenuous state is magnified when George,
elevated to the symbolic level, becomes the
universal representative of theology and ethics.
This ineffectual, pedantic little man stands
alone against the swollen tide of Jumpers--
"Logical postivists, mainly, with a linguistic
analyst or two, a couple of Benthamite
Utilitarians . . . lapsed Kantians and empiricists generally . . . and of course the usual
Behaviourists . . ." (pp. 50-51). George himself
admits his bottom rank: "I was lucky to get the
Chair of Moral Philosophy . . . . Only the chair
of Divinity lies further below the salt, and
that's been vacant for six months . . ."
(p. 51). Furthermore, even with this lone
defender, God's position is eroding, for George
has turned Him into "a philosopher's God,
logically inferred from self-evident premises"
(pp. 39-40). Consequently, God has fallen victim
to the tricks of language--another failure among
man's inventions. George confesses that "words
betray the thoughts they are supposed to express"
(p. 46). By George's own semantic twists, God
becomes a "theological soubriquet" for the "first
Cause" (p. 27); or, as "the first term of the
series," George explains, "God, so to speak, is
nought" (p. 29). At the height of his
frustration, George cries out: "How does one
know what it is one believes when it's so
difficult to know what it is one knows. I don't
claim to **know** that God exists, I only claim
that he does without my knowing it, and while I
claim as much I do not claim to know as much;
indeed I cannot know and God knows I cannot"
(p. 71). However despondent, George's words ring
with atrophying heroism when juxtaposed with
Dotty's admission: "And yet, Professor, one
can't help wondering at the persistence of the
reflex, the universal constant unthinking appeal
to the non-existent God who is presumed dead"
(p. 35).

Morality suffers from the same confusion.
How can the world of **Jumpers** right its wrongs
when no one can agree on what is wrong? George
is the solitary spokesman for moral absolutes; he
summarizes the culture's dilemma while stating

his agreement with his namesake: " . . . by
insisting that goodness was a fact, and on his
right to recognize it when he saw it, Moore
avoided the moral limbo devised by his
successors, who are in the unhappy position of
having to admit that one man's idea of good is no
more meaningful than another man's . . ."
(p. 67). A principal cause of this moral
confusion is again--language. George says that
every year the symposium's subject is the same,
"Man--good, bad, or indifferent?" but "there is
enough disagreement about its meaning to ensure a
regular change of topic" (p. 46). Unfortunately,
George's egocentric and unfeeling reactions to
Dotty and the others indicate that his own
morality is smothered by pendantry.

At the end of Act II, theology and ethics
seem bereft of their last defender. George
discovers that he, not Dotty, has killed
Thumper--with the arrow shot to prove God's
existence. In the shock of realizing himself a
killer, George steps backward, and
"CRRRRRRRRUNCH!!!" he kills his tortoise, Pat.
His sobs are amplified and blend into the Coda,
where the prostrate George is gripped by a
bizarre dream. Has George suffered a total
collapse? Or has he merely found escape?

Even in George's dream, Archie is in charge.
Symbolically, Archie is leadership--the
repository of man's hopes and abdicated responsibilities. And Archie has led all segments of
society down the path of expediency and
amorality. Archie's intellectuals--education--
are corrupt and ineffective, jumping from one
pose to another at Archie's convenience and
command. According to George, they are all as
mad as McFee, who thinks lying and murder are
merely antisocial, not inherently wrong. The
general acceptance of such beliefs is witnessed
by their philosophical classification--"Orthodox
mainstream" (p. 49). The ineptitude of all these
thinkers is exposed when Archie reveals the basis
of their selection. For the new chairman of the
Philosophy Department, he wants "someone of good
standing; he won't have to know much philosophy"
(p. 69).

As leader of the Radical Liberals winners of
the recent election, Archie also represents
politics--the foundation of man's self-govern-
ment. But like morality, "Democracy is all in
the head," Archie has told Dotty (p. 34). In
fact, Dotty explains, the election was actually a
coup d'état. When George protests that he
voted, she retorts: "It's not the voting that's
democracy, it's the counting" (p. 35). Language
plays its tricks again. As a result of this
"election," the Church Commissioners were
dispossessed, the Newspaper proprietors found
themselves in a police car (p. 37), Clegthorpe--
agricultural spokesman and agnostic--has been
appointed Archbishop of Canterbury (p. 38), and
early next week "the Police Force will be thinned
out to a ceremonial front for the peacekeeping
activities of the Army" (p. 65). The image of
the failure of politics is intensified by
recalling that the Rad-Libs are "a mixed bunch"
(p. 47), more than just party workers and
academics. Moreover, in the first scene the
whole pyramid of Rad-Lib Jumpers has been seen to
collapse under the removal of logic--the death of
McFee. In the Coda the pyramid is rebuilt with
Archbishop Clegthorpe, "the highpoint of
scientism" (p. 39), as its pinnacle. But once
more a gunshot-- violence--intervenes.
Clegthorpe is toppled, and the pyramid disintegrates. Are Archie's Jumpers like a pile of
dominoes, doomed to fall each time Someone
somewhere gives a nudge? (p. 29).

Dotty, of course, stands for escapism. She
is sex, show business, and romance--rolled into
one. Her songs about Juney moons, her millions
of undaunted admirers, her flirtations and
infidelities speak of man's wishes--his fantasies
of beautiful bodies and perpetual love-making
under a spangled moon. But this symbol too has
collapsed. Dotty faltered in the middle of her
act and addressed herself to the mystery of
another absolute: ". . . why must the damned
show go on anyway?" (p. 39).

Summoned by fearful anonymity is Bones--
symbol of law, order, and justice. He is
supposed to be evenhanded and incorruptible, able

to detect the evil-doers and empowered to right
their wrongs by punishment. Alas! Bones, the
implacable law, is also human. Victimized by
Dotty's charms, Bones instructs Archie to temper
justice with romantic illusion, dirty tricks, and
prejudice: "Put her in the box and you're halfway there. The other half is, get something on
Mad Jock McFee, and if you don't get a Scottish
judge it'll be three years probation and the
sympathy of the court" (p. 64). Finally, made
vulnerable by his fantasies, Bones--the full
majesty of the law--is frightened into retreat by
Dotty's blackmail. But the mystery remains: who
killed McFee? And the criminal is still at large.
Is there no protection under the law?

The secretary and Crouch, of course,
represent the mute, lowly ones who only watch and
serve. That American Jumper, Richard Nixon,
might have called them the silent majority. But
they are victims too. Stripping on the flying
trapeze, the secretary symbolizes man swinging
between the darknesses of ignorance and false
hopes, from the innocence of the womb to the
reality of the tomb. The moments of light in
between represent those flashes of insight which
strip him, little by little, of his beliefs and
illusions. Crouch, representing the servile
ones, is so blinded by his workaday world that he
doubts neither his own inferiority nor the
Jumpers' expertise. Unseeing, he **"backs into
the path of the swing and is knocked arse over
tip by a naked lady"** (p. 18). He never knows
what has hit him until he is blacked out and
broken in the crash. But in the Coda, Crouch has
become Chairman of the Symposium. Do the meek
inherit the earth?

Catalysts to it all are the moon men--
science and technology raised to the ultimate
power. The scientific method was intended to
provide the objectivity that would unlock the
secrets of the universe. Instead it unloosed an
invasion by machines--television cameras
exploring the surface of the moon and the skin of
Dotty's body. Can external coverings reveal the
soul--of Dotty or the moon? It unloosed astronauts in goldfish bowls violating God's heaven,

landing their amorality on the moon. In the
Coda, Archie puts rationalizations into Captain
Scott's mouth. He orders Scott to explain his
"instinctive considerations" with "special
reference" to his "seniority" over Oates, their
"respective usefulness to society," and his
responsibility to himself. Captain Scott has
only to answer, "That's it" (p. 84). The
spectacle of these astronauts fighting on the
moon caused McFee to doubt himself. Before his
murder, he confided to Crouch: "I am giving
philosophical respectability to a new pragmatism
in public life, of which there have been many
disturbing examples both here and on the moon"
(p. 80). Perhaps the most far-reaching effect
was on Dotty: the moon was no longer fantasy
land, no longer Juney or spooney or crooney. For
Dotty it was all over once man set foot on the
moon and could see us "whole, all in one go,
little--local" with all our absolutes looking
like "the local customs of another place"
(pp. 74-75). Dotty's final declaration
paraphrases into an awesome interrogative: What
is going to happen when the people on the bottom
discover that the truths they have taken on trust
now have edges?

Dotty's concern adds to the principal
accumulated questions: Is God? Is man good, bad
or indifferent? What do **good** and **bad**
mean? And, of course, who shot McFee? Stoppard
lets Archie give the answer: "Unlike mystery
novels, life does not guarantee a denouement; and
if it came, how would one know whether to believe
it?" (p. 81). Thus, the play states that life is
a mystery no one can solve. Stoppard's advice
seems to be--dream! look on the better side!--
because the Coda ends on an optimistic note.
Dotty sings again, perched on "a spangled
crescent moon" (p. 87). George exclaims that
even disbelivers agree that "life is better than
death, that love is better than hate" (p. 88).
And Archie revives an extended version of the old
paradox that the half empty cup is also half
full. He sanctions: "Do not despair--many are
happy much of the time . . ." (p. 88). Or does
the Coda merely suggest that life, like this
play, is one bizarre dream after another?

One thing is clear: Stoppard's Absurd
"Whodunit" about the multiple mysteries of life
is an almost perfect blend of form and content.
Moreover, in production the fast pace and over-
lapping images of **Jumpers** create a three-ring
circus effect. The swinging trapeze, the songs,
the jokes, and the nudity mix bits of vaudeville,
musical comedy, and burlesque into this legimate
stage play. The result is that Absurdism,
usually so depressing to audiences, emerges in a
new configuration with entertainment.

Notes

1. Tom Stoppard, **Jumpers** (London, 1972), p. 76.   All page references are to this edition.

2. Richard Corrigan, **The Theater in Search of a Fix** (New York, 1973), pp. 257-58.

The Universe as Murder Mystery:
Tom Stoppard's Jumpers

G. B. Crump

The reaction of reviewers to Tom Stoppard's
Jumpers, produced in England in 1972 and in
America in 1974, reflects the critics' suspicion
that in his plays Stoppard indulges in startling
stage antics, erudite allusions, and involved
puns in order to disguise deficiencies in insight
and make shallow plays appear profound. A
comment in a recent handbook of modern writers
typifies this attitude: "Stoppard's plays reveal
good ideas theatrically well developed but
intellectually unexplored (reflecting a lack of
grasp of his material), a clever ear for merging
his predecessors' . . . effects, and a frothy,
infectious, vacuous excitement."[1] Much the
same assessment is discernible in an extended
critique of **Jumpers** by John Weightman. He
complains that, although the play is striking and
theatrical, "quite a bit of the action did not
seem necessary." He singles out the murder of
McFee, the central incident in the plot, claiming
that it has no relation to the play's ideas and
is merely a convenient stratagem for sustaining
audience interest: "You only have to kill a
character pointlessly in Act I to have a corpse
to play about with for the rest of the evening
and to run a gratuitous thread of suspense
through the whole action."[2]
The image of Stoppard as a superficial
dilettante is at odds with his friend Derek
Marlowe's account of the pains the author takes
in his work: "For Tom, writing a play is like
sitting for an examination. He spends ages on
research, does all the necessary cramming, reads
all the relevant books, and then gestates the

results."[3]   Nevertheless, the real issue is not
Stoppard's industry in studying his sources but
whether his labors lead to a meaningful and
aesthetically satisfying whole or merely to a
"vacuous" exercise in showing off. **Jumpers**,
one of Stoppard's most erudite works, illustrates
the problems his use of research can pose for the
reviewer. The philosopher-protagonist, George
Moore, spends most of his time arguing for a
belief in God and moral absolutes and against the
materialism and moral relativism of the
"jumpers," the logical positivists who compose
the philosophical establishment at his university. Besides being uncertain about the relevance
of the murder plot to this argument, reviewers
were unsure about the very basic question of
which side, if either, Stoppard intended to have
win the argument.[4] In an article on Stoppard,
Kenneth Tynan has asserted that "there is no
question where Stoppard stands" in the debate.
He "votes for the spirit," and indeed the "main
purpose" of **Jumpers** is "to affirm the
existence of God," to defend "transcendent moral
values," and to attack the "pragmatic materialism" of the jumpers. In support of his
interpretation, Tynan quotes Stoppard's public
endorsement of "Western liberal democracy . . .
based on a moral order derived from Christian
absolutes."[5] But it does not necessarily
follow that the playwright is arguing for the
validity of a Christian moral order in
Jumpers. Other difficulties posed by the
play are why Stoppard chose to name his hero G.
E. Moore after the British intuitionist philosopher, and whether Bones, a major character, is
merely an appendage to the mystery plot or
relates to the philosophical debate in a
significant way.
        An explication of **Jumpers** in the light
of the major tenets of logical positivism will
show that the murder of McFee is integral to
George's debate with the materialists, that the
debate also includes Bones, that nothing in the
play is gratuitous or pointless, and that, far
from adding complications or allusions solely for
the sake of dazzling the audience, Stoppard

fashions the language and action of **Jumpers**
into a highly particularized and apt portrait of
the intellectual and moral uncertainty modern man
feels when confronting his world.   An integral
part of this portrait is the implication that
George, however sympathetic his character and
attractive his beliefs, fails in his efforts to
give life a satisfying meaning through philosophy.   Further, since **Jumpers** does form a
unified and meaningful whole, not all of
Stoppard's works may be dismissed as shallow
displays of stage pyrotechnics.
     Although George classifies his antagonists
as "Logical positivists, mainly," he also
includes in their number "a linguistic analyst or
two, a couple of Benthamite Utilitarians . . .
lapsed Kantians and empiricists generally . . .
and of course the usual Behaviourists"6--that
is, nearly all the groups prominent in the
"orthodox mainstream" of British philosophy in
the forty years since, in George's view, "it went
off the rails" (p. 46).   Much of the satire in
Jumpers extends beyond logical positivism to
materialistic philosophy in general.   Logical
positivism originated in Vienna in the 1920s but,
with the rise of Hitler, its center shifted to
England, where it merged with a well-established
tradition of British analytic philosophy
represented in the early twentieth century by G.
E. Moore, George's namesake, and Bertrand
Russell, whose Theory of Descriptions is
mentioned in **Jumpers**.   One might argue that
the roots of logical positivism are British since
Ludwig Wittgenstein, the Austrian whose
Tractatus Logico-Philosophicus (1921) was one
of the most powerful influences on the movement,
had studied with Moore and Russell at Cambridge.
In addition to Moore, Russell, and Wittgenstein,
Jumpers alludes to British philosophers A. J.
Ayer and Gilbert Ryle (p. 35), and it is the
British branch of the movement Stoppard
satirizes.
     The world of **Jumpers** is carefully
constructed to give dramatic form to some of the
questions pondered by the logical positivists.
For instance, a distinguishing trait of logical
positivism is its focus on language.   This focus
was inspired by Wittgenstein's **Tractatus**,

which is concerned with the relation between a
logical language and the world of which that
language purports to give us a picture;
distortions in the language that shapes the
picture, Wittgenstein believed, can lead to an
unclear picture of reality.[7]   Similarly,
Russell has described the British branch of
logical positivism as a "school of linguistic
analysis," which holds "that all philosophical
perplexities are the outcome of slovenly use of
language."[8]   In **Jumpers**, much of the action
and humor hinges on linguistic ambiguities and
confusions.   These confusions mirror larger
ambiguities present in the reality represented in
the drama.   For instance, the double meaning
implied in Dorothy's remark that "she's all right
in bed" (which may mean that she feels secure as
long as she is in bed or that she is sexually
adroit) and Archie's reply that "there's
something in that" (p. 70) reflects the
uncertainty about whether he is Dorothy's lover
or her doctor.   The play is constructed of a
whole tissue of such uncertainties, which the
language compounds and perpetuates.

     The most pervasive verbal joke in
Jumpers is the "cognomen syndrome," a
psychological condition in which one's name
corresponds to one's role in life.   Archie
(archer) Jumper is a gymnast.   Crouch is a
servant aspiring to become a jumper-philosopher.
Duncan McFee suffers the fate of the murdered
king in **Macbeth**.   Inspector Bones tries to
deal directly with the bare bones of reality.
Dotty is "dotty."   George seems doomed to embrace
some of the ethical principles of G. E. Moore
because he has the same name.   Although the
convention of descriptive names stretches back in
English drama as far as Jonson and the morality
plays, its use here alludes to an indirect
consequence of Russell's Theory of Descrip-
tions--"that ordinary proper names function as
descriptions [in Russell's sense]"[9]--and to
such philosophical concerns as the relation
between names and descriptive phrases, between
names and what they denote, and between the
reference and the sense of a word.[10]

Similarly, George's gibe that it is for "reasons
which will be found adequate by logical spirits"
that G. E. Moore was never in when George called
(p. 67) points to what P. F. Strawson,. in an
attack on Russell's theory, calls "the lingering
superstition that a name is logically tied to a
single individual."[11] If this were true,
then Stoppard's George Moore would actually be
G. E. Moore, an adequate reason why he cannot be
in two places at once. Bones's remark that
"there's only ever been one Dorothy Moore"
(p. 57) repeats this joke, the wife of G. E.
Moore having also been named Dorothy. Thus
Stoppard's tricks with language in **Jumpers**
are not purposeless games or incidental
flourishes of wit but part of his depiction of
logical positivism.

The best known statement of the logical
positivist position in English is **Language,
Truth and Logic**, published in 1935 by A. J.
Ayer, and Stoppard almost certainly consulted it
in preparing to write **Jumpers**. In addition
to its having virtually the status of a text-
book,[12] Stoppard alludes to it in the title
of George's work **Language, Truth and God**
(p. 58), and Archie's initials suggest Ayer's
famous first and middle initials. One of Ayer's
illustrations in the revised introduction of 1946
may have supplied Stoppard with the seed of the
idea for his play: "The statement that I have
blood on my coat may, in certain circumstances,
confirm the hypothesis that I have committed a
murder, but it is not part of the meaning of the
statement that I have committed a murder that I
should have blood upon my coat."[13] That is,
a man may kill without getting bloody or have
blood on his coat without being a murderer. At
the end of **Jumpers**, we are invited to
conclude that George's secretary murdered McFee
because of the blood on her coat, but we immediately learn the coat is actually stained with the
blood of Thumper, the rabbit (a fact which would
nevertheless not preclude her being the
murderer); further, Archie, George, Crouch, and
Dorothy also have motives for shooting McFee.
The central tenet of logical positivism is the

principle of verification, which holds that no
statement is "literally significant" or
"meaningful," no statement is truly about the
world unless its truth or falsity can be
empirically verified. As Ayer puts it, "We say
that a sentence is factually significant to any
given person, if, and only if, he knows how to
verify the proposition which it purports to
express--that is, if he knows what observations
would lead him . . . to accept the proposition as
being true, or reject it as being false"
(**Language, Truth and Logic**, p. 35).

As the secretary's coat demonstrates,
however, observations can be ambiguous, untrust-
worthy, and inconclusive. Ayer's coat
illustration may have brought home to Stoppard
the limits of what can be affirmed about life if
one adheres to the principle of verification and
may also have suggested a means of dramatizing
the limits of various philosophical approaches to
reality. "To begin at the beginning," George
reasons, is to ask "is God?" (p. 24). Just as
the universe and George's argument begin with
God, **Jumpers** begins with the murder of McFee
and its mysterious perpetrator. This congruence
signals that the mystery of McFee's murder is a
metaphor for the essential mysteries of creation.
In a murder mystery, the chief questions are "Who
done it?" and "Why?" Some of our fundamental
questions about life are the same: Who done it?
Who created the universe and to what purpose?
The ways that Archie, Bones, and George set about
solving the murder represent various philosophical approaches to answering these larger
questions.

Dorothy plays a special role in the murder
investigation. Although at times she herself
expresses a pragmatic philosophy of sorts--"Here
is my consistent proposition / Two and two make
roughly four" (p. 86)--Dorothy is chiefly
concerned with the consequences of the murder
rather than its solution and therefore must be
distinguished from the three philosopher-
detectives. Moreover, she forms the center of
emotional interest for the men. For these
reasons, Dorothy occupies a unique position in
the play's structure. In one sense, she

represents man's nature uncomplicated and
unrefined by intellect, his emotions and
appetites: she is an entertainer and spends most
of the play in the bedroom, a place of sleep,
sexual intercourse, and luncheon trays. Dorothy
has been psychologically traumatized by the
triumph of rationalistic materialism in the
modern world, epitomized by the ascendancy of
logical positivism in philosophy and radical-
liberalism in politics and by technological
achievements such as moon landings. A symptom of
the trauma is her loss of the ability to croon
romantic songs about the moon after man's lunar
landing destroyed the planet's aura of poetry and
romance. Her collapse into insanity signifies
the persistence of emotional and spiritual needs
which seem irrational viewed from a "sane" and
materialistic perspective. She longs for
something incredible rather than the "credible
and all too bloody likely" acrobatics of the
jumpers (p. 20). She wants to believe in God,
the soul, or right and wrong, absolutes
incredible to the philosophically up-to-date
jumpers, who accept as credible only what is
verifiable.

  Dorothy's plight, symbolized by her need to
dispose of McFee's body, corresponds to that of
modern man, caught with life and death on his
hands and in need of a reason for continuing to
function in a grim and chaotic world from which
the spiritual consolations of the past have been
withdrawn. The moments of most intense feeling
in the play are those in which she pleads for the
emotional support that might make life worth
living. Her involvements with George, Bones, and
Archie betoken three types of personal relations
from which one might extract such support and
also three stages in the historical development
of the relationship between man and woman.
George offers traditional married love, involving
physical and emotional connections and a fair
amount of realism about one's partner. Bones's
idealistic love is callow and romantic in the
Nineteenth Century style, while Archie offers a
crassly physical relationship of the modern type.
All the men fail Dorothy in varying degrees, both

as lovers and as philosopher-detectives trying to
give her a convincing and sustaining picture of
reality.

Dorothy, along with the secretary, also
forms part of the puzzling reality the men strive
to interpret. Both women play scenes in the
nude; a metaphor for the **ding an sich**, this
physical exposure hides more than it reveals.
Stoppard invests the women with an air of enigma
which, like the world, defies male ratiocination.
The opening scene makes this point in a parable:
all the party guests but Crouch are aware of the
secretary's striptease, but each time he turns
her way, she has just swung her trapeze elusively
into the darkness. Elsewhere in the play the
secretary is stolid and **"poker-faced"**
(p. 14), never speaking and registering little
emotion. The conclusions of Bones and George
that Dorothy is a murderess are never verified,
and the play leaves unanswered questions about
her relations with the three leading men. It is
not clear, as George himself says, "what on earth
made **her** marry **him**" (p. 35), or whether
Dorothy's charge of rape against Bones is true or
concocted in order to blackmail him. Although
the available evidence suggests the hypothesis
that Dorothy is having an affair with Archie, the
same evidence could conceivably support her
explanation that Archie is her psychiatrist. As
the anecdote about Wittgenstein's comment on the
rotation of the earth shows (p. 75), a single
observed fact may have more than one possible
explanation, and the most obvious is not
necessarily correct. Faced with such ambiguity,
George asks the question the entire play poses:
"How the hell does one know what to believe?"
(p. 71).

The answer Inspector Bones gives to that
question represents that of the man on the
street, for he embodies the intellectual
processes of ordinary people just as Dorothy
expresses their emotional need. Bones's approach
to solving the murder (and, by extension, the
mystery of reality) is direct but altogether too
simple for the complex issues involved. It is
that of a detective whose main interest is show

.B. Crump   161

business (in other words, appearances). The
precise analytical methods and elaborate
distinctions of philosophy are mumbo-jumbo to
him: when George introduces himself as a
logician, Bones thinks he has said magician
(p. 44). Differences between schools of
philosophy are likewise lost on him: "You bloody
philosophers are all the same" (p 59), he says of
George and McFee. Bones's habit of scrambling
names sometimes shows an intuitive grasp of the
truth--as when he calls Archie Sir Jim (gym) and
Sir Archibald Bouncer. But it also suggests the
lack of precision in sense and reference to which
everyday language is prone and which formal
philosophy strives to avoid.
     Bones's hope of arriving at a correct
solution to the murder rests with his sentimental
faith in a lover's insight into the motives of
Dorothy and his adherence to the detective's code
of integrity and disinterestedness. "This is a
British murder enquiry," he says, "and some
degree of justice must be seen to be more or less
done" (pp. 65-66). Because circumstantial
evidence implicates Dorothy, Bones will go only
so far to get her off, in spite of his crush on
her; he looks for signs of temporary insanity but
will not buy a phony suicide. Nevertheless, his
passion wars with his integrity and prejudices
his conclusions. When he describes Dorothy as "a
delicate creature, like a lustrous-eyed little
bird you could hold in your hand, feeling its
little brittle bones through its velvety
skin--vulnerable . . . highly strung" (p. 58),
his language, hopelessly compromised by maudlin
sentiment, reveals that he does not clearly
perceive even her, let alone the crime. After
all, the presence of the corpse does not in
itself prove guilt, and Bones may **want**
Dorothy to be guilty so that he can come to her
rescue with the insanity plea. Asked why he
suspects her, he can only reply that "I have a
nose for these things" (p. 66). The example of
Bones demonstrates that no tenable conclusions
about reality can be reached by relying, as the
average man does, on instinct and emotion
bolstered by casual observation.

The logical positivist perception of reality
is reflected in Archie's handling of the murder.
In **Jumpers**, Stoppard depicts logical positivism as providing the intellectual impetus behind
the modern drift toward materialism, utilitari-
anism, and state socialism. Archie is a
composite figure embodying various prophets of
this secular drift--psychiatrist, lawyer,
bureaucrat, and physical culturist as well as
philosopher. Under the leadership of jumpers
like Archie, the radical liberals embark on their
program to "rationalize" all social and religious
institutions and even patterns of thought. God
and the soul, their existence unverified, no
longer have any reality. The fear of temporal
law having therefore replaced respect for divine
authority, the Chair of Divinity is offered to a
policeman. Archie regards Dorothy's soul-sick-
ness as a neurosis to be treated by a machine
that examines her skin: in much the same way,
logical positivism holds that the basic nature of
the world can be understood by studying its
"skin," the language through which we perceive
it. The socialists appoint as Archbishop of
Canterbury an agricultural minister who will feed
bodies rather than save souls. Since statements
of moral principle are viewed as expressions of
the speaker's feelings rather than the setting
forth of absolutes, the university's Chairs of
Ethics and Logic are kept separate.

Using one of G. E. Moore's favorite
reasoning tactics, **reductio ad absurdum**,
George ridicules the materialism of the jumpers
with a one-sentence summary of their philosophy:
"No problem is insoluble given a big enough
plastic bag" (p. 40). Archie's response to
McFee's murder proves this summary to be
accurate: he disposes of the corpse in a large
plastic bag, blackmails Bones with the alleged
rape of Dorothy, and certifies in his capacity as
coroner that McFee crawled into the bag and shot
himself. Archie is ruthlessly efficient in
coping with life's immediate contingencies and
therefore more immediately helpful to Dorothy
than George and Bones. But the riddle of "who
done it" he ignores. His final pronouncement

about the murder rests on the logical positivist
principle that no question about reality is worth
asking unless one knows how to answer it: "We
will never even know for certain who did shoot
McFee. Unlike mystery novels, life does not
guarantee a denouement; and if it came, how would
one know whether to believe it?" (p. 81). Logical positivism can offer answers to the questions
of life because it excludes unanswerable
questions. In **Language, Truth and Logic,**
Ayer designates all propositions that are neither
"tautologies" (definitions) nor empirical
hypotheses as "metaphysics." Any propositions
about non-material reality (such as God, the
soul, or the ideal) are metaphysics, including
almost all statements made by theologians, poets,
and even philosophers. For Ayer, such questions
about the universe as "who done it" are not the
proper concern of philosophy, which "as a genuine
branch of knowledge, must be distinguished from
metaphysics" (p. 41), and he does not conceal his
contempt for those who have tried to answer them:
"The labours of those who have striven to
describe . . . [a transcendental] reality have
all been devoted to the production of nonsense"
(p. 34).

     Jumpers demonstrates some of the
drawbacks to the logical positivist attitude
toward reality. For one thing, treating McFee's
death as a problem of waste disposal leaves no
room for sorrow over McFee the man, the unique
individual who will never again know life on this
earth. Archie's first reaction to his
colleague's death is glib and callous: "It's a
great pity," Dorothy quotes him as saying, "but
it's not as though the alternative were
immortality" (p. 50). The play ties this
careless devaluation of life to the "emotive
theory of ethics," the logical positivist
doctrine that ethical statements are expressions
of the speaker's feelings, not of absolutes, and
the corollary principle that morality is the
totally relative product of one's culture. As
Ayer puts it in **Language, Truth and Logic,**
"in so far as [statements of value] are not
scientific, they are not in the literal sense
significant, but are simply expressions of

emotion which can be neither true nor false."
Thus, curiously, "a strictly philosophical
treatise on ethics should . . . make no ethical
pronouncements" (p. 103). Stoppard represents
this position as leading to the abandonment of
ethics altogether. In this way McFee's espousal
of the emotive theory of ethics contributed to a
climate of amorality in which his own murder
became more likely.

A second drawback is that logical positivism
cannot, by virtue of its materialistic assumptions, give Dorothy the spiritual comfort and
reassurance she craves. It can dispose of the
body but not of the spiritual dilemma of needing
to believe and being unable to. Dorothy's need
is reflected in her lament for the loss of our
absolutes: "We are no longer the still centre of
God's universe . . . and all our . . . thou-
shalts and . . . thou-shalt-nots . . .
look. . . . Like the local customs of another
place. When that thought drips through to the
bottom. . . . There is going to be such . . .
gnashing of unclean meats, such covetting of
neighbours' oxen and knowing of neighbours'
wives. . . . Because the truths that have been
taken on trust, they've never had edges before"
(p. 75). Archie's response is that required by
his logical positivism, the cliché response of
the psychiatrist-- "When did you first become
aware of these feelings?" (p. 75). It is
inadequate because it treats Dorothy's agony as
purely subjective, ignoring the madness of the
external world, the historical crisis of belief
that triggered it. In the same way, Archie's
materialism means that he can offer Dorothy sex
but not love. This is why she turns to George
for comfort both here and elsewhere in the play.

As a philosopher, George proposes to "set
British moral philosophy back forty years"
(p. 46), to restore it to its pre-Wittgenstein
views. He counters the emotive theory of ethics
by arguing that although men have believed
various things to be good at different times and
places, their particular beliefs have meaning
only in relation to the concept "good" whose
existence all men have intuitively recognized.

This argument resembles that of G. E. Moore in
his **Principia Ethica**; there Moore argued
that good is an unanalyzable quality like the
color yellow. Good is good; yellow, yellow. We
cannot define these qualities, but we can
recognize them when we experience them and can
therefore legitimately ask such questions as
"What things are good in themselves?" and "What
things can produce good?"[14]

Although the original George Moore could
find no convincing evidence that God exists, the
George of **Jumpers** affirms God's existence on
several traditional grounds--that He is a first
cause, that He is needed as an authority for
moral absolutes, and that His existence can be
inferred from life just as the existence of a
circle can be inferred from the idea of a polygon
with an infinite number of sides. George would
prefer a "philosopher's God, logically inferred
from self-evident premises" (pp. 39-40) and
independent both of organized religion and man's
emotional need to believe. But, unlike Archie,
he also possesses an authentic passion to know,
even in matters where complete knowledge is not
possible; he fears more than anything the
unknown--death, for instance, rather than dying
(p. 69). In his argument that God can be
inferred from life, at the furthest boundary to
which reason can carry him, George abandons
rationality and makes a jump of his own, an
existential leap of faith: "Now and again . . .
in some quite trivial moment, it seems to me that
life itself is the mundane figure which argues
perfection at its limiting curve. And if I doubt
it, the ability to doubt, to question, to
think, seems to be the curve itself.
Cogito ergo deus est" (p. 72).

Even to George himself, it sounds like he
believes because he believes: "All I know is
that I think that I know that I know that nothing
can be created out of nothing, that my moral
conscience is different from the rules of my
tribe, and that there is more in me than meets
the microscope--and because of **that** I'm
lumbered with this incredible, indescribable and
definitely shifty **God**" (p. 68). In these

passages, George speaks to and for that element
in man's nature which craves sureties in spite of
reason and evidence. He is not so out-of-step
with his contemporaries after all. Wittgenstein
summarizes "the whole sense" of the **Tractatus**
in these words: "What can be said at all can be
said clearly, and what we cannot talk about we
must pass over in silence" (**Tractatus**, p. 3).
Chiefly concerned with the limits of what can be
said and reasoned, Wittgenstein was also something of a mystic, aware that things exist "we
cannot talk about," things beyond the limits
reached by reason.[15] George's convictions
about God lie beyond the boundary where
analytical philosophy halts and mystical theology
takes over.

As a result, George, though he may not have
a more rational argument than the logical
positivists, has more of what we might call soul.
He contrasts with McFee, who "never put himself
at risk by finding mystery in the clockwork," and
whose death, for that reason, "left nothing
behind but a vacancy" (p. 72), a gap in the pyramid of jumpers. Stoppard has said that
Jumpers originated with the image of a pyramid
of acrobats with one missing (Tynan, p. 82). The
appropriateness of the image to characterize the
logical positivists is evident, for it connotes
not their momentary defiance of material laws in
the act of intellection but their ultimate
subjection to them.

Several details of **Jumpers** testify to
George's philosophical competence. His ability
to interpret Dorothy's mimes in their running
game of charades signifies a grasp of reality
which goes beyond the narrowly literalist range
of logical positivism. In her first charade, for
instance, she actually appears to be dead, but he
correctly recognizes she is miming, in spite of
her earlier cries of "murder" (p. 30). In the
dream-like **Coda**, where George and Archie
debate their philosophical positions, Archie's
presentation is a paragraph of gobbledygook, a
parody of the formal languages devised by
logicians to insure the precision of their
statements (it is, in fact, a highly ambiguous

conglomeration of interwoven puns). After the
audience at the debate cheers Archie's nonsense,
George offers a spirited and cogent refutation of
logical positivism in which he argues that the
principle of verification is a two-edged sword.
In practice, the logical positivists make many
value judgments which cannot be verified--that
socialism and technological progress offer the
best hope for feeding the world and that
gymnastics is healthy, to name only two. But how
can they be sure that a well-fed world and good
health are to be desired? If they can agree to
the relatively simple proposition that the
Bristol train left from Paddington only "if they
were actually there when it left--and even then
only on the understanding that all the observable
phenomena associated with the train leaving
Paddington could equally well be accounted for by
Paddington leaving the train," how can they
"claim to **know** that life is better than
death, that love is better than hate" (p. 87),
both very complex propositions? Given their
strict requirements for affirming a truth, what
cannot finally be doubted?

These details favorable to George are
undercut by others which suggest that he fails as
a husband and as a detective. The nature of the
failure is implied in Stoppard's choice of G. E.
Moore as a model for his hero. Although respect-
ed as a philosopher, Moore was notorious among
his acquaintances for what one writer calls "an
almost childlike naiveté concerning ordinary
affairs."[16] In **Russell and Moore**, A. J.
Ayer quotes J. M. Keynes on Moore's
"unworldliness and his indifference to the
'qualities of a life of action'" (p. 137) and
points out that Moore himself conceded that his
work took its "main stimulus" not "from direct
reflection on 'the world or the sciences' but
rather from what other philosphers had said about
them" (p. 141). All these traits are displayed
by the George of **Jumpers**. The self-reflexive
nature of his thought is represented by his
lecturing before a mirror; he is talking only to
himself. The opening stage directions stipulate
that either Dorothy's bedroom (which looks out on

the world through French windows and television)
or George's study must be blacked out, thereby
dramatizing the radical separation between the
abstract conceptual world of his philosophizing
and the "real" world of her breakdown and McFee's
corpse. Because of his isolation, George
consistently learns of developments in the public
drama of the radical-liberal coup and the private
drama of the murder indirectly, through others.

George's love for the rarefied atmosphere of
abstract logic results in a destructive indifference to human concerns. He dismisses political
events as insignificant, yet they have great
influence on the actual lives of people. In the
Coda, he is unwilling or unable to defend the
new Archbishop of Canterbury, who, like Thomas
à Becket, faces martyrdom when he begins to
take his role as spiritual leader seriously. In
view of Dorothy's special role in the play, the
fact that George is her husband rather than a
mere lover like Bones or Archie suggests that he
has a closer relationship to "reality" and ought
to better comprehend the trauma she suffers. But
George repeatedly fails Dorothy as a husband.
When she cries first "Murder!" and then "Rape!"
Bones and Archie go to her aid, but George
disregards her cries for help, responding only
when they get so loud that they disrupt his train
of thought. In the larger sense, he overlooks
her crisis of unbelief: **"Please don't leave
me!** I don't want to be left, to cope" (p. 41),
Dorothy begs him (almost as if George himself
were God), but belief in God is for him a
philosophical issue, not a pressing human need.
When Dorothy promises to stop seeing Archie and
weeps on George's breast, his heart is described
in the stage directions as **"uncomprehending"**
(p. 41), and he returns to his study rejecting
her invitation. George's eloquence in the
Coda is unable to restore Dorothy's lost
sense of romance, and the play ends with her
farewell to the "spoony Juney moon" (p. 87), a
symbol for the ideal of undying marital love and
fidelity. This gesture suggests that she will
turn from her husband to her lover. George's
indifference helps to destroy his marriage and,

G.B. *Crump*   *169*

by extension, the civilizing forces of moral
tradition and social stability that the
institution of marriage embodies.

In the instance of George, philosophy has
degenerated into sterile academic debate divorced
from the issues actually troubling man. For this
reason, he cannot fill Dorothy's need for spiritual assurances, and she must perforce turn to
Archie, who can at least help in disposing of the
corpse. George's misordering of human priorities
is epitomized by the fact that he is more worried
about Thumper and Pat, the rabbit and tortoise he
uses to refute Zeno's paradoxes, than about
Dorothy and McFee.

As a detective, George is no more astute
than Bones. He is the last person in the play to
learn there has been a murder, his ignorance
continuing through several scenes in which others
discuss the killing with him but he misunderstands because of various linguistic confusions:
for George as for Bones, language is a trap. At
one point, he accepts Archie's improbable suicide
story. George's eventual solution to the murder
is cast in the same language and issues from the
same arbitrary intuitive leap as his conclusions
about God: "There are many things I know which
are not verifiable but nobody can tell me I don't
know them, and I think that I know that something
happened to poor Dotty and she somehow killed
McFee, as sure as she killed my poor Thumper"
(p. 78). The last part of this deduction undercuts the reliability of George's overall
solution, for the audience eventually learns that
George himself shot the rabbit by accident when
he mistook Dorothy's cry of "fire" (a noun) for a
command to fire (imperative verb) his bow and
arrow.

Going to answer the door and expecting to
greet Archie, George says to his turtle, "Now
might I do it, Pat" (p. 43). The line echoes
that of Hamlet as he passes up his chance to stab
the praying Claudius. Like Hamlet, George is
guilty of thinking too much, and because he is so
absorbed in resolving issues solely on the
conceptual plane, he is never able to dispatch
his rival Archie and regain Dorothy's affections.

When George discovers Thumper impaled on his
arrow, he utters his own cry for help, for the
emotional support he has denied Dorothy. Though
a final humanizing touch, that cry once more
emphasizes George's ineffectuality in the realm
of action.

    Whatever may be Stoppard's personal views
about God, **Jumpers** does not endorse George's
position at the expense of those of Bones and
Archie. It does not show a brilliant Sherlock
Holmes outwitting the bumbling representatives of
Scotland Yard and triumphantly proving that the
murderer is the one person we would never
suspect. At the end, we have not discovered the
identity of the murderer or the nature of his
motive, but have merely listened to several
inconclusive speculations and received some
inkling of the plethora of possible culprits, the
variety of their motives, and the ambiguities of
the evidence. McFee's puzzling murder forms a
dramatic image of a reality as striking, as full
of menace, and as enigmatic as the sharp sound
made by the closing of the secretary's purse.
That sound of closure is all the answer man gets
when he seeks knowledge of life's ultimate
mysteries, yet the presence of the detectives in
Jumpers testifies that he will never stop
seeking.

Notes

1.   Martin Seymour-Smith, **Who's Who in Twentieth Century Literature** (New York: McGraw-Hill, 1976), p. 355.

2.   John Weightman, "A Metaphysical Comedy," **Encounter,** 38 (April 1972), 44-45. Other reviewers who argue that there is no real relation between the murder and the ideas are Harold Clurman, **Nation,** 218 (18 May 1974), 637; Stanley Kauffmann, **New Republic,** 170 (18 May 1974), 18, 33; and Gary Jay Williams, "Misbegotten Moons," **National Review,** 26 (1974), 377.

3.   Quoted in Kenneth Tynan, "Profiles (Tom Stoppard)," **New Yorker,** (19 December 1977), p. 80.

4.   In his review in the **Nation,** for instance, Harold Clurman says he thought George was being satirized in the English production but decided Stoppard was endorsing George on seeing the American production. See **Nation,** 218 (18 May 1974), 637.

5.   Tynan, pp. 85-86.

6.   Tom Stoppard, **Jumpers** (New York: Grove Press, 1972), pp. 50-51; hereafter cited in the text.

7.   See Bertrand Russell's introduction to Ludwig Wittgenstein, **Tractatus Logico-Philosophicus,** 2nd ed., trans. D. F. Pears and B. F. McGuinness (New York: Humanities Press, 1961), pp. ix-x; hereafter cited in the text.

8.   Bertrand Russell, **Wisdom of the West** (1959; rpt. New York: Fawcett, 1964), p. 401.

9.   A. J. Ayer, **Russell and Moore: The Analytical Heritage** (Cambridge, Mass: Harvard University Press, 1971), p. 37. Russell set forth his theory in an essay entitled "On

Denoting" in **Mind** (1905). It is reprinted in
Problems in the Philosophy of Language, ed.
Thomas M. Olshewsky (New York: Holt, Rinehart,
1969), pp. 300-311.

10. For a general discussion of these
issues, see Gilbert Ryle, "The Theory of
Meaning," originally published in **British
Philosophy in the Mid-Century**, ed. C. A. Mace
(1957); rpt. in Olshewsky, pp. 131-50. With the
exception of **Language, Truth and Logic**, for
which the case is strong, it is not very fruitful
to speculate at length on what books Stoppard
might have read in preparing to write
Jumpers. Nevertheless, the general review in
Ryle would be the sort of study he might look
for, and there is at least one specific passage
that suggests he might have read Ryle, who is
alluded to in the play. See note 13.

11. P. F. Stawson, "On Referring," 1950;
rpt. in Olshewsky, p. 329.

12. Gustav Bergmann, **The Metaphysics of
Logical Positivism** (Madison, Wis.: University
of Wisconsin Press, 1967), p. 3n.

13. A. J. Ayer, **Language, Truth and
Logic**, 2nd ed. (1946; rpt. New York: Dover,
1952), p. 14; hereafter cited in the text. The
idea of using the murder mystery may also have
come from Ryle, who speaks of the word **analysis** in the phrase **linguistic analysis** as
having "a good Scotland Yard ring to it." See
Olshewsky, p. 150.

14. George Edward Moore, **Principia
Ethica** (1903; rpt. Cambridge: Cambridge
University Press, 1968), p. 7.

15. For this point, I am indebted to my
friend Don Hart, who has assisted me with the
philosophical concepts throughout my essay.

16. John O. Nelson, "Moore, George Edward,"
Encyclopedia of Philosophy, 1967 ed.,
p. 373.

Seriousness Compromised by Frivolity: Structure and Meaning in Tom Stoppard's **Travesties**

Rodney Simard

No one familiar with Stoppard's drama would ever doubt the authorship of **Travesties**, his celebrated play of 1974, but many, while delighting in the overt theatricality of the play, have been baffled by its message in the seeming confusion of its form. Loosely based on the historical fact that James Joyce, Lenin, and Tristan Tzara were all in Zurich during World War I, the play is a pastiche of styles and modes in delightful, if confusing, disarray. Usefully, however, Stoppard has been quite articulate in discussing his intentions for the work, which, he says, "asks whether the words 'revolutionary' and 'artist' are capable of being synonymous, or whether they are mutually exclusive, or something in between."[1] This is the sort of question that impelled his two previous full-length plays, **Rosencrantz & Guildenstern Are Dead** and **Jumpers**, and a consideration of Stoppard's success in **Travesties** can profitably begin with an examination of the drama's place in his canon.

Travesties, in many ways, represents a culmination of the early part of Stoppard's career. Based in Oscar Wilde's **The Importance of Being Earnest**, the play recalls the play-within-a-play mode of **Rosencrantz** as well as **The Real Inspector Hound**; as an examination of aesthetics and the role of the artist, it can be seen as a logical extension of **After Magritte** and **Artist Descending a Staircase**; but structurally and thematically, it bears a close resemblance to **Jumpers**, its immediate predecessor. In a famous quotation,

Stoppard has outlined his goals for this period:
"What I try to do, is to end up by contriving the
perfect marriage between the play of ideas and
farce or perhaps even high comedy."[2] Comment-
ing on his success with this goal, Felicia
Hardison Londré has observed that,

> Dialectical thought provides some impetus
> for advancing the action in **Jumpers**, but
> it is the externalization of that thought in
> theatrical images that makes this play the
> supreme dramatic achievement in Stoppard's
> canon to date. **Travesties** repeats the
> pattern, and falls only a little short of
> that mark as a piece of writing, although it
> may have the edge over **Jumpers** in the
> theater.[3]

Stoppard recognizes the similarity of the two
plays and admits his intentions were similar:

> You start with a prologue which is slightly
> strange. Then you have an interminable
> monologue which is rather funny. Then you
> have scenes. Then you end up with another
> monologue. And you have unexpected bits of
> music and dance, and at the same time people
> are playing ping-pong with various intellec-
> tual agruments. . . . and there are senses
> in which **Travesties** is a great advance
> on **Jumpers**. . . .[4]

Despite the self-deprecation inherent in these
remarks, he has also commented that "most of
Travesties--not as a structure and a play but
speech by speech--still seems to me as good as I
can ever get."[5]   When the similarity of the
argument in **Artist Descending a Staircase** and
Travesties was pointed out to him, he
remarked, "If it's worth using once, it's worth
using twice," but more tellingly, he also
commented that,

> One of the impulses in **Travesties** is to
> try to sort out what my answer in the end
> would be if I was given enough time to think

> every time I'm asked why my plays aren't
> political, or ought they to be? Sometimes I
> have a complete comical reaction, and I
> think that in the future I must stop
> compromising my plays with this whiff of
> social application. They must be entirely
> untouched by any suspicion of usefulness. I
> should have the courage of my lack of
> convictions.[6]

The flippancy of this remark, however, has been
belied by the serious political observations in
many of his later plays, notably **Professional
Foul, Every Good Boy Deserves Favor,** and
Squaring the Circle. Travesties' dual
concern is with art and politics, and even though
Stoppard was early criticized for being
apolitical, no one has ever doubted the moral
concerns of those early plays, for any
consideration of art is inherently moral in his
work. Asked about "the impotence of political
art," he stated that,

> . . . art--Auden or Fugard or the entire
> cauldron--is important because it provides
> the moral matrix, the moral sensibility,
> from which we make our judgments about the
> world. . . . that's what art is best at.
> The objective is the universal perception,
> isn't it? By all means realize that
> perception in terms of a specific event,
> even a specific political event, but I'm not
> impressed by art **because** it's political.
> I believe in art being good art or bad art,
> not relevant art or irrelevant art.[7]

An explication of these ideas about art and its
relation to politics is the subject of
Travesties, one that is reflected in
Stoppard's construction of the play as well.
Margaret Gold argues that **Travesties**
represents "a new chapter in the history of the
comedy of ideas,"[8] and John William Cooke calls
the play "Stoppard's theater of chaos."[9] This
chaos of ideas is precisely his concern, for as
Craig Werner observes, by "centering his

attention on the interaction of the mythologies
of Art (represented by Joyce), Political
Revolution (represented by Lenin), and Radical
Individualism (represented by Tristan Tzara),
Stoppard unveils the limitations of the twentieth
century's most cherished systems of
belief."[10]   But Stoppard theatricalizes these
important ideological concerns in the ways
characteristic of his early career.   In
Travesties, however, we can see even more
than the culmination of the early Stoppard in his
dazzling theatricality, for a subtle shift in his
treatment of political matters suggests a new,
increased awareness of the realities of human
existence.   The play may be based in an opposition between art and politics, but Stoppard's
treatment of these twin themes, as embodied in
his characters, evinces a more sympathetic
treatment of political concerns than ever before;
despite his austere depiction of the Lenins, they
emerge as the most realistic characters in the
play and his treatment of them is sympathetic.
They may be solemn, but compared to the flippancy
of his portrayal of the artists, they attain a
high stature and seriousness in the audience's
eyes.   (In fact, the play has often been
criticized for this point; many critics have
suggested that his characterization of the Lenins
is too literal, that their historical accuracy
breaks the flow of the play, exposing a lack of
genuine dramatic conflict.)   Oppositions abound,
but no one side ever emerges as the clear victor.
Stoppard's ideas are presented with his
characteristic ambiguity, but they are easily
apprehendable: it is his structure that has
tended to confuse and dismay both his audiences
and readers.

      The play is based in a dialectic between
oppositions: art and politics, artists and
revolutionaries, World War I and Zurich, Tzara
and Henry Carr, Lenin and Joyce, the past and the
present, **The Importance of Being Earnest** and
Ulysses.   Thomas Whitaker observes that the
play "uses its symmetries not only to speed up
the farce but also to engage at length the
antithetical doctrines that have shaped modern

art and politics."[11] Modernism is the issue
he focuses on, and he appropriates the historical
figures of Lenin, Tzara, and Joyce because
modernism was, to a large extent, the history of
individuals who believed in a new form of
expression that would have a positive moral and
social force. In different ways, each man
believed he was accurately reflecting contemporary consciousness and that his contribution was
the proper and most effective reflection of the
time. To showcase this clash of ideologies,
Stoppard chose an early masterpiece of modern
drama as the basis of his own work, and his
superimposition of **Travesties** on Wilde's play
parallels the juxtaposition of aesthetic and
political theories he dramatizes. It also echoes
Joyce's use of **The Odyssey** for his
Ulysses.

Stoppard's first level of concern in this
play is with art and the role of the artist, or,
as he says, "it asks whether an artist has to
justify himself in political terms **at
all**,"[12] a question he had already answered
for himself six years earlier: ". . . artists do
not in fact need to justify themselves--they are
producing something which crystallizes and makes
concrete something in the air."[13]
Travesties is the dramatization of this
belief, an inner debate within the playwright
himself. He has commented that, in the play,

> I found that various voices of my own which
> were on a collision course made up whole
> scenes of **Travesties** for me, if you
> like. Henry Carr's skepticism about the
> valuation which artists put on themselves is
> very much my own skepticism. But then
> Joyce's defense of art is mine, too . . . .
> And even in the case of Tristan Tzara . . .
> I went into that having as I thought to
> create his arguments from nothing since I
> had no sympathy with them to start with. He
> wasn't speaking for me at all. But in the
> event I found some of the things Tzara had
> to say quite persuasive.[14]

Each of these voices is heard at length in the
play, and the debate between various points of
interpretation forms the essential dramatic
conflict of the work. Art, as a concept,
dominates the conversations of the characters,
and as their discussions begin to shape the role
of the artist, the second major concern of the
play, politics, takes form and focus. In the
voices he created for this play, Stoppard begins
to answer his own question: "artist" and
"revolutionary" are parallel if not synonymous
roles, although their effects are quite
different.

     Because this is a memory play, and therefore
subjective in much the same way as **The Glass
Menagerie**, we apprehend this debate through the
filters of Old Carr's creative recollection of
the events (which Old Cecily reminds us at the
end of the play are basically false or confused).
Carr functions as our eyes and ears, and by
making him the protagonist, Stoppard invites--or
rather demands--that we experience the play from
his perspective. Carr's is a moderate position,
the perception of the common man and, to a large
extent, our perception as audience. In fact,
despite the presence of the three revolutionary
"artists" who each expound on their notions of
art, Carr is given much more commentary on this
basic theme than the others. Early in the play,
he cites the drama's main concern and opposition
in a typically Stoppardian pun: "Truth of the
matter, who'd have thought big oaks from a corner
room at 14 Spiegelgasse?--now here's a thing:
two revolutions formed **in the same street.**
Face to face in Spiegelgasse! **Street of
Revolution! A Sketch.**"[15] To Carr, Lenin
was "an essentially simple man, and yet an
intellectual theoretician, bent, as I was already
aware, on the seemingly impossible task of
reshaping the civilized world into a federation
of standing committees of workers' deputies"
(23). He adds, "To those of us who knew him
Lenin's greatness was never in doubt" (24),
although we later learn that he had never known
him (the travesty of memory and subjective
perceptions on history).

The other "theoretician" determined to
reshape "the civilized world" was Joyce, a
revolutionary in the world of art. Because of
the litigation surrounding his role in
Earnest, Carr did have good reason to recall
him: "To those of us who knew him, Joyce's
genius was never in doubt. To be in his presence
was to be aware of an amazing intellect bent on
shaping itself into the permanent form of its own
monument--the book the world now knows as
Ulysses!" (22). In the parallelism of his
assessment, we have an equation between the art
of **Ulysses** and the Russian Revolution in
Carr's mind, which, historically, were both
revolutionary events. The question Carr (and
Stoppard) poses is: which was the more important
of the two creative geniuses?

As a minor artist who has pretentions to
acting ability while also being a diplomat and
man of politics, Carr presents us with his answer
from his dual perspective, colored, however, by
his resentment of Joyce. Nonetheless, he
presents a traditional assessment of the role of
art and the artist in society. To Carr, as to
most of society, "art doesn't change society, it
is merely changed by it" (74), and "For every
thousand people there's nine hundred doing the
work, ninety doing well, nine doing good, and one
lucky bastard who's the artist" (38). However,
his perceptions run deeper and he can also say
that "It is the duty of the artist to beautify
existence" (37), and that "An artist is someone
who is gifted in some way that enables him to do
something more or less well which can only be
done badly or not at all by someone who is not
thus gifted" (38), a remark that is a direct
quotation from Donner in **Artist Descending a
Staircase**.[16] When provoked by Tzara, he
brings art into relation with revolution:

> The nerve of it. Wars are fought to make
> the world safe for artists. It is never
> quite put in those terms but it is a useful
> way of grasping what civilized ideals are
> all about. The easiest way of knowing
> whether good has triumphed over evil is to
> examine the freedom of the artist. The

> **ingratitude** of artists, indeed their
> hostility, not to mention the loss of nerve
> and failure of talent which accounts for
> "modern art," merely demonstrate the freedom
> of the artist to be ungrateful, hostile,
> self-centered and talentless, for which
> freedom I went to war, and a more selfless
> ideal for a man of my taste it would be
> difficult to imagine. (39)

Despite his vendetta against Joyce, Carr states
the moderate, common position, outlining the
distinction between art and politics. Art is a
reflection of "civilized ideals," created by one
who is simultaneously "lucky," and "gifted," who
beautifies existence; his freedom is an absolute
measure of "good." Like Lenin, he deplores
modernism in the arts, if not in politics, for
also like Lenin, he is willing to fight to
preserve that freedom of creative expression even
if he fails to appreciate or understand it.
Unlike Lenin, Carr makes no political demands on
art, accepting it as an aestheticizing experience. The revolutionary fights for civilization,
embodied in the artist; theirs are symbiotic if
distinct roles.

This moderation is in opposition to the
radicalism of Tzara, the anti-aesthetic Dadaist
who believes the war has destroyed traditional,
rational values. He asserts that "anti-art is
the art of our time" (39), and he tells Joyce
that "Your art has failed. You've turned
literature into a religion and it's as dead as
all the rest, it's an overripe corpse and you're
cutting fancy figures at the wake. It's too late
for geniuses!" (62), saying, in short, "Art for
art's sake—I defecate!" (48). He counters
Carr's "bourgeois" views with:

> When the strongest began to fight for the
> tribe, and the fastest to hunt, it was the
> artist who became the priest-guardian of the
> magic that conjured the intelligence out of
> the appetites. Without him, man would be a
> coffee-mill. Eat—grind—shit. Hunt—
> **eat**—fight—**grind**—saw the logs—
> **shit**. The difference between being a
> man and being a coffee-mill is art. (47)

Without realizing it, he has come to complete
agreement with Carr's notion of the artist as a
representative of civilized ideals. Then, as he
becomes political in his explication and begins
to attack the capitalistic corruption of art, the
realization hits him (literalized on stage by a
change in lighting), and he says: "Without art
man was a coffee-mill: but with art, man--is
a coffee-mill!" (47), lapsing into a string of
dada nonsense. Unlike the essentially realistic
Carr, Tzara is the failed romantic, one who wants
to believe in values he thinks have lost their
value. He calls for a revolution of aesthetics:
"Nowadays, an artist is someone who makes art
mean the things he does" (38), also echoing
Donner in **Artist**; to him, an artist is
someone whose duty it is "to jeer and howl and
belch at the delusion that infinite generations
of real effects can be inferred from the gross
expression of apparent cause" (37). Carr
believes that revolution serves the artist, Tzara
the opposite: "Artists and intellectuals will be
the conscience of the revolution" (83). Carr
realizes the essential similarity of their
positions, aware that both believe in the
connection between art and politics, and tells
him that "All this dancing attendance on Marxism
is sheer pretension. You're an amiable bourgeois
with a chit from Matron and if the revolution
came you wouldn't know what hit you. You're
nothing. You're an artist. And multi-coloured
micturition is no trick to those boys, they'll
have you pissing blood" (83). But the idealistic
Tzara is also aware of some basic realities of
the time, for, as he says, "as a Dadaist myself I
am the natural enemy of bourgeois art and the
natural ally of the political left, but the odd
thing about revolution is that the further left
you go politically, the more bourgeois they like
their art" (45); he also knows that Lenin "is a
reactionary in art, and in politics he was
brought up in a hard school that killed weaker
spirits, but he is moved by a vison of a society
of free and equal men. And he will listen"
(83).
     Both understand the relation of revolution
to art, but while Carr believes in cause and

effect, Tzara believes in effect and cause. Each
position is meaningless in reality, however, for
as Donner remarks in **Artist**, "We tried to
make a distinction between the art that celebrated reason and history and logic and all
assumptions, and our own dislocated anti-art of
lost faith--but it was all the same insult to a
one-legged, one-armed, one-eyed regiment of the
maimed" (30). Both men believe in the value of
art and the need for the freedom of the artist,
but debate about the nature of art and the role
of the artist pales in comparison to the reality
of fighting and sacrificing for essential
human freedoms. Carr and Tzara stand in
between the poles of opposition represented by
Joyce and Lenin, the artist and the politician,
uniting revolutionary art and politics in the
play, and their debate does much to illuminate
the polarization of the two major figures of
modernism.

Even though he wasn't included in the
original plan for the play, Joyce's presence
dominates (at least Act I). He early makes his
aesthetic position clear: "As an artist,
naturally I attach no importance to the swings
and roundabout of political history" (50), having
just presented his own version of **Mr. Dooley**
to illustrate the point. Later, during conversation with Tzara, shortly after performing various
magic tricks, Joyce literalizes his actions in
his defense of art: "An artist is the magician
put among men to gratify--capriciously--their
urge for immortality" (62). His art has no
purpose, for it is pure and self-referential, and
as an artist, he has no real purpose that isn't
"capricious." Speaking of his work on
Ulysses, he says, "It is a theme so overwhelming that I am almost afraid to treat it.
And yet I with my Dublin Odyssey will double that
immortality, yes by God **there's** a corpse that
will dance for some time yet and **leave the
world precisely as it finds it** . . ." (62-63).
Politically, this stance is unconscionable, but
it is also a defense that Stoppard says "is the
most important speech in the play. It's
showbiz, but the speech is there because of its

place in the argument."[17]   Joyce's art is
absolute, and the world will take care of itself,
detached from him, illustrating Carr's earlier
remark to Tzara: "My dear Tristan, to be an
artist **at all** is like living in Switzerland
during a world war.   To be an artist **in
Zurich**, in 1917, implies a degree of
self-absorption that would have glazed over the
eyes of Narcissus" (38).   While we admire Joyce's
genius and recognize the aesthetic revolution he
brought about, we cannot defend him on moral or
political grounds, except to say, as he implies,
that he is above such considerations; Joyce's art
makes its own statement, complete within itself.

        Lenin, however, has much to say on the
subject, and it is his presence that dominates
Act II.   His stance is clear, and clearly
political: "Today, literature must become party
literature.   Down with non-partisan literature!
Down with literary supermen!   Literature must
become a part of the common cause of the
proletariat, a cog in the Social Democratic
mechanism . . ." (85).   In her role as his
disciple, Cecily is more complete in her
explanation:

        Art **is** society!   It is one part of many
        parts all touching each other, everything
        from poetry to politics.   And until the
        whole is reformed, artistic decadence,
        whether in the form of the perfectly phrased
        epigram or a hatful of words flung in the
        public's face, is a luxury which only
        artists can afford. (74)

This revolutionary impulse is a powerful moral
force, one difficult to counter with an aesthetic
argument.   Lenin, however, is aware of this
inherent conflict, for as Nadya tells us, "He
wrote little about art and literature, generally,
but he enjoyed it" (86), and as Lenin himself
remarks, "We are good revolutionaries but we seem
to be somehow obliged to keep up with modern art.
Well, as for me I'm a barbarian.   Expressionism,
futurism, cubism . . . I don't understand them
and I get no pleasure from them" (86-87).

Obviously, Lenin would not have enjoyed
Ulysses, just as Stoppard's Joyce is
apparently indifferent to the Russian Revolution.
In this sense, "artist," and "revolutionary" are
mutually exclusive, but Lenin is not immune to
the seeming contradiction. He speaks of the
beauty of Beethoven's **Appassionata** and his
reaction to it:

> It always makes me feel, perhaps naively, it
> makes me feel proud of the miracles that
> human beings can perform. But I can't
> listen to music often. It affects my
> nerves, makes me want to say nice stupid
> things and pat the heads of those people who
> while living in this vile hell can create
> such beauty. Nowadays we can't pat heads or
> we'll get our hands bitten off. We've got
> to hit heads, hit them without mercy, though
> ideally we're against doing violence to
> people . . . Hm, one's duty is infernally
> hard . . . (89)

This position is also morally difficult, and
Lenin is aware of the power of art; however, his
priorities are political: the creation of a
better world, a world perhaps not unlike the
Zurich in 1917 that enables Joyce to write his
Ulysses. Stoppard asks us, as he is asking
himself, does the nature of the society allow art
to be created or does the art function to shape
the society? The problem here is rather like the
question of the chicken and the egg, and the only
solution Stoppard offers us is not in the opposition of Lenin and Joyce, but primarily in the
difference and debate between Carr and Tzara. As
Tim Brassell has observed, "The play does not
merely circumnavigate the beliefs of the three
main characters: it arranges them in such a
fashion as to spotlight the various directions
open to twentieth-century art."[18] Like the
nature of the entire play, however, no easy
solutions are offered and all the action is
located within an individual mind. This play
ends in the ritualistic resolution of the comedic
dance, followed by the coda in which some
semblance of historical accuracy is established.

Coppelia Kahn argues that "Stoppard implies
. . . that any comparison between action that
effects a change in the real world and art that
creates an imaginary world is inappropriate," and
that "art must always be at counterpurposes with
society or it is not art."[19] Stoppard's
political beliefs, as reflected in the character
of Lenin, are clear in this case. He has said
that he was trying in **Jumpers** to demonstrate
that "all political acts have a moral basis to
them and are meaningless without it," which "goes
against Marxist-Leninism in particular, and
against all materialistic philosophy. I believe
all political acts must be judged in moral terms,
in terms of their consequences." Specifically,
he believes that "the repression which for better
or worse turned out to be Leninism in action
after 1917 was very much worse than anything
which had gone on in Tsarist Russia."[20]
Thus, while Stoppard's political sympathies are
explicit, Lenin functions in the play as the
advocate of social responsibility in art, while
still suggesting a political concern new in the
Stoppard canon.

Act I of **Travesties** is dominated by
Joyce and the dialectic about art; Act II
concerns Lenin and the belief, as voiced by
Cecily, that "the sole duty and justification for
art is social criticism" (74), to which Carr, as
raisonneur, counters, "a great deal of what
we call art has no such function and yet in some
way it gratifies a hunger that is common to
princes and peasants" (74). Lenin, himself, is
reactionary in his aesthetic tastes, and his
mastery of modernism is purely political, in
Stoppard's view as negative as Dada in the arts.

Most critical debate about Lenin, however,
is not thematic, but structural. All the
characters in the play, except the Lenins, are
"travestied," that is, receive parodic
treatment,[21] which makes the Lenins stand out
and seem to receive a different handling.
However, like Zurich, the War, and the
Revolution, they function to give the play its
basis in historical and objective reality, much
the same way that **Hamlet** stands behind
Rosencrantz and the Rad-Lib victory forms the
foundation of **Jumpers**. Lenin is the touch-

stone against which the primary revolution and
war (in this play) are measured--the revolution
in modern art and the contest between different
values represented by Joyce, Carr, and Tzara. In
terms of Stoppard's structure, Lenin's role is
crucial as well. Stoppard has explained:

> What I am trying is this. What I'm always
> trying to say is 'Firstly, A. Secondly,
> minus A.' What was supposed to be happening
> was that we have this rather frivolous
> nonsense going on, and then the Lenin
> section comes in and says, 'Life is too
> important. We can't afford the luxury of
> this artificial frivolity, this nonsense
> going on in the arts.' Then he says,
> 'Right. That's what I've got to say,' and
> he sits down. Then the play stands up and
> says, 'You thought **that** was frivolous?
> You ain't seen nothin' yet.' And you go
> into the Gallagher and Shean routine. That
> was the architectural thing I was
> after.[22]

Lenin is a symbol of revolution, as is Zurich.
His realistic presence is sobering, as is
Cecily's opening lecture in Act II, but he
functions to underscore the essential seriousness
in the manic frivolity of the play.[23]
     The audience cannot afford to make too much
of the historical accuracy of the play (which is
severely flawed by Carr's memory) or of the
actual personages of Carr, Bennett, Tzara, Lenin,
and Joyce, for **Travesties** is a dialectic
between ideologies, not history, and like Carr's
mind and memory, the play collapses chronological
time.[24] Stoppard himself tells us that "my
characters are all mouthpieces for points of view
rather than explorations of individual psychology. They aren't realistic in any sense. I write
plays of ideas uneasily married to comedy or
farce."[25] Gold summarizes this position:
"Joyce weighs in for the supreme value of art,
and Lenin for politics as an absolute. Carr and
Tzara exist in a situation where they attempt to
mediate between those extremes, with Tzara
standing for both art and politics, perhaps, and
Carr standing for neither."[26]

Structurally, Carr is at the center of the play, just as Switzerland is at "the still centre of the wheel of war" (26), and, as Stoppard reminds us, most of the play "**is under control of Old Carr's memory, which is not notably reliable, and also of his various prejudices and delusions**" (27). The play is internal, within Carr's mind, and the two sets represent the duality of his perceptions: memory and actuality. Carol Billman emphasizes that "a person is in control of the history he tells," that "he is a living reminder of the erratic subjectivity of the history-teller and the relativity of his product."[27] This point of view supports Stoppard's thematic concerns as well, for, as Pearce argues, **Travesties** "raises the fundamental question of whether reality lies in dream or in life," and that "reality is the ultimate object of travesty's imitation, but the travesty calls reality itself into question. Stoppard's play travesties Wilde's, which travesties life. It travesties history as well, which seems to travesty its own principles of cause and effect, of probability."[28]

Carr, revolutionary in nothing, is the common man, the observer of the great who surround him, and it is through his reactions to the various values and behavior of the other characters that we as audience receive our information. As protagonist, he functions to demonstrate modern aesthetic theories as they affect the average person, but his reactions are all superficial, suggested in his clothing fixation (although Stoppard may be hinting at a clothes philosophy much like that in **Sartor Resartus** here). Carr presents us with the other characters, whom we know only as he reflects the ideologies for which they stand. As Werner asserts, "from a Leninist perspective, Carr, however, much controlled by his class situation, represents economically motivated modern man. . . . From the Dadaist point of view he is an individual with theoretically unlimited idiosyncracies, however repressed. From a Joycean perspective, he provides something of the material of a Leopold Bloom."[29] He is,

first, what he represents to each of the three
masters of modernism, and, second, he is who
presents them to us; in essence, he and his
perceptions constitute the entire play.

    While we identify with the ordinariness of
Carr, representing as he does the common man, we
cannot identify with him as an individual, for
the form of his perceptions is simply too
bizarre. But the actual structure of the play,
presented as Carr's egocentric and perhaps senile
memories, is also Stoppard's technique, and
Stoppard states that his goal was to "write a
play which was an anthology of different sorts of
play. . . . I mean different kinds of style,
different kinds of idiom."[30] **Travesties**
contains burlesque, parody, limerick, rhyme,
song, allusion, and imitation in its form, which
has caused some problems for its audience; it
seems to have no one style, no definite theory of
communication. But this multiplicity, which
reflects the dialectical oppositions in its
subject matter, also reinforces its theme. As an
audience, we are invited to judge and select for
ourselves, for Stoppard remains aloof from the
material he presents in the play; choice is an
individual matter in art, as in life.

    But this multiplicity, Stoppard's
"anthology," also serves to suggest another
debate of modernism, one not in the actual
content of the play but in its very form: the
contrasts between modernist movements in drama.
Based in the early classic of the modern theater,
The Importance of Being Earnest,
Travesties was absolutely contemporary when
conceived, spanning, like Carr, the gap between
the beginnings of modernism and a reflection on
those theories from a postmodern perspective.
According to Pearce, the play "becomes multiple
reflections on dramatic theory and practice" and
contains echoes of Beckett, Brecht, Ionesco, and
Shaw, as well as Wilde.[31] While presenting
this anthology of modern dramatic styles,
Travesties also parallels the major work of
the character whose aesthetic theories dominate
the dialectic: Joyce's **Ulysses.**

    T. S. Eliot notes that **Ulysses** was
perceived, quite wrongly, in early reviews as

Dadaist, and in his defense of the novel, he
states that its form "is simply a way of
controlling, of ordering, of giving a shape and a
significance to the immense panorama of futility
and anarchy which is contemporary history,"[32]
a process that is paralleled in **Travesties**.
The play again becomes self-referential, as it is
metadramatic in its catalogue of dramatic styles.
Wilde's switched bags, one with the baby and the
other with the novel manuscript, become, in
Travesties, switched chapters, one from Lenin
and the other the "Oxen of the Sun" section of
Ulysses, wherein Joyce underlies his content
by writing in a catalogue of English prose
styles. Another more obvious example is in
Joyce's confrontation scene with Tzara (56-60), a
series of questions and answers with a dual
effect: on one level, Stoppard shows Joyce in
his Lady Bracknell role from **Earnest**, a
parallel not extended very far in the "travesty"
of Wilde; however, the technique also clearly
recalls the catechism mode of the "Ithaca"
section of **Ulysses**. Just as Joyce transmuted
the ordinary into the immortal by paralleling it
with a classic work of art in his novel, Stoppard
places the ordinary Carr at the center of his
play, itself juxtaposed on an earlier work. As
Pearce notes, the play "refers itself as well to
other multiple reflections of life and art. Its
primary technical analogue is Joyce's
Ulysses, appropriately, since envy of that
work is the source of Carr's story."[33] In
the same way that **Ulysses** emerges from the
play as the triumphant product of the aesthetic
debates that form its primary subject matter,
"Stoppard in his travesty of **Ulysses** becomes
that intellect shaping itself in its own
monument, mirroring itself among the multiple
reflections of its **mimesis**."[34]
      In **Travesties**, Stoppard takes on the
major theories of life and art in the twentieth-
century and does much to illuminate and reconcile
them in his dramatization of ideology, both in
the content and form of his play. This is an
audacious goal, but one that he achieves admirably, and once having done it he moved into a new

phase of his career, with parallel but decidedly
different concerns. **Travesties** will
undoubtedly continue to delight and baffle its
audiences because of the fantastic scope of its
concerns. Yet it can still be approached and
apprehended as simply as the art it explicates,
for as Gold reminds us, it is just "a theatre-
piece that meditates upon its own dramatic
origins and at the same time dramatizes questions
concerning the proper relation of politics to
art."[35]

Notes

1.   Tom Stoppard, "Ambushes for the Audience: Towards a High Comedy of Ideas," **Theatre Quarterly**, 4 (May-July 1974), 11.

2.   Stoppard, "Ambushes," p. 2.

3.   Felicia Hardison Londré, **Tom Stoppard** (New York: Ungar, 1981), p. 49.

4.   Quoted in Ronald Hayman, **Tom Stoppard**, 3rd ed. (London: Heinemann, 1979), p. 12.

5.   Quoted in Hayman, p. 12.

6.   Quoted in Hayman, p. 2.

7.   Stoppard, "Ambushes," p. 14.

8.   Margaret Gold, "Who Are the Dadas of **Travesties**?" **Modern Drama**, 21 (1978), 59.

9.   John William Cooke, "The Optical Allusion: Perception and Form in Stoppard's **Travesties**," **Modern Drama**, 24 (1981), 525.

10.   Craig Werner, "Stoppard's Critical Travesty, or, Who Vindicates Whom and Why," **Arizona Quarterly**, 35 (1979), 228.

11.   Thomas Whitaker, **Tom Stoppard** (New York: Grove, 1983), p. 119.

12.   Stoppard, "Ambushes," p. 16.

13.   Tom Stoppard, "Something to Declare," **The Sunday Times** (London), 25 February 1968, p. 47.

14.   Quoted in Nancy Shields Hardin, "An Interview with Tom Stoppard," **Contemporary Literature**, 22 (1981), 156.

15. Tom Stoppard, **Travesties** (New York:
Grove, 1975), p. 24; subsequent references to
this edition will appear in parentheses in the
text.

16. Tom Stoppard, **Artist Descending a
Staircase**, in **Four Plays for Radio** (London:
Faber, 1984), p. 23; subsequent references to
this edition will appear in parentheses in the
text. Also compare Carr's remarks (46) with
Beauchamp's (46).

17. Quoted in Hayman, p. 9.

18. Tim Brassell, **Tom Stoppard: An
Assessment** (New York: St. Martin's, 1985),
p. 160.

19. Coppelia Kahn, "**Travesties** and the
Importance of Being Stoppard," **New York
Literary Forum**, 1 (1978), 192, 196; several
other critics also share this interpretation.
See, for example, Werner, p. 236; Kenneth Tynan,
"Withdrawing with Style from the Chaos," **Show
People: Profiles in Entertainment** (New York:
Simon, 1979), p. 111; and Lucina Paquet Gabbard,
The Stoppard Plays (Troy, NY: Whitson,
1982), p. 116.

20. Stoppard, "Ambushes," p. 12.

21. Kahn, p. 194, however, suggests that
Lenin travesties himself in his Swedish deaf-mute
plan.

22. Quoted in Hayman, p. 10.

23. Brassell, pp. 158-59, argues powerfully
that one of Stoppard's main concerns in
Travesties is "to suggest how art can be
overshadowed and even controlled by the currents
of political activity--even when his own
brilliance may be jeopardized in the process. In
this way the role of Lenin completes the
intermittent debate on art and revolution; even
though he never converses with the other
characters, his is the most important single
contribution."

24.   Carol Billman, "The Art of History in
Tom Stoppard's **Travesties**," **Kansas
Quarterly**, 12 (1980), 48-49; see also Cooke,
p. 533, who says that "of course, we inevitably
do think of these figures as historical
characters, because we rely not simply on Carr's
memory but also on our own. Like Carr, we too
have 'intentions' about Lenin, Joyce, and Tzara,
hardly more or less fictionalized than Carr's."

25.   Quoted in Tynan, p. 100.

26.   Gold, p. 64.

27.   Billman, p. 50; see also Rodney Simard,
**Postmodern Drama: Contemporary Playwrights in
America and Britain** (Washington: American
Theatre Assn.-UPA, 1984), pp. 49-74, for a
discussion of subjective reality in Stoppard; and
Cooke, p. 532, who argues that "individual
perception is not only a theme of the play, but
also an activity which occurs in it, and
therefore, each element of the play, and thus the
play itself, depends upon this same process.

28.   Howard D. Pearce, "Stage as Mirror: Tom
Stoppard's **Travesties**," **Modern Language
Notes**, 94 (1979), 1148, 1153.

29.   Werner, p. 231.

30.   Quoted in Hayman, p. 143.

31.   Pearce, p. 1155; see also Jim Hunter,
Tom Stoppard's Plays (New York: Grove,
1982), p. 127, who observes that "there is
probably no precedent for so lively and original
an artist choosing so regularly to work in and
out of classics, clichés, and popular culture:
the nearest parallels are in the
twentieth-century visual arts."   Also, see
Billman, p. 48, and Gold, p. 62, who suggest that
"**Travesties** seems to pick up where Shaw's
Heartbreak House leaves off."

32.   T. S. Eliot, "**Ulysses**, Order, and
Myth," in **Selected Prose of T. S. Eliot**, ed.
Frank Kermode (New York: Harcourt, 1975),
p. 177.

33.   Pearce, p. 1153; see also Whitaker,
p. 122, who observes that **Ulysses**, "which
transmutes fragments of art and life into a
multi-faceted and quasi-eternal object, is now
being imitated by a play that is itself derived
from reference to Wilde's **The Importance of
Being Earnest** and accounts events in Zurich
about 1917."

34.   Pearce, p. 1157.

35.   Gold, p. 59.

The Structure and Function of Tom Stoppard's
Travesties

Weldon B. Durham

The critical response to **Travesties** has focused on the play's statements about the relation between art and politics and on the truth of apparent assertions about historical incidents. For instance, Lucina P. Gabbard concludes that **Travesties** "demonstrates symbolically that art and entertainment are not effective tools for revolution and serious politics," and that the play "contradicts Lenin's notion of life's being too serious for art; instead it proclaims that art and entertainment possess a magic that the seriousness of life cannot do without." In Gabbard's view, **Travesties** answers dramatic questions and makes thematic statements.[1] Indeed, it does, but answering questions and making statements is not this play's reason for being. Eric Bentley has written of The Importance of Being Earnest, the dominant object of travesty in **Travesties**, that "nothing is easier than to handle this play without noticing what it contains."[2] It might be said that nothing is easier than to handle **Travesties** noticing little **else** than what it contains.

Stoppard's comments on his playwriting technique call attention to a "universal perception" which is the objective of his plays;[3] to "incredibly carefully thought-out structural pivots"; and to "a highly compressed form in the mind of the artist," a "nucleus" which "dictates what the tentacles do at the extremities of his conscious gift."[4] Clive James has asserted in an essay Stoppard has publicly admired that the character Moon in Stoppard's **Lord Malquist & Mr Moon** "is a guarantee that the supposedly

passionless intricacies of Stoppard's plays have
all unfolded from a preliminary intuition of
extreme intensity."[5]

Stoppard told Ronald Hayman in an interview
published in 1977: "One of the impulses in
Travesties is to sort out what my answer would
in the end be if I was given enough time to think
every time I'm asked why my plays aren't political, or ought they to be?"[6] But perhaps even
more poignantly, Stoppard remarked to Janet Watts
while writing the play: "I've never felt that
art is important. That's been my secret
guilt."[7] However, by 1976, Stoppard could tell
interviewer Steve Grant of **Time Out** that he
no longer felt guilty about being an artist.[8]
No sophisticated investigator would conclude from
these remarks alone that Stoppard had, in
Travesties, concretized and stylized his
engrossment in guilt over his calling as an
artist, thereby freeing himself from that
psychological burden, but the coincidence is
provocative. If **Travesties** and **Jumpers**
are only a little more substantially similar than
Stoppard has admitted in print,[9] then
Travesties might profitably be examined as if
it were rooted in feelings of guilt and as if the
composition of it had functioned to disemburden
Stoppard of guilt about his calling. Writing a
play or in any way fictionalizing or dramatizing
one's engrossment in a "preliminary intuition" or
in a "universal perception" allows an author to
"encompass" that perception, that is to maximize
consciousness of it. To allow the play to be
publicly performed and published is to seek to
share with audiences and readers the engrossing
intuition, to make them sensible of it through
stylization of the components of the play:
locale, character, structure, theme, and
language.[10] This essay will focus on the
locale and structure ("what the tentacles do at
the extremities of his conscious gift") of
Travesties in an effort to illuminate the
nuclear perception Stoppard was apparently trying
to work up into a functional form.

Travesties gazes with giddy double vision
on Oscar Wilde's 1895 farce, **The Importance of
Being Earnest.** Why Wilde's monument to
indolent drollery? According to Eric Bentley,

"the general conclusion has been that Wilde merely decorates a silly play with flippant wit." But Bentley goes on to direct attention to the "serious" social satire imbedded in the humor.[11] Wilde established a sophisticated outpost on the frontier between innocent playfulness and bitter criticism, between farce and satire, between empty witticisms over cucumber sandwiches and fiery rhetoric on a soapbox at Hyde Park corner. Such an outpost should compel the attention of a newspaperman, an author adept at parody and beset by guilt over having responded to a call to be an artist. **The Importance of Being Earnest** was the nearly perfect mirror into which Stoppard might have gazed as he sought to perfect his portrait of himself as an artist.

The locale of the action of **Travesties** sustains and amplifies the motive of the play. Zurich is a city imaginatively conceived in the image of art itself: "to be an artist **at all** is like living in Switzerland during a world war. To be an artist **in Zurich, in** 1917, implies a degree of self-absorption that would have glazed over the eyes of Narcissus."[12] On the other hand, "Switzerland," like art, "will not go away" (p. 26). Switzerland, like art, is blessed with a "reassuring air of permanence" (p. 26). Stoppard has said elsewhere that the function of art is to provide "the moral matrix . . . from which we make our judgments about the world."[13] Indeed, Joyce declares that "Zurich has become the theatrical center of Europe. Here culture is the continuation of war by other means" (p. 51). In another place, Zurich is the "still centre of the wheel of war" (p. 26). Zurich contains the fripperies of Henry Carr, the bizarre playfulness of Tristan Tzara, and the political obsessions of Lenin, just as does Stoppard's art. Stoppard's dramaturgy embraces these characters and characteristics as attributes, merely, while the play remains self-rather than other-absorbed, not toiling for social and political change, but poised as a still centre of moral sensibility. The drawing room of Henry Carr's apartment ("THE ROOM") and a section of the Zurich Public Library ("THE

LIBRARY") refine and particularize the image of
Switzerland as central **and** peripheral; however, the specific function of each of these
places can best be examined in relation to the
structure of the action.

Commentators who attend to the structure of
the full-length plays nearly universally remark
upon Stoppard's devotion to paradox and dialectic
as structural matrices. Statement is opposed to
counter-statement, as Stoppard urges one's
perceptions toward a transcendence of both A and
not-A, a transcendence that embraces A and not-A,
but reaches beyond these partial visions toward a
mystery. Richard Corballis's thesis in **Tom
Stoppard: The Mystery and the Clockwork** is
that the plays are binary in form: "an abstract,
artificial view of the world ('A') is pitted
against the flux of reality ('B'), and the
audience is invited to eschew the 'clockwork' of
the former in favour of the 'mystery' of the
latter."[14]   Later, Corballis observes that
"**Travesties** adheres to his [Stoppard's] customary structural pattern, which consists of a
pair of polar opposites straddled by something in
between." Corballis cites Margaret Gold to the
effect that Joyce is for art and Lenin for
politics, while Carr and Tzara mediate between--
Tzara standing for both art and politics, Carr
for neither.[15]   Both Corballis and Howard D.
Pearce have erected signposts indicating the
structural means by which **Travesties** functions. Pearce observes that **Travesties** is a
mirror, for:

> We are given back, in the imitative event,
> ourselves as well as the structures of our
> relationships with others. And we are cut
> loose from the event, realizing temporal
> mobility in the play of imagination. The
> mirror of stage does not singly imitate some
> object, but primarily puts us in play in a
> complex of referential structures. It does
> not merely show us an image of the world,
> but, like the mirror essential to seeing
> ourselves, puts us into that play of
> relationships.[16]

If Pearce's interpretation of the function of the
play as a mirror is reasonable (and I believe it
is), then **Travesties** has allowed Stoppard to
see himself, perchance to know himself "in play
in a complex of referential structures." But, I
would amend Pearce's interpretation still
further, for the play mirrors the structure of
our relationships with others, not only referentially, but also intra-referentially. One can
catch a glimpse of what the play has done for
Stoppard by looking closely at the way parts of
the play offer not only a fun house mirror of
The Importance of Being Earnest and myriad
other objects, as most commentators have done,
but also by looking closely at the way parts of
the play mirror one another.

While the play as a whole is a travesty of
The Importance of Being Earnest, each of the
two acts of the play is devoted to burlesque
deflation of earnestness of a certain sort. Act
I is the "art" act, while Act II is the
"politics" act. The absurd fripperies of Act I
build in a sequence that culminates in the scene
between Joyce (as Lady Bracknell, more or less)
and Tzara (as Jack). The subject of the question
"What is the meaning of this?" is not love,
however (as it is in **The Importance of Being
Earnest**), but poetry, specifically Dadaist
poetry (with which Joyce is covered). After
Joyce has bit by bit divested himself of the
poetry which has befallen him, he conjures from
the hat where he places the paper bits a white
carnation, some silk hankies, and, to illustrate
his answer to his own question regarding Dada's
gift of pictorial art, he extracts from the hat
the flags of Spain, the U. S. A., France, Italy,
and Russia. As the conjuring ends, Tzara's
growing rage peaks in curses ["My God, you
supercilious streak of Irish puke! . . . (p. 62)]
which mirror Carr's curses of Tzara ["My God, you
little Rumanian wog. . ." (p. 40)] and Tzara's
curses of Carr ["My God, you bloody English
philistine. . ." (p. 47)]. He then smashes
"whatever crockery is at hand," which violence
must be topped by the intensity and verve of
Joyce's eloquent defense of art: "An artist is

the magician put among men to gratify--
capriciously--their urge for immortality. . ."
(p.62ff).

In Act II, instruction displaces entertainment; in the intermission, "The Library" has
displaced "The Room," and the play resumes with
Cecily's lecture on Lenin. The playful mood of
Act I has been displaced by the recitation of
virtually unadorned "facts." The inverted mood
of the play is momentarily righted in a scene in
which Carr (as Tzara) makes a pass at Cecily, but
Cecily's function as teacher is assumed and
carried on by Nadya in a narrative concluding
with an account of Lenin's escape from Zurich.
Appropriately, this act climaxes in a segment of
the play including Lenin's oration (pp. 85-86),
Nadya's comments on it, and Nadya's continuing
account of Lenin's attitudes toward art, which is
punctuated by Lenin's enactment of portions of
her memoir. Implementation of Stoppard's stage
directions (p. 85) would make it clear to an
audience that Lenin's oration on artistic freedom
is the climax of Act II just as Tzara's smashing
of crockery would make it clear that Joyce's
reply is the climax of Act I. The two ideas of
the function of art articulated in these climac-
tic moments--to gratify through caprice man's
urge for immortality and to serve socialism
through sympathy with the working millions--are
the poles of the situation Stoppard explores in
Travesties.

Each of the two acts of **Travesties** is
divisible into five episodes. A discussion of
the complex relations among the episodes will be
facilitated by this diagram:

| ACT I | ACT II |
"Joyce and Art"	"Lenin and Politics"
A. Prologue: "The	A. Prologue: "The
Library" Joyce, Lenin,	Library" Cecily's lec-
and Tzara at their	ture. Joyce, Carr (as
places, composing.	Tzara), Lenin, and Nadya.
(pp. 17-21)	(pp. 66-70)

B. "The Room" as Old Carr begins his memoirs; seque to Zurich, 1917; travesty of **Earnest** begins with Carr-Bennett time slips cued to "I have put the newspapers and telegrams on the sideboard, sir." (pp. 21-32)

B. Carr as Tzara to spy on Lenin involved in a series of time slips as he makes a pass at Cecily. Time slips cued to "I don't think you ought to talk to me like that during library hours." (pp. 70-79)

C. Previews of later scenes between Carr and Tzara ("Rumanian nonsense") and between Carr and Joyce (in limerick form at manic pace); then Old Carr resumes his memoir; Young Carr and Tzara appear as Algernon and Jack in "What brings you here?," two long scenes and a connecting interlude involving Old Carr. (pp. 32-47)

C. Nadya continues Cecily's lecture--a narrative leading to Lenin's escape includes Carr's plans to stop the escape. (pp. 79-84)

D. Art as magic: the product of chance rather than reason or technique. Joyce offers Carr a role in **Earnest**; Tzara offers Gwen a poem; they are engaged. Joyce (as Lady Bracknell) confronts Tzara (as Jack), then conjures. (pp. 47-63)

D. Art as the product of state policy: Lenin's speech; Nadya's commentary on Lenin's views on art and artists. (pp. 85-89)

E. Concluding the
Joyce/art half of the
play: Off-stage voices
indicate off-stage
action slips back to
Tzara's entrance (as
Jack) to Carr (as
Algernon) at the
beginning of episode
D, p. 47; Old Carr
recalls the production
of **Earnest**, its
reception, and
subsequent conflict
with Joyce; "anybody
hanging on just for
the cheap comedy of
senile confusion might
as well go because I'm
on to how I met Lenin
and could have changed
the course of history"
cues the subject of
Act II. (pp. 63-65)

E. "The Room."
Dislocation of the play
begins and progresses
through 12 verses of "Mr.
Gallagher and Mr. Shean"
setting for parody of
Gwendolyn-Cecily scene;
Carr (as Tzara) is
exposed; manuscripts
confuse Carr and Tzara;
Joyce identifies manu-
scripts, which are
returned to the rightful
owners; lovers dance ("a
complete dislocation of
the play"); Carr
concludes that the lesson
of Zurich, 1917 is that
one is either an artist
or a revolutionary.
(pp. 89-99)

While the climax of each act is situated in
the fifth episode, other structural parallels are
evident. Each of the acts begins with a prologi-
cal episode--that is, each act begins with an
event or series of events which set the tone for
events to follow. Episode A of Act I reveals
"The Library" where Joyce, Lenin, and Tzara are
composing. The quiet, conventional scene is
first "dislocated" when Tzara cuts the paper upon
which he has been writing into word-sized bits,
dumps the bits in a hat and draws out the words,
one by one, their chance arrangement resulting in
a poem he reads in a loud voice. Joyce dictates
his apparently nonsensical composition to Gwen,
while Tzara makes another chance poem, which he
reads out one dislocated word at a time.
Cecily's rapid movements across the stage,
Tzara's exit, Gwen's exit, Nadya's entrance, and
her conversation with Lenin in Russian, all serve

to arouse audience expectations for the alogical
action to follow. Episode A of Act II seems
designed to reorient the audience to a new style.
Cecily waits patiently for the audience to come
in and sit down, then she begins to lecture on
Marx, the Russian reception of **Das Kapital**,
Lenin's first exposure to the book, and so on, in
an orderly but most untheatrical way. If the
prologue of Act I leads an auditor to expect
magic and other forms of nonsense to follow, then
the prologue of Act II leads an auditor to expect
information and argument.

Of course, neither expectation is immediately fulfilled, for Episode B of each act introduces a contradictory tone. The antic behaviors
of the first episode of Act I are followed by
Carr's rambling and senile discursus on how he
met Joyce, how he met Lenin, and how Dada came to
Zurich. Cecily's lecture is punctuated by the
appearance of Carr in disguise as Tzara to spy on
Lenin, and the second episode features Carr (as
Tzara as Jack Worthing as Jack's fictitious
brother, "Ernest") courting Cecily in the style
established as the mode of Act I.

Each act features a courtship: Tzara woos
Gwen with a poem in Episode C of Act I; Carr
makes a pass at Cecily in Episode B of Act II.
Naturally enough, each act ends with an episode
which functions as a denouement. Old Carr, true
to the promise of his monologue in Episode B,
wraps up his account of meeting Joyce and
announces he will go on to treat the subject of
how "he met Lenin and could have changed the
course of history." Episode E of Act II pursues
the parody of **Earnest** to the extreme of
setting the famous Gwendolyn-Cecily scene to the
tune of "Mr. Gallagher and Mr. Shean," wraps up
the business of the misplaced manuscripts, brings
the **Earnest** lovers together for a comedic
dance, and concludes with Old Carr's estimate of
the lesson he learned in Zurich in 1917: one is
either an artist **or** a revolutionary.

The structure of Act II is not, however,
simply a mirror of the structure of Act I; in
significant ways Act II is structured inversely
to Act I. It might be said that the two halves

of the play are related to one another the way
Joyce's costume in Act I is related to his
costume in Act II. In Act I, Joyce wears the
jacket from one suit and the trousers from
another; in Act II, he wears the other halves of
the outfit. Imagine the visual effect, and one
glimpses an emblem of the structure of the play.

The function of Episode A of Act I
resembles the function of Episode E of Act II in
that both are consciously designed to shock and
disorient an audience. Tzara's absurd method of
composition, Gwendolyn's farcical flutterings and
shushings, and the Russian-language dialogue of
Nadya and Lenin level expectations for a
conventional experience, to say nothing of the
impact of the surreal situation in which are
brought together Joyce, Lenin, Tzara, and a
character from **The Importance of Being
Earnest**. As I have observed, Episode E of Act
II is structured to climax in a comic revel, the
effect of which is "a complete dislocation of the
play" (p. 97). The link between the final
episode of Act I and the first episode of Act II
is less problematic. Old Carr narrates the end
of the Joyce story and promises to relate the
story of how he met Lenin. Act II provides the
Lenin story, but Carr doesn't tell it.

Episode B of Act I features Old Carr composing
his memories of two revolutionaries: Joyce and
Lenin. When the travesty of **Earnest** begins,
the content of the conversations between Young
Carr (as Algernon Moncrieff) and Bennett is
focused on the war and the Russian Revolution,
particularly on the latter. The episode presents
an artistic **reductio ad absurdum** of
revolution and revolutionaries. Episode D of Act
II presents a revolutionary's deflation of art
and artistry.

Episode B of Act II offers an inverted image
of many of the incidents and ideas presented in
Episode D of Act I. Both episodes feature a
scene of courtship: Tzara woos Gwendolyn and
Carr woos Cecily. But while Tzara and Gwendolyn
converse in language borrowed from Shakespeare,
Carr and Cecily engage in heated arguments over
the duty and justification of art and over the

relevance of Marxism (while Carr undresses Cecily
in his imagination!). Nevertheless, each couple
ends its scene in an embrace. In Act I, Carr
believes the operettas of Gilbert and Sullivan
(**Patience!, Trial by Jury!** . . . , **Pirates of
Penzance**) are evidence of England's world
leadership in dramatic art; in Act II Carr
counters Gwendolyn's assertion that "Art is a
critique of society or it is nothing!" with more
allusions to Gilbert and Sullivan operettas. In
both acts Oscar Wilde is unkindly characterized
(as "an Irish-coxcomb and bugbear of the Home
Rule sodality" by Cecily in Act I and as an
"Irish Gomorrahist" by Carr in Act II). Through
both episodes runs the unifying thread of the
issue of the nature and function of art: in Act
I "all poetry is a reshuffling of a pack of
picture cards, and all poets are cheats" (Tzara:
p. 53) or art has the quasi-religious function of
gratifying the urge for immortality (Joyce:
p. 62), while in Act II "Art **is** society!"
(Cecily: p. 74).

     So, while Act I makes comic fools of Joyce
and Tzara and denigrates through parody the kind
of art and the idea of art to which each is
associated, Act II, using the technique of
docudrama, illustrates the totalitarianism
implicit in Lenin's views of art, and, using
again the devices of travesty, undercuts the idea
of art as social criticism. Finally, no model
artist and no conventional idea of art emerges
unscathed from Stoppard's rending exploration of
the ideas of art and the ideal of the artist.
Such is the effect of the mirror structuring of
incidents that virtually every image of art
entering the world of this play is distorted for
comic effect and every aesthetic or political
impulse motivating the behavior of characters is
blunted or deflected. This analysis of the
significance of the locale and of the structure
of the action of **Travesties** lends more weight
to the position that Stoppard's full-length plays
are expressions of a writer agonized by uncertainty and paradox. In **Travesties** as in
Jumpers statement is opposed to counter-
statement. The imperatives of art are poised

against the imperatives of politics, but the
dialectic seems to lead to no synthesis--no
transcendence beyond these partial truths toward
a mystery. Neither art as the whimsical product
of detached self-absorption, nor as the magic
that accounts for the "difference between being a
man and being a coffee-mill," (p. 47) nor as the
repository of acquired wisdom, nor as a critique
of society, nor as a "cog in the Social
Democratic mechanism" (p. 85), nor as an
emotional stimulant making one "feel proud of the
miracles that human beings can perform" (p. 89),
nor art as any synthesis of any of these
functions can be the idea at the root of
Travesties. If Joyce's costume may be taken
as an emblem of key structural relationships in
the play, then the crockery Tzara smashes to
punctuate his curses of Joyce may be an emblem of
the motive of the play. After condemning Joyce
for turning "literature into religion," Tzara
proclaims:

> It's too late for geniuses! Now we need
> vandals and desecrators, simple-minded
> demolition men to smash centuries of baroque
> subtlety, to bring down the temple, and thus
> finally, to reconcile the shame and the
> necessity of being an artist! (p. 62)

Yet Tzara is not allowed to have the last word.
Joyce's physical immobility adds to the precision
of his cutting "You are an over-excited little
man, with a need for self-expression far beyond
the scope of your natural gifts" (p. 62), and his
eloquent defense of his motive to double the
immortality of Ulysses yet to leave the world
unchanged deflects Tzara's thrust and disarms the
Dadaist. No function of art is allowed to dominate the consciousness of the reader or viewer of
Travesties. "To travesty" is certainly the
motive of the play, and Stoppard's personal
situation as its composer seems surely to have
been dominated by a need to "reconcile the shame
and the necessity of being an artist."
    Travesty has a double function as regards
the writer's motive. It allows the writer to

venerate the object of the travesty while at the
same time gaining release from its hold on the
imagination. The travesty is an expression of
the writer's dependence on the object as well as
an expression of his independence from it, or,
more pointedly, of his **desire** for liberation
from it.[17] Writes Jim Hunter: "Allusion and
travesty are at the heart of Stoppard's work.
They assert irreverence for sacred cows, the
artist displaying his freedom; they work by
rebounds, one off another; and they are forms of
homage."[18] In a similar vein, Lucina P.
Gabbard concludes that "the plays individually
deal with a myriad of separate, significant
questions; but from the telescopic view, all ask
one question: Why is man unable to be free--of
inadequacy, of conformity, of guilt, of
uncertainty, and of oppression?"[19] In
Gabbard's view, "the deepest-seated
characteristic of the Stoppard plays is their
basis in . . . the wish to be free and the wish
to know" (p. 11). Thomas R. Whitaker joins this
chorus with this observation: "Even when seeming
ambivalent on almost every issue, Stoppard's work
has always implied a firm belief in freedom of
expression."[20]
     This analysis of the locale and structure of
Travesties suggests that art is both central
and peripheral in the world as re-created in
Stoppard's imagination. As was the Oscar Wilde
of **The Importance of Being Earnest,** so is the
Stoppard of **Travesties** compulsively alienated
by earnestness of any sort. Freedom from literary imperatives for drama--meaning, coherence--as
well as freedom from political imperatives for
literature--social relevance, political sub-
stance--are needs **Travesties** is structured to
fulfill. Stoppard has organized his materials as
an elaborate stylization of his quandary as an
artist compelled to live with unreconciled
feelings about his calling. "I JUST DON'T KNOW"
he seems to say[21] as he asks the auditor to
join him in the task of "smashing centuries of
baroque subtlety" as regards the role of art in
society.

Notes

1. Lucina P. Gabbard, **The Stoppard Plays** (Troy, New York: Whitston Publishing Co., 1982), pp. 116-17.

2. Eric Bentley, **The Playwright as Thinker** (New York: Reznal and Hitchcock, 1946), p. 172.

3. Tom Stoppard, "Ambushes for the Audience," **Theatre Quarterly,** 4 (May-July 1974), 13.

4. Cited in Ronald Hayman, **Tom Stoppard** (London: Heinemann, 1977), p. 2.

5. Clive James, "Count Zero Splits the Infinite," **Encounter,** 45 (November 1975), 74.

6. Hayman, p. 2.

7. Janet Watts, "Tom Stoppard," **Guardian** (21 March 1973), p. 12.

8. Steve Grant, "Serious Frivolity," **Time Out** (18 June 1976), p. 7.

9. Hayman, p. 12. See also Weldon B. Durham, "Symbolic Action in Tom Stoppard's **Jumpers**," **Theatre Journal,** 32 (May 1980), 169-79.

10. For a discussion of the idea of literature as "symbolic action," see Kenneth Burke, **The Philosophy of Literary Form,** rev. ed. (New York: Vintage Books, 1957).

11. Eric Bentley, pp. 172-77.

12. Stoppard, **Travesties** (New York: Grove Press, 1975), p. 38. Subsequent page numbers in parentheses in the text refer to this edition of the play.

13. "Ambushes for the Audience," p. 13.

14. Richard Corballis, **Tom Stoppard: The Mystery and the Clockwork** (New York: Methuen, 1984), p. 15.

15. Corballis, p. 77.

16. Howard D. Pearce, "Stage as Mirror: Tom Stoppard's **Travesties**," **Modern Language Notes**, 94 (1979), 1157.

17. Travesty was a staple of the English and American stage of the nineteenth century, when burlesque treatments of **Hamlet, Macbeth, The Merchant of Venice, Othello,** and **Richard III** were quite common. In many respects **The Importance of Being Earnest** is a travesty of W. S. Gilbert's **Patience** (1881), itself a travesty of popular sentimental comedies such as T. W. Robertson's **Caste** (1867).

18. Jim Hunter, **Tom Stoppard's Plays** (London: Faber and Faber, 1982), p. 132.

19. Gabbard, p. 152.

20. Thomas R. Whitaker, **Tom Stoppard** (New York: Grove Press, 1983), p. 132.

21. "My plays are a lot to do with the fact that I JUST DON'T KNOW . . ." ("Ambushes for the Audience," p. 3).

Travesties: Plot and the Moral Tilt

Shirley Shultz and Russell Astley

Since Tom Stoppard is perhaps our première
virtuoso of the play of ideas, it is no wonder
that critics and reviewers have focused on the
ideas in his plays. This approach has led to the
now widely-held opinion that the debates featured
in the plays conclude inconclusively, that they
intentionally end in a balance of doubt, and that
therefore the plays themselves render no final
judgments. (This interpretation is most
prevalent with regard to plays up to
Travesties; many writers detect growing
explicit commitment after this.) We have no wish
to dispute assertions that the debates **per se**
are purposely inconclusive. But we do want to
deny that it follows from this that the play is
therefore inconclusive, and we want to claim that
views narrowed to the merely intellectual have
missed the way certain intrinsic dramatic
elements give a moral--even ideological--tilt to
the outcomes of Stoppard's plays. The particular
play we examine here is **Travesties** and we
concentrate on one of the most neglected of these
intrinsic elements, the plot itself.

The charge of plotlessness is often lodged
against Stoppard's plays. In "Plays Without
Plot: The Theatre of Tom Stoppard," for example,
Gabrielle Scott Robinson writes that "Stoppard
expresses his basic sense of disorder . . .
indirectly . . . by a lack of development and
coherence in his plots, which are constructed
episodically of a chain of arguments and
counterarguments."[1] And with regard to
Travesties in particular, Kenneth Tynan
proclaims the total absence of "the sine qua non
of theatre; namely, a narrative thrust that

211

impels the characters . . . toward a credible
state of crisis, anxiety, or desperation."[2]
Even Stoppard's notorious raiding of other works
and genres seems to meet with a lack of specifically literary curiosity. Bobbi Wynne
Rothstein, for instance, maintains that Stoppard
borrows and modifies plots and other literary
elements only in order to draw attention to
patterns, rules and other such formal gamelike
features in and for themselves.[3] Views like
these, where they are not plainly false,
nevertheless lead us to ignore much of Stoppard's
achievement in **Travesties**. What they tend to
distract us from is what the plot in that play
actually comprises and what work that complex
plot is doing. One of the things it is doing, we
will argue, is effecting a moral tilt.

   At least two questions about the borrowed
plot in **Travesties** need to be asked and
answered: Why does Stoppard use the **Earnest**
plot in the first place? and why isn't it
sustained once imported? The short answer to
both is that the appropriation of the **Earnest**
plot is rooted in the psychology of an internal
author whose design cannot be realized within the
confines of that plot. Stoppard has confessed
that while writing **Travesties** he was aware of
feeling "uneasy in trying to work out questions
that involve **oneself**, in terms of authentic
geniuses."[4] His artistic solution to this
embarrassment is to interpose a **persona**
between himself and the historical figures of
Joyce, Lenin, and Tzara. The consciousness of
the authentic non-genius Henry Carr thus becomes
the prism[5] through which issues relating to the
conflict between art and politics get sorted out
and displayed. To understand what happens to the
plot we need to understand the character dynamics
of its internal author.

   Carr as fantasizer/rememberer creates
virtually the entire play. In his consciously
professed beliefs he epitomizes the bourgeois
conventionality of his day. Yet his repressed
negative experiences of the war and other
repudiated feelings clash with his beliefs and
ironically undercut them. Most of his inner

dissonances can be recognized as versions of the
inveterate rivalry of pleasure and duty which is
also the principal moral dialectic of **The
Importance of Being Earnest.** He attempts to
deal with these inner problems by externalizing
them in the larger-than-life figures of a
fanciful reconstruction of his youth. Old Carr
presents, as leading man of this fantasy "play-
within-the-play," a Young Carr who upholds a
stern morality while indulging in frivolous
pleasures; at the same time he projects a Tristan
Tzara who is a dedicated anarchist yet who
affects a dandyism which Young Carr himself more
authentically exemplifies. Proud of his
"triumph" in the role of Algernon in Joyce's
production of **Earnest** and of his knack for
limericks, Carr is an artiste manqué who uses
the figure of Joyce partly to magnify this
frustrated component of his personality.
Basically, Carr projects these particular
repudiated or unrealized bits of himself onto
artists because his enjoyment of being invalided
out of the horrors of the first world war into
placid, pleasant Zurich stirs in him a guilt too
distressing to confront squarely. And he
resentfully criticizes the non-combatant artists
for their very lack of such guilt. On the other
hand, he projects onto Lenin his own moralistic
sense of the good as tedious, even painful duty
which is at odds with our natural delight in
beauty.
        Despite survivor-guilt and resentment of
artists, Carr is nostalgic for his **Earnest**
moment of stardom and his courting of Cecily--
which in retrospect loom as the twin pinnacles of
a long life of very modest satisfactions. To
glamorize stardom and courtship he seizes upon
Earnest. However, insofar as he must deal
with his guilt and resentment he cannot use it
unalloyed. He therefore blends his **Earnest**
with a conventionally melodramatic spy thriller,
casting himself as hero, a transformation which
has the effect of elevating his private conflicts
to the level of international urgencies. And,
compensating for his actual obscurity, he
pictures himself as an important public figure,
British Consul in Zurich and Friend of the

Famous. On this world-historical stage the
personal conflict of pleasure and duty realizes
itself more naturally as a public debate on
international art and politics. This elevation,
in turn, has the further effect of endowing
Carr's **Earnest** with an air of generality
which its original did not possess. Old Carr, in
fact, re-constitutes the **Earnest** world as a
nostalgic caricature of the pre-World War I West.
He dreams a social order that could securely
indulge in frivolous pastimes and **art pour
l'art**. But it is, at both private and public
levels, an order of gaiety maintained by the
strict exclusion of all that is grave and
passionate in human life, and these excluded
elements will not allow it to proceed
untroubled.

Act I centers around aesthetics and
pleasure, and the plot tends to exploit scenes
from Wilde both to occasion debates on art and
love and to establish a love story. This
Earnest world is repeatedly derailed by
intrusions of Carr and Tzara's personal
passions--Carr's horror about the war and Tzara's
fury against what art has become--and has to be
started up again and again by Carr's undiscour-
ageable will. But the eruptions are never
serious enough to overwhelm the love story or
chase **Earnest** from the stage for very long.
In Act 2, however, the emphasis shifts from
aesthetics and pleasure to politics and duty and
weightier criticisms are registered, especially
in regard to the position and character of Lenin.
This new austerity does succeed in chasing the
fun-loving **Earnest** world from the stage for
long stretches of dramatic time. **Earnest**
steals back only in disguised form, as Carr's
ludicrous spy thriller with romance subordinated
and, at the crisis, sacrificed to political
obligation. This previously downplayed aspect of
the plot now swells and transfigures the
Earnest line and, hence, exerts a more
ominously profound effect than the temporary
disruptions of Act 1.

In fact the melodramatic spy twist to Carr's
comedy inevitably implicates it in a clear scheme

of moral evaluation. Good and bad may be
irrelevant to or remain unresolved in comedy or
farce; in melodrama they are of the essence.
Insofar as we play along with a melodrama we must
accept--however ironically--its moral schema: we
must identify its hero and its villain if we are
simply to make out the plot. Here Carr is the
hero, Lenin the villain. And thus a moral tilt
imposes itself upon the action that grounds the
otherwise morally inconclusive debate. Can we
merely shrug off this moral weighting when we
leave the theater and put together our "final"
response to Stoppard's play? There is reason to
think not. Doubtless we do discount exaggera-
tions on both sides, but surely no one would want
to claim the play gives us any warrant for
reversing the sides. Although we laugh off
Carr's naive elaborations and self-serving
distortions of history, we are left with a
residual feeling that he represents something
basically decent, if ineffective, while Lenin in
retrospect continues to look fanatic and all too
effective. This feeling, as the following analysis of the plot will show, is in no sense
extrinsic to the play.

Carr's naive image of a sophisticated,
hedonistic Zurich is established in Act 1 by an
obvious recall of the first scene of **Earnest**.
Old Carr adorns his younger self with the
polished style of Wilde's Algernon, promoting
himself to the position of Consul (which he
however treats with Wildean nonchalance) and
demoting the historical consul, Bennett, to
something not far from his own real-life
position. He dramatizes the critical year of his
life as if it had all occurred within the
glittering world of the one play he was a great
success in. But memories intrude and derail the
fantasy. Most time-slips occur because Carr
experiences as violent passion some aspect of his
repressed conflict between duty and pleasure, so
that he momentarily loses his grip on the
immediate, self-glamorizing story line. He
nevertheless wants desperately at this stage to
stay focused on the pleasures of the bourgeoisie
and to paper over or simply ignore the ugly

realities of the trenches and the Russian
Revolution. When Carr tries to fit Tzara into
his **Earnest** scheme, its world again proves
too fragile to contain forceful negative
emotions. Tzara shatters the Wildean mold with
his passionately destructive message of anti-art,
"**shouting, raving**" the word "dada" over and
over.[6]

As mentioned above, however, the momentary
disruptions Carr and Tzara cause do not threaten
to annihilate the **Earnest** world. Moreover,
the characters remain securely identified
respectively with Algernon and Jack. The other
major character in the **Earnest** scheme is
Joyce, associated with Wilde's dominating
matriarch, Aunt Augusta. This world's fixation
on aesthetic pleasure virtually entails a
prominent role for this archetypal artist. The
only character who does not figure in the
Earnest scheme at all is Lenin. And it is
the dramatic presence of Lenin--both as
antagonist to artistic freedom and as source of
changes more sweeping and radical than the
momentary disruptions Tzara and Carr
occasion--that catalyzes the nearly total
transformation of **Earnest** into a spy
thriller.

In Act 2 the levity of the first act's
Wildean Zurich is displaced by a new center of
gravity. The formal symmetry of the two acts
emphasizes the contrast. There are three
elements of each act which are notably symmetrical: the frames, the prologue to Act 1 and its
reenactment in Act 2, and the dominant settings.
Act 1 is framed by Old Carr's monologue near the
beginning and his monologue at the end, both of
which refer to his performance in **Earnest**.
The Act 2 frame consists of Young Cecily's
introductory monologue in the form of a lecture,
and, at the end of the act, Old Cecily's
lecturing of Old Carr to expose the fantastic
unreality of his story. The substitution of
speakers underlines the shift of focus from Young
Carr's performance in **Earnest**--that is to
say, from art or aesthetic pleasure--to history
and the performance of duty. The dominant

impression of the play's prologue in the Zurich
library is an evocation of the nonsensical
activities associated with Dada; in the second
act virtually the same scene is re-enacted but
now fraught with unmistakeable world-historical
political significance. Also this time, with
Cecily "pedantically" translating every word of
Lenin and Nadya's conversation, we are forced to
understand what Lenin is about, and we cannot
laugh it off as mere nonsense. To further mark
how **Earnest** has become a spy thriller, Young
Carr, now a spy disguised as the Dadaist Tristan
Tzara, wears the very costume he had earlier
decided on for his role as Algernon (52). The
two acts are also set in two very different sorts
of rooms, the insulated, dandyish **Earnest**
world of Carr's drawing room giving way to the
public library, now associated with the wider
world of political seriousness.

     The spy plot itself observes the traditional
form of the well-made play (with easily identifiable exposition, inciting moment, complication,
crisis, and denouement) as well as many of the
more specific conventions of its genre. Though
its transformation of the Wildean world only
comes to dominate our attention in Act 2, the
ground has already been thoroughly prepared by
the first act's way of recalling the first two
scenes of **Earnest**. In fact, Old Carr
appropriates the whole first scene between Lane
and Algernon from Wilde's play principally as
exposition for his own spy adventure by
substituting for Wilde's nineteenth century
erotic topics twentieth century political ones,
specifically the world war and the revolution in
Russia. The "inciting moment" occurs when the
Minister in Berne sends a telegram suggesting
that Carr "take all steps to ascertain . . .
[Lenin's] plans." Thus Young Carr like the
conventional spy "gets his assignment," and the
outlines of a regulation spy thriller begin to
take form. The naive personal relations of the
Earnest world are here infected at the start
by the threat represented by Lenin. And in the
last replay of the Tzara/Jack entrance, Tzara
explains his "Jack" identity with reference to

Lenin. To get a card at the Library without
alienating the anti-dada Lenin, who happened to
be present, Tzara had pretended to be his own
(invented) older brother. The double-identity
dodge gives Carr the idea to disguise himself as
"Jack" Tzara's prodigal brother, Tristan, the
better to spy on Lenin. Stoppard's Cecily
contrasts here with Wilde's in initially
capturing Young Carr's attention mainly as a
possible means to carry out his "assignment" to
investigate Lenin.

With the shift in Act 2, the **Earnest**
elements are subsumed more fully than in Act 1 by
conventions of the spy melodrama, and the threat
grows more ominous. Carr and Cecily re-enact
Algernon and Cecily's meeting in Wilde's play.
But the scene does not merely hint at the spy
thriller as did the Wilde scenes in Act 1; it now
entirely fulfills a well-known spy-story convention: Carr as secret agent meets the obligatory
beautiful woman "on the other side" with whom
the spy of the classic kind becomes romantically
involved.

Even the conflict between Carr's personal
pleasure in Cecily and his public obligations as
a spy is congruent with a classic formulation of
the spy's character as "filled with rebellion on
the inside while showing complicity on the
outside. . . ."[7] Indeed, Carr's whole
invention of the spy thriller is an attempt to
demonstrate enthusiastic complicity with his
society while his hypocrisy about his duty and
his exhibition of his repressed thoughts betray
the rebellion of the inner man, as shown for
example in his hallucinatory transformation of a
Leninist scolding by Cecily into an erotic
striptease.

Limited to the **Earnest** world, Cecily's
misunderstanding of Carr's real identity would
likely have led to a series of amusing complications eventually straightened out in a festive
ending. As part of the spy thriller, however,
this misunderstanding has more serious consequences which lead, in fact, to Carr's failure in
his great mission. Carr-as-spy pops up from
behind the desk hiding Cecily and Carr-as-lover,

establishing thereby that he is overhearing
Lenin's secret plan to return to Russia.
However, busy off-stage a moment later with
Cecily's weeping over Jack/Tzara's refusing
Tristan/Carr's hand in brotherly reconciliation,
Young Carr loses his one opportunity to learn
that the plan to leave from Berne he has
overheard has been abandoned and a new one to
leave from Zurich formed the very same day.
Carr's pursuing his mission with this wrong
information evokes yet another cliché of the
spy genre, namely, the red herring to throw the
hero off the track.

  To be absolutely sure we do not miss the
point, the stage goes suddenly dark except for a
light on Old Carr, who stops the action to
underline the crisis of his story of Young Carr,
British spy. Old Carr spells out his dilemma,
basically a conflict of love and duty: "I'd got
pretty close to [Lenin], had a stroke of luck
with a certain little lady and I'd got a pretty
good idea of his plans, in fact I might have
stopped the whole Bolshevik thing in its tracks,
but--here's the point. **I was uncertain.**
What was the right thing? And then there were my
feelings for Cecily." Carr then presents his
role in the classic mold: on the success or
failure of the hero's assignment hangs the fate
of civilization. "So there I was, the lives of
millions of people hanging on which way I'd move,
or whether I'd move at all, another man might
have cracked . . ." (**Travesties**, p. 81).
Here surely is Tynan's "sine qua non": a
theatrically highlighted "state of crisis,
anxiety, or desperation." To deny it
"credibility" would be to deny the play the right
to its own imaginative premises.

  Knowing only the abandoned plan, Young Carr
deliberates his course of action. His inner
debate is externalized as an unlocalized and
non-temporalized conversation with his alter-ego,
Tzara, off in one corner of the stage while, on
another part of the stage, Nadya continues a
"documentary," equally unlocalized in time or
space, of the actual new plans being formed. We
see a split-stage on which two pseudo-dialogues
proceed in counterpoint.

The countdown to Lenin's departure recalls
another aspect of the typical spy thriller:
there must be a "ticking time bomb, a countdown,
by which pursuit, delay, movement are measured in
absolute terms . . . . Without a timetable, one
cannot know how late it is."[8] The dates Nadya
carefully lists in documentary style evoke the
suspense of the enemy's flight, while Carr
unaware vacillates. The psuedo-dialogues draw
toward a simultaneous ironic conclusion: Young
Carr patriotically chooses duty over love and
decides to risk alienating Cecily by telegraphing
his inside information to the Minister to prevent
Lenin's escape. But as he reaches his decision
to telegraph Berne, we hear the famous train
chugging out of Zurich, bearing Lenin to the
Finland Station and his role as "leader of
millions" (**Travesties**, p. 96).

The young spy has failed in his mission; the
counterspies, Tzara and Bennett, by passing on
Allied secrets, have sabotaged his mission and
abetted Lenin's (**Travesties**, pp. 72–73); and
Joyce has aided the enemy by his principled
disengagement. Lenin, the enemy, has escaped.

In hindsight Old Carr shows that he now
understands clearly that Lenin **was** an
important enemy by having him appear alone in a
spotlight. Looking exactly as Old Carr earlier
recalls him from the famous May 1920 photo
(**Travesties**, pp. 23–24), Lenin recites
totalitarian, repressive prescriptions for art
and society. Much of the material in this and
the other Lenin sections is taken from sources,
some of which Nadya cites, written or published
long after the events in this play are depicted
as having taken place. It is necessary to insist
on the anachronism because it indicates that Old
Carr, the ambient mind, knows these things only
in this second-hand way, thus underscoring Young
Carr's inevitable lack of comprehension of the
full seriousness of the threat.

Despite his knowledge, Old Carr ignores
Lenin and imposes his own solution to the
conflicts between duty and pleasure, politics and
art by re-establishing the dominance of the
Earnest plot. But after such knowledge, what

forgiveness? The denouement Carr finally
presents must now appear incredibly naive and, as
Cecily points out, even pathetic. The Wilde
world itself is made to seem yet more ludicrous
when the tea-service tiff of Wilde's Cecily and
Gwendolen becomes a music-hall routine with
choreographed tea-drinking. Carr and Tzara
enter, both carrying folders. As in **Earnest**,
after the confusion of identities is straightened
out, there is "one more question," which in
Travesties becomes the ladies' desire to know
what their suitors thought of the manuscripts
they read. Carr and Tzara's misdirected negative
criticisms alienate the women, who proclaim such
"intellectual differences . . . an insuperable
barrier!" (**Travesties**, p. 94). This barrier
is immediately lifted as the switched manuscripts
of Joyce and Lenin are correctly recognized and
the negative criticisms disarmed by the return of
the works to their appropriate contexts of art
and politics respectively.

The scene dissolves into a period dance and
a joyful ending for all--except Lenin. Old Carr
drives his courtship tale to the same happy
though superficial conclusion as occurs in
Wilde's comedy, with all love knots appropriately
tied. But he does so at the cost of banishing
Lenin from the stage altogether. Because his
tale of espionage ends in anticlimactic failure,
he must expunge the shadow of the Bolshevik
menace from the brightly lit carousel of his
Wildean festive ending. This solution suggests a
resolution to the play's debate that is really
consonant with Joyce and Carr's view: art and
revolutionary politics cannot or should not be
confused; they are, in terms Stoppard himself
proposed, "mutually exclusive."[9] But it is
only in the bright fairyland of Carr's
Earnest, aloof from the exigencies of a real
Europe, that such a resolution could conceiveably
seem satisfactory. And to underline the
fantastic nature of everything so far, Old Cecily
waltzes in at the play's end with her bucket of
cold historical fact to dash against Carr's cozy
illusion.

Yet in a larger sense, the world-historical
images Old Carr's egotistic melodrama deploys

strongly suggest a generalized reading whose
forces and figures have representative significance. Carr is himself defined against the
unfreedom of the kind of totalitarian society
implied by Lenin's personality and principles.
In response to the artists' self-absorption, Carr
strikes what is perhaps the archetypal Western
anti-totalitarian attitude: he assumes the role
of defender of everyone's right to be wrong.
Thus, as he moves among these near-mythical
figures at the center of epoch-making events,
Carr too takes on an aura of the emblematic. In
the countdown scene, for example, it is comic
megalomania when Carr fantasizes that the fate of
millions depends on his decision whether to stop
Lenin, thereby deflecting the Russian revolution
toward democracy and, by assuring Russia's
continued help to the Allies, shortening the war.
But at the same time something very like a
political cartoon of mythic dimensions is
suggested in which Carr stands for the West
debating with itself at inordinate length, in a
style all too typical of democratic procedures,
at the precise moment when threats to its way of
life call for decisive action. At this emblematic level the roles in Carr's melodrama of failed
heroism cohere to constitute a moral allegory or
abbreviated myth of the fall of twentieth century
Western civilization and the characters become
exemplary. From the examples of Carr and Joyce,
we may draw the lesson that those who believe in
this civilization are ill-prepared to defend it.
From the examples of Tzara and Bennett, we may
observe that others, in the shelter of its
freedoms, work to destroy it and aid the cause of
enemies such as Lenin.

But **Travesties** is a comedy, not a
political tract. Its ideological presumptions
are buffered by the usual ifs and buts of
non-didactic art: If **Travesties** were a work
avowedly about the career of the West in this
century, it would present this ideological view
of the international drama; but the play actually
puts before us only one man's self-aggrandizing
and plainly false fantasy version of that drama,
from which we can logically conclude nothing

about history. Art, however, does not live by
logic alone. Partly **because** we are not
attending to the larger ideological melodrama
which is the scaffolding or framework for the
foregrounded misadventures and conflicts of views
among individual characters, this background
remains in the unscrutinized realm of the
taken-for-granted.

    There can be little doubt that
Travesties illustrates Stoppard's own view of
art and politics. Shortly before he finished
writing the play in 1974 he declared that,
although the criterion for judging art should be
aesthetic and not ethical or political, he was
not opposed to political art.[10] Contrary to
what may be too hastily assumed, the Stoppard of
that time already saw art as an agent of change.
But he distinguished between short- and long-term
effects.[11] Stoppard held that "art . . . is
important because it provides the moral matrix,
the moral sensibility, from which we make our
judgments about the world."[12] Old Carr keeps
compulsively restarting the Wilde world's
merry-go-round after each breakdown without ever
squarely facing and conquering the causes of the
intrusions. When, however, he presents Young
Carr as finally understanding the real danger to
his pleasure-loving freedom and his duty to
arrest that danger, it is too late to prevent
Lenin's return to Russia, and hence the door is
opened to the totalitarian transformation of
Western civilization already portrayed by
Stoppard as a **fait accompli** in the dystopian
future of **Jumpers**. Carr seems to be
acquiescing in his failure when he again returns
to the Wilde plot on the heels of the scene
revealing his failure to stop Lenin. He
contrives a solution to the debate on art and
politics, but it is a solution so frail that it
is secure only in a travesty of the Wildean
satire of prelapsarian Western society. Through
its morally weighted melodramatic plot,
Travesties has managed to show us a great
deal of the Stoppardian moral--and ideological--
matrix.

Notes

1. **Educational Theatre Journal,** 29
(March 1977), 37.

2. **Show People: Profiles in
Entertainment** (New York: Simon and Schuster,
1980), p. 109.

3. "Playing the Game: The Work of Tom
Stoppard," Diss. University of Rhode Island, 1979,
p. 40ff.

4. Ronald Hayman, **Tom Stoppard** (Totowa,
N. J.: Rowman and Littlefield, 1977), p. 117.

5. **Prism** was once the working title of
Travesties. See Hayman, p. 117.

6. Tom Stoppard, **Travesties** (New York:
Grove Press, 1974), p. 47.

7. Robin Winks, **Modus Operandi: An
Excursion into Detective Fiction** (Boston:
David R. Godine, 1982), p. 54.

8. Winks, p. 52.

9. "Ambushes for the Audience: Towards a
High Comedy of Ideas" (Tom Stoppard interviewed
by the editors), **Theatre Quarterly,** 4 (May –
July 1974), 16.

10. "Ambushes," p. 14.

11. Janet Watts, "Interview with Tom
Stoppard," **Guardian,** 21 March 1973, p. 12.

12. "Ambushes," p. 14: see also pp. 15, 16.

Breaking the Stalemate:
The Stoppard Comedies Since **Travesties**

Katherine E. Kelly

It is no longer news that something has
changed in the Stoppard comedies since 1974, but
little of the commentary on the "politicizing of
Tom Stoppard" has recognized in this change a
major readjustment of subject and treatment
amounting to a shift in his poetic.[1]
Travesties, Stoppard's 1974 defense of art's
disinterestedness, marks the end of his early
play of ideas. It was a form characterized by
heavy borrowing from the structures and speeches
of other works of art, by a meticulous detachment
from the points of view expressed by the characters and by a symmetrical dividing of stage space
usually into two distinct playing areas, each
devoted to one of the two or more ideas at war in
the action. Writing **Travesties** appears to
have freed Stoppard to loosen the style and
context in which to examine the relation between
art and politics. The three plays central to
this shift include the musical docu-drama **Every
Good Boy Deserves Favor**, the television play
Professional Foul and the dramatic twins
Dogg's Hamlet, Cahoot's Macbeth, all written
between the summer of 1977 and the spring of
1979, and all set in the East in countries
resembling the U.S.S.R. and Czechoslovakia, where
Stoppard had spent one week with a representative
of Amnesty International in 1977.[2] I will
argue that together, these three political
comedies accomplish the poetic shift and lay the
groundwork for the more ambitious stage plays,
Night and Day (1978) and **The Real Thing**
(1982) that have followed them.[3]
In many respects, the three eastern
transitional plays invert the conventions of the

earlier plays of ideas, but they also signal a
new loosening of style and argument that
coincides with the playwright's growing interest
in situational ethics and in the dialectical
tension between experience and belief. In one of
the most obvious inversions of his earlier works,
Stoppard's political plays remove the action from
the West to the East, where the moral paralysis
of characters like George Moore is replaced by
the moral confidence of characters like Pavel
Hollar and Alexander Ivanov. Through this
geographical transfer, Stoppard locates his
characters in a fictional culture that offers
them a clearer sense of moral alternatives, of
right and wrong actions and beliefs, than that
afforded by the West. His characters trapped in
totalitarianism ironically enjoy greater freedom
from intellectual paralysis than their "free"
western counterparts who struggle to know what it
is that they believe and why they think that they
believe it.

        Written and aired in 1977, **Professional
Foul**, Stoppard's first television play since
The Engagement (1970), takes as its central
situation a naive westerner's visit to
Czechoslovakia where he is temporarily entrapped
in a government plot to jail a dissident. The
camera takes us on board a plane bound for Prague
where Professor Anderson, J. S. Mill Professor of
Ethics at the University of Cambridge, is preparing without much enthusiasm to speak officially
at a philosophy colloquium and guiltily planning
with a great deal of enthusiasm to attend the
World Cup Soccer Match where he hopes to see the
British defeat the Czechs. As he converses with
another philosopher on board the plane, we catch
glimpses of earlier Stoppardian characters. Like
George Riley of **Enter a Free Man**, Anderson
prefers daydreams to practical problem solving
and erotic magazines to the colloquium's
brochure. Like Henry Carr, the less than
reliable narrator of **Travesties**, Anderson
suspects the "easiness" of avant-garde philosophy. Like Albert, the university drop-out of
Stoppard's 1969 radio play, **Albert's Bridge**,
Anderson has a passion for fixity and order
aroused by the suspicious "wagging" of the

airplane's wings: "Solid steel. Thick as a bank
safe. Flexing like tree branches. It's not
natural."[4] As oblivious as Albert to the
actual properties of metal under stress, Anderson
can not be expected to recognize that the steel's
flexibility is also the guarantee of its
strength. But unlike Stoppard's earlier heroes,
the Cambridge Don does eventually learn to bend
under pressure in the course of the action,
discovering the strength that comes from
flexibility. Anderson differs from earlier
heroes in other ways, as well, having grown in
distinction and confidence since his incarnation
as George Moore of **Jumpers** fame. While Moore
admits to cutting "a ludicrous figure in the
academic world," Anderson is admired by a younger
colleague aboard the plane, in spite of his
apparent boredom with the chief philosophical
questions of the day. Unlike Moore, who was kept
as a sort of humanist "pet" by the Rad-Libs,
Anderson has a recognized place among doers of
contemporary philosophy. Once in Prague, the
Cambridge Don will behave like a typical, if more
refined, Stoppardian philosopher until the play's
final scenes, when he will overcome hesitation,
come down off the fence and act on his beliefs.

Once Anderson reaches Prague, the action
splits just about evenly between scenes involving
westerners and scenes of Czech life, the former
played comically, the latter seriously. This,
too, shows the playwright varying an older
pattern, substituting for the argument-objec-
tion-reply sequences in the earlier plays a more
subtle and implicit argumentation relying upon
the syncopating effect of alternating serious and
comic scenes. Scenes 6 and 7, the structural
fulcrum of the play, show this large dialectical
swing between East and West, seriousness and
comedy, at its most powerful. As Scene 6 opens,
Professor Anderson is stopping briefly at Pavel
Hollar's apartment in Prague to return to his
former student a manuscript Hollar had hoped
Anderson would smuggle out of the country.
Anderson has refused to help Hollar, a critic of
his government's human rights policies, on the
grounds that it would be "bad manners" for him to

do so while a guest of the Czech government.[5]
But what he learns at the Hollar apartment and
later, from Hollar's wife and son, changes his
views of both manners and morals. This serious
sixth scene takes us away from the western hotel
and into the Czech's apartment, where Anderson
soon realizes he has mistakenly blundered into a
secret police search for evidence to incriminate
the Czech dissident. The arrival at the apartment, the atmosphere of fear and suspicion, the
confusing presence of secret police, the babble
of Czech and broken English all convey quickly
and intensely to Anderson and to the viewer the
terror of the police operation, the details for
which Stoppard took in part from documented
evidence, public testimony and personal experience.[6] Once inside the apartment, the police
detain Anderson, who reluctantly gives his
tickets to a plainclothesman and resigns himself
to listening to the match on Mrs. Hollar's radio.
The two actions—the police search and the Match
of the Day—proceed simultaneously and simultaneously reach a point of crisis that amounts to a
complex commentary on Czech and British rules for
fair behavior. Moments after the English-speaking Colonel advises Anderson that Hollar is being
charged with a currency offense like "an ordinary
criminal," British soccer player Broadbent
commits a foul against Czech player Deml to
prevent him from scoring a certain goal. The
symbolic foul committed in the game invites a
comparison of the soccer ethos, in which individual players act unfairly for the good of the
team, with the ethos of the Czech ruling regime,
in which the individual's rights are sacrificed
to a common "good." Not a scene or gesture in
this play functions gratuitously, so fine is
Stoppard's control of his material. A tense
scene shot through with comic touches, it closes
on an ominous note, as the police produce
currency that they will use to incriminate
Hollar. Frightened and "out of his depth,"
Anderson leaves the hotel abruptly, seeking the
safety of the western enclave. In spite of its
superficial resemblance to a scene in
Jumpers, where George Moore fails to come to

the aid of Archbishop Clegthorpe who is
mysteriously executed by the Rad-Libs, this scene
marks a change in Stoppard's staging of moral
conflict. The tone struck is far more serious
than it is comic; the action far more lifelike
than explicitly theatrical; and Anderson's
failure of nerve is far more forgivable than is
the aloofness of his earlier incarnation as an
absent-minded professor.

In creating the syncopation of seriousness
and comedy referred to earlier, Stoppard follows
this dark scene with a light parody of British
journalism. Upon returning to his hotel,
Anderson overhears British sports reporters
dictating their stories of the soccer match.

> Dickinson and Pratt were mostly left
> standing by Wolker, with a W, and Deml, D
> for dog, E for Edward, M for mother, L for
> London--who could go round the halls as a
> telepathy act, stop. Only Crisp looked as
> if he had a future outside Madame Tussaud's.
>   (p. 91)

There's more to the comedy than the parody
of sports journalism. Anderson, too, has just
lost a game. While Hollar's future grows more
ominous, Anderson's hesitation to help him grows
more conspicuous. In subsequent scenes, the
oppression and urgency of the East impinges on
the West with increasing speed and intensity,
driving Anderson to commit his own professional
foul by smuggling Hollar's thesis out of
Czechoslovakia in an unsuspecting colleague's
briefcase. Anderson's new willingness to commit
a foul stems directly from his experience in
Czechoslovakia where the regime's denial of the
individual's rights constitutes a wrong deeper
and more far reaching than his own and justifies
his own wrongdoing. This assessing of relative
wrongdoing has not, until these eastern plays,
received sustained and serious treatment. But it
figures centrally in most of the post-
Travesties plays, where the characters have
accepted the contingent nature of their moral
decisions, while operating under the conscious
fiction that they are permanent and absolute.

Stoppard reworks the definition of free expression as a primary right in each of the political comedies that defines his style shift, and in each thematic pressure significantly changes his characteristic form. **Every Good Boy Deserves Favor**, set entirely in an eastern prison cell made to resemble a mental hospital in contemporary Russia, shows us Stoppard's new poetic at its most lyrical, somber and intense. While preserving the rhythm of alternating comic and serious scenes found in **Professional Foul**, this piece compresses the pattern and overlaps its effects to intensify the claustrophobia intermittently transmitted in the television drama. The chief means for controlling mood and rhythm occurs through the extraordinary presence of a symphony orchestra in the play, acting as character, setting and symbol by turns and occasionally all at once. The success of the collaboration between Stoppard and André Previn's London Symphony Orchestra would seem to lie in each artist's willingness to concede to the other some part of the expressive range of his own medium. In Stoppard's case, he fitted the play with a radically new minimal dialogue style that rides on and with Previn's sympathetic score much like an operatic libretto, here motivating and there responding to the music.

The story reads like a fraternal twin of **Professional Foul**, only in this piece Stoppard takes the spectator directly into the cell of Alexander Ivanov, being held in a mental hospital for having written about the imprisoning and torture of his friends in similar hospitals. While in prison, he begins a hunger strike to protest his confinement, which the authorities attempt to end by admitting Ivanov's son, Sacha, to see him and beg him to stop. Close to death by the play's end, Ivanov is miraculously saved by the semanticist Colonel Rozinski, who mistakenly declares both Ivanov and his identically named (but actually insane) roommate cured of their respective delusions. Like **Professional Foul**, the thematic struggle lies in the conflict between the collective good and the

individual's rights. Like Pavel Hollar,
Alexander Ivanov and his son, Sacha, are composite portraits of actual people Stoppard has known
and stories that have been written by eastern
intellectuals about the procedures used in mental
hospitals turned prisons.[7]
    In presenting this situation, Stoppard moves
the action between three playing areas--school-
room, doctor's office and Ivanov's cell--without
relying on formal scene breaks. The musical
score signals shifts in place as well as feeling.
The fluidity of the action marks a sharp break
with the earlier plays, frequently set on a
symmetrically divided stage. Here, the orchestra
engulfs the characters whose entrapment within an
orchestrated society is visually before the
audience from the moment the action begins.
    In part as an accommodation to the
potentially overwhelming orchestra, Stoppard
developed for this piece a poetic dialogue of
relative simplicity, economy and intensity that
has become a hallmark of his political plays, and
which has survived in abbreviated form in both
Night and Day and **The Real Thing**. Like
the Hollars' powerful, broken English in
Professional Foul, the Ivanovs' spare speech
rings with authenticity and conviction.
Alexander completes his autobiography in four
sentences:

>My childhood was uneventful. My adolescence
>was normal. I got an ordinary job, and
>married a conventional girl who died
>uncontroversially in childbirth. Until the
>child was seven the only faintly interesting
>thing about me was that I had a friend who
>kept getting arrested.   (p. 21)

    But the dialogue style does more than
provide a character note. Rhetorical simplicity
in the eastern plays mimics on the linguistic
plane the expression of an essential moral
principle taken to be self-evident: that the
individual's right to free expression is a
primary right preceding other rights. The
central conflict in this piece is between
Alexander, who publicizes the jailing of artists

in mental hospitals and the authorities, who
pervert language in reporting their "official"
versions of reality. The struggle between these
two versions of fact drives Alexander to refuse
to change his story and to begin a hunger strike
to force the authorities' hand.

The types of speech in this play range from
simple narrative reporting of the sort quoted
above, to Sacha's teacher's didactic instruction,
"Open the book. Pencil and paper. You see what
happens to social malcontents" (p. 15), to
Alexander's lyric encoding, "I want to get back
to the bad old times when / a man got a sentence
appropriate to his crimes" (p. 30), to Ivanov's
insane ranting "A trombone is the longest
distance between two points!" (p. 34), and
include comic passages among the most bitter
Stoppard has written to date, "If you don't eat
for a long time," Alexander tells the audience,
"you start to smell of acetone, which is the
stuff girls use for taking the paint off their
fingernails" (p. 23). These varieties of speech,
compounded with the varying and fluid effects of
the orchestra, give Stoppard an extraordinary
range of expression, from light comedy to farce
to dark comedy, which he exploits in precise
harmony with the orchestra. One of the most
poignant and powerful of these musical and verbal
combinations occurs repeatedly as the slow,
silent starvation of Alexander is counterpointed
by a musical-poetic motif, "Everything will be
all right," Sacha's repeated wish for a return to
harmony with his family and the official society.
Alexander sounds an elegantly simple warning note
at the play's close, after he has been released
by the farcical Colonel:

> Sacha (**sings**):   Papa, don't be crazy!
>   Everything can be all
>   right!
>
> Alexander: Sacha--
>
> Sacha (**sings**):   Everything can be all
>   right!   (p. 39)

For the moment, everything will be all right.
But the future is uncertain. The somber closing

music of the symphony overrides Sacha's
insistence on a bright future and drowns his
hopefulness in a dark swell of deep sound. For
the most part, Alexander and Sacha's dialogue
bears little resemblance to the earlier speech of
Stoppard's philosophers and aesthetes such as
George Riley's quasi-poetic reveries and
Rosencrantz and Guildenstern's Beckettian music
hall banter. The new compressed speech helps
Stoppard to create a new character type: the
ordinary person forced by circumstances to
express and defend a moral position. In striving
to express this position, Stoppard creates a
dialogue with poetic depth, stretching his comedy
vertically in the direction of tragedy.

The dark tone of the political comedies
alternates with extremes of farce humor in the
third of the political plays that together define
Stoppard's style shift. In **Dogg's Hamlet,
Cahoot's Macbeth** (1980)[8], Stoppard assigns
comedy to the first half and farce satire to the
second half of the two-part play. Written for Ed
Berman's Inter-Action community arts program,
this play relies on favorite Stoppardian
techniques of pastiche and parody, but with a
difference. Where extensive parody in the
earlier plays afforded Stoppard a vantage point
in "no-man's-land," between each of his major
character's points of view, here, what appears at
moments in the play's second half to be a parody
of **Macbeth** begins to take shape as a stinging
satire of Czechoslovakian censorship mounted from
the vantage of actors forbidden to work on the
stage. While the situation enacted in both parts
of this play could be described as a natural-
seeming action, the explicitly artificial
dialogue is borrowed from at least three literary
sources--Shakespeare, Wittgenstein and Pavel
Kohout.[9] In addition, two of the plays'
dialects, Elizabethan English and "Dogg," substitute for each other during the action. The shift
in tone and treatment from **Dogg's Hamlet** to
Cahoot's Macbeth recapitulates the larger shift
from the early to more recent Stoppard plays:

light gives way to dark comedy, spoof hardens as
satire, farce exaggeration shrinks to a style
nearer realism, the political innocence of the
Dogg-speaking schoolchildren yields to the
political experience of unemployed and harassed
artists.

      Dogg's Hamlet, a slight spoof built from
two other spoofs, **Dogg's Our Pet** (1971) and
The Fifteen-Minute Hamlet (1976), both also
written for Berman's program, acts out on stage
an illustration of the language game from
Wittgenstein's **Philosophical Investigations**,[10] including the language Dogg and
the building of a speaking platform that becomes
the context for the mini-**Hamlet** following it.
The latter was written to be performed as a piece
of street theater on Ed Berman's double-decker
bus. **Dogg's Hamlet** combines these two pieces
by staging an action in which a group of
Dogg-speaking schoolboys helps an
English-speaking lorry driver build a platform on
which they all speak Elizabethan in a
speed-through version of **Hamlet**. By the
play's conclusion, lorry driver Easy has learned
Dogg--a dialect that will link him to the second
part of this play. Little in this dramatic
burlesque can be called political; however, the
second half reverses the order of the
Shakespeare/Easy plots, opening with an
abbreviated but serious **Macbeth** and closing
with its translation into Dogg in the context of
a sustained satire of the bullying tactics of
Czech censors. The origins of **Cahoot's
Macbeth** lay in Pavel Kohout's 75-minute
Macbeth, condensed as a piece of "living-room
theater," an underground form that grew up in
post-1968 Prague. Inspired by Kohout but working
his own comic vein, Stoppard transforms the
tragic language and style of **Macbeth** by two
simultaneous actions--the visit of a Czech secret
policeman, a reincarnation of the real inspector
hound who bursts on the scene to stop subversive
activity, and the subsequent arrival of Easy and
his lorry full of lumber. Easy now speaks only
Dogg, into which dialect the actors translate
Macbeth to escape detection by eavesdropping

censors. This comic mining of Shakespeare's
tragedy of ambition provides Stoppard with the
means to ridicule the warped ambition of Czech
officials and to celebrate the actors' moral
courage and comic resourcefulness.
     In response to repeated interruptions of
their skeletal **Macbeth,** the actors do not
give up their production but incorporate their
visitors into the fiction which soon becomes a
satire of official censorship disguised as an
Elizabethan tragedy. In a final dramatic shift
of style and language, the actors translate
Elizabethan English into Dogg and transform
Easy's lorry with its blocks and slabs to Birnham
Wood over the Inspector's protests, "May I remind
you that we're supposed to be in a period of
normalization here" (p. 74). The actors and Easy
triumph, as, at the conclusion of the play, the
Inspector and the policemen are caught up within
the fiction, building the platform in a free play
of art that they had come to interrupt. In a
country where repression is cloaked under the
guise of normalization, Shakespeare's tragedy is
cloaked under the guise of Dogg, a language used
to escape and ridicule tyranny.
     While less ambitious than the two comedies
previously described, **Dogg's Hamlet, Cahoot's
Macbeth** carries forward the same style shift
that distinguishes them from Stoppard's earlier
plays. Carefully turned witticisms have been
replaced by other fictional dialogues, including
an actor's "plain speaking" denouncement of
official repression:

     If you're afraid to risk the infection of an
     uncontrolled idea, the first time a new one
     gets in, it'll run through your system like
     a rogue bacillus. Remember the last time.
                                        (p. 62)

     Seriousness and spoof succeed one another in
a rhythmic pattern that pulls the comedy in the
direction of satire. The protagonist Cahoot
fights official interference with citizens' right
to free expression--the central self-evident
principle thematically uniting all three of the

political plays. And in all three works, details
of plot and staging draw on documented evidence
provided by eastern artists as well as Stoppard's
personal experiences while a visitor in the
U.S.S.R and Czechoslovakia.

It is no surprise that the two major
Stoppard plays written for the stage in the late
1970s and early 1980s also show evidence of this
shift. **Night and Day** opened in late October
of 1978, approximately one year after the
television premiere of **Professional Foul** and
the stage premiere of **Every Good Boy Deserves
Favor**. Stoppard also sets **Night and Day**
outside of western Europe and focuses its play of
ideas squarely on the problem of free expression,
defined as press freedom.

Without these intervening plays, **The Real
Thing** (1982) would appear to break sharply with
Stoppard's earlier style. And in his thematic
preoccupation with love in this play--romantic,
betrayed, unrequited and passionate--Stoppard
does break new ground. But his stylistic choices
in staging and expressing the theme of love
belong clearly to his more recent work. Stoppard
returns to England as the setting for his
romantic comedy and chooses a playwright as his
central character who finds himself in a post-
Travesties predicament: how can he define and
express "real" love and genuine commitment in a
realistic style without resorting to theatrical
clichés? Playwright Henry's dilemma is also
familiar--how can he write about and defend
marital fidelity without appearing to be a prig
or a glib moralist? How can he know "the real
thing" when love and commitment mean different
things to different people? How can he balance
the comic and serious treatment of cuckoldry, the
oldest of comic predicaments? Stoppard manages
to save his playwright from ridicule by giving
him an ironical awareness of his weaknesses, the
sort of dignified self-consciousness typical of
the post-**Travesties** hero. The irony of the
play's treatment of love goes further than the
character of Henry. Virtually all of the
characters are involved in the theater in some
way, either as actors or writers, which gives

Stoppard the opportunity to remind the spectator
that this play is investigating the artistic
problems posed by the genre itself.   While
confessing to Annie that he's having trouble
trying to write "her" play, presumably a play
about their love for one another, Henry considers
his options:

> Perhaps I should write it completely
> artificial. Blank verse. Poetic imagery.
> Not so much of the 'Will you still love me
> when my tits are droopy?' 'Of course I
> will, darling, it's your bum I'm mad for,'
> and more of the 'By my troth, thy beauty
> makest the moon hide her radiance,' do you
> think?[11]

Both the "Will you still love me" and the "By my
troth" choices become part of the play as the
dialogue of each of its three inner plays--
House of Cards, Brodie's play and Ford's **'Tis
Pity She's a Whore**--weaves in and out of the
frame play.[12]   In contrast to these styles of
speech, the dialogue of the frame play appears
relatively natural, or "real."   But even this
distinction between real and artificial is
reversed when Annie and Billy, co-stars in the
Ford play, begin an actual love affair while
rehearsing in Scotland.   Ford's lines in the "By
my troth" manner come to represent the real and
the artificial simultaneously.   For a time, at
least, two types of love hold the stage--Annie's
and Billy's and Henry's and Annie's.   Is one of
them more real than the other?

Stoppard makes no final judgment on "the
real thing."   And in this we recognize the author
of the early plays.   But he does consolidate a
number of the aesthetic and psychological
problems raised in the play with the intensity
and confidence characteristic of his more recent
work.   Annie's love for Billy may or may not be
as "real" as her love for Henry, but she
eventually tires of Billy.   Playwright Henry's
absolute commitment to Annie as his "true love"
survives her affair with Billy because Henry is
willing to suspend his own moral code in favor of

hers and to accept whatever uncertain outcome
time will bring to their marriage. His ability
to commit himself in spite of this uncertainty
draws him together with Stoppard's eastern heroes
and with Professor Anderson who learned to juggle
conflicting moral choices without succumbing to
paralysis. His love for Annie puts him in the
awkward position of attempting to rewrite a play
by Private Brodie whom Henry considers a fraud
incapable of writing a genuine line of "real"
dialogue. The central aesthetic question being
raised in the play springs from Henry's dilemma
as ghost writer. Annie accuses him, "You're
jealous of the idea of the writer. You want to
keep it sacred, special, not something anybody
can do" (p. 52). Henry the playwright seems to
speak for Stoppard when he responds to Annie's
charge by comparing the successful writing of a
play of ideas with the successful batting of a
cricket ball:

> This thing here which looks like a wooden
> club, is actually several pieces of particu-
> lar wood cunningly put together in a certain
> way so that the whole thing is sprung, like
> a dance floor. It's for hitting cricket
> balls with. If you get it right, the
> cricket ball will travel two hundred yards
> in four seconds. . . . What we're trying to
> do is to write cricket bats, so that when we
> throw up an idea and give it a little knock,
> it might . . . **travel**. (p. 53)

None of the characters in **The Real Thing**
gives the final word on playwrighting any more
than on love. But neither does the play end in a
stalemate on the subject. Henry firmly believes
in the artist's unique talent, but under threat
of losing Annie he compromises this belief to act
as Brodie's ghost writer. Henry believes in the
sacredness of the word, but he learns to write
science fiction movies to finance his alimony
payments to his first wife. Although Henry's
idea of the writer as uniquely talented
occasionally seems defeated by what he writes, he
learns to live with that contradiction.

The Real Thing clearly follows after and
even functions as a culmination of the post-
Travesties pieces, pushing the style shift
already documented to an aesthetic and thematic
resting point. The summary quality of the play
grows from its repeated references to Stoppard's
own work and reputation. The effect is that of a
dramatic commentary by the playwright on
playwrighting. Henry repeatedly refers to his
professional reputation in terms that critics
have applied to Stoppard. Henry's disaffected
wife Charlotte accuses him of failing to write a
decent part for a woman. Henry admits that he
doesn't know how to write love, echoing a
criticism that Stoppard does not know how to
portray human affections in his plays. Henry's
daughter Debbie accuses him of substituting lines
for speech, "Don't write it, Fa. Just say it"
(p. 68). People have said of Henry's plays that
they "prefer the early stuff" just as critics
have bemoaned Stoppard's "turn towards the
pulpit" in the late 1970s.

In its implicit handling of the shifting
perspectives afforded by art on life and by life
on art, in the characters' strong commitments to
their beliefs, in the repeated use of music and
simplistic love lyrics to express the delicate
humor of love's banality and, finally, in its
repeated references to itself as a conscious
commentary on playwrighting, Stoppard's **The
Real Thing** consolidates the shift away from
conceptual paralysis and formal rigidity towards
a new flexibility in thought and staging.

Notes

1. The phrase is Milton Shulman's, taken from his review of **Professional Foul** in the London **Times** of 23 April 1978, D3. See Andrew K. Kennedy's "Tom Stoppard's Dissident Comedies," **Modern Drama**, 25, 4 (December 1982), 469-76, for a description of the novel elements in **Professional Foul** and **Every Good Boy Deserves Favor** and for the tentative suggestion that these plays may constitute a new genre of political comedy. In **Beyond Absurdity: The Plays of Tom Stoppard** (New Jersey: Association of University Presses, 1979), Victor Cahn stresses the continuity rather than the discontinuity of Stoppard's vision in the political comedies. See especially pp. 143-52.

2. Milton Shulman quotes from Stoppard's own report of this crucial 1977 trip to Russia in "The Politicizing of Tom Stoppard," **New York Times**, 23 April 1978, sec. 2, pp. 3, 27. See Stoppard's own account of what he experienced in "The Face at the Window," **The** (London) **Sunday Times**, 27 February 1977, p. 33.

3. In making this argument, I will necessarily pay selective attention to these pieces. Interested readers can find a more complete discussion of their plots and sources in the commentary cited in Note 1, above, and in the following: R. J. Buhr, "Epistemology and Ethics in Tom Stoppard's **Professional Foul**," **Comparative Drama**, 13, 4 (Winter 1979-80), 320-29; Ruby Cohn, "Tom Stoppard: Light Drama and Dirges in Marriage," in **Contemporary English Drama** (New York: Holmes and Meier, 1981), pp. 109-20; C. J. Gianakaris, "Stoppard's Adaptations of Shakespeare: **Dogg's Hamlet, Cahoot's Macbeth**," **Comparative Drama**, 18, 3 (Fall 1984), 222-40; Felicia Londré, **Tom Stoppard** (New York: Frederick Ungar, 1981), especially pp. 142-64; Kenneth Tynan, "Withdrawing with Style from the Chaos," **New Yorker** (December 19, 1977), pp. 41-111; Thomas Whitaker, **Tom Stoppard** (New York: Grove Press, 1983); and Hersh Zeifman, "Comedy of Ambush: Tom Stoppard's **The Real Thing**," **Modern Drama**, 26 (1983), 139-49.

4. Stoppard, **Every Good Boy Deserves Favor** and **Professional Foul** (New York: Grove Press, 1978 [first printing]), p. 45. Subsequent references will appear in the text.

5. For a detailed analysis of Anderson's moral dilemma, see Richard J. Buhr's "Epistemology and Ethics."

6. See Shulman, above.

7. Stoppard describes these sources in notes accompanying the RCA Recording of this piece, RCA ABLI-2855, 1978.

8. Stoppard, **Dogg's Hamlet, Cahoot's Macbeth** (London: Faber and Faber, 1980). Subsequent references will appear in the text.

9. Stoppard describes his debt to Czech writer Kohout in the introduction. For a close account of Stoppard's Shakespearean borrowing in this piece, see Gianakaris's "Stoppard's Adaptations."

10. The key passage in **Philosophical Investigations** would seem to be the following:

> Let us imagine a language. . . . meant to serve for communication between a builder A and an assistant B. A is building with building-stones: there are blocks, pillars, slabs and beams. B has to pass the stones, and that in the order in which A needs them. For this purpose they use a language consisting of the words "block," "pillar," "slab," "beam." A calls them out;--B brings the stone which he has learnt to bring at such-and-such a call.--Conceive this as a complete primitive language.

Ludwig Wittgenstein's **Philosophical Investigations**, trans. G.E.M. Anscombe (London: B. Blackwell, 1953), p. 3.

11. Stoppard, **The Real Thing** (London: Faber and Faber, 1982), pp. 40-41. Subsequent references will appear in the text.

12.   For a fuller description of Stoppard's literary sources, see Hersh Zeifman's "Comedy of Ambush."

Unlikely Bedfellows: Politics and Aesthetics in
Tom Stoppard's Recent Work

Joan F. Dean

Throughout Stoppard's plays questions
concerning the artist, his responsibilities, and
his work frequently surface. His characters are
often painters, writers (including poets,
journalists, and dramatists), musicians, or
actors. Some are based on historical personages;
some cut from whole cloth; one or two even
suggest a close connection with Stoppard himself.
Many of these characters are directly concerned
with the creative, artistic process. Others,
notably the many actors who populate his plays--
Dorothy Moore in **Jumpers** (1972) and the
players in **Rosencrantz** (1967)--are not
primarily imaginative, but interpretive artists.
Still others, like the journalists in **Night and
Day** (1978), are marginally connected with art
itself: first, because like other writers, they
work in the medium of language and, second,
because they share similar responsibilities with
imaginative artists who deal with political
questions.
Stoppard's own recent works also address
political issues. Especially since **Jumpers**,
his characters inhabit well-defined social and
historical contexts--hyperbolic and futuristic as
they may be--rather than timeless, abstract, or
universal realms. **Travesties** (1974), like
Artist (1972), is set in Zurich during World
War I just before the Russian Revolution.
Night and Day deals with a political situation in Africa in a specific phase of post-
colonial development. **Professional Foul**
(1977), **Every Good Boy Deserves Favour**
(1977), **Cahoot's Macbeth** (1979), and

Squaring the Circle (1984) all examine the
plight of those trying to work under the
oppression of totalitarian governments in the
late twentieth century. These four all rely
heavily upon specific situations in
Czechoslovakia, the Soviet Union, or Poland in
the very recent past. Among Stoppard's works,
these are his most explicitly political. The
Real Thing (1982) is set in present-day England
against a backdrop of anti-nuclear, anti-Estab-
lishment agitation. In each case, the social and
political backdrop is essential to the thematic
concerns--specifically those regarding the nature
of playwrighting--in a way that is not at all
characteristic of the plays before Jumpers.

Over the past decade, these two recurrent
themes, politics and playwrighting, have become
curiously interrelated. Stoppard's efforts to
sway what Henry in The Real Thing calls "that
axis of behaviour where we locate politics or
justice"[1] focuses on communist repression in no
fewer than five works: Professional Foul,
Every Good Boy Deserves Favour, Cahoot's Macbeth,
Squaring the Circle, and, to a lesser extent,
Travesties. The immediate concern with the
affairs and responsibilities of the artist appear
in Artist, Travesties, and The Real Thing;
Night and Day deals with journalists rather
than artists.

Despite critical charges that his early
characters were subordinate to the ideas they
represented, Stoppard's more recent characters
often face the same challenges as the playwright
himself. They take up questions that Stoppard as
a journalist, a playwright, an individual has
addressed in interviews, non-fictional articles,
and lectures. A dramatist, to be sure, has many
more options open to him than a journalist, but
the dramatist has the additional responsibility
of creating art. Insofar as the playwright
concerns himself with political matters, he can,
as Stoppard often does, disseminate information
and shape opinion. Moreover, in Night and Day,
Every Good Boy Deserves Favour, Cahoot's
Macbeth, and Squaring the Circle, freedom
of artistic expression and freedom of the press

are portrayed as dual manifestations of the same
basic liberty. Those freedoms of expression are
critical for Stoppard. Speaking before the
National Press Club 1979, Stoppard asserted: "A
reasonable litmus test for any society in my view
[is] is it a society where you can publish within
the law?"[2]   Ultimately, in Stoppard's works
the responsibilities of the political playwright
are not unlike those of the political reporter.

In his recent works, on the one hand,
Stoppard's characters persistently encounter
problems related to the nature of drama--specifi-
cally, those pertaining to the relationship
between dramatic representation and reality,
between life and art.   On the other hand, artists
and others (journalists, the narrator in
Squaring the Circle, et al.) are often forced
to account for or to justify themselves and their
work. While these two questions are distinct,
they are hardly unrelated. This is especially
true for those works that deal directly with
specific political situations. The possibilities
for oversimplifying or misrepresenting a
political situation are strong; the consequences
of such distortions are potentially disastrous.

The pitfalls of the intentional fallacy are
particularly troublesome in evaluating Stoppard's
characters. There are no straw men in his plays
and few characters, like Brodie in **The Real
Thing**, who elicit an immediate dislike. The
creation of villainous or even unsympathetic
characters would undermine one of the foundations
of Stoppard's dramatic technique: what he
himself has referred to as a "kind of infinite
leapfrog."[3] Characters with diametrically
opposed views are pitted against one another, but
both sides of the argument are given strong
voices. **Jumpers** provides the best example in
the contrast between the dapper though unctuous
Sir Archibald Jumper and the sincere but hapless
George Moore. Whereas Archie is powerful,
successful, and thoroughly cynical ("At the
graveside, the undertaker doffs his hat and
impregnates the prettiest mourner. Wham, Bam,
thank you Sam"[4]), George succeeds neither in
marriage nor in academe. Yet, as Kenneth Tynan
observes, George's ineffable faith in man's
spirit and the existence of a moral order
approximates Stoppard's own convictions:

In that great debate there is no question
where Stoppard stands. He votes for the
spirit--although he did not state his
position in the first person until June of
this year [1977], when in the course of a
book review, he defined himself as a
supporter of "Western liberal democracy,
favouring an intellectual elite and a
progressive middle class and based on a
moral order derived from Christian
absolutes."[5]

Yet though it may be helpful to link Moore and
Stoppard on this point alone, to identify
Stoppard and Moore is patently foolhardy.

Moreover, the fact that Stoppard writes
comedy rather than tragedy presents another
obstacle to examining the playwright's aesthetic
and political position. Aristophanes and all who
followed him not withstanding, comedy, especially
in post-WWII British drama, is too often seen as
escapist entertainment rather than politic
commentary. As Catherine Itzin amply demonstrates in her study **Stages in the Revolution:
Political Theatre in Britain Since 1968**, the
British stage has frequently and forcefully been
used as a political platform for issues ranging
from gay rights to government funding of the
arts, from anti-war and anti-nuclear views to the
I.R.A.[6] But the vast majority of these political plays are overtly polemical and decidedly
mirthless--two characteristics that immediately
distinguish them from Stoppard's works. Their
single-mindedness and dreariness are implicitly
mocked in **The Real Thing** by Brodie's dogmatic
television script.

In **Artist**, a radio play, and its
full-length theatrical descendent,
Travesties, Stoppard focuses on questions
concerning the artist and his relationship to
society that he had only touched upon in earlier
works. While none of the characters in
Artist reappear in **Travesties**, the former
is clearly a preamble to the latter in its
themes, setting, and comments about the artist in
society. Both plays deal with characters who as

artists find that global conflict raging about
them and who, to varying degrees, attempt to
ignore it by seeking refuge in Switzerland.   In
Artist the aural images of the war are all
too obvious: the discussions concerning art are
punctuated by "a convoy of rattletrap
lorries,"[7] explosions, the thundering hooves of
the German cavalry.   In **Travesties** the
reminders of war appear in Carr's personal
experience in the trenches, Lenin's exile in
Zurich, and Joyce's insistence that "[a]s an
artist, naturally I attach no importance to the
swings and roundabout of political history."[8]

     Whereas **Artist** is principally focused on
a story of unrequited love and the difficulty of
expressing that love in art, **Travesties** more
pointedly confronts the relationship between art
and politics and the artist's responsibility to
his society.   As I have shown elsewhere,
Travesties pits the proponents of socialist
realism (Lenin), Dadaism (Tzara), art for art's
sake (Joyce), and conventional bourgeois art
(Carr).[9]   Among these views, Lenin's view of
art is the one most discredited in **Travesties**
because it is contradicted by Lenin's own
response to art.   The appropriate, doctrinaire
response on art is learned rather than felt by
Lenin.   He initially prefers the bourgeois
Pushkin to the revolutionary Mayakovsky;
Beethoven's "Appassionata" "makes [him] want to
say nice stupid things and pat the heads of those
people who while living in this vile hell can
create such beauty" (89).

     Yet the most substantial hinge between
Artist and **Travesties** lies in the
repetition of two statements concerning art and
the artists.   Donner, the artist in love with
Sophie who ultimately commits himself to
realistic painting, and Henry Carr both offer
definitions of the artist: "An artist is someone
who is gifted in some way that [which] enables
him to do something more or less well which can
only be done badly or not at all by someone who
is not thus gifted" (**Artist**, p. 83;
Travesties, p.   38).   That definition
anticipates Henry's comparison of those who craft

cricket bats and those who write plays in **The
Real Thing**. Donner, an artist capable of
realistic painting, Carr, and Henry agree that
the prerequisite of the artist is the mastery of
his medium; what is often simply called talent.

   Travesties also shares with **Artist**
nearly identical statements appearing in very
different contexts concerning the artist's
standing in and responsibility to society. As
Carr says in **Travesties**: "What is an artist?
For every thousand people there's nine hundred
doing the work, ninety doing well, nine doing
good, and one lucky bastard who's the artist"
(46). Carr is suspicious of, if not hostile to,
art. He distrusts art because he fears that he
may not understand it, that it may be a ruse
perpetrated by artists. Stoppard's **Squaring
the Circle** and **The Real Thing** also present
characters who distrust art, often for political
reasons.

   Squaring the Circle follows the pattern of
Professional Foul (both television plays),
Cahoot's Macbeth, and **Every Good Boy Deserves
Favour** in focusing expressly on a specific
political situation. Unlike **Jumpers** and
Night and Day, **Squaring the Circle** does not
distance the work in an imaginary setting, but
directly addresses a political reality as well as
the problems involved in presenting that
situation. In the course of **Squaring the
Circle** Stoppard communicates an enormous amount
of purely factual information: the history of
Poland since 1720, the reason Poland is less
likely to receive loans from Western governments
than other equally economically imperiled
countries, why moral leadership in Poland has
been in the hands of the Church, the fact that 70
per cent of Polish agriculture is privately
owned. This is no mean feat. At a time when
most of the media coverage, at least in America,
depicted the conflict between the Polish unions
and the country's communist government in highly
charged emotional terms, **Squaring the Circle**
approaches its subject with an even-handedness.
The play's approach to its subject seems
predicated on the conviction that before the

audience can undertake political action, it must
factually and objectively understand the
situation. As much as the image that General
Jaruzelski presents to the Western world may fit
the caricature of a Communist puppet dictator,
complete with sinister tinted glasses,
overbearing demeanor, and Fearless Leader
uniform, and Lech Walesa may appear as his
perfect foil--with his work clothes, unkept
mustache, and insistent family--these are not the
basis on which Stoppard draws their characters.
Both are far more complex because they are
presented not just as symbols, but as individuals. Audience expectations are continually
reversed, for **Squaring the Circle** does not
focus on the charismatic personality of Walesa,
but rather on the complexities and ambiguities of
the situation in Poland. Here, perhaps more
convincingly than in any other play, Stoppard
demonstrates how thoroughly he has researched his
subject.

     In some ways **Squaring the Circle**
contains Stoppard's most "Brechtian" dramaturgy.
(Ironically, its politics are decidedly anti-
Brechtian or at least anti-communist.) The
dramatic progress of the work expediently guided
by the direct address of the Narrator. But that
progress is repeatedly thwarted, qualified, or
interrupted by the voice of the Witness who
objects to or criticizes the dramatization of a
particular situation. Despite its didacticism,
Squaring the Circle, like all of Stoppard's
political plays, does not intend to galvanize the
audience to action.

     The difficulty of accurately reporting or
recreating a political situation becomes a
thematic concern, just as it had in **Night and
Day**. Stoppard's attention is expressly focused
on the problem of presenting the words and deeds
of actual people with honesty. His preface to
Squaring the Circle confirms his sensitivity to
this inherent dilemma:

          Documentary fiction, by definition, is
          always in danger of seeming to claim to know
          more than a film maker **can** know.
          Accurate detail mingles with arty detail,

> without distinguishing marks, and history
> mingles with good and bad guesses. . . . It
> was the fear of just such imponderables and
> just such confusion between large specula-
> tion and small truths . . . that led me to
> the idea of having a narrator with
> **acknowledged fallibility.**[10]

Technically, this is not an innovative device in
Stoppard's dramaturgy. The most obvious
precedent is Henry Carr, the "narrator" as well
as a character in **Travesties**. Carr's memory,
the stage directions record, "occasionally jumps
the rails and has to be restarted at the point
where it goes wild" (27). Stoppard's own work
employs other analoguous dramatic devices, many
of which evoke Pirandello's manipulations of
dramatic reality. For Stoppard, as for
Pirandello, multiple perspectives or renditions
are not only stylistic devices, but because of
their very nature and tacit commentary on drama
itself, they become an important thematic
component of these works.

As early as **Rosencrantz**, characters
concerned themselves, often in an alarmingly
disinterested way, with various explanations or
interpretations of events. Rosencrantz, for
instance, offers a "list of possible explanations"[11] for his run of incredibly bad luck
at coin-tossing. In **After Magritte** (1970)
various characters, all eyewitnesses, provide
radically different descriptions of the identical
event. But in the works since **Jumpers**, those
that are more directly concerned with political
or aesthetic issues, Stoppard moves through
different planes of dramatic reality to indicate
how restricted any single perspective on a
political situation must be.

Stoppard's solution to th dilemma of this
limited perspective in **Squaring the Circle**
was the creation of the Witness who periodically
interrupts the narrator to challenge his
authority. The very presence of the witnesses
raises the question of "the qualified reality"
(9) which is all any account, whether it aspires
to the status of art or claims to be wholly

documentary, can achieve. Any perspective is
necessarily limited--be it by camera position (in
the case of a film documentary), by editing, or
by inherent if inadvertent bias--and the best,
the most objective and fair-minded solution for
Stoppard is to acknowledge that fact.
Consequently, in **Squaring the Circle** the
exchanges between the narrator and the Witness
make explicit the problem Stoppard as a
playwright and commentator confronted.

The Narrator is closer to Stoppard than
virtually any of his earlier characters.[12]
Like the playwright, the Narrator operates from a
position of presumed authority. Throughout most
of the history of drama, until very recently in
fact, one of the conventions governing the use of
direct address (soliloquies, asides, choric
statements, etc.) was that the character speak
the truth, or at least what he perceived to be
the truth at that moment. But Stoppard, through
the Narrator, not only acknowledges but also
exploits that assumption.

Much of the humor in **Squaring the Circle**
lies in the conscious manipulation of the
dramatic conventions governing veracity in direct
address and awareness of the clichés of
television journalism or its "docu-dramas." The
Narrator often explains or tries to justify the
interjection of literary images, such as a chess
game or a game of cards, as a matter of artistic
license. When the party bosses appear dressed as
gangsters, the Witness objects:

> WITNESS: What's all this gangster stuff?
> NARRATOR: It's a metaphor.
> WITNESS: Wrong. You people--
> NARRATOR: All right.
>   (54)

The Witness is not about to allow the imposition
of simplistic or clichéd images, no matter how
convenient, on his reality. He resists all
attempts of the Narrator (and author) to reduce
the political circumstances to an easily
accessible, tidy scenario. During the confrontation of General Jaruzelski, Walesa, and Cardinal
Glemp, which is portrayed as a card game, the

Narrator admits: "Everything is true except the
words and the pictures" (84).

Stoppard meticulously develops the ironies
inherent in the political situation in **Squaring
the Circle**. The play opens, for example, with
the striking contrast between the official,
public language that Leonid Brezhnev might have
addressed to Edward Gierek ("Comrade! As your
friends and allies in the progress towards the
inevitable triumph of Marxist-Leninism, we are
concerned, deeply concerned, by recent departures
from Leninist norms by Polish workers manipulated
by a revisionist element of the Polish
Intelligentsia!" [21]) and what is closer in tone
to, but certainly not exactly, the actual words
uttered by Brezhnev: "What the hell is going on
with you guys? Who's running the country? You
or the engine drivers? Your work force has got
you by the short hairs because you're up to your
neck in hock to the German bankers, American
bankers, Swiss bankers--you're in hock to **us**
to the tune of . . . is it millions or
billions. . . ?" (22).

In **Every Good Boy Deserves Favour**, the
incompetence of the authorities and their
desperate attempts to conceal that incompetence,
forces the play's action to the borders of farce.
Bureaucrats posing as doctors struggle to
disguise their bungling just as Feydeau's
philanderers fought to safeguard their illicit
liaisons. Only the stupidity and hypocrisy of
the authorities assure the nominal, momentary
(and hollow) happy ending of **Every Good Boy
Deserves Favour**. Similarly, the ending of
Professional Foul, recalling the recovery of
Miss Prism's long-lost handbag and, in its
self-conscious artificiality, obliquely suggests
that such contrived happy endings are not about
to resolve the oppression depicted. But in
Squaring the Circle there is not only a more
sustained, methodical delineation of the
political issues, there is far less of the
frenetic action of farce, very little of the
intricate wordplay and wit so often identified
with Stoppard, and none of the sleight-of-hand
happy endings found in **Professional Foul** or
Every Good Boy Deserves Favour. **Squaring the
Circle** ends when the political situation
reaches an impasse, not a resolution.

Thematically, **Squaring the Circle** deals
with the political reality in Poland as well as
the difficulty of writing about that situation.
Stoppard's **The Real Thing** considers the
difficulty of writing not only about politics,
but also about love.

The Real Thing moves between the illusive
and the real, the impersonal and the personal,
the false and the true. Its opening scene
initially lures the audience into mistaking House
of Cards for the real thing, or **The Real
Thing**. Conflating Henry's play and Stoppard's
play is as natural and as dangerous as conflating
Henry and Stoppard, the character and his
creator. This is not the only opportunity the
audience has to conflate art and life. In The
Real Thing Stoppard again interpolates scenes
from other works as a play-within-a-play much as
Hamlet is used in **Rosencrantz** or Earnest in
Travesties. The intimate conversations of
Stoppard's characters flow into the rhetorical
formality of Ford's **'Tis Pity She's a Whore**
or Strindberg's **Miss Julie**.

Life, of course, does imitate art. When in
The Real Thing Annie and Billy drift into the
dialogue taken from Ford's **'Tis Pity She's a
Whore**, Billy, at least, is sincere in borrowing
from a character to express his own feelings. In
the next scene in **The Real Thing**, Henry's
first wife, Charlotte, reminds Henry that she
lost her virginity to the actor playing Giovanni
to her Annabella, fuelling Henry's suspicions
about Annie's infidelity.

Moreover, **House of Cards** establishes the
image of a suspicious husband searching through
his wife's possessions for evidence of adultery
that is twice replayed in the course of **The
Real Thing**. First, Charlotte, Henry's ex-wife,
reports that her affair with an architect (a
profession shared with the jealous husband in
House of Cards) ended when he was unable to
find her diaphragm in their home while she was
away. Later, Henry himself ransacks Annie's
belongings, presumably with the same goal in
mind, while she is in Glasgow playing Annabella
to Billy's Giovanni. The crucial difference is

that in a highly emotional state, the razor-sharp
wit of the characters in **House of Cards**
yields to the untidy and unliterary anger of
characters who present themselves as more real,
or at least more human. As Hersh Zeifman
observes, "the reaction of the 'real' husband to
his wife's betrayal is, in both cases, utterly
opposite to the graceful wit under pressure
displayed by the theatrical husband in **House of
Cards**."13
     The ambivalence of the play's title,
referring both to true love and true art, is
indicative of not only the play's structure, but
its subject as well. Those subjects--love and
art--are approached with a reverence anomalous in
Stoppard's canon. Rarely does Stoppard treat his
subject with such vulnerable sincerity and without the detachment of witty barbs.
     The Real Thing contains some of Stoppard's
most direct statements concerning love as well as
the nature of the artist and his creation. In
Henry, Stoppard has created a character who
suggests not just tangential but direct
comparison with his author. Among all Stoppard's
characters, Henry offers the most tempting
invitation to identify a character as the
spokesman of his creator. Beside age,
profession, and an interest in cricket, Henry and
Stoppard share similar if not identical notions
of playwrighting. Outside of his interviews, the
most forthright statements from Stoppard
concerning playwrighting come from Henry. None
of Henry's ideas on art in general or
playwrighting contradict or are at variance with
what Stoppard has said about playwrighting in
interviews. Moreover, Henry's comments on drama
are unrefuted, even unqualified by any other
character in **The Real Thing**. The only
possible opposition to Henry's ideas on
playwrighting lies with Brodie, a singularly
dislikable character, who ends with dip rather
than pie on his face.
     Yet Henry is hardly a self-serving
idealization of the playwright. Unlike what
Tynan has said of Stoppard's meticulous
preparation, Henry "doesn't like research" (21).

Certainly, the little of what we know of **House of Cards** suggests Stoppard's characteristic wit and wordplay, but its subject, self-knowledge through pain, is hardly typical of his work. Although Henry respects language to the point of twice correcting his friend's grammar, he is not above writing a hack screenplay to earn the money to pay his alimony. He does, in fact, eventually doctor Brodie's play for television production. But he never manages to write the play he has promised Annie, largely because, as he says, "Loving and being loved is unliterary. It's happiness expressed in banality and lust" (40). As tempting as it is, identifying Stoppard and Henry is as misguided as mistaking **House of Cards** for **The Real Thing**.

For Henry the real thing is as illusive and rare in love as it is in art. Just as he doesn't "believe in debonair relationships" (72), he objects to the single-mindedness of Brodie's dramatic effort. Henry, in fact, despises Brodie as "a lout with language" (54), and Brodie's play as invective drivel. In regard to "politics, justice, patriotism," Henry believes:

> There's nothing real there separate from our perception of them. So if you try to change them as though there were something there to change, you'll get frustrated, and frustration will finally make you violent. If you know this and proceed with humility, you may perhaps alter people's perceptions so that they behave a little differently at that axis of behaviour where we locate politics or justice; but if you don't know this, then you're acting on a mistake. Prejudice is the expression of this mistake. (53-54)

What Henry here suggests is precisely what Stoppard's political works, especially and most successfully **Squaring the Circle**, attempt to do. Polemical works are likely only to polarize already divided groups. But if properly used, words "can build bridges across incomprehension and chaos" (54). For both Henry and Stoppard political action is wedded not to a particular

ideology or cause, but to moral intelligence and
sensibility. Without that fusion, political
statement can easily become, as it does for
Brodie, violence.

Moreover, if political statement is to be
expressed artistically, both Henry and Stoppard
would argue that precision with language and
talent are necessary. Henry's already famous
comparison of writing and crafting a cricket bat
recall what Donner in **Artist** and Carr in
Travesties say about the artist's talent:

> This thing here, which looks like a wooden
> club, is actually several pieces of particu-
> lar wood cunningly put together in a certain
> way so that the whole thing is sprung, like
> a dance floor. . . .
> What we're trying to do is to write cricket
> bats, so that when we throw up an idea and
> give it a little knock, it might . . .
> travel. . . .
>   (52)

In the ability to make an idea "travel" lies the
possibility of quickening the moral and political
sensibilities of the artist's audiences. And
therein lies the power as well as the genius of
Stoppard as a dramatist.

The dramatic device most characteristic of
Stoppard's approach to both political and
aesthetic problems is to establish a dramatic
reality on one plane and then to qualify, deny,
or undercut it by introducing a higher plane
which announces itself as closer to the Truth.
The structure of his recent works, especially
those which address political or aesthetic
questions, reflects the games of leap-frog played
by characters who offer "an argument, a
refutation, then a rebuttal of the refutation,
then a counter-rebuttal. . . ."[14]

Established, fixed texts--the official party
line in the case of **Squaring the Circle**,
Shakespeare's **Hamlet**, Wilde's
Earnest--only partially illuminate a given
situation. Yet another perspective is provided
by the vastly more personal, intimate and

individualized portraits of Stoppard's
characters.

The introduction of multiple perspectives on
a single situation is hardly a recent development
in Stoppard's work; **After Magritte** provides a
much earlier example as various characters
attempt to report what they saw. But in
Squaring the Circle and **The Real Thing** this
device effectively interpolates alternative
versions of reality specifically to indicate the
ambiguities and complexities of human situations
that variously deal with art, love, or politics.
In earlier works, this same device was used but
to vastly different ends: the text of
Shakespeare's **Hamlet** was interpolated into
Rosencrantz and fragments of Wilde's
Earnest appeared in **Travesties**. In
Squaring the Circle and **The Real Thing**
Stoppard's deft manipulation of dramatic
realities and interpolated scenes has realized a
new maturity in suggesting the limits of art and
the complex relationship between art and life.

In 1975, Stoppard told Charles Marowitz:

I'm not impressed by art **because** it's
political. I believe in art being good art
or bad art, not relevant or irrelevant art.
The plain truth is that if you are angered
or disgusted by a particular injustice or
immorality, and you want to do something
about it, **now**, at **once**, then you can
hardly do worse than write a play about it.
That's what art is bad at.15

Despite the political content in the works since
Jumpers, there is nothing in any of
Stoppard's works that contradicts this statement.
His sights have always been on the "axis of
behaviour where we locate politics or justice"
(53-54); his concern for the integrity of art has
always preceded his political statements.
Political commitments are matter left for the
audience to discover in their own moral
sensibility.

Notes

1. Tom Stoppard, **The Real Thing**, rev.
ed. (Boston: Faber and Faber, 1983), p. 53-54.
Subsequent references given in the text refer to
the edition listed in the notes.

2.   Stoppard, National Press Club Luncheon,
11 October 1979, Washington, D.C.

3.   Stoppard, "Ambushes for the Audience,"
Theatre Quarterly, 4 (May- July 1974), 6.

4.   Stoppard, **Jumpers** (New York: Grove
Press, 1972), p. 87.

5.   Kenneth Tynan, **Show People** (New
York: Simon and Schuster, 1979), p. 89.

6.   Catherine Itzin, **Stages in the
Revolution: Political Theatre in Britain Since
1968** (London: Methuen, 1980).

7.   Stoppard, **Artist Descending a
Staircase in Albert's Bridge and Other
Plays** (New York: Grove Press, 1977), p. 106.

8.   Stoppard, **Travesties** (New York:
Grove Press, 1975), p. 50.

9.   Joan Dean, **Tom Stoppard: Comedy as a
Moral Matrix** (Columbia: University of Missouri
Press, 1981), pp. 75-84.

10.   Stoppard, **Squaring the Circle**
(Boston: Faber and Faber, 1985), pp. 7-8.

11.   Stoppard, **Rosencrantz & Guildenstern
Are Dead** (New York: Grove Press, 1967),
p. 16.

12.   Stoppard's introduction makes clear that
he saw himself as the Narrator. See p. 9.

13.   Hersh Zeifman, "Comedy of Ambush: Tom
Stoppard's **The Real Thing**," **Modern Drama**,
26 (1983), 147.

14. "Ambushes for the Audience," p. 7.

15. Charles Marowitz, "Tom Stoppard--The Theater's Intellectual P. T. Barnum," **The New York Times**, 19 October 1975, sec. 2, p. 5.

Tom Stoppard's Children

Richard Corballis

Tom Stoppard loves his children. He has
often said so, once even going so far as to
assert that "one should stop for the children and
not make the children stop for the writing."[1]
Television has captured him kicking a ball about
with the kids, and the play that many regard as
his masterpiece (**Travesties**) was written "For
Oliver, Barnaby, William and Edmund."

Only in recent years, however, has
Stoppard's philopaedia taken on a dimension which
is of interest to critics and reviewers. In six
recent plays--**Professional Foul, Every Good Boy
Deserves Favour, Night and Day, Dogg's Hamlet,
Cahoot's Macbeth, Squaring the Circle** and **The
Real Thing**--children appear among the
dramatis personae. And in most cases they
play a major part in defining the moral issues
which are at stake.

The child with the most straightforward role
is Sacha Hollar in **Professional Foul**. Sacha
is the son of Pavel Hollar, the persecuted dissident with whom George Anderson becomes involved
during a visit to Prague. Sacha features in only
two scenes, and he speaks in only one of them--
the nocturnal interview with Anderson following
the arrest of Pavel. The scene (and therefore
the character of Sacha) seems redundant at first
sight. Sacha's explanation that the currency
offence of which his father is accused is a
trumped-up charge is unnecessary; the audience
already appreciates this. And the plan which he
outlines for the return of his father's thesis
via the mysterious Jan is completely gratuitous.
Jan never appears--is never heard of again, in

fact. And even if he had turned up as promised
for the last day of the **Colloquium
Philosophicum** it seems very unlikely that
Anderson would have entrusted the thesis to him.
During the interview with Sacha, Anderson insists
that Pavel wanted the thesis taken to England,
and his repetition of this point seems to
indicate that he is now determined to see the job
done. Moreover, the device he hits on for
getting the thesis out (hiding it in McKendrick's
bag) is actually effected before he leaves for
the **Colloquium** the next morning. So even if
Jan had turned up, Anderson would have had
trouble conveying the thesis to him.

Viewed in terms of plot, then, this whole
episode constitutes something of a loose end, and
one imagines that Stoppard must feel a little
uncomfortable about it, since he once confided to
Ronald Hayman:

> I really hate gratuitousness. On
> television--and I have enough technical
> knowledge about how plots work--if I see
> something which is a cheat on the one hand
> or a left-over on the other, or a little
> loose end, it destroys the entire edifice,
> as far as I'm concerned. To me it's like a
> bridge which is going to fall down in five
> minutes.[2]

Viewed in terms of theme, on the other hand,
the character of Sacha is vitally important. The
play is about "the conflict between the rights of
individuals and the rights of the community"[3]
and Anderson is obviously expressing the author's
own opinions when--in his truncated address to
the **Colloquium Philosophicum** near the end of
the play--he argues that the conflict is "a
pseudo-conflict" because the rights of the
community are "a secondary and consequential
elaboration" of the rights of the individual.
According to Anderson the force which sanctions
these individual rights is neither the will of
God nor some form of social contract but an
innate "sense of right and wrong which precedes
utterance." And the best way to establish the

existence of this common sense of justice is by
appealing to people who are not "clever enough"
to be skeptical about their natural impulses.
Children fall into this category:

> A small child who cries 'that's not fair'
> when punished for something done by his
> brother or sister is apparently appealing to
> an idea of justice which is, for want of a
> better word, natural. (p. 176)

The same point is made by two other characters in
the play: Chetwyn and Pavel Hollar himself.
Chetwyn's character is lightly sketched, but his
commitment to the cause of the Czech dissidents
(which ultimately gets him into hot water) proves
that his heart is in the right place. In the
scene which immediately precedes Anderson's
encounter with Sacha, Chetwyn talks with Anderson
(and McKendrick) about ways of tackling awkward
moral dilemmas:

> CHETWYN: A good rule, I find, is to try
>   them out on men much **less**
>   clever than us. I often ask my
>   son what **he** thinks.
> ANDERSON: Your son?
> CHETWYN: Yes. He's eight. (p. 165)

Hollar's discussion with Anderson earlier in
the play covers much the same ground as
Anderson's address to the **Colloquium** at the
end. (In fact Anderson's address must resemble
Hollar's thesis very closely, although there can
be no question of direct influence since the
thesis is written in Czech.) Here is how the
strictly academic part of their discussion ends:

> HOLLAR: You see, to me the idea of an
>   inherent right is intelligible.
>   I believe that we have such
>   rights, and they are paramount.
> ANDERSON: Yes, I see you do, but how do you
>   justify the assertion?
> HOLLAR: I observe. I observe my son for
>   example.
> ANDERSON: Your son?
> HOLLAR: For example. (p. 141)

So the point is thrice made that the child
is father to the man in ethical matters. And
Sacha, the son whom Hollar observes, has been
dragged into the play to demonstrate the point.
His demonstration is not very sophisticated, of
course; he does little except protest his
father's innocence. But this is enough to spur
Anderson to action. Immediately after his
encounter with Sacha, Anderson borrows a typewriter and sets to work on a polemical paper to
replace his scheduled address to the **Colloquium**. The implication is that his decision to
take a stand on Hollar's behalf has been brought
about by the intervention of Sacha--"a small
child who cries 'that's not fair.'"

In **Every Good Boy Deserves Favour**, which
was written in the same year as **Professional
Foul**, there is a child of similar age who is
again called Sacha. The play's protagonist is
Sacha's father, Alexander, whose dissidence has
been rewarded with devastating spells of confinement in a couple of Soviet mental hospitals.
Sacha's main function is to provide a present
reenactment of the sort of behaviour which has
got Alexander into trouble in the past. His
dissidence is on a smaller scale, of course, but
it impresses the audience for reasons which were
spelled out in **Professional Foul**. Sacha is
obviously too young to be susceptible to the
Teacher's claim that dissidents are merely
"malcontents" and "fanatics" who deliberately
indulge in "anti-social" behaviour (p. 105); in
his case the dissidence is natural and
instinctive. And his example in turn confutes
any doubts that the audience may have about
Alexander's motives.

So far the roles of the two Sachas seem
roughly similar. But there is an important twist
in the tail of **Every Good Boy Deserves
Favour**. Bullied incessantly by the Teacher,
and intimidated by the lunatic Ivanov (who
impersonates the Doctor when Sacha visits the
hospital late in the play), Sacha's resolve
finally weakens and he takes up the slogan of his
father's persecutors:

Papa, don't be rigid!
Everything can be all right! (pp. 120-21)

The fact that he **sings** these words is a
further indication of his capitulaton. The play
is built upon three simple equations: music =
Soviet orthodoxy; dissonance = dissidence; and
(thanks to the inclusion of mad Ivanov) music
(and therefore Soviet orthodoxy) = madness. At
the beginning of the play Sacha is, like his
father, "tone-deaf," as we see when he beats his
triangle "**randomly**" and his snare-drum
"**violently**" (pp. 104, 110). By the end, he
has learnt to sing along with the orchestra,
which indicates that he is now a part of the
crazy Soviet system.

Sacha's change of heart is brought about not
by persuasion so much as by naked fear--fear for
the safety of his father. Stoppard still seems
to feel that children are immune to sophistry; he
would still like us to believe with Professor
Anderson that

> when, let us say, we are being persuaded
> that it is ethical to put someone in prison
> for reading or writing the wrong books, it
> is well to be reminded that you can persuade
> a man to believe almost anything provided he
> is clever enough, but it is much more
> difficult to persuade someone less clever.
> (p. 176)

In **Every Good Boy Deserves Favour** Stoppard
does, however, acknowledge that children are
particularly vulnerable **physically**; it may be
difficult to persuade them to betray their better
instincts, but it is easy to frighten them into
doing so. This recognition helps to make **Every
Good Boy Deserves Favour** a bleak and moving
play, though it is, of course, not Sacha's
capitulation but the final isolation of Alexander
(and the music which accompanies it) that moves
the audience most.

Young Alastair Carson in **Night and Day**
is a much less significant character than either
of the Sachas. It is true, I suppose, that he
exerts more influence on the course of the plot
than does Sacha Hollar. (It is Alastair who
alerts Wagner to the fact that Mageeba is coming
to the Carson house to negotiate with Shimbu, and
so the responsibility for the show-down between
Wagner and Mageeba in Act II is ultimately his.)

But Alastair lacks Sacha's thematic
significance; he is not paraded as the living
proof of one of the play's primary contentions.
Instead he exhibits a sort of passive version of
Sacha's active virtue. Early in the play he
serves as a catalyst for revealing the moral
propensities of others. Wagner, the union bully
who is the nearest thing in the play to a
villain, alternately ignores Alastair and
patronizes him abominably, whereas Guthrie, the
quiet, matter-of-fact photographer who ultimately
emerges as something like the hero, treats him
with affection and respect.

Only in the revised version of the script
(published as a second edition by Faber and Faber
in 1979) does Alastair get a chance to campaign
more actively in the cause of morality, and still
he does so only by proxy. Towards the end of the
debate about newspapers conducted by Ruth, Wagner
and Mageeba, Wagner expresses the view that "a
newspaper is too important to be merely a rich
man's property," since the rich man may insist on
the suppression of facts and views which are
uncongenial to his attitudes. Ruth, who favours
free enterprise, responds vehemently:

> How strange. I had no idea that it was the
> millionaires who were threatening your
> freedom to report, Dick. I thought it
> was a millionaire who was picking up the
> bill for your freedom to report. In
> fact, I was discussing this very thing with
> somebody only yesterday--who could it have
> been?--Oh, yes, it was Alastair 4

And she proceeds to use Alastair as a stalking-
horse for her attack on Wagner.

> His theory--Alastair's theory--is that it's
> the very free-for-all which guarantees the
> freedom of each. 'You see, Mummy,' he said,
> 'you don't have to be a millionaire to
> contradict one. It isn't the millionaires
> who are going to stop you, it's the Wagners
> who don't trust the public to choose the
> marked card.' (p. 83)

And so on.

Ruth is obviously exploiting Professor Anderson's point that "a child would know the difference." It is difficult to escape the impression, however, that this is exploitation in the worst sense of the word, and that the notion of the child as ethical arbiter has here become a mere rhetorical device rather than a sincere postulate. The children in **Professional Foul** (young Chetwyn as well as Sacha Hollar) are really put to the test on ethical issues, but it is clear enough that Alastair's meditations on the media are the invention of his mother. Moreover, this flaw in the presentation is matched by a flaw in the content; Ruth (quoting Alastair) is nowhere near as convincing on the subject of newspapers as are Hollar, Anderson and Alexander on the subject of ethics.

Hollar, Anderson and Alexander are not absolutely irrefutable, of course; a professional philosopher could no doubt demolish them as easily as Jonathan Bennett demolished their predecessor (George Moore in **Jumpers**).[5] But **within the context of the play** no effective challenge is offered to their arguments. Ruth's views **are** effectively challenged, however--not only by Wagner (and Mageeba and Guthrie) but by Ruth herself.

Still quoting Alastair, Ruth proceeds to argue that Wagner's fear about rich newspaper proprietors suppressing facts and views which are uncongenial to them is unwarranted because the proprietors only get rich by pleasing the general public. To Wagner's response (that "a man can be rich from oil or real estate and subsidize a paper on the profits") she contrives a rather feeble answer (that millionaires are not homogeneous in their attitudes). But her original argument was susceptible to an objection quite different from Wagner's, namely her own complaint (voiced in Act I and again at the end of Act II) that pleasing the public results in an unacceptable degradation of journalistic standards.[6]

Night and Day is, by Stoppard's standards, a dark and equivocal play. The heroes of both

Professional Foul and **Every Good Boy Deserves Favour** end up physically and morally triumphant, even if there is something hollow and ominous about the way Alexander wins his freedom. But Ruth, the central character of **Night and Day**, is compromised in almost every sense by the end of the play. She is about to conform to her own definition of a tart by going off to sleep with Wagner a second time, and she has failed to score points--other than for vehemence --in the debate about journalism because of the contradiction between her insistence on a free press and her conviction that certain subjects ("the women's page, and the crossword, and the racing results, and the heartbreak beauty queens") are unworthy of attention. (Guthrie gently points to the flaw in her argument when he reminds her that "information, in itself, about **anything**, is light"--p. 92, my emphasis.)

Ruth's inconsistencies are accentuated by her dishonest treatment of Alastair's opinions. The play does not undermine the idea that children have an instinctive sense of right and wrong; it simply points out that unscrupulous adults can abuse this faculty and indicates the dismal consequences which can attend this abuse.

In **Professional Foul**, **Every Good Boy Deserves Favour** and **Night and Day** the child's instinctive "idea of justice" is never seriously questioned.[7] When children are attended to things end happily; when children are coerced, exploited or ignored things end unhappily--that, as Miss Prism or the Player (in **Rosencrantz**) might have put it, is what Stoppard means, at least in the period 1977-79. It was in this period, of course, that he first began to take a position on important topical matters (civil rights and trade unionism), and it was no doubt comforting for him to have a sure criterion to help him set out his views.

Subsequently his attitude to children has become a little more skeptical. This may have something to do with the progression of his two oldest boys from childhood to adolescence. It also seems to reflect a dawning awareness on his part that neither public issues (in **Squaring the Circle**) nor private ones (in **The Real Thing**) are susceptible to the kind of clear-cut analysis offered in these earlier plays.

Before we turn to this more complex pair of
plays, however, we must briefly consider the work
that divides them from the trio already
discussed: **Dogg's Hamlet, Cahoot's Macbeth.**
Dogg's Hamlet, the first half of the diptych,
contains no fewer than four children, but they
bear no resemblance to Alastair Carson or the
Sachas. Able, Baker, Charlie and Fox Major are
simply cartoon characters, labelled alphabetical-
ly and played (for laughs) by adults. Clearly
these children have no special insights; their
sole function is to spout the language which
Stoppard has invented for the occasion. The only
character of any substance in **Dogg's Hamlet**
is Easy, the English-speaking adult who ventures
unwittingly into the bizarre world of the
Dogg-speakers. Likewise in the more serious
sequel, **Cahoot's Macbeth** (from which the
children are banished entirely), Easy emerges as
the hero who enables the dissident Czech actors
to complete their subversive production of
Macbeth despite the Inspector's attempts to
stop it.

There is an easy explanation for the
surprisingly negligent treatment of the children
in this play. **Dogg's Hamlet** is an expanded
version of "Dogg's Our Pet," which was written in
1971. Although Stoppard's heroes were often
childlike at this early stage of his career
(George Moore in **Jumpers,** for example, and
Charlie in "Dogg's Our Pet"), he did not explicitly propound the theme of the noble infant until
1977 (in **Professional Foul**). Albert (in
Rosencrantz) is another early example of a
child devoid of special insights.

Actually it can be argued that "Dogg's Our
Pet" constitutes an attack on the very notion
that there can be any meaningful intuition which
"precedes utterance." The play seems to have
been written as a counterblast to Ted Hughes's
"Orghast," which Stoppard saw performed by Peter
Brook's company in 1971. As Stoppard himself
explained at the time, "Orghast aims to be a
leveller of audiences by appealing . . . to the
instinctive recognition of a 'mental state' within a sound."[8] He found that the play "largely

failed to transmit on an instinctive level the
meaning which had been put into it on an
intellectual level," and so he invented his own
language (Dogg) where the "intellectual level" is
all-important and the audience gets to understand
what is meant by ignoring their instincts and
attending only to "philological clues."

Eight years later, when "Dogg's Our Pet"
became **Dogg's Hamlet,** Stoppard had come to
rate the instincts above the intellect--at least
in moral matters, and there is a latent tension
between the old and the new in **Dogg's Hamlet,
Cahoot's Macbeth.** In the first part, as in
"Dogg's Our Pet," Dogg is a language which one
picks up by exercising one's intellect; in the
second part Dogg is more akin to "a clinical
condition," and "you don't learn it, you catch
it."[9] It is, in short, a metaphor for
subversion, which is something that appeals
instinctively to some (the dissidents) and not to
others (the Inspector and his cronies). If
instead of the childlike Easy, Stoppard had put a
child in charge of the transmission of Dogg in
Cahoot's Macbeth, he would have brought the
play more closely into line with its immediate
predecessors (**Professional Foul,** etc.), but
he would also have exacerbated the tension
between the two parts; a noble infant like the
Sachas would look out of place in the company of
Able, Baker, Charlie and Fox Major.

It was perhaps this uneasy juxtaposition of
intellect and instincts which caused Stoppard to
play down the child motif in his next study of
communism in action: **Squaring the Circle.**
The children in this case belong to Lech Walesa,
and his affection for them is one of the first
points made in his favour. But only once do
these children have anything significant to say,
and what they do say quickly becomes a casualty
of the play's unusual narrative strategy.

This strategy was designed to circumvent the
residual problem of all documentary drama--that
(as Stoppard puts it in his introduction) "we
don't **know** what happened and what was said"
(p. 9). Too scrupulous to emulate Shakespeare,
Hochhuth and others by simply presenting his own

version of the facts, Stoppard opted to filter
his portrait of contemporary Poland through the
eyes of "a narrator with **acknowledged fallibility**" (p. 10). And to emphasise that this
fallibility is real, and not just a theatrical
gimmick, Stoppard originally planned to take the
part of the narrator himself. (This idea was, as
he puts it, "vetoed by the Americans".)

To demonstrate the narrator's fallibility,
Stoppard has him criticized and corrected from
time to time by a series of characters played by
a single actor and referred to collectively as
"the Witness." (Just how the Witness knows "what
happened and what was said" is not clear,
incidentally.)

Towards the end of the play there is a shot
of the Narrator **"watching several of the**
WALESA CHILDREN **playing with a ball,"**
(p. 84). The children reflect on the naiveté
of their father's friend Jacek Kuron, who "thinks
if he leaves the Party alone . . . the Party will
leave him alone." The Witness's voice is heard,
complaining that the scene is "a cheap trick,"
and the next scene elaborates this point. The
Witness agrees with the children that Kuron is
misguided, and--in what looks very much like an
affectionate parody of **Professional Foul**--he
concedes that "children are always right":

> Right and wrong are not complicated--when a
> child cries, "that's not fair!" the child
> can be believed. (p. 84)

But he maintains "it was still a cheap
trick"--presumably because the issues at stake go
beyond the "uncomplicated" business of "right and
wrong." Kuron is technically "right," but, like
so many of Stoppard's characters (McKendrick in
Professional Foul, for example), he has got
things "upside down" in that he puts theory
before practice, and--as the Witness complains
here--"theories don't guarantee social justice,
social justice tells you if a theory is any
good."

Kuron and Walesa are both on the side of the
angels (i.e. Solidarity), but they disagree about

tactics, Kuron being an intellectual and Walesa a
man of action. This difference is indicated
clearly at the beginning of Part Two. In the
first scene of this Part Kuron is released from
prison to the accompaniment of this speech from
the Narrator:

> Kuron went straight to Gdansk. For two
> decades the drama of his intellectual life
> had been the attempt to square the Communist
> circle inside the cornerstones of democratic
> socialism, and now the show had started
> without him. (p. 49)

In the next scene Walesa makes his first
appearance. The contrast between him and Kuron
is almost overstated; Walesa has "never read a
book," and his next ambition is to "Eat dinner."
(His affection for his children is also stressed
here.)

Kuron is treated more sympathetically than
many of Stoppard's intellectuals, but Walesa is
obviously the real hero of the play. Stoppard
stops short of absolute adulation, however;
Walesa is shown to be rash and autocratic on
occasions, and he is certainly naive to believe
(like Kuron, incidentally) that Solidarity can
operate within the Party system--that the circle
can be squared. Conversely, the Party leaders
are not depicted as out-and-out villains. Gierek
in particular has a human face (which he shows in
his real office) as well as a Party face (which
he shows in the fake office used for television
broadcasts). And his successors, Kania and
Jaruzelski, show distinct traces of benevolence.
It is really only the Russians who are uniformly
unbending.

Squaring the Circle depicts a world
where historical and political exigencies distort
moral and ethical issues. The child's instinctive sense of right and wrong is therefore
scarcely relevant, and it is not really
surprising to find the motif relegated to an
ironic aside.

Stoppard began work on **Squaring the
Circle** at the same time as he was finishing

work on **The Real Thing.** Here too he almost
seems to go out of his way to avoid invoking the
child's instinctive sense of right and wrong.
There is, of course, no child in the play, but
there is a character who (like Stoppard's eldest
children in 1982) has not progressed far beyond
adolescence.

The central character is a debonair and
articulate playwright called Henry. By his first
marriage (to Charlotte) Henry has a daughter,
Debbie, who is neither debonair nor articulate;
she "goes riding on Barnes common looking like
the last of the Mohicans,"[10] and she is fond
of uttering "persuasive nonsense" and **"ersatz**
masterpieces" which put Henry in mind of
"Michelangelo working in polystyrene" (pp. 63,
64).

Debbie is much older than Alastair, the
Sachas and Lech Walesa's children. In fact she
is old enough to be living in a "squat" with her
boyfriend, who is either a steam-organist or a
dodgem-entrepeneur, depending on which version of
the text one reads.[11] But, despite her age,
her appearance and her unpromising idiom, Debbie
has an instinctive sense of the way in which
human intercourse should be conducted, and her
account of these instincts (in Scene Nine of the
first edition, Scene Eight of the second) has an
important effect on Henry's outlook.

Henry starts the play as a perfectionist--
especially as regards love and literature,
marriage and words. About words he has this to
say:

> I don't think writers are sacred, but words
> are. They deserve respect. If you get the
> right ones in the right order, you can nudge
> the world a little or make a poem which
> children will speak for you when you're
> dead. (p. 55)

His view of love is similarly rarified, as this
speech indicates:

> I love love. I love having a lover and
> being one. The insularity of passion. I

> love it. I love the way it blurs the
> distinction between all the people who
> aren't one's lover. Only two kinds of
> presence in the world. There's you and
> there's them. (p. 44)

Henry's idealism comes under attack from
many quarters. Early in the play Max insists,

> There's something wrong with you. You've
> got something missing. You may have all the
> answers, but having all the answers isn't
> what life's about. (p. 35)

Charlotte is making the same point when she
observes that Henry has "no place for children.
Smart talk, that's the thing" (p. 21). A little
later Henry's second wife Annie objects to the
way Henry's writing depends on "well chosen words
nicely put together. So what? Why should that
be **it**?" (p. 52). And she also complains
about his complacent attitude to their relationship: "You don't care enough to **care**.
Jealousy is normal" (p. 43).

The pressure on Henry builds, and eventually
the debonair facade cracks. In the penultimate
scene his glib and polished phrases degenerate
into an incoherent cry of pain as he contemplates
the possibility that Annie may be having an
affair with Billy: "Oh, please, please, please,
please, **don't**" (p. 79). At the same time his
complacent confidence in "the insularity of
passion" gives way to the realization that he
must allow Annie some freedom within the
relationship. She puts it this way:

> You have to find a part of yourself where
> I'm not important or you won't be worth
> loving. (p. 72)

He protests, "I can't **find** a part of myself
where you're not important" (p. 77). But he has
already allowed Annie to take a telephone call
from Billy in private, and has even covered up
for her--quite voluntarily--when this call makes
her late for work. One therefore gets the
impression that he is slowly learning to be more
flexible.

It is in order to hasten the revision of
Henry's ideas about love and language that
Stoppard introduces Debbie and reintroduces
Charlotte, who has been offstage since Scene
Three. Charlotte unsettles Henry's idealism
about love by revealing that she had nine lovers
in the course of their marriage. Henry expresses
surprise: "I thought we made a commitment."
Charlotte scoffs at his absolutism: "There are
no commitments only bargains. And they have to
be made again every day" (p. 65).
     Debbie's scene with Henry succeeds
Charlotte's in the first edition and precedes it
in the second. Again the emphasis is on these
two crucial issues, love and language. He begins
by explaining why he sent Debbie to an expensive
private school:

> I paid school fees so that you wouldn't be
> barred by your natural disabilities from
> being taught Latin and learning to speak
> English. (60)

Debbie suggests an additional motive: "I thought
it was so that I'd be a virgin a bit longer."
Henry concedes that he did indeed have this in
mind, and he sums up his twin purposes in the
neat phrase **"Virgo syntacta."**
     Debbie now proceeds to confound his hopes.
In fact she has already revealed a tenuous grasp
on English grammar by using the phrases "Me and
Terry" as the subject of a sentence. (Henry,
however, overreacts when he substitutes the
unidiomatic "I and Terry"; we sense already that
he is heading for a fall.) Debbie continues to
reel off clichés, but--unlike Max in Scene
Two--she is not cowed by Henry's purist outrage.
"Don't write it, Fa. Just say it," she sighs as
another polished phrase rolls off his tongue.
She is no longer on stage, however, to witness
her final triumph. In Scene Eleven Henry quotes
verbatim the **"ersatz masterpiece"** to
which he objected so strongly when it first
issued from her lips: "Exclusive rights isn't
love, it's colonization" (pp. 64, 77). The play
is full of echoes and recapitulations. This one

indicates the extent to which Henry's high-
mindedness about language moderates in the course
of the play. It also indicates that Debbie plays
a significant part in effecting this change.

Debbie has something to teach Henry about
love as well. She quickly reveals that the
expensive private school bolstered her virginity
as little as it bolstered her grammar; she
emerged no more **virgo** than she was
syntacta. In fact it was the putative
guardian of her syntax (the Latin master) who
deflowered her--a nice irony. From these and
subsequent couplings she has developed a worldly
attitude to love and sex which compares
favourably with Henry's priggish idealism. She
knows that there is more to "fidelity" than
simply "not having it off," and that therefore
the question which so obsesses Henry in both his
life and his plays--"Did she or didn't she?"--is
a shallow and uninteresting (not to say sexist)
one. Moreover, since she concedes that her
current lover, Ben, "does" while she herself does
only "occasionally," we may assume that she has
learnt to give her partner that freedom which
Henry still cannot concede to Annie. It is when
he does finally move towards such a concession
(in Scene Eleven) that he quotes Debbie's adage
about "exclusive rights"--an indication that in
this respect too he has learnt from her.

So far Debbie's role seems as pivotal and as
absolute as Sacha Hollar's. She instinctively
knows the truth which the central character must
acquire through painful experience--
"self-knowledge through pain," as Henry puts it,
talking of **House of Cards**. But in fact there
are crucial differences between Henry and
Anderson and between Debbie and Sacha.

The change in Henry is nowhere near as
clear-cut as the change in Anderson. Though, on
the whole, Henry's idiom becomes simpler and more
personal towards the end, he is still capable of
polished irony in his speeches to Brodie and (on
the telephone) to Max in the final scene. More
important, his determination to allow Annie more
independence is never put to the test, since she

loses interest in Billie (and Brodie) at the crucial moment. So we cannot be sure how either partner will react when next somebody takes her fancy.

As for Debbie, her guarded confession that her experience of sex has not lived up to her expectations--"it turned out to be biology after all" (p. 62)--suggests a subtextual insecurity which, if sufficiently exploited by the actress playing the part, may turn everything she says into prickly defensiveness rather than instinctive good sense. Her age, of course, encourages such speculation and so, perhaps, does her sex, since teenage girls have traditionally occasioned more concern than their male counterparts. Stoppard seems to have gone out of his way to stress her vulnerability. Clearly he did not want Henry exposed to a moral monolith like Sacha Hollar.

All sorts of question marks hover round the conclusion of **The Real Thing.** Both here and in **Squaring the Circle,** Stoppard acknowledges that life--considered in either a public or a private dimension--is too complex to be subjected to the instincts of babes and sucklings. It seems likely that children will no longer feature prominently in his plays. But they served a very useful purpose in the period 1977-82, by providing the prop which helped him out of his early phase of intellectual "leap-frog" into social and political involvement. He is now ready to throw away the prop and to engage in more complex, more adult (and therefore more satisfying) analyses of these and other problems. But without the children--without **Professional Foul** and **Every Good Boy Deserves Favour**--he would probably not have been able to progress from the froth and bubble of **Hound** and **Dirty Linen** to the complexities of **The Real Thing.**

Notes

1. Ronald Hayman, **Tom Stoppard** (London: Heinemann, 1977), p. 138.

2. Hayman, p. 142.

3. Tom Stoppard, **"Squaring the Circle"** with **"Every Good Boy Deserves Favour"** and **"Professional Foul"** (London: Faber and Faber, 1984), p. 173. All subsequent references to these three plays are to this edition.

4. Stoppard, **Night and Day** (London: Faber and Faber, 1979), p. 83. All subsequent references are to this edition. In the first edition (London, 1978) there is at this point a single oblique reference to Alastair: "I bet even Allie could work out for himself that it is the very free-for-all which guarantees the freedom of each" (p. 83).

5. Jonathan Bennett, "Philosophy and Mr Stoppard," **Philosophy**, L (1975), pp. 5-18. A supplementary critique is: Henning Jensen, "Jonathan Bennett and Mr Stoppard," **Philosophy**, LII (1977), pp. 214-7.

6. See **Night and Day**, pp. 47-48, 59-61, 91-92 of the second edition. It is difficult to know how much weight Stoppard means these arguments to carry. Readers of the play can probably convince themselves that the defences of junk journalism put forward by Milne (pp. 60-61) and Guthrie (p. 92) effectively counter Ruth's arguments. But on-stage Ruth's presence is so magnetic that the audience may well lose its critical faculties in respect of her ideas.

7. It is interesting to note that in the first edition of **Night and Day** Mageeba calls Alastair Alexander (p. 76)--the name of which Sacha is the diminutive. Thus the children of **Professional Foul**, **Every Good Boy Deserves Favour** and **Night and Day** are linked (albeit tenuously) by name. This accentuates the similarity in their roles.

8. **The Times** (London) **Literary Supplement** (1 October 1971), p. 1174.

9. Stoppard, **Dogg's Hamlet, Cahoot's Macbeth** (London: Faber and Faber, 1980), p. 74.

10. Stoppard, **The Real Thing** (London: Faber and Faber, 1983), p. 30. All subsequent references are to this edition.

11. The first edition (published by Faber and Faber in 1982) differs markedly from the second, from which my references are taken. The versions performed in London and New York differed slightly from both the published editions--and from one another.

Tom Stoppard's Dramatic Debates:
The Case of **Night and Day**

Katherine E. Kelly

The notion of entertaining an audience with
lengthy intellectual debates may strike
contemporary theatergoers as more than slightly
anachronistic. But in the history of the modern
theater, Beckett's poetics of silence and Robert
Wilson's theater of images are the exception
rather than the rule. Much of the modern theater
movement grew up with the avowed intention of
replacing the set speeches of melodrama with
intelligent argument capable of provoking the
spectator to sustained reflection upon a social
or moral problem. In his 1871 "Inaugural
Lecture," Danish scholar Georg Brandes was
adamant on this point:

> What keeps a literature alive in our days is
> that it submits problems to debate. . . . A
> literature that does not submit problems to
> debate loses all meaning . . . hav[ing] as
> little to do with development and progress
> as the fly that thought it was driving the
> wagon forward because it occasionally gave
> the four horses some harmless stings.[1]

After reading Brandes's Lectures, Henrik Ibsen's
thinking and writing for the stage underwent a
transformation. In the years following 1872, he
wrote a number of social problem plays, including
A Doll House which, in its turn, clarified
Shaw's vision of the modern theater:

> To this day [critics] remain blind to a new
> technical factor in the art of . . .
> playmaking . . . the discussion. . . . The

discussion conquered Europe in Ibsen's
Doll House; and now the serious
playwright recognizes in [it] the main test
of his highest powers, [and] the real centre
of his play's interest.[2]

Thirteen years later, Bertolt Brecht, while
building his own Epic theory of theater,
applauded Shaw's delight in disputation in his
1926 essay "Three Cheers for Shaw":

Shaw's own dramatic works dwarf those of his
contemporaries [as] they so unhesitatingly
appeal to the reason. His world is one that
arises from opinions. The opinions of his
characters constitute their fates. Shaw
creates a play by inventing a series of
complications which give his characters a
chance to develop their opinions as fully as
possible and to oppose them to our own.[3]

For Brecht, as for Brandes and Ibsen, the theater
offered a forum for discussing and reforming
society. But by the 1960s and 1970s, Tom
Stoppard had begun writing a discussion play
based on the premise that the thinking playwright
cannot endorse unqualified opinions about the
fundamental questions of his time. Coming after
Beckett's and Pinter's startling critiques of the
expressive and discursive powers of dramatic
language,[4] Stoppard conceived of his play of
ideas as a comedy of uncertainty:

My plays are a lot to do with the fact that
I just don't know. . . . Few statements
remain unrebutted. . . . There is very
often no single clear statement in my plays,
but a series of conflicting statements made
by conflicting characters, and they tend to
play a sort of infinite leap frog.[5]

Of his five major stage comedies to date, **Night
and Day** has been the least successful, perhaps
because it marks a change in Stoppard's style of
dramatizing uncertainty. And while I would not
argue that it equals **Travesties** in energy,

wit or scope, I do hope to demonstrate that it
has been underestimated both as a striking
example of a contemporary discussion play and as
a transitional work in the playwright's emerging
canon. Every element of its structure, but
particularly its debate scenes, show evidence of
a new flexibility in Stoppard's staging of
thoughtful comedy.
     While the overall effect of this work may
appear muted in relation to earlier Stoppard
plays, **Night and Day** represents a broadening
of the playwright's expressive range, already
begun in his political plays. The style shift is
one of degree--from pervasive to sporadic parody;
from extravagantly clever dialogue to deliberately flat speech; from multiple converging plots to
a primary line of action. Technical innovations
support these shifts in language and theme. The
static, two-part set of **Enter a Free Man,
Jumpers** and **Travesties** has been replaced by
a cyclorama that can swivel to change the propor-
tion of interior to exterior space, expressing
Stoppard's movement away from a static demarking
of life and illusion towards a dynamic staging of
their fusion. The play's opening scene neatly
illustrates how Stoppard's earlier techniques
have been modified to suit his shift towards a
more naturalistic style. Coincidence, for
example, one of the hallmarks of Stoppard's
comedy, works structurally in this piece as it
has in earlier works, but to quieter effect. The
opening helicopter scene orchestrates the
coincidental substitution of "real" stage objects
for an imagined stage scene, while, at the same
time, dramatizing a violent shooting nearly
identical to an incident to be narrated at the
play's close.[6] The curtain opens on what later
proves to be a dream sequence. As an African
dusk falls, a helicopter approaches from the
distance, hovering just above the stage; a jeep
drives on, headlights flashing; a machine gun
begins to fire. A British photographer jumps out
of the jeep, shouts and waves his arms to stop
the firing, but is caught by a spray of bullets.
Then the stage lights come up to simulate late
afternoon, and we see George Guthrie, the same

photographer, stretched out asleep on a garden
chair, and the individual objects of his
nightmare assume their actual identity: a telex
machine chatters in bursts like a machine gun, a
car approaches with a noise like a jeep, and the
sun shines like a spotlight on Guthrie's eyes.
Later in this scene, an actual helicopter buzzes
the verandah, causing the now awake Guthrie to
shrink in fear. As the light rises to simulate
late afternoon and Guthrie awakens, both he and
the audience discover simultaneously that the
opening scene has been a dream. Stoppard will
ambush the audience again, disguising the dream
scene opening Act 2 as a continuation of the main
plot. This drifting between night and day,
between dream world and ostensibly real world,
occurs with greater fluidity and less structural
segmentation here than in, for example, **The
Real Inspector Hound**, one of Stoppard's earlier
farces on the same theme.

    The debate scenes in this play also reflect
Stoppard's shift from complete to partial parody,
from literary allusiveness to reduced and
occasionally spare speech, from historical
reconstruction to original creation. Here, the
debates are less discrete structurally, more
distended and integrated into realistic conversa-
tional exchanges than are the debates of
Travesties or **Jumpers**, for example. Their
language and rhythm do not parody widely
recognizable literary styles, although Wagner
imitates extremes of journalistic prose. They
are timed to ensure that the plot's events will
shift the characters' and spectators' viewpoints
on the argument, and they are tied to a plot that
bears directly on the issues in dispute. **Night
and Day** continues Stoppard's dramatic preoccupation with absolute values, here defined as the
absolute good of the free flow of information.
But instead of parodying the search for that
absolute, Stoppard refines it through his
characters' repeated attempts to describe the
proper relation between free expression and news
reporting.

When two British journalists and a
photographer gather in Jeddu at the home of
British mine owner Geoffrey Carson to cover a
rebellion against Kambawe's ruling dictator, they
discover themselves on opposite sides of a
fundamental question: how free is Britain's
press and at what price should its freedom be
secured? Dick Wagner arrives shortly after the
slumbering photographer Guthrie has awakened on
the Carson's verandah. Wagner, a reporter for
the London **Globe**, is a stylized type of the
hard-bitten, veteran journalist who calls himself
a "fireman" covering "fires." "I don't file
prose. I file facts" (p. 32). Wagner's
political views are similarly hard-edged and
rigid--at the outset of the action. Journalists,
he says, are "working to keep richer men than us
richer than us, and nothing's going to change
that without worker solidarity" (p. 33). The
loyal unionist Wagner meets young Jacob Milne, a
freelance **Globe** writer at the Carson house,
soon after Milne has scooped the brewing
rebellion and obtained an interview with the
elusive rebel leader Colonel Shimbu. When Wagner
discovers that Milne opposes closed shops for
journalists' unions and refused to join what used
to be his local chapel in Grimsby, England, he
uses the Carsons' telex to wire the **Globe** his
protest over the employment of non-member Milne.
The fiery debate between Wagner and Milne
accompanying this action is grounded both in the
general conflict between materialism and idealism
already familiar in Stoppard's works[7] and in
the particular British press dispute over the
closed shop. Wagner, the materialist, advocates
protecting his freedom of expression by
exercising maximum economic control of the
newspaper industry through unionization. Milne,
the idealist, substitutes for Wagner's economic
concern, a philosophical preoccupation with the
press's ideal function as the "last line of
defense for all the other freedoms" (p. 63).
While attempting to protect the reporter's
freedom from management's interference, Wagner's
unionists would subject it to the workers'
control, says Milne. In part because of its

special function, Milne (here speaking for
playwright Stoppard) classifies journalism as a
sacred activity exempt from the parochial
squabbling of union strikes and negotiations. So
polarized are Wagner and Milne that they exhaust
their verbal resources in a mere few lines of
debate, exchanging the epithets "scab" and "trot"
as the argument heats up. Only the arrival of a
Globe wire ironically congratulating Milne on
his Shimbu interview saves him from the tough
Australian's flying punch.

The emotional heat of this exchange has
another source in Britain's self-conscious
scrutiny of its press in the 1970s. At the
center of this scrutiny lies the controversy over
the closed shop whose advocates favored the line
adopted by the National Union of Journalists
(NUJ), most of whose members had long favored
100% membership agreements to strengthen their
negotiating position against employers. In the
NUJ's view, the application of this membership
policy was to be purely industrial. However,
opponents of the closed shop feared that under
such 100% membership conditions, the NUJ could
use its strength to limit access to the press by
people other than union members, and, in extreme
instances, could result in controlling editors
and in censoring the news.[8]

Neither of Stoppard's spokesmen on either
side of this issue cuts a wholly appealing or
credible figure. Milne's articulate defense of
the ideal function of the press relies heavily on
principle, only slightly on practice. Even his
clothes--safari suits and tennis shirts--betray
his youthful romanticism. Wagner, on the other
hand, speaks and moves aggressively, proves to be
jealous and opportunistic and overly fond of
slogans when expressing complex ideas. Ruth
Carson, Geoffrey's intelligent and sexy wife,
spots the weakness in both men, nearly laughing
aloud at Milne's high-mindedness and openly
scorning Wagner's vulgarity--and that in spite of
having gone to bed with the Australian on a
recent trip to London.[9] Stoppard conditions
the audience's response to this first debate in
the terms of his newer style, substituting for
the shrivelling humor of parody a psychological

rendering of the characters' flaws. Even
idealist Milne, we discover, is motivated by a
grubby egoism:

> Carson says there's fifty reporters in
> Jeddu. They've got themselves thoroughly
> lumbered. . . . (**Reading from the** Globe)
> " . . . sources close to President
> Mageeba . . ." Sheer desperation . . .
> Richard Vahgner. I bet I've made him sick.
> (p. 25)

And Wagner's competitiveness exceeds Milne's.
The veteran wires his protest of Milne's
employment only after discovering that Milne has
scooped him on the rebel's story. Vanity and
self-interest compromise the journalists'
statements of their professional ideals and
complicate the audience's response to their
expression. Stoppard uses this first debate to
relate free expression as an absolute value to
its imperfect exercise in an imperfect
profession.

The second of the debate scenes begins
unobtrusively by extending the first and ends by
submerging the argument in Ruth's sexual desire.
In a dialogue with Ruth the realist, Milne
amplifies the difference between himself and
Wagner, shifting the terms of debate from
politics to the principle of free expression.
But Ruth, embittered by the papers'
sensationalistic coverage of her divorce and
remarriage to Carson, dismisses most actual
newswriting as "junk journalism" written by
vulgar egoists. Milne agrees with her, but takes
the argument one step further:

> Milne: No matter how imperfect things are,
>   if you've got a free press every-
>   thing is correctable, and without it
>   everything is concealable.
>
> Ruth: I'm with you on the free press.
>   It's the newspapers I can't stand.
>
> Milne: You don't have to tell me. . . .
>   It's the price you pay for the part
>   that matters.

> "Ruth":   I like that one who's doing all the
>   talking.
>
>   . . . .
>
> Milne: Junk journalism is the evidence of a
>   society that has got at least one
>   thing right, that there should be
>   nobody with the power to dictate
>   where responsible journalism
>   begins.   (pp. 65-67)

Intrigued by Milne's conviction, Ruth's attention
jumps track from the cerebral to the sensual.
Milne exits the scene pursued by Ruth's provocative stare. Stoppard reinforces the play's
central idea--reconciling principles and human
nature--by submerging the press debate in Ruth's
erotic subtext. The argument, like the play's
setting, shifts from daylight rationality to
twilight fantasy, from the rational to the
psychological, preparing us for its continuation
during the farce interlude opening Act 2. The
Act 2 debate questions the nature and cost of
freedom--specifically sexual freedom--in the
terms set by Ruth's realism and Milne's idealism.
Cunningly staged as a continuation of the real
action, only the scene's conclusion discloses
that the audience has been watching two Ruths:
the actual Ruth, a witty, bored colonial wife
stuck in Kambawe, and her imagined self, "Ruth,"
a pastiche of cinema seductresses Talullah
Bankhead, Elizabeth Taylor and Marlene Deitrich.
Designing the action to fool his audience into
taking the unreal for the real, Stoppard
underscores the relative realness of the play
world in which life-like people must make
life-like choices and ethical trade-offs when
attempting to live by their principles. One of
Stoppard's most divided and therefore interesting
characters, Ruth manages during this debate
simultaneously to interrogate and seduce the
figures of her dream:

> Ruth: It's a bit metaphysical to feel
>   guilt about the idea of Geoffrey
>   being hurt if Geoffrey is in a
>   blissful state of ignorance--don't
>   you think? . . . .

> Milne: You shouldn't try to make it sound
>   like a free ride. "Geoffrey will
>   never know and I'm not his chattel
>   so there's nothing to pay." There
>   are no free rides. You always pay.
>
> Ruth: Take it, then, and pay. Be a
>   bastard. Behave badly. (pp. 76-77)

Milne tells Ruth that his fantasies of going to
bed with her exist "in a parallel world. No day
or night, no responsibilities, no friction,
almost no gravity" (p. 75). Like George Moore's
dream Coda that concludes **Jumpers**, Ruth's
dream scene distills the play's major intellectual question and poses it from a slightly
different vantage point: What is the cost of
freedom? It comes cheaply only in dreams.

The implications of this debate scene are
not what they first appear. By seducing Milne,
"Ruth" seems to make a clear choice, albeit a
make-believe one, to sacrifice her marriage to
the pragmatist Geoffrey for the sake of the young
idealist Milne. But in the relatively more
"real" frame play, Ruth's moral rules change as
events take their course. Early in the action,
she explains to Wagner that having gone to bed
with him once was a forgiveable slip, but twice
would make her a tart. And yet, at the play's
close, she is inviting him to spend the night
with her--again. The parallel world of "Ruth's"
seduction scene takes us directly into the
familiar hiding place of the Stoppardian "Moon"
character whose frustrated desire for moral
clarity often locks the dreamer into his dream
world. But where the Moon of Stoppard's earlier
works rarely escapes his self-constructed dream,
Stoppard's Ruth moves easily back and forth
between the "real" and the imaginary. Stoppard
no doubt placed "Ruth's" and "Milne's" fidelity
debate after Milne's exit and before the
announcement of his death in order to keep
Milne's beliefs before the audience while writing
him out of the action. Ruth later will present
Milne's opinions disguised as her son's in the
play's concluding debate on press freedom, initi-
ated by the arrival of Kambawe's President
Mageeba.

This last debate scene, focussing squarely
on the issue of press freedom, broadens the terms
of the pro- and anti-union dispute by introducing
Mageeba's anti-British, anti-democratic standards
of press control. These standards collide with
those held, however implicitly, by Wagner, whose
head gets badly knocked during the course of his
Mageeba interview. The British educated Mageeba
stays at least one step ahead of Wagner during
their exchange, not simply outguessing Wagner's
attempts to flatter him with a series of anti-
communist clichés but managing to use Wagner as
a publicist in his own campaign against the rebel
leader Shimbu. Like the Lenin and Tzara couple
of **Travesties,** Stoppard plays off the ruth-
less political leader against a naive westerner
who understands little of the lethal force behind
the man whose story he hopes will bring him
temporary fame.

Mageeba is no straw dog. His authority
grows from his familiarity with the British press
and its practices. When Carson advises Wagner to
quote the President on the "lobby basis,"[10]
Mageeba has an informed opinion of that
convention at hand:

> I don't believe in that. . . . I know the
> British press is very attached to the lobby
> system. It lets the journalists and the
> politicians feel proud of their traditional
> freedoms while giving the reader as much of
> the truth as they think is good for him.
>
> (p. 94)

For the first time in the play, British practices
are presented from a wholly alien point of view.
And we recall that Mageeba has pointedly rejected
the British model of rule and of rights for his
own country. As he tells Wagner and Ruth, his
own post-revolutionary newspaper, the **Daily
Citizen,** represents a compromise between
all-out totalitarian control of information and
the anarchic chaos he identifies with private
enterprise:

> I did not believe a newspaper should be part
> of the apparatus of the state. . . . But

neither could I afford a return to the whims
of private enterprise. . . .   What then?
. . . .   Freedom with responsibility, that
was the elusive formula we pondered. . . .
From the ashes there arose . . . a new
Daily Citizen, responsible and
relatively free.   (p. 99)

Mageeba's cynical definition of "freedom"
sacrifices the most basic principle of a free
press--that it report "the facts" regardless
whose interests they serve. In Mageeba's view,
the press is never neutral; either it helps him
rebuild his country his way or it hinders him.
Thus his grim view of the **Globe's** interview
with his enemy, Shimbu, a view he demonstrates
with a mute gesture:

(**He leans toward** WAGNER.) Do you know
what I mean by a relatively free press, Mr.
Wagner?

Wagner: Not exactly, sir, no.

Mageeba: I mean a free press which is
           edited by one of my relatives.
           (**He throws his head back and
           laughs. . . .** MAGEEBA **brings
           the weighted end of his stick down
           on** WAGNER's **head.** WAGNER
           falls on the floor.)
                                         (pp. 99-100)

Stoppard times Mageeba's attack on the press's
right to disclose information to shock both the
audience and characters into recognizing its
status as the primary right in the press debate.
Wagner's and Milne's dispute over unionization
suddenly diminishes in the face of the fundamental split dividing the British from the Kambawean
principle of press freedom. The walking stick
ends the relatively free exchange of ideas.
    The shock following Mageeba's outburst is
amplified when Guthrie enters and tells Wagner
that Milne is dead. What has been until this
point a theoretical dispute on the nature and
value of free expression is shown to have flesh
and blood consequences in the lives of actual

journalists. Milne has not only professed a
belief in the free flow of information but also
risked his life for it. These two shocking
revelations synchronize the dramatic and
intellectual moment of climax with Ibsenesque
economy. Offstage, events have taken an
irreversible turn, while onstage the discussion
has reached a point of impasse. The breaking
war, Milne's death and Mageeba's stick exert
opposing pressures on the journalists, on the one
hand, to leave the country for safer ground, and,
on the other hand, to remain there to tell the
story. Stoppard again integrates action and
discussion by orchestrating the characters'
reactions to Milne's death as a means of
clarifying their choices. Both journalists opt
to stay and face whatever danger the war and
Mageeba may pose, although Guthrie decides more
readily than Wagner. When Carson warns Guthrie
that Mageeba may not think the **Globe** is on
his side, Guthrie responds, "We're not here to be
on somebody's side, Geoffrey. That was World War
Two. We try to show what happened. . . . And
sometimes people bitch about which side we're
supposed to be on . . ." (pp. 106-7).

But Ruth cannot let Guthrie's position go
unchallenged. Resurrecting her earlier exchange
with Milne, she confronts the photographer, "I'm
not going to let you think [Jake] died for free
speech and the guttering candle of democracy--
crap! You're all doing it to impress each other
and to be top dog . . ." (pp. 107-8). In answer
to Ruth's cynicism,[11] Guthrie, the play's
unobtrusive hero, delivers its most thematically
crucial lines:

> I've been around a lot of places. People do
> awful things to each other. But it's worse
> in places where everybody is kept in the
> dark. It really is. Information is light.
> Information, in itself, about anything, is
> light. That's all you can say, really.
> (pp. 108-9)

The deliberate flatness of George's speech marks
Stoppard's departure from the rhetorical flourish

of the central speeches in earlier works such as
Rosencrantz & Guildenstern Are Dead, Jumpers
and **Travesties**, and it gives to Guthrie's
lines the ring of authenticity. Both the play's
messenger and its soothsayer, Guthrie fits his
plain talk to the equally plain and essential
truth he utters. It follows that his decision to
stick out his assignment in Kambawe comes
lightning fast. Having sorted out his loyalties,
he avoids the excesses of Wagner's jaded
maneuverings and Milne's naive enthusiasm,
balancing his ideals with the weight of his
experience.

Wagner, on the other hand, decides to stay
in Kambawe only when provoked by a telex message
whose content and timing further testify to
Stoppard's playing of irony and coincidence in a
lower key: "Milne copy blacked by subs, full
chapel and machine room support. Total
confrontation and dismissal notices tonight,
weekend shut down definite. Wotwu . . .
Battersby" (p. 110). Stoppard's use of the verb
"blacked" neatly ties Wagner's protest to a
blocking of light. Wagner's success in excluding
Milne's non-union copy from the **Globe's**
weekend issue has rebounded: his own story will
be kept out as well. But more significant for
the play's argument is the irony with which
Stoppard here distinguishes Milne's somewhat
naive pursuit of "light" and Wagner's dogged
pursuit of darkness. By timing the message to
follow on the heels of Guthrie's report of
Milne's death, Stoppard attempts to throw the
balance of sympathy with Milne's opposition to
the closed shop. Even Wagner's staunch pro-union
position appears to shift after reading the
cable. Not only does he refuse to withdraw his
labor in agreement with union practice but also
he pays tribute to Milne by composing his
obituary to be relayed to the **Grimsby
Messenger.**

The press debate is over, if not resolved.
Guthrie's equation between information and light,
the carefully timed arrival of the **Globe**
telegram, and the menacing threat of Mageeba's
brand of censorship throw the play's weight

against the closed shop and in favor of
encouraging a proliferation of newspapers with a
variety of ideological lines. But while the
Milne-Guthrie view prevails in the press debate,
Milne's idealism loses in the fidelity debate.
Just as the rules of union politics have become
academic to Wagner in the face of Milne's actual
death and the promise of a breaking story, so has
absolute fidelity become pointless to Ruth:

> Wagner: I thought you didn't want to be a
>   tart . . .
>
> Ruth: How do I know until I've tried it?
>   I name this bottle "Cutty Sark."
>   (p. 112)

With the death of idealist Milne, Ruth further
relaxes her moral rules in favor of standards
more finely tuned to the contingencies of the
real world.[12] The fidelity debate ends
ambiguously with Ruth christening both the scotch
and herself "Cutty Sark," "Cutty" punning on the
Scottish colloquial for immoral woman.[13]
Evoking this traditional association between
scotch, lust and regret, Stoppard closes the play
with an ambiguously artificial tableau--the
piano-player plus singer scene--that looks both
like one of Ruth's cinematic hallucinations and
like an uninterrupted continuation of the frame
play. Either of the two Ruths could be directing
this scene, or the two may have merged in the
closing parody of the torch singer drowning her
sorrows in music and booze.
    The debate strategy in **Night and Day**
marks a crucial shift in Stoppard's play of
ideas, most obviously signalled by a stylistic
turn towards naturalism, and corresponding to a
new thematic preoccupation with reconciling the
idealist's search for moral absolutes with the
pragmatist's acceptance of moral flexibility.
Stoppard chooses as his metaphor for this
reconciliation a contemporary debate on the
implications of the closed shop for Britain's
free flow of information. And, although the
weight of the play's press debates seems clearly

to condemn the closed shop, the play's closing
scenes substitute for the particular press
question the general moral question underlying
it: How can the individual make responsible
moral choices under conditions of change and
uncertainty? And what strategies can the
playwright use to render the problem of choice
compelling and credible? No single scene,
character or debate holds the answer to that
question. Instead, the movement within
individual debate scenes and between those scenes
and the play's visual and narrative events
carries the sense Stoppard hopes to communicate
of thought shifting under feeling and of night
fading under the light of day.

Notes

1. Quoted from Eric Bentley, ed., **The Theory of the Modern Stage**, trans. Evert Sprinchorn (London: Penguin Books, 1972), p. 388.

2. G. B. Shaw, "The Quintessence of Ibsenism" (1913 expanded edition) in **Major Critical Essays**, Vol. 19 (New York: William H. Wise & Co., 1931), p. 145.

3. Bertolt Brecht, "Three Cheers for Shaw," in Willett, John, ed. & trans. **Brecht on Theatre** (New York: Hill and Wang, 1964), p. 11.

4. Andrew Kennedy summarizes this critique in his **Six playwrights in search of a language** (Cambridge: Cambridge University Press, 1975), see especially Chapters 3 and 4.

5. Tom Stoppard, "Ambushes for the Audience: Towards a High Comedy of Ideas," **Theatre Quarterly**, 4 (May-July 1974), 6-7.

6. Stoppard, **Night and Day** (New York: Grove Press, 1979). The dream helicopter scene is described in stage directions on pp. 1 and 2. Subsequent citations will be to this edition and will appear in the text. Philip Gaskell's important history of the revisions made to the script of this play between the years 1978-80 testifies to Stoppard's determination to change his production style. See "**Night and Day**: The Development of a Play Text," in Jerome J. McGann, ed., **Textual Criticism and Literary Interpretation** (Chicago: University of Chicago Press, 1980), pp. 162-79.

7. Kenneth Tynan describes this conflict as it appears in Stoppard's early (unpublished) 1964 television play, **This Way Out With Samuel Boot**, in which two Boot brothers represent the extremes of materialism and idealism. See Tynan's "Withdrawing with Style from the Chaos," **The New Yorker** (19 December 1977), pp. 57, 60. The Moon character generally aligns him or

herself with the human spirit as manifested in art against the forces of materialism as manifested in deterministic ideologies.

8. For a more complete summary of this controversy, see the **Royal Commission on the Press Final Report** (Her Majesty's Stationery Office: London, 1977), especially Chapter 17, "Closed Shop in Journalism." A more partisan summary of the controversy that shares Milne's disapproval of the closed shop appears in **Index on Censorship**, 4 (2) (1975) 72-75, a periodical Stoppard reads.

9. Stoppard strengthened Wagner's appeal both as a spokesman for the closed shop and as a lover for Ruth in several post-rehearsal changes to the Faber edition of the text. In the most striking of these, Stoppard gives Wagner a speech that proves him not only equal to Ruth's sarcasm and snobbery but of a temperament similar to hers (See Wagner's speech, pp. 55-56 in the 1979 Grove Press edition).

10. The "lobby basis" of attributing information refers to the British practice by which journalists withhold attribution when reporting politically sensitive news to avoid embarrassing themselves or their sources should such reports prove false. My thanks to Professors James Gindin and Graham Hovey of the University of Michigan for their interpretation of this jargon phrase.

11. In her otherwise perceptive essay, **"Night and Day,"** in **Gambit**, 10 (37) (1980), 77-86, Judy Simons overlooks Stoppard's careful attempt to balance Milne's idealism with Ruth's cynicism, identifying the latter as the play's dominant view. (See this essay for parallels between **Night and Day** and Stoppard's earlier work.)

12. For a different interpretation of Ruth's motivation, see Jim Hunter's essay, **"Night and Day,"** in Harold Bloom, ed., **Tom Stoppard** (New York: Chelsea House Publishers, 1986), pp. 119-26.

13.   Stoppard no doubt chose this phrase for
its having been immortalized in Robert Burns's
mock-heroic poem "Tam O' Shanter," whose moral
warns of the high price to be paid for life's
joys:

> Whene'er to drink you are inclin'd,
> Or cutty-sarks run in your mind,
> Think, ye may buy the joys o'er dear,
> Remember Tam o' Shanter's mare.

(Quoted from James Kinsley, ed., **The Poems and
Songs of Robert Burns**, 2 [Oxford: Clarendon
Press, 1968], p. 564.)

Comedy of Ambush:
Tom Stoppard's **The Real Thing**

Hersh Zeifman

When the curtain rises on **The Real
Thing**, Tom Stoppard's most recent comedy, we
see a solitary figure, Max, seated in his living
room: "[h]e is using a pack of playing cards to
build a pyramidical, tiered viaduct on the coffee
table in front of him."[1] Suddenly we hear
the off-stage front door being opened; Max calls
out "Don't slam--" (p. 9), but before he can
finish his sentence, the door slams and his
viaduct of cards collapses. The door-slammer is
his wife, Charlotte, who appears briefly before
disappearing into the hall to hang up her
topcoat. Charlotte has just returned from a
business trip to Switzerland--or so she claims;
the problem is that, during her absence, Max has
ransacked her private belongings and discovered
her passport in her recipe drawer:

CHARLOTTE:	You go through my things when I'm away? (**Pause. Puzzled.**)
MAX:	I liked it when I found nothing. You should have just put it [your passport] in your handbag. We'd still be an ideal couple. So to speak.
CHARLOTTE:	Wouldn't you have checked to see if it had been stamped?
MAX:	That's a very good point. I notice that you never went to Amsterdam when you went to Amsterdam. I must say that I take my hat off to you, coming home with Rembrandt place mats

299

> for your mother. It's those
> little touches that lift
> adultery out of the moral arena
> and make it a matter of style.
> (p.13)

Without her passport, Charlotte has obviously not
been abroad; where **has** she been, then, and,
more important, with whom? Charlotte refuses to
answer, and the scene draws to a close with her
picking up her suitcase and walking out.
Abandoned, Max reaches down to open the present
she had brought him from her supposed trip to
Switzerland. When he sees what it is, he begins
to laugh: it is "a **miniature Alp in a glass
bowl. He gives the bowl a shake and creates a
snowstorm within it**" (p. 15). End of Scene
One.

Despite Dotty's putative affair with Archie
in **Jumpers**, despite Ruth's acknowledged
infidelity with Wagner in **Night and Day**,
Stoppard has never before written a play focusing
primarily on middle-class adultery. Yet if the
theme of his new comedy seems at first glance
somewhat startling and unexpected, the style is
reassuringly Stoppardian. The entire panoply of
Stoppard's trademark comic devices is abundantly
present in the scene: witty puns, elegant jokes,
comic misunderstanding. Here is Max, for
example, launching into a long, funny, seemingly
irrelevant encomium on the superiority of Swiss
watches:

> And they've done it without going digital,
> that's what I admire so much. They know
> it's all a snare and a delusion. I can
> remember digitals when they first came out.
> You had to give your wrist a vigorous shake
> like bringing down a thermometer, and the
> only place you could buy one was Tokyo. But
> it looked all over for the fifteen-jewelled
> movement. Men ran through the market place
> shouting, "The cog is dead." But still the
> Swiss didn't panic. In fact, they made a
> few digitals themselves, as a feint to draw
> the Japanese further into the mire, and got

on with numbering the bank accounts. And
now you see how the Japs are desperately
putting hands on their digital watches.
It's yodelling in the dark. They can yodel
till the cows come home. The days of the
digitals are numbered. (pp. 11-12)

The scene is, moreover, cunningly patterned and
allusive, another Stoppardian signature.
Stoppard opens his play by deliberately echoing
the close of Ibsen's **A Doll's House**, the most
reverberating door-slam in all of drama.
Charlotte's entrance on this fateful day, like
Nora's exit, thus symbolizes the shattering of a
marriage; the structure of Max and Charlotte's
life together falls apart in front of our eyes,
as surely as Max's house of cards collapses.
     Scene Two takes us to a different living
room, a messier one. As the scene opens, Henry
is discovered searching his shelves of records
for a particular piece of music; Charlotte
enters, wearing Henry's dressing gown. Is Henry
Charlotte's lover, then, the man with whom she
has betrayed Max? He appears to be, and yet
there are too many jarring details which puzzle
us. To cite just one example: Max eventually
turns up and, though there is some awkwardness,
there is not the kind of sexual tension we expect
in a confrontation between cuckolded husband and
gloating or embarrassed lover. What is going on
here? Gradually we learn the truth. Henry is a
playwright--a playwright with a reputation for
being witty, clever, "intellectual," much like
Stoppard--and he is not Charlotte's lover, but
her husband. Charlotte and Max are actors; the
scene with which the play opened was not "real
life," but a scene from Henry's current play,
House of Cards, in which Charlotte and Max
are starring. The "real" situation of Stoppard's
play is thus very different from what we at first
assumed: the focus is still on love and marriage
and adultery, but Charlotte and Max are **not**
the main characters. It is Henry who is the
"real" adulterer here; as the scene progresses,
we discover that he is having an affair with
Annie, an actress married to Max. But is their
love "the real thing"? What **is** "the real
thing" when it comes to love?

The rest of the play attempts to answer these questions--or rather, as is typical of Stoppard's plays, it bounces the questions around in a kind of endless debate, with no single "answer" shown to be indisputably right. Different characters hold different views on love, **embody** different views. For Henry's teenage daughter, Debbie, for example, love has nothing to do with sexual fidelity: "Exclusive rights isn't love," she pontificates, "it's colonization." Henry's reply is instructive: "Christ almighty. Another **ersatz** masterpiece. Like Michelangelo working in polystyrene" (p. 63). The **ersatz**, the fake, the artificial, versus "the real thing": this is Stoppard's primary concern in the play, specifically in relation to the theme of love. But if love holds center stage here, there are numerous side acts which prompt the same sort of questioning and which parallel and enrich the central theme: "real" music versus sham, for instance; "real" sex versus mere biology; the "real" self versus various masks; the "real" motivations behind political commitment; and, most significant of all, "real" writing versus trash.

In a sense, all of Stoppard's major plays are about defining "the real thing"; the only element that varies from play to play is the nature of the particular "reality" under debate: philosophy, art, political freedom, the press. What remains constant is the debate formula itself, and the method of dramatizing it. Stoppard involves his audience in that debate not just intellectually, but viscerally. Thus the very structure of his newest play--not simply its thematic content--dramatizes the difficulty inherent in determining precisely what "the real thing" is; once again, the **form** of a Stoppard play mirrors its theme. Consider, for example, the Pirandellian opening of **The Real Thing**. For the entire first scene, we think we know exactly where we are: the play will be about the effect of Charlotte's adultery on her marriage to Max. Halfway through the second scene, however, the ground shifts beneath our feet; what we **thought** we were seeing in the first scene

turns out to be an "illusion," a scene from
Henry's play. Stoppard is deliberately shaking
his audience up, like Max's miniature Alp in a
snowstorm. When the snow settles, we discover we
have been tricked; just when we think we have
latched on to "the real thing," the reality
alters. We have, in effect, been ambushed; and
that is precisely Stoppard's aim. "I tend to
write," he once noted, "through a series of
small, large and microscopic ambushes--which
might consist of a body falling out of a
cupboard, or simply an unexpected word in a
sentence"[2]--or, as in the present case, an
opening scene which, structurally, brings into
immediate question the whole thematic concept of
what is "real" and what is not.

This kind of ambush in Stoppard's plays is
fundamentally comic--an audience laughs when it
discovers it has been tricked, laughs at the
sheer audacity of the trick. But it is also
disconcerting; it is so easy to be tricked, so
difficult to know precisely what is "real."
Stoppard uses this kind of structural dislocation
repeatedly in **The Real Thing.** In Act Two,
for example, Annie asks Henry to help rewrite a
television play in which she is thinking of
appearing; the play is autobiographical, written
by a friend of hers, a Scots soldier named
Brodie, currently in jail for committing criminal
acts during an antinuclear protest. Henry is
unsympathetic both to Brodie's politics and to
his playwriting. In Henry's opinion, Brodie's
play is execrably written, and he proceeds to
quote a few lines to make his point. In the
passage he quotes, Brodie, entering a train
compartment while en route to the protest,
encounters a young woman, Mary, reading a book
(it is the part of Mary which Annie considers
playing):

> HENRY: (**Reading**) "Excuse me, is this
> seat taken?"
> "No."
> "Mind if I sit down? . . . Do you
> know what time this train is due to
> arrive in London?"

> "At about half-past one, I believe,
> if it is on time."   . . .
> "You put me in mind of Mussolini,
> Mary. People used to say about
> Mussolini, he may be a Fascist, but
> at least the trains run on time."
>   (pp. 47-48)

Despite the play's stilted language, Annie
disagrees violently with Henry's contemptuous
dismissal of Brodie's work, and the scene ends
with the two of them having a blazing row before
finally making up.
    We then shift immediately into the following
scene:

> ANNIE **is sitting by the window of a moving
> train. She is immersed in a paperback
> book.**
>
> BILLY **walks into view and pauses, looking
> at her for a moment. She is unaware of his
> presence. . . . He speaks with a Scottish
> accent.**
>
> BILLY: Excuse me, is this seat taken?
> (ANNIE **hardly raises her eyes.**)
> ANNIE: No.
> (BILLY **sits down next to or opposite her.
> . . . She doesn't look up from her
> book.   . . .**)
> BILLY: You'd think with all these Fascists
>   the trains would run on time.
> (ANNIE **looks up at him and jumps a mile.
>   She gives a little squeal.**)
> ANNIE: Jesus, you gave me a shock.
> (**She looks at him, pleased and amused.**)
>   You fool.
> (BILLY **drops the accent.**)
> BILLY: Hello. (pp. 54-55)

Stoppard is teasing us mercilessly here. When
the scene begins, we **think** what we are
watching is a scene from a play--Brodie's play,
from which Henry has just finished reading. We
have been fooled once before, after all, and are

not about to make the same mistake twice. In
fact, we make the **opposite** mistake; it turns
out that the scene is **not** part of Brodie's
play, it is "really" happening. Annie is on her
way to Glasgow to rehearse a new play; Billy is
an actor travelling to Glasgow for the same
production. Billy, we discover, has also read
Brodie's play; when he sees Annie in the train
compartment, immersed in her book, he is unable
to resist taking advantage of the situation by
putting on a Scots accent and lapsing into the
appropriate lines from the parallel moment in
Brodie's play. This scene **reverses** the
Pirandellian trick of the opening scene, but the
point, of course, is the same: what appears to
be "the real thing" may be an illusion, and vice
versa.
    The comic ambush of such Pirandellian
playing with reality sets us up for the image of
theater as **illusion** which runs through
Stoppard's entire play. Dramatists write
constantly about love, but can its "real" essence
ever accurately be captured on stage? Henry is
doubtful, at least as far as his own playwriting
is concerned:

> I don't know how to write love. I try to
> write it properly, and it just comes out
> embarrassing. It's either childish or it's
> rude. . . . Perhaps I should write it
> completely artificial. Blank verse. Poetic
> imagery. . . . I don't know. Loving and
> being loved is unliterary. It's happiness
> expressed in banality and lust. (p. 39)

Does this mean, then, that all drama dealing with
love is, by definition, artificial, not "the real
thing"? Stoppard explores this issue through a
further series of comic ambushes, deliberately
juxtaposing the "real life" love scenes between
Henry and Annie, now divorced from their
respective mates and married to each other (or,
at any rate, living with each other), with love
scenes from specific plays. Thus, in Act One,
Annie launches into a passionate scene from
Strindberg's **Miss Julie**, a play she is about

to perform and whose lines she is shown trying to
memorize. And in Act Two, Annie is seen
rehearsing a production of Ford's **'Tis Pity
She's a Whore**, with Billy playing Giovanni
opposite her Annabella.

In the original text of **The Real Thing**,
the particular play being cannibalized by
Stoppard was left, in both instances, deliberately unidentified--somewhat in the manner of
Christopher Hampton's **The Philanthropist**,
which never actually names the Molière play to
which it is so pointedly indebted. The closest
Hampton comes is having one of his characters
describe a recent visit to La Comédie
Française:

> BRAHAM: Last time I went, I had this
> enormous American lady sitting next
> to me, and just as the lights went
> down, mark you, and they were
> banging that thing on the stage,
> she leant across and said, "excuse
> me, I haven't had time to read my
> programme, would you mind telling
> me what the play is about, because
> I just can't understand a word
> they're saying." So I said, "Well,
> madam, it's about a man who hates
> humanity so much that he would
> undoubtedly refuse to explain the
> plot of a world-famous play to an
> ignorant tourist."
>
> ARAMINTA: You didn't really?
> BRAHAM: She thanked me. Profusely.
> ARAMINTA: Which play was it?
> BRAHAM: (**coldly**) Three guesses.[3]

In his revised text, however, Stoppard takes pity
on us. Thus the references to **Miss Julie** are
specifically identified through a few deft
alterations in dialogue: reading the part of
Strindberg's Jean, Henry is made to say "'You
flatter me, Miss Julie'" (p. 39), instead of the
original's less enlightening "'You flatter me'";
and Annie's comment about the eroticism of **Miss
Julie**'s subtext, "Mine [i.e., the play she is
rehearsing] is supposed to be steaming with
lust," is altered to "My Strindberg is steaming

with lust" (pp. 39-40). Our initial allusion to
'Tis Pity She's a Whore, on the other hand,
remains a teasingly oblique passage in which
Henry, reminding Annie that she cannot possibly
do Brodie's play because of a conflicting
theatrical engagement in Scotland, amusingly
confuses one famous play about incest with
another:

> HENRY: Anyway, I thought you were
> committing incest in Glasgow.
> ANNIE: I haven't said I'll do it.
> HENRY: I think you should. It's classy
> stuff, Webster. I love all that
> Jacobean sex and violence.
> ANNIE: It's Ford, not Webster.[4] (p. 46)

But at the end of this scene in the revised text,
Stoppard clarifies the potential confusion by
having Henry declare "I'll come to Glasgow and
I'll sit in your dressing-room . . . while you're
doing **'Tis Pity She's a Whore**" (pp. 53-54).
Regardless of whether these plays are named or
unnamed, however, the audience is not being
deliberately tricked in quite the same way as in
the Pirandellian opening, for in these instances
we are never in any doubt that what we are
witnessing is indeed a play-within-a-play.
Stoppard's ambush here is of a different kind.

In the first act of **Travesties**, Joyce,
echoing Lady Bracknell echoing the "Ithaca"
episode of **Ulysses**, catechizes Tzara about
the history of Dada:

> JOYCE: Did [Hugo] Ball keep a diary?
> TZARA: He did.
> JOYCE: Was it published?
> TZARA: It was.
> JOYCE: Is it in the public domain by virtue
> of the expiration of copyright
> protection as defined in the Berne
> convention of 1886?
> TZARA: It is not. . . .
> JOYCE: Quote discriminately from Ball's
> diary in such a manner as to avoid
> forfeiting the goodwill of his
> executors.[5]

With a work like **'Tis Pity She's a Whore,**
Stoppard has no such copyright worries, and he is
therefore free to reproduce two key love scenes
from Ford's play in **The Real Thing.** In Scene
Six, Annie and Billy are shown rehearsing the
scene in which Ford's lovers first declare their
mutual passion; in Scene Eight, they enact the
scene in which Annabella and Giovanni have just
consummated their love.[6] What is the point of
such specifically theatrical interpolations?
     In the case of Stoppard's allusions to
'Tis Pity She's a Whore, both the play itself
and the circumstances in which it appears in his
text are clearly seen as artificial--not "the
real thing." The language Ford's lovers speak is
blank verse, a language totally alien to
contemporary life; in addition, both Annie and
Billy are known to be merely **acting** when they
speak those words. Presumably, only the most
unsophisticated theatergoer confuses the identity
of actor and role. When Annie kisses Billy, for
example, it is **Annabella** kissing
Giovanni: the gesture has nothing to do with
how Annie "really" feels about Billy. By the
same token, Annie's playing a "whore" (by which
term Ford meant an adulteress--or, to use
Angelo's lethally precise term in Shakespeare's
Measure for Measure, a "fornicatress")[7]
obviously does not imply that she herself is a
whore. I am belaboring the obvious here because
it is precisely the obvious Stoppard is so intent
on ambushing. For during the course of their
rehearsals in Glasgow, Annie and Billy begin an
affair; when they then declare their passion for
each other in the words and embraces of Ford's
theatrical lovers, who are we watching make
love--Annabella and Giovanni, or Annie and Billy?
It is **Annie,** as well as Annabella, who is
expressing her love here; **Annie,** as well as
Annabella, who has become a whore. The
"artificial" and the "real," theater and life,
have begun to overlap and merge, to bleed into
one another: which is "the real thing"?
     A similar kind of ambush underlies
Stoppard's brief quotations from **Miss Julie.**
Again, the theatrical interpolation is introduced

in such a way that its artificiality is
specifically emphasized. Intent simply on
memorizing her lines, Annie "reads" the part of
Julie **"without inflection"** (p. 39), while
Henry cues her by reading, equally mechanically,
the part of Jean. Strindberg's intensely erotic
love scene, in which Jean and Julie flirt
passionately with each other (as Annie describes
it, "Then he sort of bites my finger and I do the
heavy breathing and he gives me a quick feel,
kisses me on the neck . . ." [p. 40]), is thus
delivered by two "actors" acting dispassionately.
Likewise artificial is the dialogue itself: the
words are self-consciously "stagy," a fact to
which Strindberg (and by extension, of course,
Stoppard) explicitly draws our attention.
"'Where did you learn to talk like that?'" the
aristocrat Julie inquires of the flowery-tongued
valet Jean.   "'Do you spend a lot of time at the
theatre?'" (p. 39).   And yet, for all its
artificiality, Strindberg's play is later "used"
by Henry to express his genuine love for Annie, a
love he finds difficult to declare in "real
life": "We'll do that bit . . . you breathe,
I'll feel . . . (**She pushes him away.**)"
(p. 40).[8] Who, ultimately, is acting here--
Jean or Henry? By attempting to embrace Annie
via Strindberg's play, Henry deliberately blurs
the boundaries between the "artificial" and the
"real," leapfrogging from theater into life--just
as Billy, under the guise of ostensibly "rehearsing" in the scene on the train Giovanni's
declaration of love for Annabella, expresses
thereby his **own** attraction to **Annie.**

And if theater keeps ambushing "real life,"
so "real life" constantly evokes theater:
Stoppard's play is a two-way mirror. Thus, just
after the **Miss Julie** quotations, Henry
bravely risks his own "voice" by declaring his
love for Annie in a moving, sincere passage
seemingly no longer mediated by theatrical
borrowing:

>   HENRY: I love love. I love having a lover
>   and being one. The insularity of
>   passion. I love it. I love the way
>   it blurs the distinction between
>   everyone who isn't one's lover.

                    Only two kinds of presence in the
                    world. There's you and there's
                    them.
                    I love you so.
          ANNIE: I love you so, Hen.
          (They kiss. The alarm on HENRY's
          wristwatch goes off. They separate.)
                                                  (p. 43)

That alarm startles us--not simply because it is
an unexpected sound breaking a tender love scene,
but because the fact that it breaks the scene
emphasizes that what we have been watching is
indeed a **scene**: a "theatrical" moment
deliberately created and then shattered. The
sound of the alarm is like the voice of a direct-
or yelling "Cut!" We have heard that sound
before--specifically in the opening moments of
Genet's **The Maids**, where it similarly
destroys the illusion of reality. When **The
Maids** begins, we think we are watching a
confrontation between Madame and her maid Claire,
but the sudden ringing of an alarm clock "wakes
us up" to the reality of the situation: what we
were watching was, in fact, not "real," but a
"theatrical" charade in which the maid Solange
"played" Claire while the maid Claire "played"
Madame.[9] As hard as we try, there appears to
be no escape in **The Real Thing** from this
dilemma of determining "the real thing": is
Henry's "real" love declaration more or less
genuine than the "artificial" love scene from
Miss Julie with which it is so cunningly
counterpointed?
        The love scenes from Ford and Strindberg
thus function, structurally, as deliberately
theatrical, "artificial" models against which we
are meant to judge the "real" love of Stoppard's
central characters. The most important of these
theatrical models for Stoppard is **House of
Cards**, that witty, intricately patterned play
written by Henry ("Henry Ibsen," as his daughter
calls him [p. 61]) which we saw dramatized in
Scene One. According to Charlotte, Henry's play
may be amusing, but it is utterly phony, too
clever by half (and where have we heard that
before?); it tells us nothing about how people in
love "really" behave. To some extent,

Charlotte's complaint expands to indict theater
generally: all plays are artificial, and thus so
are the images of love they present:

> CHARLOTTE: Having all the words to come
> back with just as you need them.
> That's the difference between
> plays and real life--thinking
> time. You don't really think
> that if Henry caught me out with
> a lover, he'd sit around being
> witty about Rembrandt place
> mats? Like hell he would. He'd
> come apart like a pick-a-sticks.
> His sentence structure would go
> to pot, closely followed by his
> sphincter. You know that, don't
> you, Henry? Henry? No answer.
> Are you there, Henry? Say
> something witty. (pp. 21-22)

Is Charlotte's complaint justified?
Stoppard proceeds to test her hypothesis by, in
effect, twice replaying that opening scene,
wrenching it out of the sphere of obvious theater
into the sphere of supposedly "real life." Thus,
in Scene Three, the "real" Max discovers the
"real" adultery of his "real" wife. The scene
opens with Max sitting alone in his living room;
we hear the off-stage front door being opened,
and his wife Annie appears briefly before
disappearing into the hall to hang up her topcoat. When she returns, Max confronts her with
Henry's semen-stained handkerchief which he has
found in their car. The Max we see here behaves
very differently from the witty, suave Max we saw
"acting" in Scene One: he weeps, hurls abuse at
Annie, and flings himself on her **"in something
like an assault which turns immediately into an
embrace"** (p. 36). In Scene Nine, Stoppard's
second replay, the "real" Henry likewise
discovers the "real" adultery of his "real" wife.
The scene opens with Henry sitting alone in his
living room; we hear the off-stage front door
being opened, and his wife Annie appears briefly
before disappearing into the hall to hang up her
topcoat. Annie has just arrived on the morning
train from Glasgow--or so she claims. Why then

was Henry told she had checked out of her hotel
when he telephoned the previous evening? Again,
Henry's reaction here is far removed from that of
his theatrical persona in **House of Cards**;
crumbling emotionally in front of our eyes, he
indeed "come[s] apart like a pick-a-sticks."

In his plays, Henry knows all the right
words to come back with, waxing witty about place
mats and digital watches and much else besides.
Even outside his plays, Henry's verbal response
is sharp and instantaneous when the pain does not
threaten him **personally**; he has no trouble
writing "dialogue" for Charlotte, for example,
when her lover accuses her of infidelity after
discovering she had taken her diaphragm with her
on a brief out-of-town trip:

> HENRY: What did you say?
> CHARLOTTE: I said, I didn't **take** my
>   diaphragm, it just went with me.
>   So he said, what about the tube
>   of Duragel? I must admit he had
>   me there.
> HENRY: You should have said, "Duragel!
>   --no wonder the bristles fell
>   out of my toothbrush." (p. 65)

But when the adultery is "real"--not in a play,
and not somebody else's problem--Henry finds
himself mute with pain. The theatrical brittle-
ness of Noël Coward-like dialogue so evident in
House of Cards cracks under the strain of "real
life":

> HENRY: I don't believe in behaving well. I
>   don't believe in debonair relation-
>   ships. "How's your lover today,
>   Amanda?" "In the pink, Charles,
>   how's yours?" I believe in mess,
>   tears, pain, self-abasement, loss of
>   self-respect, nakedness. (p. 71)

"The real thing" would thus appear to be very
different from Henry's theatrical version of it.

It is obvious that both replays are
initially set up so that, structurally, each
explicitly mirrors the opening scene; it is

equally obvious that the reaction of the "real"
husband to his wife's betrayal is, in both cases,
utterly opposite to the graceful wit under
pressure displayed by the theatrical husband in
House of Cards. The structural similarities
would thus appear to be deeply ironic, underscoring the disparity in emotional truth between
theater and life; we finally seem to have
discovered "the real thing." But have we? Are
those structural similarities there paradoxically
to **clarify** the distinction between the artificial and the real, or rather to **cloud** it?
Stoppard has one more ambush up his sleeve, for
the claims of theater cannot be so easily
dismissed. Thus, in the first replay, Max
discovers his wife's infidelity through an
incriminatingly dropped handkerchief. At the
very heart of this "real" scene, then, we are
implicitly reminded of theater--of a highly
theatrical, and therefore artificial, Moor who
likewise bemoaned (and in blank verse!) the loss
of his wife's handkerchief. Is Max's love, Max's
pain, greater than Othello's? Is this discovery
scene necessarily more "real" than Shakespeare's
theatrical discovery scene? Or, for that matter,
than the discovery scene in the equally theatrical **House of Cards?** In Henry's play, the
husband signals his jealous suspicion of his
wife's adultery (she has ostensibly been on a
business trip to Switzerland) by bombarding her
with a barrage of off-center questions: "How's
Ba'l?" (p. 10); "How's old Geneva, then? Franc
doing well?" (p. 11); "Good sale? . . . Was the
sale good? The sale in Geneva, how was it? Did
it go well in Geneva, the sale?" (p. 12).
Henry's play is apparently the epitome of artificiality, yet the "real" Max signals **his**
jealous suspicion of his wife's adultery (she has
ostensibly been at a rehearsal) through a
syntactically duplicate series of questions:

```
MAX:    How's Julie?
ANNIE:  Who?
MAX:    Julie. Miss Julie. Strindberg's
        Miss Julie. Miss Julie by August
        Strindberg, how is she? (p. 35)
```

Similarly, while the pain felt by Henry is
naked, intense and terribly moving, is it too,
like Max's, necessarily more "real" than the
suffering of his theatrical alter ego in **House
of Cards**?   In both "real life" and Henry's
play, the betrayed husband ransacks his wife's
belongings; as Annie comments, in a direct echo
of the opening scene, "You should have put everything back. Everything would be the way it was"
(p. 69).   In both "real life" and Henry's play,
the accused wife feels she has been burgled, and
later claims no longer to know her husband. And
the "real" scene ends with Henry alone on stage,
opening the present his wife has brought him from
her adulterous trip to Glasgow: it is a tartan
scarf (p. 72).   Unlike his theatrical counter-
part, Henry does not laugh. But an audience,
however much it genuinely aches for him, might be
tempted to: life has a disconcerting habit of
imitating theater. Stoppard has ambushed us once
again.

Nor are Max and Henry the only characters
who replay variations on that opening scene. At
the end of Act One, the "real" Annie is seen
"methodically and unhurriedly" (p. 43) ran-
sacking Henry's personal belongings, a gesture
which closes the act by echoing its beginning:
she too mimics the despair and jealousy of the
protagonist of the theatrical **House of Cards**.
Stoppard, that irrepressible joker, has stacked
the deck. Theater, then, far from being a
necessarily artificial distortion of love's
complexities, may, in fact, be uniquely capable
of most truthfully reflecting them. Like Major
Monarch and his wife in Henry James's tale "The
Real Thing," a parable of the conflict between
art and life from which Stoppard presumably
derived both the title and theme of his play, we
are forced to bow our heads "in bewilderment to
the perverse and cruel law in virtue of which the
real thing could be so much less precious than
the unreal. . . ."[10]   And **is** the
supposedly unreal so unreal after all?
Stoppard's ambushes never cease: **The Real
Thing** keeps circling endlessly back on itself,
a play constantly playing with various plays-
within-the-play. Dizzy from this series of comic

ambushes of our perceptions and preconceptions,
we thus find ourselves at the end invariably
questioning, among a host of other "realities,"
the precise nature of love--as Stoppard, of
course, intended. Love speaks in many different
tongues, with many different accents. Which of
them, finally, is "the real thing"?[11]

Notes

1. Tom Stoppard, **The Real Thing** (Boston
and London: Faber and Faber, revised 1984),
p. 9.   All further page references will be cited
in the body of my text.   When I originally wrote
this paper in the fall of 1982, I based my
reading of the play on the text of **The Real
Thing** which had only just been published
(London: Faber and Faber, 1982).   Since it had
been published to coincide with the play's London
premiere (November 1982), I knew that I was
dealing, in effect, with a prerehearsal text, and
that the play as **performed** would have
doubtless differed significantly, given
Stoppard's usual theater practice, from the text
of that first edition.   Such was indeed the case,
as subsequent editions of the text (1983, 1984)
reflected the actual performance texts of the
play in London and New York, respectively.   I
have accordingly made some slight revisions to
this paper (first published in **Modern Drama,**
26 [June 1983]) in order to bring it into line
with the most recently published edition of the
play.

2. Tom Stoppard, "Ambushes for the
Audience: Towards a High Comedy of Ideas,"
Theatre Quarterly, 4 (May-July 1974), 6.

3. Christopher Hampton, **The
Philanthropist** (London: Faber and Faber,
1970), p. 36.

4. In the original text of **The Real
Thing,** Annie was herself a bit confused here
(as was Stoppard), for her last line read: "It's
Ford, not Webster.   It's Elizabethan not
Jacobean."   Webster's **The Duchess of Malfi**
(c. 1613-1614) is indeed Jacobean, but Ford's
'Tis Pity She's a Whore (published 1633) is
Caroline, not Elizabethan.   Stoppard's error
continued in the play's second edition but was
finally corrected in the third edition, where
Annie's comment "It's Elizabethan not Jacobean"
was eliminated.

5. Tom Stoppard, **Travesties** (London: Faber and Faber, 1975), p. 58.

6. Cf. John Ford, **'Tis Pity She's a Whore**, ed. Mark Stavig (Arlington Heights: AHM Publishing, 1966), I.ii.180-216; II.i.1-16.

7. **Measure for Measure**, in **Shakespeare: The Complete Works**, ed. G. B. Harrison (New York: Harcourt, Brace & World, 1968), II.ii.23.

8. Stoppard appears to have used no published translation of **Miss Julie** for his Strindberg quotations. In Michael Meyer's translation of the play (London: Eyre Methuen, 1976), the passage Stoppard cites is on pp. 112-113.

9. Jean Genet, **The Maids**, trans. Bernard Frechtman (London: Faber and Faber, 1975), p. 13.

10. Henry James, "The Real Thing," in **The Portable Henry James**, ed. Morton Dauwen Zabel, rev. Lyall H. Powers (Harmondsworth: Penguin, 1977), p. 134.

11. The initial writing of this paper was made possible by a grant from the Social Sciences and Humanities Research Council of Canada, whose generous support I gratefully acknowledge. An abbreviated version of the paper was presented at the MLA Convention, Los Angeles, December 1982.

Art and Experience in Stoppard's
The Real Thing

G.B. Crump

At one point in Tom Stoppard's **The Real
Thing**, the playwright hero Henry is referred to
as "Henry Ibsen,"[1] but it is Henry James whom
the play evokes (whether Stoppard consciously
borrowed his title from the James story or
not.)[2] James's story and Stoppard's play
examine the complex and problematic relation
between life and art, the mysterious process
whereby one becomes the other, and the paradox
that, even in mimetic art, what appears true to
actual fact may not make for the most
aesthetically satisfying illusion of reality.
Both affirm that one function of art is
representation and that art is rooted in
experience, but both also attest to the
prodigious gulf separating the actual from the
represented. That gulf lies at the heart of
Stoppard's play, determining both its structure
(which interweaves episodes from Henry's life
with scenes from his drama) and its double focus
(on aesthetic issues and love).
At first, art occupies the foreground.
Hersh Zeifman has discussed some of the ontological questions Stoppard raises by paralleling
acted and real scenes (for instance, Scene One,
which appears to depict a "real" Max discovering
his wife's adultery but is later disclosed to be
an excerpt from Henry's play performed by Max,
echoes Scenes Three and Nine, where the real
husbands Max and Henry learn about Annie's actual
adultery).[3] As Zeifman shows, Stoppard employs
such juxtapositions to contrast the reactions of
the real and imaginary husbands to adultery and
to ask whether life or art is after all more

real. But the art-life opposition among these
three scenes or between Scene Six (Annie meeting
Billy on the train) and passages from the train
episode in Brodie's play enacted in later scenes,
is matched by other parallels and contrasts among
episodes in the "real life" portion of the drama.
The similarities among Scenes Two, Four, Five,
and Eleven, all opening with Henry in the living
room and his wife of the moment entering from the
bedroom, emphasize that the scenes chart stages
in Henry's evolving relationship with his wives.
The opposition between this set of scenes and
Scenes Three and Nine, where the husband is in
the living room and the wife enters from outside,
makes a point about "real life"--namely that
adultery, the intrusion into a marriage from
outside, is only a catalyst making manifest
hidden changes which have already occurred inside
the marriage.

Stoppard may have felt this pronounced and
elaborate linking of scenes to be necessary
because **The Real Thing** is a realistic play
and he has generally been more skillful at
inventing metaphorical and symbolic structures
than at sustaining realistic actions. The plots
of **Rosencrantz & Guildenstern Are Dead,
Travesties**, and **Jumpers** were substantially
borrowed from other plays or highly conventional
genres. He had their actions as givens. In
contrast, the action he invents for his previous
major realistic work, **Night and Day**, never
really succeeds in tying its public subject,
journalistic ethics, to its private subject, the
heroine's sexual longings.

The structure of parallel scenes in **The
Real Thing** is the author's strategy for
overcoming unity problems caused by a double
focus implicit in the ambiguities of the drama's
title. Like James, Stoppard recognizes that the
phrase **real thing** has different meanings when
applied to life and to artistic representations
of life. In James's story, the upper-class
couple his artist narrator hires as models for
title figures are named the Monarchs, signifying
not only that they are "true" aristocrats but
also that nothing rules us so completely as the
real. The Monarchs are life, the things in

itself, the "real thing," the time-space bound
actual, with all the unique ontological status
that entails. Nevertheless, in the artist's
illustrations they are less real-seeming than
servant-class models. For writers like James and
Stoppard's special favorite Oscar Wilde, **art**
is in some ways the real thing, more real than
life, more selective, more organized, more
typical, more essential, more permanent. As
Wilde writes in "The Decay of Lying," "Hers
[art's] are the 'forms more real than living
man,' and hers the great archetypes of which
things that have existence are but unfinished
copies."[4] Both these applications of the
phrase "real thing" are central to Stoppard's
play, and he exploits its romantic connotations
as well. He examines whether Henry's love for
Annie is the real thing, the one romantic
attachment so profound and authentic that it
makes all other relationships seem transient and
secondary. These various senses of the title
(and others emerging in the play) do not
completely coalesce; their connection with the
same phrase is largely accidental; and because
the aesthetic and romantic aspects of the play
which they are associated with do not always
coalesce either, **The Real Thing** never
achieves the tight metaphorical unity of a
Jumpers. Indeed, as it progresses, the
romantic story gradually drowns out the treatment
of aesthetic questions.

Stoppard's treatment of art in the drama
seems designed to rebut or otherwise respond to
attacks on his early successes; thus, **The Real
Thing** brings into focus and comments by
implication on a series of debates carried on in
the criticism of Stoppard's work as a whole--
whether art should make serious, often political
statements about the world or may be deliberately
frivolous,[5] whether it should be realistic and
refer to the external world or may sometimes be
autonomous fantasy referring to the world
indirectly if at all, and whether it should have
pragmatic value or can be important solely as an
orderly structure of language and imagery. As
these debates suggest, **The Real Thing**
dramatizes a clash between a critical tradition

which holds that art should be political and the
tradition of literary aestheticism to which Joyce
and Wilde, major influences on Stoppard,
belong.[6]
     In the political critics' reading of
Stoppard's career, early successes like
Rosencrantz, **Jumpers**, and **Travesties** may
have ostensibly serious subjects (the absurdity
of man's lot, the death of God, the artist's
relation to history), but the plays are
self-indulgent and individualistic, wallowing in
fashionable despair and discounting the efficacy
of collective action. Stoppard's use of farce
and an inconclusive pattern of argument and
counter-argument--"a series of conflicting
statements . . . [in] a sort of infinite
leap-frog" ("Ambushes," 6-7)--further undercuts
any serious examination of his subjects. His
well-known claim for the moral significance of
art--"art . . . is important because it provides
the moral matrix, the moral sensibility, from
which we make our judgments about the world"
("Ambushes," 14)--reflects the romantic-aesthetic
conviction that art shapes our perception of the
world, in effect creating the world for us in our
imaginations. As Wilde puts it, "Things are
because we see them, and what we see, and how we
see it, depends on the arts that have influenced
us" (**Artist as Critic**, p. 312). This
formulation makes truth entirely too subjective
for proponents of a political drama who claim to
perceive a truth located in the external world.
The early Stoppard ultimately fails, they argue,
because he does not take political (usually
left-leaning) positions, because he does not
believe art can change the **objective** world,
and because he does not deal with the "public"
man. The happy shift toward political subjects
in works like **Night and Day** proves that he
has finally seen the light.[7]
     Richard Corballis interprets Stoppard as
treating Henry, the spokesman for aestheticism in
the **The Real Thing**, ironically in order to
disavow the aesthetic tradition and endorse an
engagement with reality.[8] But the debate over
Brodie's play actually allows Henry to refute
important assumptions underpinning the political

criticism of Stoppard's early work, and many of
Henry's counter-arguments reaffirm the author's
ties to the aesthetic movement. The most
fundamental assumption of political criticism
(especially Marxist criticism) is that literature, like economics and history, is validated by
its grounding in material reality: the material
world is real and knowable, and literature
conforms to it in some way. The value of a
literary work resides in the correctness of what
it says about the external world. These assumptions are reflected in Annie's defense of
Brodie's propaganda piece: "It's raw, but he's
got something to say" (65), "something to write
about, something real" (68). Billy comments in
the same vein, "He sounds like rubbish, but you
know he's right" (78). A variation on this idea
is the argument that a work must be about, and
take its importance from, a subject. Charlotte
objects that her character in Henry's play
House of Cards is a cliché, "a quiet,
faithful bird with an interesting job, and a
recipe drawer, and a stiff upper lip" (20) as if
the quality of the work hinged completely on its
subject. In this conception of art, the message,
the content, or the subject is the real thing,
not the treatment. The motive for writing should
be to proclaim the something one has to say and
thereby to change the world. Brodie writes his
play to flaunt the leftist conscience he acquired
in prison, and Annie wants to stage it in order
to speed Brodie's release.

     Henry, however, challenges the grounding of
political judgments in a material reality. In a
speech reminiscent of some of Stoppard's own
pronouncements, he says of a coffee mug, "There
is something real here which is always a mug with
a handle. . . . But [with] politics, justice,
patriotism. . . . There's nothing real there
separate from our perception of them. . . . If
you know this and proceed with humility, you may
perhaps alter people's perceptions so that they
behave a little differently at that axis of
behaviour where we locate politics or
justice. . . "(71). Understandably, Annie
attacks Henry because any message his work

contains is a remote, inessential by-product of a
craft commitment: "Even when you write **about**
something, you have to think up something to
write about just so you can keep writing" (68).
For Henry, content is never the only thing, or
the main thing, or the real thing; this is why he
can successfully rework Brodie's play, even
though he does not agree with one word of what it
says.   And when he writes to accomplish a clear,
practical end, as with the script he writes to
finance alimony payments, the results are bad
art.   If it were not for having to pay alimony,
he laments, "I'd be writing the real stuff"
(73).

Although Annie and others occasionally score
off Henry in the aesthetic debate, as when she
accuses him of using skill with words as a status
weapon or of winning the debate by arbitrarily
defining its terms (68), the plot weights the
argument in Henry's favor.   Brodie's political
ideas do come across, in Henry's words, as
"extremely silly and bigoted" (65), and even
Brodie himself agrees that his play, as Auden
would say, made nothing happen, did not get him
released from prison (111).   Moreover, Henry
manages to convince Annie on all points,
passionately pro-Brodie though she is.   She
quickly recognizes that the play needs polishing
by Henry, the real author.   When she tells Brodie
the T. V. production "did work" (110), she means
as a play, not as a means of freeing him, and it
works only because of Henry's polishing.

Central to **The Real Thing's** assault on
the notion that a literary work's value inheres
in its political subject is a conception of
language Stoppard substantially owes to the
aesthetic tradition.   The political position
implies that content and style are separable and
that language is a secondary appendage to the
literary work.   If the purpose of a play is to
say something, the language becomes no more than
a necessary evil for getting it said or at least
a transparent medium through which to refer to
the subject outside the work.   Style for style's
sake would be art for art's sake; it would be the
frivolous decadence of Wilde, writing in **The**

Importance of Being Earnest that "in matters of
grave importance, style, not sincerity, is the
vital thing" (Act 3). Through his metaphor of
the cricket bat, Henry defends finely crafted
language as the instrument making the message
effective: "What [writers are] . . . trying to
do is to write cricket bats, so that when we
throw up an idea and give it a little knock, it
might . . . **travel**" (69-70). Brodie's
manuscript is "a lump of wood . . . and if you
hit a ball with it, the ball will travel about
ten feet" (70). Again the drama bears Henry out:
his position is more convincing than Brodie's
partly because it has the force of Henry's
stylish wit behind it, as when he likens Brodie's
play to "being run over very slowly by a
travelling freak show of favourite simpletons,
the india rubber pedagogue, the midget
intellectual, the human panacea" (71).

        Ultimately, even such a marginally
functional justification of language understates
its importance, for as Wilde wrote and **The Real
Thing** confirms, "language . . . is the parent,
and not the child, of thought" (**Artist as
Critic**, p. 359): style does not just make it
possible for meaning to be transmitted, it
veritably shapes meaning. This shaping occurs in
the language of everyday life as well as art and
in the way we think about our own meanings as
well as in the way others interpret them. For
instance, Henry offers the words "**lacuna**" and
"**prejudice**" to complete Annie's sentence that
"It's a very interesting . . ." that he never
writes about "the utter tedium" of unrequited
love (47); she replies, "I've lost it now" (48),
meaning she no longer knows what she intended to
say. Contrary to her assertion, this exchange
(and similar ones on 54 and 66-67) establishes
that her idea has no existence apart from the
words in which it is expressed because the words
she might select would determine the idea.
Lacuna would suggest that Henry has not experienced unrequited love and thus cannot write about
it, whereas **prejudice** would suggest he does
not want to think about it because of guilt over
stealing Annie and insuring that his friend Max's
love for her will go unrequited.

The play's stress on language, then, is not
merely a matter of Henry's fastidiousness about
mixed metaphors like Max's phrase "hammered by an
emotional backlash" (41). In a key scene, the
reductive and facile language used by Henry's
daughter Debbie reflects her moral and spiritual
shallowness. It is the linguistic equivalent of
her sexual promiscuity. Like her mother
Charlotte, she reduces the issues in Henry's play
to whether the wife was unfaithful or not
(84-85), a reading which is obviously inadequate
even from the fragment of the play we are given.
The link between false language and false
thinking is confirmed by Henry's verdict that her
witticism on free love is "Sophistry in a phrase
so neat you can't see the loose end that would
unravel it . . . flawless but wrong" (85).
Debbie's glib dismissal of love and commitment--
"Exclusive rights isn't love . . . [but]
colonization"--deserves Henry's characterization
as "another **ersatz** masterpiece. Like
Michealangelo working in polystyrene" (87). In
the same way, Henry ties Brodie's political
inanities to his linguistic insensitivity; he
"thinks, or thinks he thinks [because his
language does not give him the tools to examine
his thoughts critically], that editing a
newspaper is censorship, or . . . that
unpalatable statement is provocation while
disrupting the speaker is the exercise of free
speech. . . . Words don't deserve that kind of
malarkey. They're innocent, neutral, precise
. . . so if you look after them you can build
bridges across incomprehension and chaos. But
when they get their corners knocked off, they're
no good any more . . ." (72).
    In addition to determining meaning, words
used in a literary work have a special function
of imparting a necessary sense of artifice. The
excerpt from Henry's **House of Cards** differs
from the scenes of real life adultery principally
through its greater linguistic artfulness, its
puns and monologues. Such artifice is crucial
because the significance of artistic material is
never immediately manifest. It must be brought
out by the mediating imagination, and the very

realness of reality (like the Monarchs in James's
story, who are too big for the illustrations they
pose for) exerts a crude tyranny over the
imagination which must be subdued and tamed by
artistry. Since it is artifice which converts
otherwise banal situations like being in love or
committing adultery into occasions for revelation
and self-knowledge, literature may suffer when
linguistic conventions confuse directness with
truthfulness. When he tries to write about love,
Henry admits, "It's either childish or it's
rude. . . . Perhaps I should write it completely
artificial. Blank verse. Poetic imagery. Not
so much of the 'Will you still love me when my
tits are droopy?' . . . and more of the 'By my
troth, thy beauty makest the moon hide her
radiance. . . '" (49-50). Artifice, moreover,
does not produce sterile affectation or
short-circuit emotion. When Henry speaks of "the
first time I succumbed to the sensation that the
universe was dispensable minus one lady," Debbie
retorts, "Don't write it . . . say it. The first
time you fell in love" (86). Although her amend-
ment is more direct, more modern, his version
suggests much more about what love is like--its
exclusiveness and the irrational value it places
on the lover, for instance, as well as Henry's
rueful recognition of that irrationality.

The scene from **House of Cards** and
colorful phrases like Henry's "india rubber
pedagogue" illustrate another property of
language (especially aesthetic language)--its
tendency to become interesting in and for itself,
to become, in other words, the real thing in
human discourse. The significance of Stoppard's
admiration for **The Importance of Being
Earnest** is that Wilde's play tests whether a
literary work's claims to greatness can ever rest
solely on language, characters who are
flourishes of verbal wit, and at best
metadramatic themes.[9] Its subject is the total
unimportance of earnestness or content in art.
By implication, it asserts that "Art finds her
own perfection within, and not outside of,
herself" (**Artist as Critic**, p. 306) and is
"lying for its own sake" (**Artist as Critic**,

p. 318). In **Real Thing**, Max complains about
his long speech on Swiss watches in **House of
Cards** because it is not a realistic speech
"about" the wife's adultery; in truth, it is a
highly stylized expression of the husband's
agitation over the suspected adultery (it causes
the wife to ask, "What's the matter?" [7]), but
lines like the Japanese "can yodel till the cows
come home. The days of the digital are numbered"
(7) are pure verbal play.

Finally, **The Real Thing** subverts the
very theory of language on which political
criticism rests, suggesting that language gets
its meaning from the use to which it is put, not
from some real thing external to language it
refers to. What the characters say often has a
significance independent of any message conveyed
by the dictionary meaning of the words. For
instance, in the following excerpt from a longer
disagreement about Brodie, the last two speeches
cannot be comprehended referentially, but only as
gestures, as peace offerings designed to defuse
the tension:

> Annie: Arson is burning down buildings.
>   Setting fire to the wreath of the
>   war memorial is a symbolic act.
>   Surely you can see the difference?
>
> Henry: (**Carefully**) Oh, yes . . . That's
>   . . . easy to see. (**Not carefully
>   enough. ANNIE looks at him
>   narrowly.**)
>
> Annie: And, of course, he did get hammered
>   by an emotional backlash.
>   (**Pause**)
>
> Henry: Do you mean real leopard skin or
>   just printed nylon? (54)

Later, when Annie answers Henry's cricket bat
speech by saying, "I hate you" (70), she really
means she sees his point, is exasperated at
having her unexamined ideas exposed as foolish,
but loves him anyway. The true subject of the

ritualistic small talk in Scene Two about
politics, children, and cheese sticks is the
emotional dynamics among the characters.
Charlotte's scathing remarks about Henry's
play--if he had made her character a real
adulteress, it would still be running
(20)--actually express her animosity toward the
husband she is about to break up with.[10]
House of Cards gives an elegant literary
version of such verbal jousting when the husband
needles the wife with punning references to Basel
and Geneva (5-6).

     Behind the disagreement about whether truth
is outside words or inseparable from the words
which communicate it lies an analogous
epistemological argument about whether man can
immediately know an objective reality or whether
his knowledge in unavoidably colored and perhaps
determined by his way of perceiving reality.
This epistemological debate relates to another
issue in Stoppard criticism. Arguing that a
literary work's quality comes from the accuracy
of its political judgments draws a clear line
between the work and the world it is about and
tends to dictate that the work be mimetic and
realistic. But if all man knows of the world is
the subjective interpretation in his head and if
all he knows of art is the same, then they have a
similar subjective status; the distinction
between art and world, representation and the
represented breaks down, and with it conventional
notions of realism and mimesis. To put it in a
way defenders of Stoppard's early non-mimetic
plays have found congenial, both a drama and the
objective world present a set of signs which man
must decode, and all man can know is that
decoding, not some ultimate message or truth, if
any, behind the signs he perceives. As one
critic writes of **Travesties**, "Because we
perceive character-as-image in the same manner in
both life and art, the pattern of imagery which
emerges asserts its own existence; reality and
truth are no longer operative or valid concepts.
One cannot speak of a 'true' or a 'false'
performance. Performance just **is**."[11]
From this "semiological" perspective, all plays

by implication, and Stoppard works like
Travesties explicitly, postulate that the real
thing about a play is located not in the objective world it mimes but only in the internal
operations of the artistic structure. As Zeifman
shows, **The Real Thing**, by getting us to
believe the husband in Scene One is real and then
revealing he is fictional, forces us to perceive
that Henry's realness and the husband's status as
a literary character are only metaphorical, part
of our subjective decoding of the juxtaposed
scenes, not an objective truth. Like all
characters in drama, Henry and his creation are
conceptual abstractions played by actors and
inhabit illusions conjured out of words.

For political critics, external reality is
everything; for semiological critics, it
threatens to become nothing, a phantom existing
only in one's head. Although taking the difficulty of decoding as his conscious theme in **The
Real Thing**, Stoppard rejects the extreme
semiological position that man is not entitled to
claim any understanding of an ultimate reality at
all. The play suggests that the existence and
nature of a real thing behind all codes (whether
the reality this drama mimes or the reality of
authentic love) can and should be taken on faith.
Stoppard's decision to write a realistic drama
and Henry's resolve to seek some ultimate
emotional communion with another person constitute analogous acts of faith; this analogy links
the romantic and aesthetic strands of **The Real
Thing** and gives the play whatever unity it
possesses.

For his part, Stoppard accepts that
literature, while it may not be grounded in a
knowable objective reality, is nevertheless
grounded in the writer's experience, which is
quite real in spite of its subjective elements.
He may owe his treatment of this precept to
Joyce's classic statement of it in **Ulysses,**
where Stephen Dedalus advances the theory that
Hamlet gets its artistic power from its origins
in Shakespeare's experience of Anne Hathaway's
adultery.[12] The connection with experience
is often not a simple or obvious one like the

straightforward identification of Shakespeare
with his hero; it may be torturous and indirect,
a disguised wish fulfillment or a thinking in
contraries. The nature of the playwright Henry,
the adulterer in life, can be expressed through
the cuckolded husband of his play, for in the
broadest sense, the author fills all his
creations (just as Shakespeare is both young and
old Hamlet and Joyce is both Stephen and Bloom).
Although Henry ironically is the other man who
cuckolds Max and although as a husband he was
oblivious to Charlotte's adulteries (89), Max's
jealousy in **House of Cards** reflects Henry's
belief that real love requires total fidelity and
commitment. Like his creator, the husband
character identifies fidelity with honesty of
language: "I abhor cliché," he says, "It's one
of the things that has kept me faithful" (11).
Scene Nine confirms the husband's links to the
author, when Henry behaves the same way as his
hero upon suspecting Annie of adultery. The
happy ending of **House of Cards**, when it turns
out the wife is faithful after all, embodies
Henry's need to believe that exclusive love
insures absolute fidelity.

     Like linguistic artifice, the disguising
of the artist's experience is essential for
turning experience into art and releasing its
emotional charge. Paradoxically, if the author's
feelings are too deeply engaged, his story too
close to the facts, the experience can be too
unruly to be mastered by the imagination (just as
the Monarchs prove to be too much for James's
narrator). The first version of Brodie's play
conveys no feeling because it is **just** experience, and it is not enough, in the words of
Brodie's complaint to Henry, to have "lived . . .
[an experience] and put my guts into it"; one
must also write "it clever" (111). The need to
distance emotion in order to process experience
explains how Henry can write **House of Cards**,
a major work, for Charlotte, whom he no longer
cares about, and can produce only the Brodie
rewrite for Annie, whom he loves passionately.

     As Henry's play illustrates, the work of art
forms a theatricalized persona of the artist. As
one of the signs which must be decoded in order

to discover the writer's nature, art becomes a
metaphor through which Stoppard develops his
play's central theme--the difficulty facing human
beings who, in order to live in the world, must
try to decipher the truth about events and other
people behind the world's ambiguous signs. While
the play's insights into literary language
exemplify the intricacy of linguistic codes, its
romantic story hinges on correct or incorrect
readings of non-linguistic codes. The hero of
Henry's play incorrectly decodes his wife's
passport as proof of her adultery, whereas Max
correctly decodes the bloody handkerchief as
proof of Annie's unfaithfulness. When Henry
brings in the cricket bat to illustrate his
defense of style, Annie momentarily misreads him
as planning to paddle her with it (69), an
interpretation reflecting her misconception that
his literary standards take their authority from
his position of cultural power rather than from
their inherent validity. Henry has failed to
decode the fact of Charlotte's nine affairs, and
Charlotte's excuse for those affairs is her
misreading of him: ". . . it didn't bother you
so I decided it meant you were having it off
right left and centre and it wasn't supposed to
matter. By the time I realized you were the last
romantic [i.e. was not upset because he assumed
love meant fidelity] it was too late" (89).

The nature of people is especially
perplexing to decode because, in the imagery of
The Real Thing, all people are actors, whether
on stage or not, and one cannot always intuit the
real thing behind the clever performance (the
Max, Brodie, and Annie behind the roles of
cuckolded husband, Marxist demonstrator, and
incestuous Annabella). When Henry says he
prefers Neil Sedaka and the Supremes to classical
music, Max interprets his declaration as "sheer
pretension" (26), a pose of inverted snobbery.
In truth, Henry has been looking for classical
selections to claim as his favorites on **Desert
Island Discs** to conceal his genuine taste for
popular songs. By the time he appears on the
radio show, Annie has shamed him into playing his
real favorites by tying his musical preferences

to his love for her (30), but how could
listeners, lacking the theatre audience's special
knowledge, ever correctly decode the sincerity of
his choice? On its face, the souvenir Swiss
paperweight the wife brings the husband in
House of Cards could be either sly stage
dressing to hide her adultery or straightforward
evidence that she actually went to Switzerland on
business. When the boorish, hardnosed Brodie who
is released from prison turns out not to be the
"helpless . . . three-legged calf . . . [of a]
boy on the train" (112) Annie remembers, she
concludes he is not the real thing. "This isn't
him," she says (112), but in fact both figures
are just images of Brodie she has in her
consciousness and both are plausible on the
evidence the play gives of him. The ambiguity of
the image one presents to others increases
because public acts often originate in private
motives (authors write plays and soldiers join
political demonstrations out of love for
actresses).

    Henry's story is heroic because he struggles
to secure the real thing, a perfect knowledge of
the reality which is Annie. He seeks a reality
behind all codes and deeper than self-deluding
affectation, a role, or a theatricalized persona
like **House of Cards**, a reality, as he says,
"that hasn't been dealt out like a deck of cards"
(86). His conviction that such a reality is
attainable in spite of all the epistemological
difficulties qualifies him to be called, in the
words from the Monkees hit playing at the
curtain, **"a Believer"** (115). To Henry, being
in love has "to do with knowing and being known.
. . . Carnal knowledge. It's what lovers trust
each other with. Knowledge of each other, not of
the flesh but through the flesh, knowledge of
self, the real him, the real her, in extremis,
the mask slipped from the face. Every other
version of oneself is on offer to the
public. . . . Carnal knowledge. Personal, final,
uncompromised. Knowing, being known" (86). The
emphasis on knowing explains the importance he
attaches to unscrambling the evidence of Annie's
adultery: "I can manage knowing if you did," he
says, "but I can't manage not knowing if you did
or not" (98).

Just how Stoppard means the audience to view
Henry's desire for perfect knowledge is not
certain. The play does not indicate whether his
love for Charlotte has ever been as intense as
that he feels for Annie. If it were, his ideal
of love would more likely seem callow and
unrealistic (as Charlotte herself believes it to
be) because no relationship which is subject to
change or capable of being duplicated with any
number of women would measure up to his exalted
romantic conception; thus Henry's lament to Annie
that "the way of things is not suspended to meet
our special case. But it never is. I don't
want anyone else but sometimes, surprisingly,
there's someone . . . you know that in another
life it would be her" (97).

This speech aside, details in **The Real
Thing** hint that Stoppard wants to endorse
Henry's romantic ideal by making his love for
Annie something special. It is important enough
to end his first marriage as Charlotte's nine
affairs did not; ". . . look what your one did
compared to my nine," she says (89). But the
nine affairs also expose Henry's less-than-
perfect knowledge of the real Charlotte and,
along with her amused reaction to Debbie's loss
of virginity and reductive reading of Henry's
play, point to Charlotte's essentially worldly
and cynical nature, which is the antithesis of
his idealism. This incompatibility is ultimately
the reason their marriage fails. In contrast,
Annie resembles Henry in being an idealistic
believer; she is ready, like him, to abandon her
spouse for a more real relationship, even though,
unlike him, she still cares for her spouse. When
Max tries to get her to say the affair with Henry
"didn't mean anything" (44) and is therefore not
the real thing, he fails, just as he is
unsuccessful in talking Henry out of his preference for the Righteous Brothers hit "You've Lost
that Lovin' Feelin'" (27). Although both Annie
and Charlotte have affairs with their costars in
Ford's **'Tis Pity She's a Whore**, Charlotte's
is a casual sexual fling at seventeen, whereas
Annie's is more mature and complex. Because
Billy plays the Brodie character in the T. V.
play, she unconsciously identifies him with her

idealized image of the young Brodie as "a boy on
the train" (112), and her attraction is reinforced by their roles as the passionate lovers in
Ford's play, which depicts a seventeenth-century
version of the absolute love Henry believes
in.[13] The roles Billy plays lead Annie to
expect something loveable beneath the roles.
When that something proves not to be there, she
can give Henry the very assurance she could not
give Max: the affair with Billy "meant something," she confesses, but "less than I thought"
(107). In addition, Annie does not allow Henry's
jealousy to destroy their relationship, in
contrast to Charlotte, who breaks up with her boy
friend after an identical jealous scene (90).

     The problem which arises in the marriage of
Henry and Annie is not caused by simple
possessiveness, unrealistic expectations, or
disagreement over Brodie's writing, though these
elements are present. It arises chiefly from the
failure of both characters to understand their
genuine natures. In Scene Two, Henry's public
persona is the detached, witty man of words who
somewhat deserves Max's criticism: "You may have
all the words, but having all the words is not
what life's about" (41). Annie's persona is the
passionate believer in public causes who thinks
that words are unimportant and that her motives
for defending Brodie are unambiguously political.
In the course of their relationship, they (like
the husband in Henry's play) must learn "self-
knowledge through pain" (84), discovering and
accommodating themselves to each other's true
natures. He must learn there are limits to his
detachment, and she must learn that private
feelings touch public acts. In Stoppard's
extended metaphor, they must reconcile her taste
for classical music and his taste for popular
music, as the Procul Harum piece which echoes
Bach hints they eventually do (103-4). Shortly
after they move in together, Annie is the
possessive one, disappointed that Henry has not
written her a play, disturbed at what she thinks
is his interest in other women, and dismayed that
he shows no jealousy of her costars. Though she
misreads this last sign as indifference to her,

it actually shows his confidence that he knows
her real self, while others know only her public
self: ". . . you can be generous about what's
shared," he says later, "she walks, she talks,
she laughs . . . she's everybody's and it don't
mean a thing . . . knowledge is something else,
the undealt card, and while it's held it makes
you free-and-easy . . ." (86-87). Two years
later, Henry's confidence proves as unstable as a
house of cards when suspicion of Annie's adultery
suggests his knowledge of her is not complete.
She points out his flawed decoding of the
evidence: she has overcome her jealousy because
his presence signified that he loved her--"There
was nothing to keep you here so I assumed you
wanted to stay" (98)--and believes he should be
able to reach the same conclusion about her on
the same evidence--"I wouldn't be here if I
didn't" love you (97). Moreover, his frantic
jealousy does not fit her image of the detached
man of words who is the "real" Henry: "It's not
you. And it's you I love" (100). Still separating private feelings and public activity, she
says, "You have to find a part of yourself where
I'm not important or you won't be worth loving"
(100); that is, he must compartmentalize his
essential self, putting the lover in one place
and the witty playwright in another (she may be
indulging in a rationalization that her attraction to Billy, so closely tied to her work, is in
a separate compartment from her marriage).
        Just how the rest of the action is supposed
to resolve this conflict is somewhat vague.
Although Henry learns to bridle his outward shows
of jealousy and apparently to accept Annie's
continued presence as a sign of her devotion, he
does not relinquish his ideal of their love's
all-encompassing exclusiveness: ". . . I can't
find a part of myself where you're not
important. I write in order to be worth your
while and to finance the way I want to live with
you" (105). Henry accepts Annie's assurance that
she is still seeing Billy in order to let him
down easy because he learns to read this behavior
as paradoxical proof of her deeper love for him:
"I have to choose who I hurt," she says, "and I
choose you because I'm yours" (107). The final

scene exorcises the last vestiges of Annie's
infatuation with Brodie and confirms Henry's
devotion to her in that he has finally written
her a play. Considering his objection to
Brodie's ideas, his revising of Brodie is a
higher tribute to Henry's feelings than an
original work would be. The revision also
demonstrates that even his most peripheral
actions are bound up with his love for Annie. At
the end, the relationship between Henry and
Annie, if not immune to time and change like some
platonic ideal, is nevertheless tempered and
strengthened by time, not destroyed by it, and
the knowledge they have of each other, if still
not perfect, is nevertheless deeper and more
certain than previously. In the final analysis,
the action of **The Real Thing** bears out
Henry's proposition: "It's no trick loving
somebody at their **best**. Love is loving them
at their worst. Is that romantic? Well, good.
Everything should be romantic. Love, work,
music, literature, virginity, loss of virginity . . ." (91-92). His list significantly covers
all the major subjects in the play, and those
associated with Henry and Annie are indeed imbued
with their romantic feelings for each other.
    Stoppard's shift in **The Real Thing**
toward mimetic drama and a concern for the
emotional lives of characters and away from
symbolic modes and the drama of ideas will please
some of his critics and put off others. No doubt
audiences, reviewers, and proponents of a
literature which comments on social realities
will find the new Stoppard more accessible and
more to their taste, just as academic critics who
need to publish elaborate cryptographic analyses
in order to be promoted will find more to approve
in the early Stoppard. Nevertheless, the story
of Henry and Annie, the most affecting dramatization of a real character relationship yet found
in his work, seems disturbingly thin in its human
content. One need only compare it to **A Long
Day's Journey into Night** or even **The Glass
Menagerie** to see how thin. The characters do
not always seem psychologically complex enough,
the issues at stake significant enough, to avoid
the potential for banality inherent in the

subjects of true love and adultery. The human
drama ironically threatens to vindicate Henry's
statement that "loving and being loved is
unliterary" (50). What saves **The Real Thing**
is the witty surprises of the dialogue evoking
Wilde and Shaw, the clever manipulation of the
structure and plot to form a metaphorical
investigation into aesthetics and epistemology,
the structural and linguistic "ambushes" created
by punning and by juxtaposing real and imaginary
scenes--in other words, the very symbolic and
verbal ingenuity which marked Stoppard's
non-mimetic, early works. Whether Stoppard will
go on to write distinguished and affecting
realistic plays about characters the audience can
identify with as people remains to be seen. The
evidence of **The Real Thing** suggests that, for
now, the real Tom Stoppard still depends on
metaphorical, intellectual, and verbal powers
even when ostensibly writing realistic dramas.

Notes

1. Tom Stoppard, **The Real Thing** (London: Faber and Faber, 1983), p. 85. Further references are to this edition (the hardback edition) and will be cited in the text.

2. The similarity of titles and subjects may not prove Stoppard borrowed from James, but the parallels between the works are striking. The possible allusion to James is mentioned in Hersh Zeifman, "Comedy of Ambush: Tom Stoppard's **The Real Thing**," **Modern Drama**, 26 (1983), 145.

3. Zeifman's essay in general was a great help to me in preparing this article.

4. "The Decay of Lying," in **The Artist as Critic: Critical Writings of Oscar Wilde**, ed. Richard Ellmann (New York: Random House, 1969), p. 306. Further references are to this edition and will be cited in the text.

5. See, for instance, Philip Roberts, "Tom Stoppard: Serious Artist or Siren?" **Critical Quarterly**, 20, no. 3 (1978), 84-92.

6. The clash is echoed by Stoppard's own ambivalence. Committed in his life to political activism and wanting to believe that art can change things, he nevertheless once cited Auden's lament that his poetry did not save a single victim from the death camps ("Ambushes for the Audience: Towards a High Comedy of Ideas," **Theatre Quarterly**, 4, no. 14 [1974], 14; further references will be cited in the text). He has publicly characterized **Travesties** as asking "whether an artist has to justify himself in political terms **at all**" ("Ambushes," 16). Yet in another mood, Stoppard has said, ". . . I have no compunction about [not writing about Vietnam]. . . . **The Importance of Being Earnest** is important, but it says nothing about anything" (Quoted in Kenneth Tynan, "Tom Stoppard," in **Show People: Profiles in Entertainment** [New York: Simon and Schuster, 1979], p. 47).

7. The political argument can be found in
Roberts and in Bobbi Rothstein, "The Reappearance
of Public Man: Stoppard's **Jumpers** and
Professional Foul," **Kansas Quarterly**, 12
(1980), 35-44. Tynan traces with approval the
shift toward political subjects in Stoppard
(103-23), as does Carol Billman, "The Art of
History in Tom Stoppard's Travesties," **Kansas
Quarterly**, 12 (1980), 47-52. Stoppard's view
of politics itself, as opposed to its role in
art, is clear enough: "I believe all political
acts must be judged in moral terms, in terms of
their consequences. Otherwise they are simply
attempts to put the boot on some other foot"
("Ambushes," 12).

8. Richard Corballis, **Stoppard: The
Mystery and the Clockwork** (New York: Metheun,
1984), pp. 138-48.

9. Several critics have discussed
Stoppard's admiration for Wilde. See Margaret
Gold, "Who Are the Dadas of **Travesties**?"
Modern Drama, 21 (1978), 60-61; Ruby Cohn, "Tom
Stoppard: Light Dramas and Dirges in Marriage,"
in **Contemporary English Drama**, ed. C. W. E.
Bigsby, Stratford-upon Avon Studies no. 19 (New
York: Holmes & Meier Publishers, 1981),
pp. 116-7; and Ronald Hayman, **Tom Stoppard**,
3rd. ed. (Totowa, New Jersey: Rowman and
Littlefield, 1979), p. 123.

10. Corballis's reading of Charlotte's
speech on **House of Cards** as reflecting
Stoppard's judgment of the play (141-42)
illustrates the view of political critics that
the value of art and the meaning of language lie
in what they are "about" and reveals his desire
to playdown Stoppard's ties to aestheticism.

11. John William Cooke, "The Optical
Allusion: Perception and Form in Stoppard's
Travesties," **Modern Drama**, 24 (1981), 536.
Some of the best criticism on Stoppard is
semiological or at least challenges simple
concepts of mimesis. In addition to Cooke, see

Keir Elam, "After Magritte, After Carroll, After
Wittgenstein: What Tom Stoppard's Tortoise
Taught Us," **Modern Drama**, 27 (1984), 469-85;
Howard D. Pearce, "Stage as Mirror: Tom
Stoppard's **Travesties**," MLN, 94 (1979),
1139-58; and June Schlueter, **Metafictional
Characters in Modern Drama** (New York: Columbia
University Press, 1979).

     12. This connection reaffirms Stoppard's
debt to the aesthetes and the admiration for
Joyce he showed in **Travesties.** Several
critics have argued that Joyce's position is
either repudiated in **Travesties** or not
central to the play. See Corballis, pp. 84-86:
David K. Rod, "Carr's Views on Art and Politics
in Tom Stoppard's **Travesties**," **Modern Drama**,
26 (1983), 536-42; and Craig Werner, "Stoppard's
Critical Travesty, or, Who Vindicates Whom and
Why," **Arizona Quarterly**, 35 (1970), 228-36.
Stoppard himself has said, however, "My
prejudices were all on Joyce's side [in
Travesties]--I utterly believe in his speech
at the end of Act I on what an artist is" (Quoted
in Oleg Kerensky, **The New British Drama** [New
York: Taplinger, 1977], p. 169). Joyce was a
proponent of the human element in drama: "By
drama I understand the interplay of passions;
. . . if a play, or a work of music, or a picture
concerns itself with the everlasting hopes,
desires and hates of humanity, or deals with a
symbolic presentment of our widely related nature
. . . then it is drama" (1899) "Royal Hibernia
Academy 'Ecce Homo'" in **The Critical Writings
of James Joyce**, ed. Ellsworth Mason and Richard
Ellmann (New York: Viking Compass, 1959), p. 32.
The name of Stoppard's heroine may be borrowed
from Anne Hathaway.

     13. Stoppard is perhaps alluding to Wilde's
famous dictum that life follows art. In another
example, Charlotte plays the wife of an architect
in **House of Cards** and then moves in with an
architect after her divorce. The relationship
ends when the architect behaves like Max's
character in the play.

From Zurich to Brazil with Tom Stoppard

Felicia Hardison Londré

In **The Real Thing**, the seventeen-year-old daughter of playwright Henry Boot humors her father by steering the conversation toward his lowbrow musical tastes. She asks: "How're the Everlys getting on? And the Searchers. How's old Elvis?"

"He's dead," her father replies.

"I did know that," she says. "I mean how's he holding up apart from that?"

Her father answers: "I never went for him much. 'All Shook Up' was the last good one. However, I suppose that's the fate of all us artists."

"Death?"

"People saying they preferred the early stuff."[1]

Of course, death is the fate of artists too, as well as taxes for the successful ones. But there is also some truth in what Stoppard's playwright-protagonist says about the public's tendency to prefer "the early stuff." Most people prefer Tennessee Williams's **The Glass Menagerie** to his **Clothes for a Summer Hotel**, or Arthur Miller's **Death of a Salesman** to his **Creation of the World and Other Business**, or Samuel Beckett's **Waiting for Godot** to his **Not I**. When it comes to Tom Stoppard himself, the axiom is not quite so clear-cut. In 1986, at forty-eight, he has been a professionally-produced stage and screen writer for twenty-three years, but he continues to delight audiences and win critical acclaim with his new points of departure: it's quite

343

conceivable that everything he has written so
far--including **The Real Thing** (1982), his
1984 television play **Squaring the Circle**, and
his co-authored 1985 screenplay **Brazil**--may
someday be lumped together as "the early stuff."
  But, without indulging in too many Stoppardian
shifts in perspective, it can be conceded that
"the early stuff" is the play that brought him
international renown in 1967, **Rosencrantz &
Guildenstern Are Dead**. Of all the plays in
Stoppard's canon, this is the one that has been
awarded the most prizes, has been translated into
the most languages (over twenty), and is still
the most frequently produced. There are reasons
for these achievements that don't necessarily
have to do with artistic merit. The clever
audacity of Rosencrantz and Guildenstern's
piggy-back ride on the greatest tragedy of the
English language gained the play admittance to
the classrooms and set it up nicely for festival
productions in tandem with **Hamlet**. On a
practical level, **Rosencrantz** is a lot cheaper
to stage than Stoppard's **Jumpers** or **The
Real Thing**, and less difficult to put across
than the complex **Travesties**. Audiences enjoy
the feeling that they have digested a play of
ideas, which they get from Rosencrantz and
Guildenstern's fairly simplistic philosophizing
about death.
      Considering how well Stoppard's artistry has
matured over the years, one is tempted to dismiss
Rosencrantz and Guildenstern as having been dead
since the mid-1970s--that is, since Stoppard's
Jumpers and **Travesties** appeared. The
sparkling dialectical conceits and linguistic
virtuosity of **Jumpers** and **Travesties**, I
believe, showed up **Rosencrantz** for what it
was: a good "first play," a hint of the talent
that was to blossom so much more fully within the
next few years, a brilliant idea that--unless
it's more than brilliantly directed and
performed--is only moderately entertaining.
      Therefore, this essay will focus on Tom
Stoppard's work from **Travesties** to the
present. Although Stoppard has continued to
reveal the same preoccupations throughout his

entire career, he did not show nearly as much
artistic development in the eleven years from **A
Walk on the Water** (1963) to **Travesties**
(1974) as he did in the eleven years from
Travesties to **Brazil**. Metaphorically,
the distance travelled in those latter eleven
years is the distance from Zurich, the setting
for **Travesties**, a real city in a real period
of history, to "somewhere in the twentieth
century" **Brazil**, a state of mind. In a
certain sense, the Zurich of **Travesties** also
exists only in a man's mind, that of Henry Carr,
the character whose memory recreates the events
that occurred there in 1917-18. But Zurich does
have a reality external to the play, whereas the
"Brazil" of the 1985 film has no intrinsic
reality; it is merely a catchy tune that serves
as a mental means of escape from reality. More
literally, **Travesties**--like **Rosencrantz**
and several others--employs a borrowed structure.
Inspired by the historical fact that during the
war years in Zurich James Joyce had worked with
The English Players on a production of **The
Importance of Being Earnest,** Stoppard
constructed **Travesties** as a travesty of Oscar
Wilde's play. Since then, Stoppard has relied
more and more upon his own invention for the
plots of his plays, and as a corollary of that
growing trust in his own resources, he has become
less and less reticent about dealing with
emotions.

    Before zeroing in on that progression from
Travesties to **Brazil**, an overview of the
totality of Stoppard's work is in order.
Statistically, it comes to 9 full-length plays, 5
one-act plays, 7 radio plays, 10 or more
television plays, 6 translation-adaptations of
full-length plays originally written in other
languages, 1 novel, 3 published short stories, 4
screenplays that have been made into movies, and
a screenplay **Innocent Blood** based on a P. D.
James novel by that title that Hollywood has not
seen fit to make into a movie.[2] Another way of
looking at the totality of Stoppard's writing is
to organize it by categories; one might classify
Stoppard's stage, radio, television, and motion

picture plays to date into roughly six groups.
First, there are the plays of his apprenticeship,
the ones from **A Walk on the Water** to
Rosencrantz plus the radio and television
plays of the 1960s, all of which are to be airily
dismissed from consideration here. Another group
that can be merely mentioned in passing is the
translation-adaptations. These tend to be
increasingly free adaptations done from another
translator's literal rendering of the plays into
English. Stoppard adapted Slawomir Mrozek's
Polish play **Tango**, Federico Garcia Lorca's
Spanish play **The House of Bernarda Alba,**
Arthur Schnitzler's German plays **Undiscovered
Country** (**Das Weite Land**) and **Dalliance**
(**Liebelei**), Johann Nestroy's play in a
Viennese dialect **On the Razzle** (**Einen Jux
will er sich machen**), and Ferenc Molnar's
Hungarian play **Rough Crossing** (**Play at the
Castle**). In the beginning, Stoppard probably
took up adapting other writers' plays for the
same reason that he borrowed the structures of
Hamlet and **The Importance of Being
Earnest** for **Rosencrantz** and **Travesties:**
he knew he could come up with scintillating
dialogue, but he lacked confidence in his ability
to construct a plot. As he says in the
Introduction to **On the Razzle**, "All the main
characters and most of the plot come from
Nestroy, but almost none of the dialogue attempts
to offer a translation of what Nestroy wrote. My
method might be compared to cross-country hiking
with map and compass, where one takes a bearing
on the next landmark and picks one's way towards
it."[3] Although Stoppard has now mastered plot
construction, he continues--as he says--to "go
around with a bag of tools doing jobs between
personal plays."[4] Perhaps he does it as a sign
of respect for those foreign authors. In making
their plays newly accessible to contemporary
theatergoers, he also refreshes his own creative
drive.
      To pursue that point, digressing briefly,
one might note as another facet of Tom Stoppard's
artistry the tremendous impact of Shakespeare's
plays on his own. In fact, Stoppard seems to

have acquired the habit of paying homage to
Shakespeare, sometimes in barely perceptible
ways, in every play he writes. If it were any
other writer, one might be inclined to call it a
gimmick, but Stoppard's sense of debt to
Shakespeare appears to be deeply engrained. One
of the librarians at the Folger in Washington,
D. C., told me that when Tom Stoppard visited
there he was like a kid in a candy store.
Examples of this aspect of Stoppard's writing
range from the obvious to the obscure. Among the
hundreds of allusions that might be cited are his
choice of **Undiscovered Country** as the title
for his translation of Schnitzler's **Das Weite
Land**, literally "distant domain;" it's a phrase
from Hamlet's "to be or not to be" soliloquy:
"the undiscovered country from whose bourne no
traveller returns." A particularly delightful
allusion is from **Jumpers**. It explains why
the tortoise that George Moore uses as a visual
aid is named Pat. This enabled Stoppard to take
Hamlet's line "Now might I do it Pat," put a
comma in it, and have George Moore speak the line
to his tortoise: "Now might I do it, Pat." The
much-discussed newspaper in **Night and Day** is
named **The Globe**, presumably after
Shakespeare's theater. Act I of **Travesties**
contains a sustained exchange of dialogue that
consists entirely of lines quoted from eight
different Shakespeare plays.[5] In **Brazil**
the acronym for Ministry of Information is
stamped on every object, even the goldfish bowl,
in Kurtzmann's office. Those letters, M.O.I.,
call to mind the teasing "M.O.A.I." in the letter
that Malvolio receives in **Twelfth Night**.

    A third category of Stoppard's plays is the
frivolous comedies, plays written just for fun,
almost like a busman's holiday from more serious
playwriting. Some--like **Dogg's Our Pet** and
The (15-Minute) Dogg's Troupe Hamlet--were
dashed off as a favor for his friend Ed Berman,
who uses the pseudonym Professor R. L. Dogg so
that the children's verse he intends to write
someday will go into library card catalogues
under the heading "Dogg, R. L."[6] Stoppard
thought that anyone who could wait that long for

a bad pun to explode was someone with whom he could fruitfully collaborate, especially after Berman founded the British American Repertory Company: the acronym is BARC! Stoppard's longest exercise in frivolity, **Dirty Linen**, a play about sexual promiscuity in high places, was written to contain his short intermission sketch **New-Found-Land**, which commemorates the American-born Berman's naturalization as a British citizen. The citizenship papers are signed in the play, with the comment, "One more American can't make any difference."[7]

Stoppard's penchant for frivolity has been evident not only in the plays themselves, but in his spontaneous manner of working with actors in rehearsal. Davis Hall, an American actor who toured with BARC in 1979, recalled that "Tom Stoppard was great fun in rehearsal. Although Ed Berman had final directorial say, Tom took over at times. He would jump up to alter a line or improvise a new gag, sometimes spending fifteen minutes or more developing a bit of dialogue which he would then discard. There was a 'helmet . . . Himmler . . . Hamlet gag' in **Dogg's Hamlet** for a couple of rehearsals. Tom or Ed suggested it, Tom developed it, the actors rehearsed it, we all laughed a bit, and Tom cut it."[8]

The frivolous comedies also include some pastiches of other artists besides Shakespeare. **The Real Inspector Hound** is not only a spoof of Agatha Christie's plays, but it is also a send-up of various styles of literary criticism. **After Magritte** is a theatrical pastiche of the visual style of surrealist painter René Magritte. And this category would include a fairly recent radio play, **The Dog It Was That Died** (1982), about a British spy/counterspy; it's really a John LeCarrécature.

The frivolity of those comedies does not exclude idea-content, only overpowers it. Happily, the converse is also true: the plays in the fourth group--the ones that Stoppard himself has designated as his "intellectual plays"--do not exclude frivolity. In the category of "intellectual plays," Stoppard places

Rosencrantz, Jumpers, Travesties, Artist Descending a Staircase, Professional Foul, and **Night and Day.** There is no better illustration of the zany side of intellectualism than **Travesties,** which takes inspiration from Oscar Wilde's "trivial play for serious people"--or is it a "serious play for trivial people"? In addition, **Travesties** is what **Newsweek** reviewer Jack Kroll called "a dizzying collage of styles; joycean stream-of-consciousness, high comedy à la Oscar Wilde, an antic scene spoken entirely in limericks, another done to the tune of 'Mr Gallagher and Mr Shean,' still another that parodies the great 'catechism' chapter between Stephen and Bloom in **Ulysses.** Technically all this works because, as Stoppard says of himself, 'I fall into comedy like a man falling into bed.' But underneath the mattress is a hard board--Stoppard's lust for ideas."[9] In his book **The New British Drama,** Oleg Kerensky says that "**Travesties** is the richest and most thought-provoking of Stoppard's plays, though it is possible that the weight of argument is too much for the structure of the play. It is hard for any audience to take in all the arguments **and** enjoy the sheer humor and theatricality of the piece."[10] It is true that the play offers too much for the average theatergoer to take in at one sitting, but this is not necessarily a flaw. After all, what theatrical experience ever is the same as a literary-analytical approach to a play? Stoppard's plays may require a bit of mental effort from their audiences even as they revel in the certainty that ideas can be fun. The intellectual plays are merely the most obvious example of what his theater is really about: a celebration of the whole range of things that the mind can generate--from abstract concepts to a humorous coloration of ordinary data to, yes, even the emotions.

Plays that explore real people and genuine emotions make up Stoppard's newest category, and so far he has placed only two stage plays in it, **Night and Day** and **The Real Thing,** both of

which also fit into other categories. Stoppard
wrote **Night and Day** in 1978 to test whether
or not he was capable of writing about love, but
he hedged his bet by writing a play that also
belongs with the intellectual plays as well as in
the sixth category, political plays. Stoppard
says that **Night and Day** was "a first go" at
writing a love play; and of **The Real Thing**,
he has said: "For better or worse, that's
it--the love play? I've been aware of the
process that's lasted 25 years, of shedding
inhibition about self-revelation. I wouldn't
have dreamed of writing about it ten years ago,
but as you get older, you think, who
cares?"[11] **The Real Thing** opened on
Broadway in January 1984 to the most ecstatic
reception by both the critics and the public that
ever greeted a Stoppard play. In his earlier
review of the 1983 London production, Frank Rich
called it "not only Stoppard's most moving play,
but also the most bracing play that anyone has
written about love and marriage in years."[12]
It is interesting that in the years since then,
much of the critical writing on **The Real
Thing** has compared it to **Travesties**.
Although Stoppard didn't give any depth to the
love interest in the intellectual play
Travesties, he did work some fairly solid
idea-content into the love play **The Real
Thing**. A major thrust of both plays is concern
with the difference between bogus art and "the
real thing." According to Paul Delaney, "if it
is sometimes difficult to tell the real from the
ersatz, if the artificial can sometimes deceive
us into believing it to be real, that in no way
suggests that the real thing does not exist and
cannot, upon discovery, be recognized."[13]
"Like **Travesties**, **The Real Thing** celebrates a
non-propagandistic art, praises art which 'works'
aesthetically whether or not it 'works' in terms
of social utility."[14]

Here we begin to overlap into the final
category of plays, the "political plays." It is
in this category that we see the clearest line of
development from **Travesties** to **Brazil**.
In 1967, when Stoppard's **Rosencrantz** gave him

overnight celebrity, the other emerging British
playwrights were David Storey, Edward Bond, Simon
Gray, Peter Nichols, and Howard Brenton, to be
followed shortly by David Edgar, David Hare,
Trevor Griffiths, Howard Barker, Stephen
Poliakoff, and others who were moving beyond the
"kitchen sink" and "angry young man" plays of the
late 1950s to the extremes of social revolution
and demolition of traditional value systems.
Stoppard pointedly stood apart from the fray,
refusing to use the theater to promote any
specific point of view. This is not to say that
his comedies ever lacked for idea-content; he
liked to think of them as "plays that make
serious points by flinging a custard pie around
the stage for a couple of hours."[15] Still,
he was dogged by the insinuations of reporters,
critics, and fellow playwrights that he should be
writing socially-conscious or "political" plays.
Gradually, irresistibly, he was drawn to the
problem of the artist's responsibility to
society. Should the artist uphold the ideal of
"pure art" or should he become "socially
committed" by espousing a particular political
position through his work? Although
Travesties is not classed as one of the
political plays, it served--much as **Night and
Day** did on the subject of love--as a "first
go," a major impetus of which was Stoppard's need
to resolve for himself the question of whether
the artist has any obligation to justify himself
in political terms. He did this by playing off
against one another the four different attitudes
toward art held by four actual historical figures
who, by coincidence, all lived in Zurich during
World War I. Henry Carr has a non-intellectual
attitude toward art: he likes what he likes, and
any relationship between what pleases him and
what is socially useful is merely coincidental.
Carr does offer in rough form some of the
arguments for the integrity of art that are
expressed in more polished images by Henry Boot
in **The Real Thing**. James Joyce celebrates
art for art's sake; he is able to remain quite
disengaged from current events, secure in the
knowledge that what he is doing has its own

intrinsic merit. Tristan Tzara is a revolutionary in art, expressing his rejection of social
conditions by smashing conventions in art and,
when possible, demolishing established.
masterpieces as well. Lenin is a political
revolutionary with traditional tastes in art;
whatever the intrinsic value may or may not be,
he wants an art that he can understand and thus
keep in its place. This polemic may not be what
the audience member remembers most about
Travesties, but it's important enough that
Stoppard remarked facetiously: "I think that in
the future I must stop compromising my plays with
this whiff of social application. They must be
entirely untouched by any suspicion of usefulness. I should have the courage of my lack of
convictions."[16]

      But, in fact, Stoppard did not lack
convictions. As Paul Delaney has noted, "his
ambiguities are intended neither to dazzle nor
confuse but 'to be precise over a greater range
of events.'"[17] Stoppard described his
customary technique as "a series of conflicting
statements made by conflicting characters, and
they tend to play a sort of infinite leap-frog.
You know, an argument, a refutation, then a
rebuttal of the refutation, then a counter-
rebuttal . . ."[18] Whereas in **Travesties**,
"the characters, as debaters and antagonists, are
equally matched,"[19] **The Real Thing** does
not hold back from giving the weight of a better
argument as well as the more sympathetic
characterization to Henry Boot, the spokesman for
Stoppard's own point of view, over Brodie, for
whom "art" is nothing more than a blunt
instrument of social change.

      While Stoppard still likes to write
arguments, "scenes where there are two people
with bats, banging this ball across a net at each
other," Stoppard admits: "I am more opinionated
that I used to be."[20] When he got beyond the
question of the function of the artist in life,
and into issues with a political application on
which he actually took sides, Stoppard turned out
to be a conservative. However, his point of view
has never been merely topical or "axe-grinding."
Mel Gussow notes that "in contrast to such

left-leaning British playwrights as David Hare,
Howard Brenton, and David Edgar, he does not use
the theatre as a platform."[21] David Hare has
said, "I never find him politically narrow in any
way. His friendship and encouragement and
generosity to writers of all persuasion are
legendary. We have far more in common than in
conflict."[22] And, according to Mike Nichols,
"he has no apparent animus toward anyone or
anything. He's very funny at no one's expense.
That's supposed not to be possible."[23]
          The issue that has most engaged Stoppard and
made a committed artist of him is that of human
rights and the violation of those rights in
totalitarian countries. Stoppard's political
plays all deal with this issue. Although it is
clear in all of them where his own sympathies
lie, their ideological bias in no way diminishes
their aesthetic value. These plays exhibit
Stoppard's mature craftsmanship. There is an
economy of means manifested in his increasingly
tight construction, in scenic devices that
metaphorically underscore content, and in a more
sculptural sense of language that grows out of
the paring away of some of his habitual trickery
and superficial demonstrations of cleverness. By
and large, the political plays constitute some of
Stoppard's best work. These are the television
plays **Professional Foul** (1977) and **Squaring
the Circle** (1984), the short play **Cahoot's
Macbeth** (1979), the experimental play-with-
live-orchestra **Every Good Boy Deserves Favour**
(1977), **Night and Day** (1978) and the movie
Brazil (1985). The issue of political
repression under a dictatorship is there in
Night and Day, although it is subsidiary to
an examination of the problems of moral
responsibilities and practical failings of a free
press. **Every Good Boy Deserves Favour** is set
in a Soviet insane asylum where a political
dissident shares a cell with a genuine mental
patient who hears an orchestra in his head; the
latter's delusion is represented on stage by an
actual full-sized live symphony orchestra.
Stoppard's metaphor for the logic of the
dissident is geometry. Although the triangle as

a geometrical figure is less tangible than the
triangle as an instrument in the orchestra, there
are absolute definitions of geometrical figures.
The principles upheld by the dissident are as
incontrovertible to a sane person as the rules of
geometry, but the totalitarian state uses its
power to distort even geometrical logic for its
own self-interest. Stoppard again used geometry
as a metaphor in his television play tracing the
1980-81 workers' Solidarity movement in Poland.
The premise of **Squaring the Circle** is that
the concept of a free trade union like Solidarity
is as irreconcilable with the Communist bloc's
definition of socialism as is the mathematical
impossibility of turning a circle into a square
with the same area. The earlier television play
Professional Foul uses a soccer match as
metaphor for examining questions of human rights
in opposition to the "ethics" of the totalitarian
state.

Cahoot's Macbeth, while based upon
Shakespeare's tragedy, uses the metaphor of
language as an arbitrary construction. Words,
like the building blocks that are delivered in
the course of the play (cubes, bricks, slabs, and
planks), can be used to different purposes,
either as an instrument of repression or as a
vehicle of escape to freedom by the human spirit.
Cahoot's Macbeth is dedicated to
Czechoslovakian playwright Pavel Kohout who,
before he was exiled from his country in 1980,
wrote to Stoppard about the underground
theatrical activities he was carrying on to help
some politically oppressed actors. The totalitarian regime had prohibited some outstanding
Czech actors from performing in public as a
punishment for their having signed a human rights
petition. Kohout's solution was to offer "Living
Room Theatre": a 75-minute abridgement of
Macbeth performed by five actors with a
suitcase full of props for small groups in
private homes.

Cahoot's Macbeth begins with a serious
rendition of a shortened **Macbeth**, performed
in pinpoints of light. When the Witches vanish,

the lights go up to reveal that the performance
is being given in an apartment living room. The
action proceeds briskly to the murder of Duncan,
but Macbeth's line, "I have done the deed. Didst
thou not hear a noise?," is answered by a police
siren approaching the house.[24] An Inspector,
whose knock on the apartment door coincides with
the knocking at the gate in **Macbeth**,
interrupts the performance, interrogates the
actors, addresses the "bug" in the ceiling, and
tells the Hostess: "If you had any pride in your
home, you wouldn't take standing-room-only in
your sitting room lying down (53-54)." He warns
the troupe that their performance is seen by the
authorities as a provocation: "When you get a
universal and timeless writer like Shakespeare,
there's a strong feeling that he could be
spitting in the eye of the beholder". . .(60).
He orders the actors to resume their performance
while he watches, but he leaves after the
coronation of Macbeth, which he takes to be a
happy ending. A truck driver named Easy arrives
with a load of cubes, bricks, slabs, and planks.
He pops in and out of view coincidentally with
Macbeth's vision of Banquo's ghost. Easy speaks
only Dogg's language, in which English-sounding
words actually mean something else. Cahoot is
able to translate and the actors quickly pick it
up, so that when the Inspector returns, the
actors foil him by switching into Dogg for the
remainder of their performance of **Macbeth**.
For example, Macbeth's "Tomorrow and tomorrow and
tomorrow" speech begins:

> Dominoes, et dominoes, et dominoes,
> popsies historical axle-grease,
> exacts bubbly fins crock lavender. . . .
> (77)

In response to a telephone call from the "bug,"
the Inspector exclaims: "How the hell do I know?
But if it's not free expression, I don't know
what is!" (75). Easy's wooden blocks are
unloaded from the truck and passed hand-to-hand
through the window just when Birnam Wood comes to
Dunsinane in the play-within-the-play. A step

unit is built for the coronation of Malcolm, but
the Inspector continues to call for blocks, with
which he builds a wall of columns across the
front of the stage. This brilliant visual
metaphor that ends the play makes a clear
statement: artists under a totalitarian regime
are physically walled in, but their thoughts and
creative imaginations will always find some form
of expression--a whole new language if necessary.
      That capacity for escape through thought and
imagination is very much the point of the movie
Brazil.   The mild-mannered protagonist Sam
Lowry works in a flunkey's job for the state; he
escapes the drabness of that technology-
encumbered, Orwellian 1984-like world through his
dreams of flying about a clear blue sky,
sometimes with a beautiful blond woman in a gauzy
gown.   A bureaucratic error that results in an
innocent man's torture and execution jars Sam
into action.   His attempts to thwart the
machinery of the state take him to the victim's
chair in the torture chamber, but he is
miraculously rescued by a so-called "terrorist."
His escape from pursuers becomes more and more
surrealistic, but he finally attains happiness
with the woman he loves in a peaceful green
valley under a blue sky.   Only in the last moment
of the film do we see that he is actually still
strapped down in the torture chamber, and we
realize that everything from the rescue on has
occurred only in Sam's mind.   "He's got away from
us," says one of the torturers, while Sam wears a
faint smile and hums the catchy 1930s tune
"Brazil."   There is a perverse kind of
exhilaration about that final moment when the
mind transports the man beyond pain, beyond
confinement, beyond the reach of a monolithic
state that has invaded every other aspect of
life.   The last freedom is that of individual
thought.   Thus we see again how far Stoppard has
come from **Travesties**, in which Carr's mind
merely recreates past events with adjustments to
suit his own ego, to **Brazil**, in which Sam
creates a separate reality from scratch.
      Before proceeding further, Stoppard's part
in the authorship of **Brazil** should be

clarified. Three screenwriters are credited:
the film's director Terry Gilliam, Charles
McKeown, and Tom Stoppard. Asked about his
contribution, Stoppard replied: "for a certain
number of weeks I was working on it in my house.
Then I gave the script to Terry Gilliam, had a
couple of meetings, and that was the last of it
until the film came out."[25] **Brazil** is
here referred to as a work by Stoppard because so
much of it has his clear imprint upon it. For
example, Stoppard has frequently spoofed the
complexity of modern life as he does in
Brazil with the many-plugged phones and
ubiquitous ducts. Sam is an ineffectual "hero"
trying to rise above those complexities in the
tradition of George Moore in **Jumpers**, or the
title characters of **Albert's Bridge** and
Lord Malquist & Mr Moon. In the latter work,
Mr Moon receives wounds in both hands; in
Brazil, Sam's beloved Jill has a bandaged
hand, Mr Kurtzmann hurts his hand so he can't
sign a check, and Sam's hand is the focus of the
torturer's work. There is also an amusingly
angled shot when Sam returns to his apartment to
find it in disarray after the Central Services
repairmen have pulled all the ducts out of the
walls and ceiling; the shot in which Sam surveys
the chaos is set up in such a way that his hand
is hidden behind a pipe with wires protruding
like veins from a severed wrist. Stoppard's
fixation on boots (a constant throughout his
work) is echoed in **Brazil** when Sam's mother
wears a leopardskin boot as a hat, and similarly,
Jill wears a black boot on her head at the
surreal funeral.

　　The movie's initiating incident is a
typically Stoppardian trivial event that
unleashes a chain of consequences. Just as in
Stoppard's early radio play **Artist Descending a
Staircase** a swatted fly causes a man's death,
so in **Brazil** a fly swatted on the ceiling
drops into a typewriter which then mistakenly
types "Buttle" instead of "Tuttle," and the very
next scene shows the innocent Mr. Buttle arrested
as he spends a quiet Christmas evening with his
family. This sequence of events is soon mocked

by a shot of the Socialist Realist-style
sculpture in the lobby of the Ministry of
Information, inscribed "The truth shall make you
free," and we see that Jill cannot get anywhere
with the truth.

Perhaps the most constant characteristic of
Stoppard's writing from **Rosencrantz** to the
present is the use of a shifting perspective on
reality. Stoppard is like the Chinese philosopher who "dreamed he was a butterfly, and from
that moment he was never quite sure that he was
not a butterfly dreaming it was a Chinese
philosopher."26 Both in structure and in
detail, his plays offer innumerable variations on
the theme that there is no such thing as a single
all-encompassing vision of reality. There are
visual incongruities like those in **After
Magritte**: what one person sees as a one-legged
blind man with a white beard and carrying a
tortoise under his arm is in reality (and with a
perfectly logical explanation) a man with shaving
foam on his face who, in his haste to run
outdoors and move his car, put both feet into the
same pajama leg and grabbed his wife's handbag
and white parasol. There are aural incongruities
like the tape that George Moore plays in
Jumpers to illustrate points in his
lecture--a romantic bit of Mozart, a braying
animal mating call, and a trumpet falling down a
flight of stone stairs--but since the audience
does not know the source of these sounds, they
are perceived in conjunction with the action in
Dotty's bedroom: Dotty and Bones facing each
other as in a dream of love, Bones raising his
head during the animal mating call and dropping
his vase of flowers when Dotty rushes toward
him.

In several plays, Stoppard's penchant for
shifting perspective is quite Pirandellian.
The Real Thing, for example, begins with a
husband-and-wife scene that we accept at face
value, only to realize in the following scene
that each of them is married to someone else and
that the scene was from a play written by the
woman's husband, in which they both perform. The
entire context of **Travesties** is the skewed

perspective of Henry Carr's self-serving memory,
but it is not until the very end of the play that
we learn to what a great extent his memory has
falsified historical events. And the play offers
a wryly clever comment on how one tends to
perceive what one is already conditioned to
perceive: the leftist-leaning Dadaist Tristan
Tzara reads a tract by Lenin, but having been
told it was a chapter by James Joyce, finds it
inimical to his views. Similarly, Carr's
pretensions to literary taste are short-circuited
by Joyce's writing when he believes it to be by
Lenin. **Squaring the Circle** begins with one
possible image of Polish first Secretary Edward
Gierek's summer 1980 meeting with Leonid Brezhnev
by the Black Sea. Two men in dark suits, hats,
and lace-up shoes walk along a deserted beach
solemnly interchanging the standard Party
platitudes. Then the Narrator interrupts to tell
us that "everything is true except the words and
the pictures."[27] Since we don't know for
certain what that Black Sea meeting was really
like, we are shown a second possibility:
Brezhnev and Gierek wear bright Hawaiian shirts
as they recline under beach umbrellas, drink pink
cocktails, and shout at each other like
gangsters.
        The very structure of **Brazil**, as
previously noted, is an alternation between one
man's mental reality and the external reality
that is constantly driving him to seek refuge in
his own mind. But there are also in **Brazil**
some delightful jokey perspective shifts, as when
what appeared to be a pretty little cottage with
a white picket fence is suddenly lifted out of
its setting by a crane, and we realize that it
was only an ugly boxcar. In his 1982 radio play
The Dog It Was That Died, Stoppard takes the
mental tempering of reality to mind-boggling
extremes with his treatment of a British
spy/counterspy who acted as "a genuine Russian
spy in order to maintain his usefulness as a
bogus Russian spy." Eventually he reaches a
point of despair. As he explains it: "I've
forgotten who is my primary employer and who my
secondary. For years I've been feeding stuff in

both directions, following my instructions from
either side, having been instructed to do so by
the other, and since each side wanted the other
side to believe that I was working for it,
both sides were often giving me genuine stuff to
pass on to the other side . . . so the side I was
actually working for became . . . well, a matter
of opinion really . . . it got lost." Advised
that he need only remember what he once believed,
the poor man replies: "I remember I was very
idealistic in those days, a real prig about
Western decadence. On the other hand I was very
patriotic and really didn't much care for
foreigners. Obviously one scruple overcame the
other, but. . . ."[28] Reduced to the same
kind of intellectual frustration, George Moore in
Jumpers cries out: "How the hell does one
know what to believe?"[29]

These examples make it sound as though
Stoppard's plays are illustrations of the maxim
that "the truth depends upon where you're
standing." But it's even more complex than that,
because Stoppard has a conservative belief in
absolute values. He calls himself "a moralist
affronted by relativism." However, his latest
stage play, **The Real Thing**, is on one level a
coming to grips with the necessity in life of
compromise. What will Henry Boot do when he
learns that his own romantic ideals and artistic
standards are not the same as those of the woman
he loves? What does Henry Carr do in
Travesties when historical truth conflicts
with emotional truth? What does Lech Walesa do
in **Squaring the Circle** when he faces the fact
that Solidarity and Communism are intrinsically
incompatible? What does Sam Lowry do in
Brazil when external reality simply will not
conform to his dream reality? In every case,
there are two choices: one can stick to a
principle or one can make a mental adjustment.

The triumph of Tom Stoppard's artistry is to
affirm for us that we, as individuals, always
have this choice. His plays are a cumulative
celebration of the possible triumph of mind over
reality. Like his characters, we have the power
within ourselves, without ever leaving home, to
travel from Zurich to Brazil.[30]

Notes

1. Tom Stoppard, **The Real Thing**
(Boston:　Faber and Faber, 1983), p. 62.

2. The full-length plays are:
**Rosencrantz & Guildenstern Are Dead, Enter a
Free Man, Jumpers, Travesties, Dirty Linen/New-
Found-Land, Every Good Boy Deserves Favour,
Dogg's Hamlet/Cahoot's Macbeth, Night and Day,
The Real Thing.** One-act plays are:　**The
Gamblers, After Magritte, The Real Inspector
Hound, Dogg's Our Pet, The (15-Minute) Dogg's
Troupe Hamlet.** Radio plays:　**The Dissolution
of Dominic Boot, "M" is for Moon Among Other
Things, If You're Glad I'll Be Frank, Albert's
Bridge, Where Are They Now?, Artist Descending a
Staircase, The Dog It Was That Died.** Television
plays:　**The Engagement, A Separate Peace,
Teeth, Another Moon Called Earth, Neutral Ground,
One Pair of Eyes, The Boundary, Three Men in a
Boat, Professional Foul, Squaring the Circle.**
Translations/adaptations:　**Tango, The House of
Bernarda Alba, Undiscovered Country, On the
Razzle, Rough Crossing, Dalliance.** Novel:
Lord Malquist & Mr Moon. Short stories:
"Life, Times:　Fragments," "Reunion," "The
Story." Screenplays:　**The Romantic
Englishwoman, Despair, The Human Factor,
Brazil.**

3. Tom Stoppard, **On the Razzle** (London:
Faber and Faber, 1982), p. 7.

4. Mel Gussow, "Stoppard's Intellectual
Cartwheels Now with Music," **The New York
Times** (29 July 1979), p. 22.

5. Tom Stoppard, **Travesties** (New York:
Grove Press, 1975), p. 54. The lines following
Gwen's recitation of the eighteenth sonnet are
from **Julius Caesar, Hamlet, As You Like It,
Hamlet, Much Ado About Nothing, Henry V, Henry
IV, Part I, Othello, Hamlet,** and **Merry Wives
of Windsor.**

6. Tom Stoppard, "Yes, We Have No Bananas,"
The Guardian (10 December 1971), p. 10.

7. Tom Stoppard, **Dirty Linen and
New-Found-Land** (New York: Grove Press, 1976),
p. 71.

8. Response to a questionnaire mailed in
June 1981 by Felicia Londré to members of the
British American Repertory Company. Another
American respondent, Stephen D. Newman, wrote:
"As Stoppard so typically put his sharing of
brainstorming sessions with the company, he was
'taking us into his lack of confidence' which is,
of course, a very flattering place to be
admitted. To watch ideas born in a brilliant
man, perhaps even to root him on, lends a
participatory pride to one's feeling about the
play."

9. Jack Kroll, "Stars over Zurich,"
Newsweek (10 November 1975), p. 66.

10. Oleg Kerensky, **The New British Drama**
(London: Hamish Hamilton, 1977), p. 164.

11. Mel Gussow, "The Real Tom Stoppard,"
The New York Times Magazine (1 January 1984),
p. 28.

12. Frank Rich, "Stoppard's **Real Thing**
in London," **The New York Times** (23 June
1983), p. C 15.

13. Paul Delaney, "Cricket bats and
commitment: the real thing in art and life,"
Critical Quarterly, 27 (1985), 47.

14. Delaney, p. 49.

15. Jon Bradshaw, "Tom Stoppard, Nonstop,"
New York (10 January 1977), p. 50.

16. Ronald Hayman, **Tom Stoppard** (London:
Heineman, 1978), p. 2.

17. Delaney, p. 45.

18. Tom Stoppard, "Ambushes for the Audience," **Theatre Quarterly**, 4 (May-July 1974), 6-7.

19. Susan Rusinko, "The Last Romantic: Henry Boot, Alias Tom Stoppard," **World Literature Today**, 59 (Winter 1985), 21.

20. Gussow, p. 28.

21. Gussow, p. 21.

22. Gussow, p. 22.

23. Gussow, p. 23.

24. Tom Stoppard, **Dogg's Hamlet, Cahoot's Macbeth** (London: Faber and Faber, 1980), p. 52. All subsequent quotations will be from this edition and will be cited in the text.

25. Duncan Fallowell, "Theatrical incest and acquisitive lust," **The Times** (London) (23 August 1985), p. 8.

26. Tom Stoppard, **Rosencrantz & Guildenstern Are Dead** (New York: Grove Press, 1967), p. 60.

27. Tom Stoppard, **Squaring the Circle** (Boston: Faber and Faber, 1985), p. 21.

28. Tom Stoppard, **The Dog It Was That Died and Other Plays** (Boston: Faber and Faber, 1983), pp. 33-34.

29. Tom Stoppard, **Jumpers** (New York: Grove Press, 1972), p. 71.

30. This article is a version of a lecture given at the University of Toledo Humanities Institute in May 1986.

Chronology

1937   Tom Stoppard is born Tomas Straussler on July 3 in Zlin, Czechoslovakia. He is the second son of Dr. Eugene˘ and Martha Straussler.

1939   Either Dr. Straussler or his wife is of partially Jewish descent. Dr. Straussler, a Bata Shoe Company doctor, transfers to Singapore, thus escaping the Nazi invasion of Czechoslovakia.

1942   Mrs. Straussler and her two sons evacuate to India as the Japanese invade Singapore. Dr. Straussler remains behind and is killed by the Japanese.

1943-6   Mrs. Straussler manages the Bata shoe shop in Darjeeling. Stoppard attends an American multi-racial school there.

1946   Stoppard's mother marries Kenneth Stoppard, a major in the British army in India. The family moves to England, where Kenneth Stoppard becomes a successful machine-tools salesman.

1946-54   Stoppard attends a prep school in Nottinghamshire, and a grammar school in Yorkshire.

1954   At seventeen, Stoppard leaves school. He joins the **Western Daily Press** as a journalist.

1958   Stoppard joins the **Bristol Evening World** as news reporter, feature writer, theater critic, film critic, and gossip columnist.

1960   Stoppard resigns from the **Bristol Evening World** to write plays and complete **A Walk on the Water**, later called **Enter a Free Man**.

1960-62   Stoppard works as a freelance journalist.

1963   Stoppard works in London as a drama
        critic for the short-lived **Scene**
        magazine. Within seven months he sees
        132 plays. He writes short stories,
        three of which are published by Faber.
        The publisher Anthony Blond commissions
        Stoppard to write a novel which is
        published in 1966 as **Lord Malquist &
        Mr Moon.** ITV transmits **A Walk on
        the Water** in November.

1964   In May through October Stoppard
        participates in a Ford Foundation
        colloquium grant in Berlin. While there
        he writes a one-act burlesque entitled
        **Rosencrantz and Guildenstern Meet King
        Lear. A Walk on the Water**
        receives its first stage production in
        Hamburg.

1965   Stoppard marries Jose Ingle, a nurse he
        had known since 1962. The Royal
        Shakespeare Company takes an option on
        Rosencrantz & Guildenstern Are Dead.
        The option expires in 1966 and several
        other managements also reject the play.

1966   **Rosencrantz & Guildenstern Are Dead**
        is produced for the Edinburgh Festival
        "fringe." BBC radio transmits **If
        You're Glad I'll Be Frank** and **A
        Separate Peace.** Stoppard's adaptation
        of Slawomir Mrozek's **Tango** is
        performed at the Aldwych Theatre in
        London.

1967   **Rosencrantz & Guildenstern Are Dead**
        is produced by London's National Theatre
        at the Old Vic. Stoppard receives three
        awards: **Plays and Players** Award for
        Best Play, John Whiting Award, and the
        Evening Standard's Award for Most
        Promising Playwright. BBC radio
        presents **Albert's Bridge.**

1968   **Rosencrantz & Guildenstern Are Dead**
        is performed in New York and receives

the New York Drama Critics' Award and
the Tony award. **Albert's Bridge** is
performed at the St. Martin's Theatre in
London. **The Real Inspector Hound** is
presented at the Criterion Theatre in
June. In December Granada television
transmits a sixty-minute thriller,
Neutral Ground.

1970   In April **After Magritte** is presented
at the Ambiance Lunch Hour Theatre club
in London. With **Hound** it makes a
West End double bill in 1972. **Where
Are They Now?**, written for BBC Schools
Radio, is broadcast in December.

1971   In December at the Almost-Free Theatre
in Soho, Inter-Action presents **Dogg's
Our Pet,** a short play which later
becomes the first part of **Dogg's
Hamlet.**

1972   Stoppard divorces Jose Ingle Stoppard
and marries Dr. Miriam Moore-Robinson,
deputy managing director of a pharmaceu-
tical company and a television
"personality." Stoppard takes custody
of the two sons from his first marriage.
In February the National Theatre at the
Old Vic produces **Jumpers.** In
November the BBC broadcasts **Artist
Descending a Staircase.**

1973   In March the Greenwich Theatre presents
Stoppard's adaptation of Garcia Lorca's
The House of Bernarda Alba (unpublished). At the Greenwich Stoppard also
directs Garson Kanin's **Born Yester-
day.**

1974   Stoppard works on the screenplay of
Thomas Wiseman's **The Romantic English-
woman,** directed by Joseph Losey.
Jumpers opens at the Kennedy Center in
Washington, D.C., and later at the Billy
Rose Theatre in New York City. In June

the Royal Shakespeare Company stages
Travesties at the Aldwych Theatre in
London.

1975   **Travesties** opens in New York City at
the Barrymore Theatre and wins the Tony
Award. In July BBC Television transmits
live a half-hour play **The Boundary**
written by Stoppard and Clive Exton.

1976   Inter-Action presents Stoppard's **The
Dogg's Troupe 15-Minute Hamlet** which
was written (or rather edited) for
performance on a double-decker bus. On
April 6 **Dirty Linen** and **New-Found-
Land** are performed at the Ambiance
Lunch-Hour Theatre Club at the Almost-
Free Theatre. The plays are transferred
to the Arts Theatre in June, and to
Washington, D.C.'s Kennedy Center in the
fall.

1977   Stoppard visits Moscow and Leningrad
with the assistant director of the
British section of Amnesty Interna-
tional. Stoppard also visits Prague.
Dirty Linen and **New-Found-Land**
begin a long run at New York City's
Golden Theatre. **Every Good Boy
Deserves Favour** plays for one night at
the Royal Festival Hall with André
Previn and the London Symphony
Orchestra. **Professional Foul** is
transmitted on British television in
September and is awarded the British
Television Critics' Award for the best
play of 1977.

1978   **Professional Foul** is presented to
American television audiences on the
Public Broadcasting System. **Every
Good Boy Deserves Favour** is revived in
London at the Mermaid Theatre. **Night
and Day** opens in November at the
Phoenix Theatre. Stoppard writes the
screenplay of Vladimir Nabokov's novel
Despair.

1979   **Undiscovered Country,** Stoppard's
            English version of Arthur Schnitzler's
            Das Weite Land, opens at the Olivier
            Theatre (the National Theatre) on June
            20. **Dogg's Hamlet, Cahoot's
            Macbeth** plays at London's Collegiate
            Theatre in July and in the fall moves to
            the Kennedy Center in Washington, D.C.,
            and then to New York's 22 Steps Theatre
            in October. In August **Every Good boy
            Deserves Favor** plays a seven-day
            engagement at the Metropolitan Opera
            House in New York's Lincoln Center.
            Night and Day makes a brief run in
            Washington, D.C., and then opens on
            November 27 at the ANTA Theatre in New
            York City. Stoppard writes the
            screenplay of Graham Greene's novel
            The Human Factor.

1981   In February **Undiscovered Country** is
            performed at the Hartford Stage Company
            in Hartford, Connecticut. In April it
            moves to the Arena Stage Company in
            Washington, D.C. **On the Razzle,**
            Stoppard's adaptation of Johann
            Nestroy's **Einen Jux will er sich
            machen,** is first performed on Septem-
            ber 1 at the Royal Lyceum Theatre,
            Edinburgh as part of the 1981 Edinburgh
            International Festival.

1982   **On the Razzle** is produced by the
            Arena Stage Company in Washington, D.C.,
            in October. **The Real Thing** opens on
            November 16 at the Strand Theatre in
            London. In December BBC radio airs
            The Dog It Was That Died, a spy
            spoof.

1984   **The Real Thing** stages a trial run in
            Boston. It opens in the Plymouth
            Theatre in New York City on January 5
            and receives the Tony Award in June. In
            May Channel 4 television in London airs
            Squaring the Circle. On October 30
            Rough Crossing, Stoppard's adaptation

of Ferenc Molnar's farce **Játék a Kastélyban,** opens at the Lyttelton Theatre in London.   Critics note that it is a rare Stoppard failure.

1985   Stoppard collaborates on the screenplay for **Brazil.** The screenplay receives an Academy Award nomination but does not win.

1986   **Dalliance,** Stoppard's adaptation of Arthur Schnitzler's **Liebelei,** opens at the National Theatre in May.

Contributors

RUSSELL ASTLEY, Professor of English at Gallaudet University, has published articles in Victorian Poetry, PMLA, and other journals.

RICHARD CORBALLIS, Senior Lecturer in English at the University of Canterbury, New Zealand, is the author of numerous articles and reviews on Renaissance drama, modern drama, and New Zealand literature. His publications include books on John Webster, Thomas Dekker, George Chapman, Witi Ihimaera, and Stoppard (Stoppard: The Mystery and the Clockwork).

G. B. CRUMP, Professor of English at Central Missouri State University, has published works on D. H. Lawrence, Tom Stoppard, R. M. Koster, and Wright Morris (The Novels of Wright Morris: A Critical Interpretation).

JOAN F. DEAN is an Associate Professor of English and Director of Honors at the University of Missouri-Kansas City. She has published extensively on contemporary British dramatists, including Peter Shaffer and Joe Orton. She has taught in London and, as a Fulbright Lecturer, at the Universite de Nancy II in France.

WELDON B. DURHAM is Professor of Theatre at the University of Missouri-Columbia. His articles on philosopher-critic Kenneth Burke and on Stoppard have appeared in Theatre Journal and in Quarterly Journal of Speech. He is also general editor of American Theatre Companies: A Historical Encyclopedia, Book I of which appeared in 1986.

LUCINA P. GABBARD, Emeritus Professor of English at Eastern Illinois University, has published books on Pinter and Stoppard and articles on Pinter, Stoppard, Albee, and O'Neill.

WILLIAM E. GRUBER is a member of the English Department at Emory University. At present he is completing a study of performance ethics in Brecht and Craig. His Comic Theaters is forthcoming from the University of Georgia Press.

JOHN HARTY, Lecturer in the English Department at
the University of Florida, is the editor of **Tom
Stoppard: A Casebook.** He served as guest
editor of **Abstracts of English Studies** 26,
Supplement (**James Joyce Quarterly** Issue). He
became Inspector Hound in a College Park,
Maryland, production of **The Real Inspector
Hound** and directed a WPFW Radio production of
The Dog It Was That Died.

J. DENNIS HUSTON is Professor of English at Rice
University and the author of **Shakespeare's
Comedies of Play.** He also has acted in a
number of Shakespeare plays, and a few modern
ones, at Rice. Some day he hopes to play
Rosencrantz or Guildenstern--Stoppard's, not
Shakespeare's.

KATHERINE E. KELLY, Assistant Professor of
English at Texas A&M University, has published
articles on the drama of Samuel Beckett, T. S.
Eliot, and Tom Stoppard.

FELICIA HARDISON LONDRÉ is Dramaturg for Missouri
Repertory Theatre and Professor of Theatre at the
University of Missouri-Kansas City. Her three
books **Tennessee Williams, Tom Stoppard,**
and **Federico Lorca** are published by The Ungar
Publishing Company. She has published articles
in **Theatre Research International, The
Theatre Annual, Slavic and East European
Arts, Studies in Popular Culture, Theatre
Journal, Theatre History Studies, Compar-
ative Drama, Research Studies,** and
Thought.

JEFFREY D. MASON is an Assistant Professor of
Theatre at California State College, Bakersfield.
He has published criticism on performance art and
American theater in **Theatre Journal** and the
North Dakota Quarterly, and he has directed
over thirty productions. He is currently working
on a study of American theater and drama in the
context of cultural myth.

GABRIELLE ROBINSON is a professor of English at
Indiana University at South Bend; her field is

comparative drama and she has written on
playwrights such as Shaw, Whiting, Nestroy, and
Schnitzler. At present she is working on a study
of contemporary farce, while also continuing her
work on patronage in Henry James.

RODNEY SIMARD, Lecturer in English and
Communications at California State University,
San Bernardino, is the author of **Postmodern
Drama: Contemporary Playwrights in America and
Britain** and **The Whole Writer's Catalog** and
Assistant Editor of **The Variorum Edition of the
Poetry of John Donne.** He has published essays
on various British and American literary figures
as well as rhetorical pedagogy.

SHIRLEY SHULTZ, Assistant Professor of English at
Gallaudet University, is working on a book on Tom
Stoppard's Symposium Comedies.

HERSH ZEIFMAN is an Associate Professor of
English at York University, Toronto. A member of
the Editorial Advisory Board of **Modern Drama,**
he has published many articles on contemporary
British drama, particularly on the plays of
Beckett, Stoppard, and Pinter.

A Selected Annotated Bibliography

The most comprehensive bibliography of
Stoppard criticism is David Bratt's **Tom
Stoppard: a reference guide** (Boston: G. K.
Hall, 1982). Bratt's book is an annotated
bibliography through 1980. The most recent
update on Stoppard criticism is Charles A.
Carpenter's "Modern Drama Studies: An Annual
Bibliography," in **Modern Drama**, 29 (June
1986), 270. Professor Carpenter's checklist
appears annually in the June issue of **Modern
Drama**.

Enter a Free Man (1968; Revised version of the
1963 teleplay **A Walk on the Water**)

Gill, Brendan. "At the Start." **The New
    Yorker**, 50 (6 January 1975), 50. The
    characters in **Enter a Free Man** "struggle
    to find words commensurate with their
    feelings and they always fail." **Enter**
    foreshadows the Stoppard plays to come.

Rosencrantz & Guildenstern Are Dead (1967)

Babula, William. "The Play-Life Metaphor in
    Shakespeare and Stoppard." **Modern
    Drama**, 25 (December 1972), 279-81.
    Stoppard's courtiers in **Rosencrantz &
    Guildenstern Are Dead** use the stage as a
    metaphor for life and think of themselves as
    actors. Rosencrantz and Guildenstern find
    themselves playing roles which are not so
    much tasteless as "baffling."

Berlin, Normand. "**Rosencrantz and Guildenstern
    Are Dead**: Theater of Criticism." **Modern
    Drama**, 16 (December 1973), 269-77.
    Rosencrantz's weakness is that it "lacks
    . . . union of thought and emotion," while
    its strength is that, because our "critical
    faculty is not subdued" while watching it,
    we arrive at insights into Hamlet's charac-
    ter, the nature of Greek and Elizabethan
    tragedy, and actor-audience relationships.
    "Stoppard is most successful when he
    functions as a critic of drama and when he

allows his insights on the theater to lead
him to observations on life. He is weakest
. . . when he attempts to confront life
directly."

Brustein, Robert. "Waiting for Hamlet." In
The Third Theatre. New York: Alfred A.
Knopf, 1969, pp. 149-53. "As is now
generally known, **Rosencrantz and
Guildenstern Are Dead** is a theatrical
parasite, feeding off **Hamlet, Waiting
for Godot,** and **Six Characters in Search
of an Author."**

Corballis, Richard. "Extending the Audience:
The Structure of **Rosencrantz and
Guildenstern Are Dead." Ariel: A
Review of International English Literature,** 11 (April 1980), 65-79. The Player
is one character through whom **Rosencrantz** can be understood. The Player
functions in two worlds: the world of the
play and the real world. Rosencrantz and
Guildenstern are spectators much like the
audience itself.

Egan, Robert. "A Thin Beam of Light: The
Purpose of Playing in **Rosencrantz and
Guildenstern Are Dead," Theatre
Journal,** 31 (March 1979), 59-69. The
Player contrasts with Rosencrantz and
Guildenstern who fail to take action.
Rosencrantz does not recast **Waiting
for Godot.** The Player's "death" scene is
thematically and theatrically important.

Levenson, Jill. "Views from a Revolving Door:
Tom Stoppard's Canon to Date." **Queen's
Quarterly,** 78 (Autumn 1971), 431-42.
Rosencrantz sets out to "examine possible solutions to a problem" (i.e., how is
one to "live reasonably in a world that
makes no sense?"). Finally the courtiers
reject all the alternatives, leaving "the
problem acutely unresolved."

Simard, Rodney. "The Logic of Unicorns: Beyond
    Absurdism in Stoppard." **Arizona
    Quarterly**, 38 (Spring 1982), 37-44.
    "**Rosencrantz** is an absurdist work, but
    it is often disconcerting in its ability to
    make one feel good at moments; **Jumpers**
    uses the same absurdist tools, but is a
    decidedly positive statement." Stoppard
    gives a debate with no conclusions. He
    "attempts to help the individual define
    himself in an age that has no definition."

The Real Inspector Hound (1968) / After Magritte (1970)

Crossley, Brian M. "An Investigation of
    Stoppard's 'Hound' and 'Foot.'" **Modern
    Drama**, 20 (March 1977), 77-86. In
    Hound and **After Magritte** the detective
    tradition is turned against itself.

Schlueter, June. "Stoppard's Moon and Birdboot,
    Rosencrantz and Guildenstern." In **Meta-
    fictional Characters in Modern Drama**. New
    York: Columbia University Press, 1979,
    pp. 89-103. Both **Rosencrantz** and
    Hound consist of metafictional charac-
    ters. "Man's confrontation with his world
    is a recurring theme in Stoppard. . . . In
    creating first a rigid structural line of
    demarcation and then violating that line
    through his protagonists' entrance into the
    inner play, Stoppard is able to use the
    play-within-a-play not simply in the tradi-
    tional way, for enhancing reality, but
    rather to suggest the nature of role playing
    and the power of illusion over reality."

Jumpers (1972)

Ayer, A. J. "Love Among the Logical
    Positivists." **Sunday Times** (London), 9
    April 1972, p. 16. **Jumpers** serves as a
    parody of philosophical writing.

Bennett, Jonathan. "Philosophy and Mr Stoppard."
    Philosophy, 50 (January 1975), 5-18.
    Jumpers only lightly touches on
    philosophy.

Delaney, Paul. "The Flesh and The Word in
    Jumpers." **Modern Language Quarter-
    ly**, 42 (1981), 369-88. ". . . Stoppard
    thinks in consciously theatrical terms. The
    ideas of the play [**Jumpers**] revolve
    around issues in moral philosophy which
    Professor George Moore will be debating in a
    departmental symposium."

Durham, Weldon B. "Symbolic Action in Tom
    Stoppard's **Jumpers.**" **Theatre
    Journal**, 32 (May 1980), 169-79. **Jump-
    ers** is unified when seen as an enactment
    of Stoppard's "engrossment in" the destruc-
    tive effects of "rationalism, pragmatism,
    and individualism" and of his adherence to
    "the Kantian proposition that playful,
    'purposeless purposiveness' can reveal
    truths inaccessible to rational, purposeful
    argument."

Hinden, Michael. "**Jumpers**: Stoppard and the
    Theater of Exhaustion." **Twentieth Century
    Literature**, 27 (1981), 1-15. ". . .
    Jumpers is by far the most literate play
    of the modern period--by no means a
    derivative work, but rather one which ties
    itself by many threads to an unraveling
    tradition of literature and thought."

Jensen, Henning. "Jonathan Bennett and Mr
    Stoppard." **Philosophy**, 52 (April 1977),
    214-17. **Jumpers** ". . . contains an
    abundance of philosophical materials," but
    "is not a significantly philosophical
    play."

Londré, Felicia Hardison. "Using Comic Devices
    to Answer the Ultimate Question: Tom
    Stoppard's **Jumpers** and Woody Allen's
    God." **Comparative Drama**, 14 (Winter

1980), 346-54. **Jumpers** and **God** deal
with the "uncertainty about God." Both
Stoppard and Allen use similar comic
devices.

Salmon, Eric. "Faith in Tom Stoppard."
Queen's Quarterly, 86 (Summer 1979),
215-32. **Jumpers** and **Travesties** are
"complementary pieces." **Jumpers** is not
an Absurdist play.

Shiner, Roger A. "Showing, Saying and Jumping."
**Dialogue: Canadian Philosophical
Review**, 21 (December 1982), 625-46.
Stoppard's plays are philosophical, and
philosophy and drama are akin. "A play can
be philosophical in the sense that
philosophical issues are given extended
treatment by explicit statement ('saying')
as well as by being 'shown'; a play can be
philosophical in the sense that philosophical issues are given extended treatment but
only by being 'shown.'" Serious moral
philosophy is spread throughout
Jumpers.

Weightman, John. "A Metaphysical Comedy."
Encounter, 38 (April 1972), 44-45.
". . . If the play [**Jumpers**] is to sound
truly modern, it must not be solemn."
Jumpers is an Absurdist play.

Travesties (1974)

Cooke, John William. "The Optical Allusion:
Perception and Form in Stoppard's
Travesties." **Modern Drama**, 24
(December 1981), 525-39. Carr's memory is
faulty and the audience gets his misconception of what happened--his optical illusion.
"The process of making meaning--be it
telling a story, writing **Ulysses**, or
composing socialist history--is the central
focus of Stoppard's play."

380   *Tom Stoppard: A Casebook*

James, Clive. "Count Zero Splits the Infinite."
    Encounter, 45 (November 1975), 68-76.
    ". . . The appropriate analogies to
    Stoppard's vision lie just as much in modern
    physics as in modern philosophy."
    Earnest moves "through **Travesties**
    like one stream of particles through
    another, the points of collision lighting up
    as pastiche."

Pearce, Howard D. "Stage as Mirror: Tom
    Stoppard's **Travesties**." MLN, 94
    (December 1979), 1139-58. Parodies in
    Travesties "reflect their objects and
    establish relationships between worlds,
    reflections, and viewers." **Travesties**
    "is like a hall of mirrors, character
    mirroring character, art mirroring world,
    stage mirroring art reflecting world, artist
    reflecting world reflecting artist, present
    reflecting past."

Rod, David K. "Carr's Views on Art and Politics
    in Tom Stoppard's **Travesties**." **Modern
    Drama**, 26 (December 1983), 536-42. "A
    careful examination of the scenes in which
    Carr's views conflict with those of Tzara,
    Joyce, and Lenin will reveal both Carr's
    centrality to the aesthetic-political debate
    and a clearer picture of the position he
    espouses. . . . However convincing Carr's
    arguments may have seemed, the situations
    that stimulated them never really
    occurred."

Sammells, Neil. "Earning Liberties:
    Travesties And **The Importance of Being
    Earnest**." **Modern Drama**, 29 (September
    1986), 376-87. The center of Stoppard's
    dramatic strategies in **Travesties** is the
    form of the play itself. **Travesties**
    critically engages with **Earnest** and the
    "manner of that engagement is its own
    statement about what art can and cannot
    do."

Werner, Craig. "Stoppard's Critical Travesty,
      Or, Who Vindicates Whom And Why." **Arizona
      Quarterly**, 35 (Autumn 1979), 228-36.
      Travesties "unveils the limitations of
      the twentieth century's most cherished
      systems of belief," in that Carr, the play's
      "central stage presence," is unmoved by all
      three of the "would-be messiahs," Joyce,
      Tzara, Lenin.

              Dirty Linen and **New-Found-Land** (1976)

Brassell, Tim. "Back to Farce." In **Tom
      Stoppard: An Assessment**. New York: St.
      Martin's Press, 1985, pp. 223-54. **Dirty
      Linen** casts "a jocular swipe at the
      discussion of the moral standards of public
      figures. . . ." Stoppard attacks political
      secrecy with sexuality and farcical devices:
      "disappearing clothes, hasty cover-ups in
      mid-sentence, misfiring missives and
      desperate and hilarious attempts to preserve
      dignity on all sides."

Davis, Jessica Milner. **Farce**. The Critical
      Idiom, no. 39. London: Methuen, 1978, pp.
      82-84, 86. The implied moral and social
      comment in **Dirty Linen** places it outside
      the usual bounds of farce.

Miner, Michael D. "Grotesque Drama in the '70s."
      Kansas Quarterly, 12 (1980), 99-109.
      Dirty Linen "uses the grotesque as a
      decorative embellishment which functions by
      reductio ad absurdum to reflect the
      political and moral chaos evidenced by the
      British and American political sex scandals
      of the 1970s."

              Every Good Boy Deserves Favor (1977)

Brassell, Tim. "Eyes East." In **Tom Stoppard:
      An Assessment**. New York: St. Martin's
      Press, 1985, pp. 179-89. Stoppard's **Every
      Good Boy Deserves Favour** is less than
      satisfactory as a piece of dramatic

construction.   ". . . Stoppard's concern was
to eschew any suggestion of opera or stage
musical and to keep his actors functioning
as actors throughout, while at the same time
ensuring that the orchestra was more than a
lavish attendant spectre."

Danfield, D. J.   "Forward with Stoppard."
    Theatre News, 11, No. 8 (May 1979),
    20-22. **Professional Foul** and **Every
    Good Boy Deserves Favor** "raise the sights
    and deepen the tone of Stoppard's work."

Professional Foul (1977)

Blumenfeld, Yorick.   "The Dramatic Relationship
    between Soccer and Freedom." **Horizon**,
    21 (April 1978), 90-92. Stoppard adds
    political and emotional commitment to
    Professional Foul. In Czechoslovakia,
    England loses a soccer match, "but Anderson
    decides that some honor may be saved by
    delivering an improvised speech to his
    conference colleagues on the ethics of human
    rights."

Buhr, Richard J.   "Epistemology and Ethics in Tom
    Stoppard's **Professional Foul**."
    Comparative Drama, 13 (Winter 1979),
    320-29. "Much more than a forum for
    Czechoslovakian dissident politics,
    Professional Foul is a culmination and
    clarification of the epistemological and
    ethical issues that have always dominated
    Stoppard's important work." Anderson
    sacrifices his absolute moral principles in
    his conflict with human rights and
    emotions.

_____.   "The Philosophy Game in Tom
    Stoppard's **Professional Foul**." **The
    Midwest Quarterly**, 22 (Summer 1981),
    407-15. ". . . Stoppard examines the
    widely accepted philosophic analogy between
    games and life through the structure of
    Professional Foul. . . . Stoppard

compels the viewer to examine whether
football [soccer] rules and ethical
principles are similar or different and
whether football [soccer] fouls and ethical
violations are justifiable or not."

Cobley, Evelyn. "Catastrophe Theory in Tom
Stoppard's **Professional Foul**."
Contemporary Literature, 25 (Spring
1984), 53-65. "For Stoppard the world is
not divided into 'either/or' oppositions; on
the contrary, he sees it as a complex
network of interrelationships where any
statement or action is a 'both-and' issue."

Kennedy, Andrew K. "Tom Stoppard's Dissident
Comedies." **Modern Drama**, 25 (December
1982), 469-76. Stoppard's comedy now
"combines moral and political commitment
with a newly stable satire of real/absurd
worlds, recognizably located in Russia and
Czechoslovakia."

Night and Day (1978)

Brassell, Tim. "The Road to Kambawe." In **Tom
Stoppard: An Assessment**. New York: St.
Martin's Press, 1985, pp. 204-22. ". . .
Night and Day is, once again, a serious
'play of ideas,' though the erstwhile
formula of its 'marriage' 'with farce or
even high comedy' appears to have been set
aside."

Rosenwald, Peter J. "The Meaning of Nonsense."
Horizon, 22 (November 1979), 38-43.
Stoppard's most recent plays include social
commitment.

Simons, Judy. "**Night and Day**." Gambit,
37 (1980), 77-86. **Night and Day** is as
directly political in its implications as
are **Every Good Boy Deserves Favour** and
Professional Foul and can be seen as a
continuation of the arguments of **Jumpers**
and **Travesties**, both of which

investigated relationships between politics,
morality and art." In **Night and Day**
Stoppard parodies journalistic styles and
attacks the abuses of journalism and the
misconceptions of public opinion.

Dogg's Hamlet, Cahoot's Macbeth (1979)

Brassell, Tim. "Back to Farce." In **Tom
Stoppard: An Assessment.** New York: St.
Martin's Press, 1985, pp. 223–56. "Comedy
. . . is the guardian angel that presides
over all of **Dogg's Hamlet**, whether in
its Wittgenstein-inspired language games" or
its compression of **Hamlet**. The reduction of **Macbeth** in **Cahoot's Macbeth**
is "the only conceivable means of presenting
the play in **any** form under the pressures
of the Czechoslovakian police state."

Gianakaris, C. J. "Stoppard's Adaptations of
Shakespeare: **Dogg's Hamlet, Cahoot's
Macbeth.**" **Comparative Drama**, 18 (Fall
1984), 222–40. Stoppard makes Shakespeare
"more accessible to audiences of another
place, time, and taste." **Hamlet** "is
clearly but limitedly adapted in **Dogg's
Hamlet** to serve as a literary and linguistic **tour de force. Macbeth,** on the
other hand, is adapted in **Cahoot's
Macbeth** to function in a vital capacity as
structural support for Stoppard's thematic
aim."

Levenson, Jill. "'Hamlet' Andante / 'Hamlet'
Allegro: Tom Stoppard's Two Versions."
Shakespeare Survey, 36 (1983), 21–28.
Rosencrantz contains components of
Hamlet, Waiting for Godot, and
Philosophical Investigations. "**Dogg's
Hamlet, Cahoot's Macbeth** suggests more
explicitly than **Rosencrantz** how
language-games—in Wittgenstein's sense—may
serve as the source and end of dramatic
art."

The Real Thing (1982)

Delaney, Paul. "Cricket bats and commitment:
    the real thing in art and life." **Critical
    Quarterly**, 27 (Spring 1985), 45-60. "**The
    Real Thing** extends and deepens the concern
    in **Travesties** and **Dogg's Hamlet,
    Cahoot's Macbeth** (1979) over the
    connection between art and politics."
    "**The Real Thing** asks if there can be
    affirmation of commitment, fidelity, trust
    between lovers who were themselves brought
    together by infidelity, the breaking of
    commitments, the betrayal of trust."

Scuton, Roger. "The Real Stoppard."
    Encounter, 60 (February 1983), 44-47.
    "Stoppard is not a dramatist--he does not
    portray characters, who develop in relation
    to each other, and generate dialogue from
    their mutual restraints. . . . His ideal of
    dialogue is an exchange not of feelings, but
    of epigrams. The real thing is never in his
    [Stoppard's] words, which contain only the
    idea of it, in the form of brilliantly
    staged metaphysical conundrums."